Contemporary Readings in Marxism

A Critical Introduction

Contemporary Readings in Marxism

A Critical Introduction

Edited by

Ravi Kumar

AAKAR

"Gefördert durch die Rosa-Luxemburg-Stiftung e.V. aus Mitteln des Bundesministerium für wirtschaftliche Zusammenarbeit und Entwicklung der Bundesrepublik Deutschland"

"Sponsored by the Rosa Luxemburg Foundation eV with funds of the Federal Ministry for Economic Cooperation and Development of the Federal Republic of Germany."

Contemporary Readings in Marxism: A Critical Introduction
Edited by Ravi Kumar

First published 2016

ISBN 978-93-5002-421-8 (Hb)

Published by
AAKAR BOOKS
28 E Pocket IV, Mayur Vihar Phase I, Delhi 110 091
Phone: 011 2279 5505 Telefax: 011 2279 5641
aakarbooks@gmail.com; www.aakarbooks.com

Printed at
Sapra Brothers, Delhi 110 092

Acknowledgements

This volume emerges as part of a process which was set in motion in 2014 when the Rosa Luxemburg Stiftung, South Asia Office and the Department of Sociology, South Asian University decided to organize a course on Marxism. In the process of organizing, Dr. Carsten Krinn, the then Resident representative of RLS and Pragya Khanna played a pivotal role as far as agreeing to organize a programme like this was concerned, while Prof. Sasanka Perera, Dean, Faculty of Social Sciences, was highly encouraging that we host such a course with such a dense theoretical content. This would not have been possible if Atul Chandra, who worked on this course as Researcher would not have taken all the pains to handle the bureaucratic pathways as well as demands from the university and RLS offices. Any course which enters the realm of formal structures cannot move forward unless there is cooperation from members of the structure and that is why it is important that I mention the late Prof. G.K. Chadha, President, South Asian University (when we organized it in 2014), current President of the University Dr. Kavita Sharma and Dr. A.K. Malik, Registrar, South Asian University.

This course and hence, this volume would not have been possible unless the resource persons had agreed to lecture and then provide us with the lecture notes to go as chapters in this volume. I must also thank K.K. Saxena of Aakar Books to have agreed to bring out this volume within the constraints of time that the formal structures provided us.

New Delhi, 2016

Ravi Kumar

Contents

Contents

Introduction

Marxism: On the Relevance of the Theory and the Need for Engagement

Ravi Kumar

A teacher from a 'premier' intellectual institution confided that while teaching social theory it was very difficult to make students read Karl Marx in the original or through secondary sources unlike the other two classical thinkers—Weber and Durkheim. Another faculty in a different situation finds it difficult to comprehend why would mention of Karl Marx and somebody like Ambedkar draw more virulent reaction than anybody else. On the other hand, when the Department of Sociology at South Asian University announced a course module on Marxism it had over four hundred applicants for thirty seats. These two instances needed a mention because they are reflective of a much deeper theoretical question that connects to not only how one approaches and comprehends theory but it also demands a more incisive introspection into how intellectual histories are moulded, legitimized and delegitimized.

Connections between theories and the stark, dark and dangerous existence of our everyday life is missing and that disconnection has been established many times over through misplaced intellectual transactions within university classrooms. The idea of knowledge as experiential and hence, to be explained as such is generally missed out as critical interpretation and engagement is replaced by straightforward reproduction of the given. There is a certain body of knowledge, which invokes as its innate characteristic the inevitable connection between the thought and the reader's experience. That is the reason why Weber and Durkheim do not incite the same reaction which Ambedkar and Marx do. The connection is automatic, intrinsic when the student brings with herself the experience of the world outside—the constitutive process of what *makes* her. The theorists inside the classroom forget this inevitable connection and become uncomfortable when the student's anger emerges like a ball of fire threatening their myopic knowledge.

Such disconnections are also indicative of a struggle that pervades the intellectual arena and then spills over within the society. Perhaps it is about the struggle as to *what* kind of knowledge is being produced by the institutionalized centres, which are in effect built to reproduce structures in the interest of the ruling class. The potential of knowledge as an instrument is in fact more distinctly recognized by the ruling classes and, hence, the emphasis on curriculum, pedagogy and character of educational institutions controlled by them. Obviously, it seeks to eliminate certain kinds of knowledge that would create subverts and challenge the existence of the system itself. And, interestingly more often than not this is not necessarily achieved through coercive mechanisms or through transformation, rather it is inbuilt in the process of the capitalist project of knowledge production itself in such a manner that after a certain point it appears natural. The student within institutions starts believing that this is how a certain theoretical enterprise exists. This has what has happened to Marxism within academia. As a well thought out 'intellectual' design it has been presented in a certain way in certain disciplines while in some others it has been pushed to the margins. For instance, Bhattacharya (2014, p. 187) says that

> contemporary practices of teaching and research in economics in India don't prepare students, teachers, and researchers to engage with the Indian political economy in a sophisticated and socially relevant way.

At a more generic level, Marxism has experienced mutations, which other theories have not faced in academia. It began with a misreading of Marxism, which spawned into categorizations and sub-categorizations of Marx's thought thereby fragmenting the very ideas that Marx wanted to push forth and paradoxically making Marxism itself a completely non-dialectical thought. While an engaged reading of Marxism should lead to grasping the continuity between his ideas expressed in *Communist Manifesto* to *Capital* and *German Ideology* to *Economic and Philosophic Manuscripts* yet while teaching students this continuity is deliberately demolished when a few pages from each of these are taught. Secondly, the moment sub-categorizations are done it takes away the idea of progress from Marxian thought. Marxism, unlike other thoughts, is an evolving thought.This is what has allowed Marxism to sustain itself as a living thought despite the death of Karl Marx. Frederick Engels trying to state the central idea of Marx behind *Manifesto* writes that Marx believed

> That the history of these class struggles forms a series of evolutions in which, nowadays, a stage has been reached where the exploited and oppressed class—the proletariat—cannot attain its emancipation from the sway of the exploiting and ruling class—the bourgeoisie—without, at the same time, and once and for all, emancipating society at large from all exploitation, oppression, class distinction, and class struggles (Preface to the 1888 English Edition)

As a reply to much oft repeated criticism of Marxism as an alien thought it is relevant to quote Marx and Engels when they wrote in the Preface to the 1872 German Edition of *Communist Manifesto* that

> much that state of things may have altered during the last twenty-five years, the general principles laid down in the *Manifesto* are, on the whole, as correct today as ever. *Here and there, some detail might be improved. The practical application of the principles will depend, as the Manifesto itself states, everywhere and at all times, on the historical conditions for the time being existing...* (emphasis mine)

In a certain sense what makes Marxism an ever-relevant thought is the fact that it deals with subjects that we encounter as our experiences in everyday lives. Also, people have identified closely with its analysis of the social, economic, political and cultural processes. It allows people to understand the viciousness of the capitalist system and every time the oppressive and tyrannical character of capital has been understood by the masses through tools provided by Marxian theory there have been mobilizations in different forms and of different scales. It was this reason which made Marx "the best hated and most calumniated man of his time. Governments, both absolutist and republican, deported him from their territories. Bourgeois, whether conservative or ultra-democratic, vied with one another in heaping slanders upon him" (Engels, 1883).

The unabated slandering of Marx and his thoughts on the non-academic front only changes its colour and tenor as it enters the intellectual domain and transforms Marx into an academic without any socio-political relevance. It is often argued citing examples of the Soviet Union and East European countries how Marxism failed. A failure discourse is generated within academic columns that puts onus on Marxian thought, something which no other thought has had to face.This is probably indicative of both the pervasive power of Marxian discourse and the bourgeois intelligentsia caught in its dilemma when they refuse to teach Marx as a thinker with a political project within the classroom while acknowledging the political nature of Marxism at the time of critiquing him. Jonathan Wolff (2002) says that "the failure of communism does not mean that all is well with Western, liberal, democratic capitalism. And it is Marx, above all, who still provides us with the sharpest tools with which to criticize existing society" (pp. 1-2). However, intellectuals have taught Marxism in a way, which led students to think that it is something better if not taught in the educational institutions. And one of the grounds on which it has been denounced is exactly what Wolff indicates—that of being a theory that 'failed'. Though one finds such an argument hardly tenable when other thinkers/thoughts would be taught who have never even been tried as social experiments and hence, had no experience of 'success' or 'failure'. In other words, is it really important to even bring in the element of it being a 'failed' theory in the context of Marxism while it is not done in case of other theories?

This misreading has often given rise to a particular kind of Marxism as Cleaver (1986) says: "What we have here is a sanitized, seminar-room Marxism that has been stripped of its political content and class anger." What is missed out in teaching of Marx and Marxism is that the theoretical endeavour was guided towards a transcendental project and possibility. Cleaver (1986) argues that Marx's concepts and theories must be read as "moments of his political analysis of capitalism as class struggle. This is what I call a political reading of Marx." Focusing on the economics/economists, Cleaver (1986) says that Marxism in understanding economy is not to be restricted to teaching/studying something like spheres of production, circulation, and distribution rather

> this approach insists that what is usually called the economic sphere is made up of moments of a political whole: the class struggle.
>
> Basic to this approach is the position that the object of Marx's study, and the only proper object for any revolutionary, is the class struggle. Let us be clear, this position denies the autonomy of the political—there is no economic sphere here and political sphere over there. The position argues that from the point of view of workers who want to overthrow capitalism there can be one and only one subject of study: the structures of their power relations with capital. Everything must be interpreted in terms of its relation to this central political issue.

While misreading of Marxism has been one major problem the idea that it should not be taught has been another serious issue. There have been voices from within academia as well as from the state, which have said repeatedly that it need not be given any kind of importance, as it has no relevance in contemporary times whatsoever. My students within the classroom in a non-intellectual, unsubstantiated manner encouraged by works of many academics do come to a naïve and untenable conclusion about how Marxism is 'ideological' and 'deterministic' and so on. These conclusions, obviously, come without any serious engagement with texts within Marxian theoretical trajectory. Anyhow, this implicitly calls for suppressing the 'ideological' (as if it is possible). Eagleton (1991) argues that

> The current suppression of the concept of ideology is in one sense a recycling of the so-called 'end of ideology' epoch which followed the Second World War; but whereas that movement was at least partially explicable as a traumatized response to the crimes of fascism and Stalinism no such political rationale underpins the present fashionable aversion to ideological critique. Moreover, the 'end-of-ideology' school was palpably a creation of the political right, whereas our own 'post-ideological' complacency often enough sports radical credentials.
>
> The abandonment of the notion of ideology belongs with a more pervasive political faltering by whole sections of the erstwhile revolutionary left, which in the face of a capitalism temporarily on the offensive has beaten a steady, shamefaced retreat from such 'metaphysical' matters as class struggle and modes of production, revolutionary agency and the nature of the bourgeois state (p. xii).

It is Marx with his companion Engels who for the first time explained the way in which capitalism as a social, economic, cultural and political system emerged. They also acknowledged how this system was not static and kept changing as revealed by their explanation of "different historical forms of capital: mercantile, agrarian, industrial, monopoly, financial, imperial and so on" (Eagleton, 2011, p. 2) hence, recognized the need for updating the analysis and ways of resisting the new forms of capital as and when they would emerge. One would hardly disagree that there have been mutations experienced by Marxism in the 20th century, which took the dialectical thrust of Marxism, wherein it talks of a whole comprises of parts interacting with and 'mutually influencing' each other in a process of producing an 'organic system'.

What has been lost is that profound understanding that looks upon productive forces not as neutral but as marked by the character of society from which they emerge. In other words, there has been a tendency to forget about the character of the relations of production. Instead, what has often been presented as Marxism is a positivism and determinism in which the development of productive forces is viewed as the cause (and tool) of all change. This conception emerged in the context of the Soviet attempt to develop as rapidly as possible because of the threat of imperialism, which is understandable, but it is a distortion of Marxism (Lebowitz in Mingliang, 2013).

The distortion did not come merely from the Soviet Union but also from what Eagleton above called the 'erstwhile revolutionary left', which has forgotten the significance or centrality of labour within the analytical realm as well as political struggles. This has, consequently, led to gradual social democratization of the political left and the thought emerging out of academia as well.

In this situation when the crisis of capitalism keeps indicating, crying with all its hoarseness, that it cannot sustain itself but as long as it is able to keep itself alive the relevance of Marxism as a thought would continue. The complexities of the production process under contemporary capitalism have paved the way for an apparently complex socio-political and cultural reality that has often been mistaken to be either the end of ideology or a post-ideological moment. However, the central characteristic of a system, which flourishes on the basic premise of how capital exploits labour to optimize surplus accumulation, continues to be in place. That has not ceased to exist although it may have become more sophisticated. And if that is so then it is really difficult to hand over the baton and acknowledge that Marxism has lost its relevance.

It is this continuing relevance of Marxism as a theoretical body of knowledge that translates into praxis that the Department of Sociology at South Asian University with support from Rosa Luxemburg Stiftung started organizing course modules on Marxism. The chapters in this volume constitute the lectures that were part of the first module on Marxism. It is for this reason that most of the chapters have a section on 'questions for further discussion'. There are also chapters, which made an effort to engage with the debates within Marxism and, thus, may appear as departures from many established ideas within Marxism. The volume is divided into two parts: while the first part deals with chapters that engage with concepts within Marxism the second part deals with the social contexts within which Marxism may be read and applied as well. This volume is not only a statement on how Marxism still remains relevant as a theoretical body of knowledge but also seeks to engage the readers with the tenets of the thought.

Engagement remains one of the fundamental goals of the course as well as this volume because the constant attempt at delegitimization of Marxian theory works on the principle of not conversing with this body of knowledge. The opponents fear to get into the works, concepts and ideas that emerge out of the theoretical body of knowledge and rather, flimsily, denounce it. It is also because it takes them out of their comfort zone and asks uncomfortable questions about our very existence itself. The engagement may take us into those uncomfortable zones but then that is the reality one must not evade. And Marxism does precisely that—asking us not to take our eyes and ears off whatever is happening around us, prompting us to seek answers to 'how' and 'why' of those events.

REFERENCES

Cleaver, Harry (1986). Karl Marx: Economist or Revolutionary?, available at https://www.marxists.org/subject/marxmyths/harry-cleaver/article.htm, (accessed September 23, 2014).

Eagleton, Terry (1991). *Ideology: An Introduction*, London and New York: Verso.

Eagleton, Terry (2011). *Why Marx Was Right*, New Haven & London: Yale University Press.

Engels, Frederick (1883). Speech at the Grave of Karl Marx, available at https://www.marxists.org/archive/marx/works/1883/death/burial.htm (accessed on September 9, 2015).

Mingliang, Zhuo (2013). The Relevance of Marxism Today: An Interview with Michael A. Lebowitz, Monthly Review, available at http://mrzine.monthlyreview.org/2013/lebowitz 210313.html (accessed on July 5, 2015).

Wolff, Jonathan (2002). *Why Read Marx Today?* Oxford: Oxford University Press.

MARXISM AND CAPITALISM

1

Historical Materialism: A Critical Assessment

Anjan Chakrabarti

Introducing 'Karl Marx'

Marx remains an immigrant among us, a glorious, sacred, accursed but still clandestine immigrant as he was all his life.

Jacques Derrida in '*Specters of Marx*'

The standpoint of the old materialism is civil society; the standpoint of the new is human society, or social humanity.

Karl Marx in '*Theses on Feuerbach*, XI'

An immigrant can never be accepted as such; he has a place but not quite; he is inside yet outside; he has a body but it is strange; he is in the bookkeeping of the state and United Nations and yet he is controversial and dangerous. Marx is an immigrant among us. As he was in life as in his global influence and presence, Marx was and remains an internationalist to the core. He is a thorn in the flesh of our mainstream understanding of what the world is and our place in it, a truly abnormal, pathological presence. He has been criticized, condemned, desecrated and even occulted. Yet, he cannot be escaped for he pointed to one aspect of human existence that has been touched upon by no other thinkers before or after him, at least not in the way he did. It is that we live in a class divided society whose basis is the phenomenon of exploitation embodying the process by which a small group of people extract and live off the fruits of surplus labour of the mass of workers. To think, theorize/explain and live otherwise is to be under one grand delusion. In this delusional cosmology, class division is non-existent or at best displaced into an outcome of natural traits in a purportedly free and harmonious society named as capitalism. The creation of this delusion cosmology is the task of Political Economy and the order/system created to foster and secure this delusion constitutes capitalist hegemony. It is this grand delusion which was the object of Marx's pointed critique of Political Economy in the book *Capital: Critique of Political Economy*. Our topic of discussion is this 'critique'.

To this purpose, Marx unpacked the location of class structure and division in a way that was fundamental to the existence of capitalism even though such class division was by no means peculiar to capitalism; feudalism and slavery are further examples of some other socio-economic forms with class divisions. Marx's conception of economy thus cannot be reduced to capitalism although it is the latter that he paid most attention to. He argued that capitalism, like feudalism and slavery, was a system based on *theft of labour*; it is definition-wise *exploitative* and hence *unjust*. The way exploitation and class division transpired in capitalism was different from that of feudalism and slave system; to demonstrate the specificity of these in capitalism was one of the purposes of Marx's endeavour in *Capital*. But then Classical Political Economy thinkers such as Adam Smith and David Ricardo have presented theories of capitalism too. So what different was Marx intending to do? Althusser and Balibar in *Reading Capital* isolate the importance of Marx's intervention thus:

> Marxist science and the Marxist researcher must take a position in the conflict ... so as to see what bourgeois ideology *necessary occults*: the class structure and class exploitation that characterize the social formation (Althusser and Balibar 1975, p. 179, emphasis ours).

The aspect of class division based on these properties was non-existent in liberal theories of politics and economics which coalesced into a well-structured Political Economy—a theory of defence of industrial capitalism. This Political Economy whose initial incarnation is named as 'classical' morphed into the neoclassical economics subsequently; unless otherwise specified, Political Economy refers to both[1]. Based on aspects such as market, competition, private property and homo-economicus (economic man), the formulated Political Economy (of capitalism) helped foreclosure[2]/occult the aspect of class as process of surplus labour, class exploitation and the question of injustice associated with it. It rendered natural and benign the class division and its debilitating effects on society. By virtue of what it necessarily occults, this Political Economy created a delusional cosmology of capitalism. Marx's *Capital* is an attempt to recast the reading of capitalism so as to defamiliarize its known interpretations and narratives. It is a challenge to the meaning, purpose and mechanics of what we understand as capitalism. This is done by unpacking, as Althusser and Balibar say, its underlying class structure and class exploitation. In the process, it paves the way to conceptualize the economy in a new way. Marx's intervention demonstrates the character of the delusion that is at the basis of theory and defence of capitalism in Political Economy. Evidently, confronting the hegemony of such a universalized picture of capitalism brings into sharp focus the importance of cultural process (production and dissemination of meanings; systems of meanings), political process (production and distribution of authority to control and regulate individuals and groups and their behaviour) and natural process (the transformation (biological, chemical, etc.) of the physical properties of matter) that are in a mutually constitutive relation with the class structure and organization of exploitation. Depending upon their specific conjunction, varieties of capitalism appear across time and space.

However, it must be remembered that Marx's intervention underscored a project of social emancipation. Marx was a child of what Eric Hobsbawm declared as 'The Age of Revolution' as also the 'The Age of Capital'; he traversed the cusp of the two; thus, history shaped Marx in as such as he shaped history. Through his critique of Political Economy, he sought to recast our understanding of socio-economic conditions in a direction where class division would pave the way for a new classless social humanity. The critique of Political Economy underlying the hegemonic formation is thus to also rethink sociality from a new standpoint. Marx not only revealed the source, function and injustices of a class divided society, but also argued in favour of transition to a new *social humanity* of an alternative kind. His critique is thus both oppositional and propositional; it telescopes a movement against and a movement for. There is another way to interpret Marx's understanding of politics. His is a *politics of paradox*: the entry point of his framework—class as process of surplus labour—also becomes the object of struggle with the intention to dissolve it—the political goal. The objective of class based politics must be to achieve classlessness. His politics is thus geared not just to end capitalism but to terminate the source of class division altogether—exploitation per se. It is not to transit from one organization of exploitation to another (say, from feudalism to capitalism or from private capitalism to state capitalism), but to exit exploitation altogether. In the sense of this systemic transgression, his critique of Political Economy is radical, discomforting and dangerous for the hegemonic, which is also why the figure of Marx lives on as a spectre-like figure threatening to penetrate and dismantle the shield of delusional cosmology qua capitalism and of all systems flourishing on class division and exploitation.

Marx and Marxism

Marx and Marxism are not the same. Rich, complex and controversial, Marxism is a political project that evolved through reading, assimilating, interpreting, applying and developing Marx's work and sought its extension into newer directions, say, Leninism, Maoism, Trotskyism, Eurocommunism, etc. Diverse strands of his works and insights filtered and diffused into new-fangled trends in anti-colonial movements, social movements, anti-capitalism, market socialism, populism, anarchism, eco-socialism, Marxism-feminism, liberation theology, autonomous movement, community economy, etc. Because of the constant sliding of meanings that transpired in the course of reading, assimilating, interpreting, applying and developing his works and insights, it is hardly surprising that their respective understandings of Marx varied and so did the extent and type of his influence. This made it very difficult to isolate or pre-fix the interpretation or influence of Marx. Marx meant different things to different people, groups and cultures. Therefore, Marx to the Western Europeans (including self-proclaimed Marxists) and Marx to the North Korean regime are not the same; or when Dalai Lama says that, "As far as socioeconomic theory, I am Marxist" he does not read and interpret Marx in the same way as Communist Party of China (CPC) would. Notwithstanding the varied ways in which Marx's thought and presence inflected the world, it is undeniable that they influenced and shaped individuals, institutions and societies at large in many countries and, as our example shows, in different ways. What Marx is and who is a Marxist and why is one a Marxist do not thus readily fit into one suit. Marxism then is a contested space and it shows off in its political history. In the twentieth century we saw political forces self-proclaimed as Marxist capturing state power which allowed them to emerge as the dominant institution and influence. But even here what is Marxism remained open-ended as history has shown; in such situations, different alternative undercurrents and effects emerged to contest the dominant rendition of 'what is Marxism', 'what is to be done', 'what is not to be done', etc. It led to internecine conflicts within the broad field of Marxism. Such conflicts reshaped the direction of Marxism and even enriched it though at times it did have the contradictory effect of undercutting the very legitimacy of its rule and influence. Thus the rise of Stalinism was a counter-current to the diverse trends and traditions that then existed in Russia and the world Marxist movement at large; its attempt to impose a universal, singular, Marxism in turn led to a set of counter-movements opposing it. Similarly, in China, the struggle between 'revolutionaries' (preferring continual mass mobilization from below) led and influenced by Mao Zedong and 'party bureaucrats/technocrats' (preferring controlled economic development) led and influenced by Deng Xiaoping within the CPC was and is well known, recurrent and at times fierce.

The point I am trying to make is that 'Marxism' is a

differentiated field that is pulled and pushed into contradictory directions from within and outside. Within Marxism, the political movements (as described earlier) have been intersected, reinforced and compensated by 'Marxian' *theories* based on diverse interpretations of Marx. Schools of thought (to name some, Austro-Marxian, Neo-Gramscian, Political Theology, Frankfurt School, Stalinism, Maoism, Modes of Production, Dependency, Analytical Marxian, Post-structural Marxism, Eco-Socialist, Feminist-Marxism, etc.) have evolved that differed in what they took from Marx and how they sprinkled it with their points of departures, insights and extensions. Insofar as its theoretical space is concerned Marxism is thereby always in movement. These theories have evolved from, in relation to and as a reaction to political movements and political orders; as such, Marxian theories and constructions / struggles / movements have remained in a relation of mutual constitution, each affecting and (re)shaping the other. They were, in their respective ways, not only adversely inclined toward mainstream Political Economy and the socio-economic order it sustained but also competed with one another. These two— critique of Political Economy and rethinking intervention and alternative—were often conjoined since the nature of critique shaped in turn the futurity that the critique sought to embrace. Thus Stalinism understood capitalism and its shortcomings as also the alternative of socialism in a unique way, something that was not palatable to other Marxist traditions and accordingly vigorously rejected.

Three broad differences emerge from *within* the space of Marxian theories. One is *over* interpretation of Marx's critique of political economy. While there is general agreement on Marx's intent and on the need to carry it forward, one also witnesses disagreement over what that critique is (its framework, modes of reasoning, objects and subjects of analysis and its insights) and how to carry it forward. This disagreement flows from differences in what is meant by Marxian theory. The second is over the idea of alternative political theories as also its associated practical path and manner aimed at achieving social emancipation from the dominant presence of class division and its underlying injustices, no matter their social forms. The third is over the question of social re-construction, of what this alternative idea of social humanity is and how to achieve it. Given the mandate, we intend to focus on the first point even though we use insights from there to reflect upon the latter two.

We will take up two Marxian theories. In this chapter, we intend to pick on a Classical Marxian approach as delivered by G A Cohen which presents and defends Marx's historical materialism in a rigorous way[3]. What makes this theory powerful and also controversial is its unabashed defence of Marx's teleological[4] theory of history. The next chapter will exclusively focus on the question of critique of political economy as seen through a particular interpretation of Marx developed by Resnick and Wolff (1987, 2006). If we associate Classical Marxism with historical materialism and dialectical materialism (as we knew it to be) then this Marxian approach may be seen as post-Classical Marxism since it is premised on neither of these. Along with the rejection of determinism, the strength of this Marxian theory is its critique of Political Economy in the spirit of Marx as described in the first section. The common objective of both chapters is to give a sample of some of the incomparable facets that Marxism brings to the menu of thought and politics. It is also to highlight the different ways in which Marxian thought make their case as also the differences in what they emphasize and why they empharize what they emphasize so differently. With this clarification let me now build the basic contours of Cohen's historical materialism and his defence of Karl Marx's theory of history.

Trajectory of the Chapter

Historical materialism is referred to as 'scientific theory of history'. To this end, we follow the intervention of Cohen (1978, 1986a, 1986b, 1988) who lays out a model of historical materialism through an interpretation of Karl Marx's 1859 Preface to *A Contribution to the Critique of Political Economy*. As per Cohen, we start with the building blocks of society in historical materialism consisting of three essential components: (i) forces of production, (ii) relations of production and (iii) superstructure of social institutions. Together they form the structure of society from where the social being arises that then determines the consciousness/mind. Let me begin by analyzing these components to put together the definition of society and then venture out to unpack its logic of transition. The relation between the various components of a society and logic of its transition are shown to be deterministic. More precisely, at various levels, society and its transition are guided by structuralism, economic and class determinism, and teleology.

One of the major points of Cohen's intervention was the introduction of functional explanation that supposedly captures the mechanism of explaining the connection between the various components of society and of why societies rise and fall. This use of logical positivism as an explanatory device is contrasted with the dialectical laws as espoused in dialectical materialism that captures the transition in many other versions of historical materialism. Cohen is shown as arguing in favour of functional explanation as against dialectical materialism which he claims is sloppy when it comes to the explanation of the rise and fall of societies. While our treatment by no means exhausts the models of historical materialism and despite the controversy surrounding it, I take Cohen as the representative type for two reasons. It is careful and rigorous in defining and explaining the concepts comprising the theory. And, the criticisms that could be directed against Cohen's version of historical materialism seem to hold commonly across all models. The last part of the essay is directed to unpack some of the major criticisms levelled against it.

Components and Definition of Society

> In the social production of their existence, men enter into definite, necessary relations that are indispensable and independent of their will, relations of production which correspond to a definite stage of development of their material productive forces. The sum total of these relations of production constitutes the economic structure of society, the real basis, on which rises a legal and political superstructure, and to which correspond definite forms of social consciousness. The mode of production of material life conditions the social, political and intellectual life-process in general. It is

> not the consciousness of men that determines their being, but on the contrary their social being that determines their consciousness. (Marx, 1859)

This constitutes the crux of what we will use to describe Karl Marx's theory of society and its history. *Society or social totality* is an articulation of the components of forces of production, relations of production (the economic structure) and superstructure, where the forces of production are given a privileged status, both at the epistemological and at the ontological level. The structure in turn determines the social consciousness. Insofar as this overarching social totality is taken as the basic representation of reality, historical materialism adopts a frame of realism implying that all essential ingredients of knowledge are present in this society and this theory allows us to know what is essential there in society to know. In short, the truth about society can be unpacked by exploring the anatomy of this society and its dynamics. Putting it in another way, as in science, the truth of society and its transition can be derived from an underlying determinant of this society and its laws of motion. As depicted metaphorically below in a topographical manner, the basic components can be seen as representing levels of society in relation to one another.

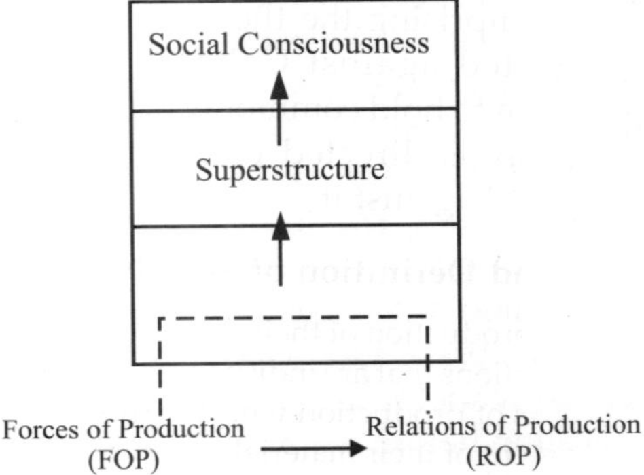

The *forces of production* consist of facilities and devices used in the process of production; it is the sum total of productive forces at the disposal of organizers of production in any society at any point in time. It includes instruments of production, raw materials, labour power, the skills and knowledge of the labour force and so forth. Labour power is devoid of any specific social content. At times, for convenience sake, the forces of production are clubbed into labour power and means of production (every other material forces other than labour power). Labour power (skill, knowledge, etc.) is considered more important than the means of production because even if the means of production are destroyed, the retained knowledge enables the labourers to recreate the means of production. Since knowledge or technology is then what remains as the most important element in the forces of production, quite often, the degree of technological development provides a rough index of the degree of development of the forces of production. These are frequently used interchangeably.

If the forces of production emphasize the material condition, the *relations of production* highlight (social) relations between people in the labour process. It describes man's practical relation with the material world in its social form. More particularly, *relations of production* take a specific social form, that of *class relations*. Cohen, unlike other Marxian theories, calls class relations of production the basis or base or foundation of society; other Marxian interpretations often refer to material forces of production as the base. Following Cohen, the base must not be confused to mean that it is the most important axis of society or of its transition; that privilege, as we shall see, is accorded to the material forces of production (quantity of means of production and labour power). In the model of historical materialism, the ***Primacy Thesis*** is that forces of production indexed by technological development is assumed to be exogenously given and determines the relations of production and everything that appears subsequently. This is akin to what may be termed as technological determinism.

One qualification before we proceed any further. Scholars interpret Marx as having used *mode of production* in different ways (Hindess and Hirst 1977, Cohen 1978 and Harvey 1982). First, he understands mode of production as the actual methods and techniques used in production under the given forms of specialization and division of labour (material mode of production). Second, mode of production captures the social properties of production process, that is, its purpose, form of producer's surplus labour and mode of exploitation (social mode of production). Third, Marx would practically refer to society (for example, in his work on *'Grundrisse'*), its entire technical and social configuration, as a mode of production (the mixed mode of production; also see Harvey). Fourth, he is interpreted as posing it as the articulation of forces of production and relations of production (Hindess and Hirst 1977). Because of its unclear nature of deployment and something that Cohen sees does not do full justice to the centrality of class relations of production in terms of economic power (I will touch on this later), he avoids using the category of mode of production.

However, and this is particularly popular in India, if we do use the term mode of production then it would infer the fourth interpretation. Following Althusser, the articulation of the forces and relations of production are also called at times infrastructure qua economic base. In that case, historical materialism would consider mode of production or infrastructure emphasizing the domain of production (the site of wealth creation) to be central. This emphasis on production (in conjunction with exchange, distribution and consumption but not as equivalent) pertains to the fact that what happens concerning production determines the rest and as such is the essential element. In this sense, the *economy* is fundamentally underlined by the organization of production prevalent in society at any historical phase, conceptualized here in terms of the mode of production. Not surprisingly, the mode of production or infrastructure is often interchangeably used for the 'economy.'

It must be said that, for Cohen, the 'economy' or economic foundation is really the relations of production and not forces of production which are the facilities and devices used in the process of production. "The sum total of relations of production in a given society is said to constitute the economic structure of that society, which is also called—in relation to the super-structure—the basis, or base, or foundation. The economic structure or base therefore consists of relations of production only; it does not include the productive forces."(Cohen 1988, p. 6)

Accepting that the separation of productive forces from the economic base, "runs against the usual construal of Marx", he nevertheless argues that, "they are below the economic foundation, the ground on which it rests" (Cohen 1988, p. 7). Even when one uses the mode of production the centrality of *primacy thesis* ensures in the structure of causality the prior presence of forces of production in relation to the relations of production.

Disputes have risen within Marxism regarding the definitional content of class relations of production, whether these are to be understood in relation to power or property or surplus labour (see the next chapter). Leaving that dispute aside for the moment, let us consider, following Cohen (1978, 1986 a, 1986b, 1988), the case whereby different relations of production can be distinguished by the fact that the direct producer (one who gives labor) may have no economic power, some economic power or total economic power over his/her own labour power and means of production. In short, class is defined in relation to the direct producer's presence or absence of economic power over the material conditions of production or forces of production (labour power and means of production). This is how Cohen differentiated the classes:

Amount of Economic Power over	His Labour Power	The Means of Production he uses
Slave	None	None
Serf	Some	Some
Proletarian	All	None
Independent	All	All

In dominant renditions of Classical Marxism, the economic power is considered as derived from the ownership/property criteria. For example, the group of people who own the means of production but not labour power is defined as the capitalist class while the other group of people who own labour power but not means of production are defined as the proletarian. Therefore class relation of production are relations of ownership; economic powers (as also forms of surplus labour and modes of appropriation) are derived from it; class as power and class as surplus labour thus get reduced to ownership deemed as encapsulating the class relations of production. But then objections have been forthcoming that ownership is a legal feature and arises at the level of superstructure (which will be explained shortly). Therefore, how can one have it at the same time in the non-legal relations of production! This is tantamount to conflating the levels of society. Cohen gets around this problem by instituting a difference between legality and control with respect to ownership of property. While accepting that 'ownership is a legal phenomenon' he claims that ownership of property can also be seen in terms of economic power as in *effective control* over the property irrespective of whether that right is legally conferred or not. Let me now explain how Cohen institutes this inversion of the above mentioned primary-secondary relation between ownership and power by offering a power theory of class. Invoking Marx, Cohen claims that

> His (Marx's) formulation implies that, at the first stage, the producer had property in a non-legal sense.
>
> Marx must have meant that he first enjoyed over his instruments effective control structurally analogous to, but unaccompanied by, legal ownership. In the usage I adopted, the said producer first had the powers which match (that is, has the same content as) the relevant legal rights of ownership, but not yet those rights themselves. My solution to the problem of legality was to represent production relations, which are commonly described in the language of ownership and rights, as, in fact relations of effective control, or powers. That a capitalist owns a particular factory is, strictly speaking, a superstructural fact. That he has effective control over it is the matching structural fact. His possession of effective control over it is his ability to dispose of it thus and so, *whatever may be that confers that ability on him* (Cohen 1988, p. 31).

Whatever may be that confers that ability on him, that is, irrespective of whether that right is socially granted or derived from the legal mandate, the structural fact is that of economic power over the forces of production enjoyed by the capitalist. The phenomenon of economic powers here, "match (that is, have the same content as) the relevant legal rights of ownership", whether officially granted or not. Those who have economic powers over means of production and labour power are assumed to have real or imputed (as if) ownership and rights over them. This is a case of reflective representation whereby economic power mirrors, captures or reflects the true meaning as it already appears in the world. Therefore, in general, as Cohen deems fit, it is legitimate to define class relations of production as economic powers over the means of production and labour power as distinct from the superstructural presence of ownership as a legal relationship.

The reason why Cohen is reluctant to use mode of production is now palpable. "The economic structure is not the way of producing, but a framework of power in which producing works...A mode of production is a way of producing." (Cohen 1978, p. 79)

Having defined the class relations of production, we now examine three related points. In class theories, when power is predicated on property relations or vice versa, exploitation (and for that matter, surplus labour, without which exploitation cannot be located) is ultimately reduced to property/power relations. Take the first instance to understand the implication. The connection would be the following: those who own means of production not only typically have economic power over them but are also, by virtue of that, necessarily exploiters. In that sense, class relations of production (defined in terms of ownership here) imply the relations of exploitation between the direct producers and non-producers. Therefore, under capitalism, only capitalists have the capacity/ability/access to exploit; this ability follows from that of class distinction made on the basis of ownership of property. The same line of argument holds for power theory of class such as that of Cohen. However, by reducing exploitation to relations of power/property structure, such approaches interrupt analysis of exploitation per se by rendering mechanisms flowing directly from the processes of surplus labour as passive, waiting to be captured or reflected by other theoretical categories (property, power, etc.). These approaches exhibit a tendency to reduce aspects related to surplus labour to aspects of power and property, rendering it as logically secondary in the hierarchy of explanation and importance. There is the tendency of disconnect of class theories of property and power with 'surplus labour' which at first tends to be demoted, then made redundant (unnecessary) and finally considered proved wrong (see Roemer 1986 for example). Cohen at least tries to maintain the connection of his power theory of class with surplus labour/exploitation unlike many of his comrades of Analytical Marxism who followed the trajectory we mentioned. In Cohen's power theory of class, the class relations of production based on more or less economic power enables the surplus labour extraction/exploitation to be created and maintained (although he expresses doubts about the labour theory of value and argues that posing exploitation does not need that theory). Nevertheless, while he foregrounds the connection between class relations of production and exploitation, the latter is reduced to the former that is, ultimately, predicated on power in the way we have explained.

Second, class here is considered as a noun—a homogenous group of people who can act. We shall come back to this point later on, but it is to be noted that class is not designated as a process but as a group of people. Class struggle is not fundamentally a struggle *over* class processes (of surplus labour) between contingent group of contextually formed collective but that what transpires *between* a priori homogenous groups of social actors (derived from their structural positions) for economic control over the forces of production.

Thirdly, at any point in time, many kinds of relations of production may exist. Cohen defines 'economic structure' as the sum total of the relations of production in a given society. However, it is one class relations of production that will be dominant with the others subordinated to it. Almost always, society or the social formation is ultimately reduced to 'dominant'production relations. Thus for example, a feudal social formation is one in which the feudal production relations is dominant and it is what principally matters in examining that order.

Another component of society is the *superstructure*, which consists of only those political, legal and cultural aspects of the society that help reproduce the relations of production. In this sense, relations of production are the (economic) foundation, a foundation on which culture and politics rise. These include the state, legal structure, education, religion, etc. For example, law facilitates the class relations of production and props up the interest of the ruling class. "In a capitalist society capitalists have effective power over means of production. What confers them that power on a given capitalist, say an owner of a factory? On what can he rely if others attempt to take control of the factory away from him? An important part of the answer is this: he can rely on the law of the land, which is enforced by the might of the state...The content of the legal system is explained by its function, which is to help sustain an economy of a particular kind" (Cohen 1988, p. 9). However, to be careful, not everything (such as art in general) is part of the superstructure. Critical is the state. It is seen as the instrument of political organization of the ruling class. In many Marxian approaches (not Cohen) it is at times seen as the collective embodiment of all other elements of superstructure. For example, law is created by the state. The state is supposed to control the political and cultural institutions as well. The objective of the state is to create, regulate and control social institutions that will reflect, justify, protect, serve and uphold the existing class relationship and through that the existing material basis of society. Thus, for example, under capitalism, a state will secure and develop the capitalist class relations of production and its existing material basis. The import, theoretical and practical, attached by Marxists to state stems from this importance they give it. Insofar as the state subsumes everything else in the superstructure, Marxian politics often tend to become state-centric. Cohen though is more careful in maintaining the distinct features and roles of each of the elements in the superstructure, and we will follow his clue.

Finally, there are forms of *social consciousness* capturing the mindset/disposition of the subjects in a manner that are consistent with the superstructure of a society. For example, the mindset favouring the norms of impersonal relations (such as impersonal exchange of property rights through market) would sustain the legal superstructure that in turn would have to be consistent with a capitalist relations of production.

Superstructure and forms of consciousness are included within the social totality but they do not have primary explanatory power so far as the reproduction, crisis or development of society are concerned. According to the theory of historical materialism, the superstructure and forms of consciousness depend on and are caused/explained by the class relations of production. This is what we call *class determinism*. If we refer to class relations of production as the economy which then determines the superstructure and consciousness, economic determinism and class determinism coincide at that level. Using a different definition, we can say that the mode of production (forces and relations of production) is causally prior to all other aspects of society. If we take the mode of production as the economic base then consciousness and superstructure are reduced to the economy. Whatever the way the levels of society are posed, this deterministic property has often been described as *economism* or *economic essentialism/determinism*. And, as mentioned earlier, the explanation of the class relations of production by the forces of production can be seen as a case of *technological determinism*. Depending upon the variations in our conceptualization of society, the levels of determinism will change. Nevertheless, they will be instrumental in determining the specific relations between the components of society.

Not only are there an embedded material/technological determinism, economic determinism and class determinism (depending upon the layers of relation) but the structure (consisting of forces of production, relations of production and superstructure) also determines the subject/consciousness producing in turn structural determinism as well. Historical materialism is evidently a structuralist model held together by functional explanation and axioms that privilege the structure (to be explained).

Within the structure of mode of production, historical materialism considers the forces of production to be independent of and causally prior (in order of explanation) to the relations of production. Primacy of the forces of production is an axiom within the historical materialist model.This sequential structure of causality produces a hierarchical order at the root of which are the material forces of production. It is the ground on which class relations of production rise and then on that foundation arise the superstructure and forms of consciousness respectively. All of these together constitute a complex social totality. However, this complex social totality has a centre or essence (forces of production) to which every other aspect of society owes their existence, even though the existence of forces of production is given *a priori* and whose privilege remains unquestioned.

Not only is there a primacy of forces of production in the conceptualization of society, but it also enjoys a privileged status in the transition of society. That is, there is an additional axiom in this model—the material forces of production develop progressively over time; this being the *Developmental Thesis*. The historical trajectory of the rest of the components of society is guided by this developmental thesis. The Primacy Thesis and Developmental Thesis foreground what is 'materialism'. The theory of history will supplement this materialism to produce historical materialism. But before proceeding to Marx's theory of history, we need to discuss an issue of central importance.

Puzzle of Historical Materialism

At this point, we land in a problem insofar as conceptualizing the relations between the structural components of society is concerned. According to Cohen, the explanatory device provided by the philosophy of dialectical materialism has not been able to resolve this problem. What then is going to be the explanatory device? The problem and the explanatory device to solve it are what we discuss below.

Recall Marx's observation in the Preface that says that "Men enter into definite, necessary relations that are indispensable and independent of their will, relations of production which *correspond* to a definite stage of development of their material productive forces". Cohen turns his attention to the term *correspondence*. Does correspondence means that the relation between forces and relations of production is symmetrical? "If relations correspond to forces, forces must correspond to relations." But then in that case, the primacy thesis entailing that, "The level of development of productive power explains the nature of the economic structure" gets violated. According to Cohen, such an interpretation of the term correspondence is inconsistent with Marx's layout in the Preface in *A Contribution to the Critique of Political Economy*. He contends that, "correspondence is not always symmetrical...'correspond' means, roughly, 'are explained by'" (Cohen 1978, p. 137). Given this asymmetry inferred in the term correspondence, one must accept that productive forces explain relations of production which he argues is clearly asserted in Marx.

But then 'correspondence' would also mean that relations of production might have influenced and through them advanced the development of the forces of production. Cohen argues that Marx gives enough indication to this effect. For example, in the Preface one finds the following, "No economic structure (set of production relations) ever perishes before all the productive forces for which there is room in it have developed...new higher relations of production never appear before the material conditions of their existence have matured in the womb of the old society itself" (Cohen 1978, pp. 140-41). This asserts that relations of production have a role in developing the forces of production and does so till it has exhausted its ability to do so fully.

The term 'correspond' then harbours a puzzle. On the one hand, it is claimed that forces of production exist independently and are causally prior to relations of production; it explains the existence of relations of production. On the other hand, it is also claimed that relations of production influence and control the forces of production. How can both be true and logically holding together in tandem?[5] Here, Cohen makes a decisive contribution to historical materialism. He argues that this type of correspondence between the different structures attributable to Marx can only be consistently explained by *functional explanation* whereby the existence of the cause is explained in terms of its effect. At stake here is the very explanation of the relations between the structures in the society and of their transition subsequently.

Functional Explanation and the Solution to the Puzzle

Cohen (1978, 1986b, 1988) distinguishes between functionalisms in general and functional explanation; he rejects the former for being sloppy and states that it is only the latter which is logically correct. Let us begin by asserting what functional explanation is not.

Statement 1: '*e* occurred because *f* occurred.' This is logically inconsistent because it represents a later occurrence as explaining an earlier one. How can what causes (*e*) an aftereffect of (*f*); Isn't it a violation of the order of causality? Because the order of causality is violated, *e* cannot be the cause and f the effect.

Statement 2: '*e* occurred because it caused *f*'. This is also wrong because by the time *e* has caused *f*, *e* has occurred, so that the fact that it caused *f* could not explain its occurrence. The problem here is that there are two times and the explanation is one.

Functional explanation, in contrast, refers to the logic of relationship in which the cause is explained in terms of the effect. The structure of causality entailing that *e* is the cause and *f* the effect holds true only under the circumstances: when *e* occurred because the situation was such that an event like e would cause an event like *f*. Generally, "something which has certain effect is explained by the fact that it has that effect." (Cohen 1988, p. 8) Two examples, as per Cohen, can be forwarded.

Example 1:

'Birds have hollow bones because hollow bones facilitate flight.'

That birds having hollow bones facilitate flight is explained by the fact that it has the effect of facilitating flight.

Example 2:

'Shoe factories operate on a large scale because of the economies large scale brings'

That shoe factories operating on large scale having the effect of economies of scale is explained by the fact that it has that effect.

Let us now apply functional explanation to the model of society in historical materialism. First, take the case of the relations between the forces and relations of production by delivering a logically consistent rendering of 'correspondence.' The numbers indicate propositions.

1. The level of development of productive power explains why certain relations and not others would advance productive power,

2. Relations which advance productive power obtain because they advance productive power,

It follows that:

3. The level of development of productive power explains the nature of the productive relations.

Proposition 1 asserts which relations of production, say of *k* type, *would* be appropriate to develop the forces of production. It states the possibility of which type of relations (or, economic structure) is appropriate to be selected and which is not. It says nothing about whether the relations will actually obtain or not. Therefore 1 does not entail the primacy of forces of production over relations of production. Now the role of functional explanation appears. Proposition 2 affirms that the fact that relations of type *k* facilitate the development of forces of production explains why that type of relations *obtain*. Thus "Production relations prevail because they are relations which advance the development of the productive forces" (Cohen 1988, p. 10). Proposition 2 explains which relations type obtain but does not capture the primacy of the forces of production over relations. 1 entails that the level of forces of production at a certain historical point will select certain and not all relations of production depending upon which of these have the capacity to raise its level further. Therefore, the order of relationship—forces of production first and then relations of production—is fixed by 1. 2 implies that, courtesy the functional explanation, only the relations of production selected by forces of production will obtain by virtue of their effects of developing the level of the forces of production. Combining 1 and 2 we get proposition 3 which guarantees the primacy of the forces of production over relations of production even as relations of production facilitate the development of the forces of production. Regarding the question as to "How productive forces select economic structures which promote their development" (Cohen 1988, p. 17), Cohen argues that he does not have a good answer and this is one area of future research. But he also contends that not knowing 'how' does in no way nullify the order of relationship between the productive forces and relations.

The above analysis, made consistent by a functional explanation, is also true for relations among the other levels of society. The economic base of relations of production at any historical time selects which superstructure, say *s*, would be suitable for its functioning (which in turn would advance the development of the productive forces); the fact superstructure can sustain and regulate the relations of production explains why the superstructure of that kind obtains. Together, they give rise to proposition 4.

4. The economic structure explains the nature of the superstructure.

Cohen argues that (3) and (4) are functional explanations because that is the only way to reconcile the following two theses:

5. The economic structure promotes the development of the productive forces, and

6. The superstructure stabilizes the economic structure.

As Cohen avers, "(5) and (6), in conjunction with (3) and (4), do force us to treat historical materialist explanation as functional... No other treatment preserves consistency between the explanatory primacy of the productive forces over the economic structure and the massive control of the latter over the former, or between the explanatory primacy of the economic structure over the superstructure and the latter's regulation of the former" (1988, p. 3).

Similarly, consciousness is explained by the superstructure and ultimately by the economic structure. Cohen invokes Marx's Preface once again where he contends, "It is not the consciousness of people that determines their being, but, on the contrary, their social being that determines their consciousness". Now Cohen goes on to the details of what Marx meant by social being (1988, pp. 37-50). He argues that, "what Marx meant by 'social being' was a particular one or a set of a person's social roles, namely, his economic role(s)." Cohen sketches the connection thus.

> The foundation is an economic structure, a set of production relations, whereas the social being of a person is his position in it; and the superstructure is a set of non-economic institutions (of law, politics, religion, education, etc.) in which persons participate with a consciousness grounded in their being. (Cohen 1988, pp. 45-46)

Superstructure being the site of stabilization and conflict, he contends that "none of this occurs except through the agency of human beings, whose actions are inspired by their ideas, but whose ideas are more or less determined by their economic roles." (Cohen 1988, pp. 45-46). This gives us the following.

7. Economic structure and superstructure determine the social being (subject) and embedded consciousness.

Finally, we combine the functional explanation connecting the relations between the various components of society with the *Development Thesis* saying that:

8. The productive forces tend to develop throughout history.

Like primacy thesis, the development thesis is taken as an axiom. Propositions (3), (5), (7) and (8) would deliver a coherent and consistent explanation of Marxian society and its theory of history as described below.

One thing is clear though. In historical materialism, whether at the level of defining the society or the logic of its transition, the essential, core, determining element is the forces of the production. And this is secured through the explanatory device of functional explanation.

Cohen sees functional explanation as *revolutionary* in two respects: "it predicts large-scale social transformations, and it claims that their course is violent." (Cohen 1986, p. 227) The aspect of large-scale transformations is due to the fact that "historical materialism puts the growth of human powers at the centre of the historical process, and it is to this 'extra-social' development that society itself is constrained to adjust." (1986, p. 227) The necessity of violence is due to the class conflict without which the above transition cannot transpire. We shall now explore both these features in details.

Transition Model I: GA Cohen's Defence of Marx's History

Cohen dismissed the idea of dialectical materialism as an explanatory device of explaining transition from one epoch to another on the basis of fettering and contradiction. Instead, he gave that privilege to functional explanation. More particularly, the roles of Primacy Thesis (3) and Development Thesis (8) as central in this underlying logic of transition are established.

Recall that the Development Thesis of historical materialism says that the forces of production tend to development throughout history. This is a historical exigency that is derived from the rationality of the people which says that people "are disposed to reflect on what they are doing and to discern superior ways of doing it" in the face of material scarcity which does not allow them to advance their wants. Given this rationality and material scarcity (both derived from nature, human and material), people will when given an opportunity tend to expand productive forces to fulfil their human wants. Not to do so is irrational which is ruled out. People's rationality works in another way. As a logical extension, they reject or accept relations of production depending upon their capacity to improve or not improve the forces of production. Again, not to do so is irrational and is hence ruled out. There are, in Cohen, two further underlying axioms which appear: that of material scarcity (that is very similar to the neoclassical understanding of economics as a choice to fulfil unlimited wants under the constraint of material scarcity) and that of the embedded principle of rationality amongst humans. Given material scarcity, there is a human agency impetus to go on developing the forces of production.

The material scarcity causing the human engine to develop the forces of production is also the reason as to why class divisions appear. This is because getting power over the productive forces means that the cost of material scarcity will not be shared equally amongst people. That is, those who enjoy effective powers over means of production will have inordinate access to the products and the surplus as compared to the rest of the population who become dependent on them. It is also the case that, "class struggle is...a principal means whereby the forces assert themselves over the relations." (Cohen 1986, p. 233) Two kinds of struggles arise: one between the mentioned two classes—ruling versus ruled—in any epoch and the second between the ruling classes versus those who want to take control over the forces of production. Note that in any era the ruled class (say, serfs under feudalism) and the class wanting to overthrow the existing ruling class (say, capitalist class under feudalism) may not be the same. Which struggle will triumph? Referring to feudalism as an example, Cohen's answer is unambiguous.

> Part of the answer is that there is a general stake in stable and thriving production, so that the class best placed to deliver it attracts allies from other strata in society. Prospective ruling classes (capitalist class, emphasis ours) are often able to raise support among the classes subjected to the ruling class (feudal lord class, emphasis ours) they would displace. Contrariwise, classes unsuited to the task of governing society (serfs; emphasis ours) tend to lack the confidence political hegemony requires, and if they do seize power, they tend not to hold it for long. (Cohen 1986, p. 233)

Other contenders like some of the feudal lords or merchants too will modify their operations on a capitalist basis and undergo a change in class character. Therefore, "the class which rules through a period, or emerges triumphant from epochal conflict does so because it is best suited, most able and disposed, to preside over the development of the productive forces at the given time" (Cohen 1988, p. 15). Accordingly, the relations of production which will procreate the economic power of the class with the above property will appear. In short, the rise and fall of classes are determined by the development of the forces of production.

Given this *Development Thesis*, the basic idea in historical materialism is that relations of production correspond to a particular stage of development of the productive forces such that peoples' wants can be satisfied. By correspondence, we mean that forces of production 'select' particular relations of production that in turn will promote the development of the forces of production as consistently explained through functional explanation. Which type? As we have already explained, it will be that associated production relations that sustain the economic power of the class which is 'best suited, most able and disposed, to preside over the development of the productive forces at the given time.' Similarly political and other cultural institutions/practices correspond to the relations of production, and forms of social consciousness arise on the received superstructure.

This *holistic* conception of society is stable if all other aspects of society, notably class relations of production, are such that they do not impede the development of the forces of production in any manner. If, at any point, relations of production do create barriers to the free development of the forces of production, a condition of social crisis arises which can be resolved only with the advent of new relations of production. Who creates the fetters of whom? Existing relations of production fetter productive forces signifying that they are no longer optimal in providing scope for the latter's development. The incompatibility or non-optimality or disequilibrium between forces and relations of production is at times captured by the notion of contradiction. Contradiction is thus a historical point of this incompatibility that arrests the development of the forces of production. It also signals that something has to give way in the relations of production as per the *Development Thesis*. This schism signifies the cusp of transition from one epoch (stage of history) to another epoch.

This new relations of production will be so selected by the forces of production that it will provide maximum scope for the productive use and development of the forces of production. Evidently, the drive of the presumed rationality of the people trying to overcome the material scarcity will ensure that such a kind of relations of production obtains. Anything else (that is, other relations of production) again will be irrational and hence are to be rejected. This change in economic structure in turn brings about a change in the superstructure, and the latter in turn brings about a change in the forms of consciousness.

Does the stage of history follow certain pattern that ties together the optimal/progressive change from one epoch to another? Here, Cohen draws upon a detailed correspondence between the images of history in Hegel and Marx. (1978, pp. 1-27, pp. 175-215) "We put forth Hegel's conception of history as the life of the world spirit, and we show how Marx took that conception, preserved its structure, and changed its content." (1978, p. 1) How? Cohen sums up their basic similarity and difference in the following two quotes:

> Hegel: History is the history of the world spirit (and, derivatively, human consciousness) which undergoes growth in self-knowledge, the stimulus and vehicle of which is a culture, which perishes when it has stimulated more growth than it can contain.
>
> Marx: History is the history of human industry, which undergoes growth in productive power, the stimulus and vehicle of which is an economic structure, which perishes when it has stimulated more growth than it can contain. (Cohen (1978, p. 26) the names Hegel and Marx, our emphasis)

It is however the case, Cohen contends, that Marx's materialism triumphs over Hegel's idealism because, unlike Hegel, his is not just a philosophy of history but a theory of history that is able to contribute to a rigorous explanation of the inner dynamics of society and its transition. But then if, "Marx's conception of history preserves the structure of Hegel's but endows it with fresh content" and we already have developed the contents in details then what is the structure in Hegel that Marx's theory of history preserves? The answer lies in the understanding of what in Hegel's, historical dialectic is appropriated in Marxian theory of history. There is a catch here too for at the same time Cohen claims that, "I do not affirm any dialectical laws" (Cohen 1988, p. 185). He seems to be suggesting that if one attributes dialectics to Marx at all then its meaning has to be on a different footing from that of Hegel and certainly dialectical materialism. The difference that he is driving at is the following. By invoking Hegel, he is not referring to laws of dialectics as in dialectical materialism. He rejects this since, as he sees, the explanatory device used to capture the relations between the levels of society and the reasoning for their transition in Marxian theory flows from functional explanation. On the question of why the stages of society (history) unfold as they do, the Hegelian induced laws (no matter their inversion) derived in dialectical materialism are dubbed as sloppy and certainly not that of Marx. That is, as Cohen sees it, Marx has a theory of history that is irreducible to Hegel. What is valuable in Hegel's concept of dialectics is its 'descriptive residue' (not its explanatory feature) which, when one starts to explain Marx's theory of history, emerges as a good imagery to capture the ascent in the stages that Marx denotes. Its value is metaphorical rather than explanatory. This imagery of Hegel is a structure of sequence of ascent of society and to which we move next.

The sequence can be discerned from the Hegelian triad of affirmation, negation and negation of negation. Broadly, it claims that the initial society (affirmation) ends up revealing contradictions, meaning that it contains within itself the seeds of dissolution (negation) leading to the creation of a more complex qualitatively superior society and also the seeds of the dissolution of that society as well (negation of negation). The contradictions do not lead to the destruction of the society but rather to its supersession to a higher stage. Roughly, Hegel divides real history constituting the *subject* (World Spirit or Reason)/*object* (nature) duality into three stages:

(a) Undifferentiated unity (when man and nature are indistinguishable but man does not know nature); primitive encounter between mind and the world; no reflection and hence no distinction between the subject and the object; sphere of innocence.

(b) Differentiated disunity (when man realizes he is different from nature but cannot conquer it); absolute distinction between mind/subject and world/object; sphere of understanding which though lacks reason in the sense that the mind does not know what to do with understanding of distinctions.

(c) Differentiated unity (when *man* knows he is different from nature and comprehends nature completely); deeper unities among understanding of distinctions

> without abandoning the distinctions themselves in the sphere of reason.

History in Hegel is the ascent of knowledge throughthese stages in the rank order intended to resolve the division and conflict between subject/object. Undifferentiated unity is the affirmation which is negated by differentiated disunity which is further negated (therefore, negation of negation) by differentiated unity. It is self-evident that given the structure of sequence one cannot skip stages (say, skip stage 2 to go straight from 1 to 3).

Marx's theory of history gels well with the image of Hegelian history. It is the sketch of the sequencing that is of interest to Marx and not the theory itself. To begin with, Marxian theory of historical materialism typically considers five basic stages/epochs of society[6] in the following rank order:

1. Primitive Communism
2. Slavery
3. Feudalism/Serfdom
4. Capitalism
5. Communism

Recall, the epochs are differentiated according to their class relations of production which in turn are explained by the material conditions of forces of production. Under historical materialism, history moves from undifferentiated unity (primitive communism) to differentiated disunity (slave, feudal and capitalist society, that is, societies divided by optimality crisis and class division/conflict) arriving finally at differentiated unity (communism or a society with no optimality crisis and consequently no class and class conflict) initiated by a series of sequential shifts in the relations of production that is in turn selected by the level of forces of production at each transition point. According to Cohen, why this movement occurs in this way has already been explained by functional explanation. Each stage in history is negated by the next one that describes the evolution of society through contradiction. The contradiction between the forces and relations of production (given by the fettering of the former by the latter) within each complex society leads to a new process of selection of another type of relations of production conducive to the development of the forces of production and subsequently superstructure and social consciousness that arise on the basis of it. That is, each contradiction is resolved to give rise to a new complex society—a higher moment of the original society—and subsequently a new contradiction within it.This new complex totality is a higher moment in the qualitative sense that the forces of production are freer to develop as compared to the previous complex social totality.

Clearly, this way of looking at history is teleological or historicist where everything in it has an underlying purpose. It reflects a rational, ordered, and progressive movement of society from a preordained origin to a predestined end. The rational element is the essence—here, the forces of production; its development signals progress which is coterminous with a higher order of society and this progressive movement starts from a given point—primitive communism—and moves with a law like ordered motion to end where history is destined to reach, finally—communism. The historical trajectory and its transition is guided by the *underlying purpose* of the development of the forces of production such that every turn, bend and shift in stages comes to be explained in terms of the more general journey of the society towards its destined end – communism; 'progress' is judged by the proximity of a stage to communism. The force is revolutionary which personifies the movement of society forward and that is reactionary which intends to hold it back. Can one skip stages? No way, answers Cohen and for that he subscribes to Marx's Preface once again, "No social formation ever perishes before all the productive forces for which there is room in it have developed; and new, higher relations of production never appear before the material conditions of their existence have matured in the womb of the old society itself." Elsewhere, he provides this quote from Marx, "If the proletariat overthrows the political rule of the bourgeoisie, its victory will only be temporary...as long as the material conditions have not yet been created which make necessary the abolition of the bourgeois mode of production" (Marx quoted in Cohen 1988, p. 15). If one agrees to it, the following interpretation follows suit. In the longer span of history,the establishment of Soviet rule was an unfortunate accident of history that was bound to fail or that the effort of Chinese Communist Party to establish capitalism was a corrective measure to rectify its accidental capture of state power in 1949 and Mao Zedong's premature adventure to establish a post-capitalist society. Till the time there is no further room for the existing relations of production to develop the forces of production, the former will not perish.

We surmise that in historical materialism developed by Cohen if essentialism/determinism is the undisputed logic of the social then historicism is the undisputed logic of transition; and as we have described above, the two logics supplement one another. The essence (forces of production) serves as the rational element in whose terms historicism operates and the historicist logic in turn captures the dynamics of transition, the inexorable ascent of human society in stages.

Under communism—the end of history—the forces of production reach a state of development such that the relations of production can no longer act as fetters to technological development. This epoch signals a change from material scarcity to material abundance such that human wants cannot be aborted. The basis of classes and consequently class struggle disappears. As Cohen states, "Marxism sees history as a protracted process of liberation–from the scarcity imposed on humanity by nature, and from the oppression imposed by some people on others. Members of the ruling and subject classes share the cost of natural scarcity unequally, and Marxism predicts, and fights for, the disappearance of society's perennial class division." (1988, p. vii) Humanity frees itself from both material and social limitations. The forces of production now has reached a stage where it need not contend with the problem of material scarcity and hence of conflicts amongst humans regarding who will have greater access and control of economic power over labour power and means of production; there is no rational purpose to be served by trying to garner such control because it fetches nothing additional for them. In contrast, here, rational organization of society comes to be based upon: 'from each according to his ability to each according to his need".

On route to the establishment of communism from capitalism, property is socialized and thereby property division is abolished. The source to draw economic power for one group as against another is taken way. Resultantly, the basis of class relations of production disappears and so does class struggle. Therefore, under communism, both the incentive and basis of class division disappear.

With the establishment of classless society, the reason for the existence of the state is no longer there. Its superstructural role as the facilitator of class relations of production becomes redundant and unwanted. Under communism, we have statelessness accompanying classlessness. In its place, different kinds of institutions aimed at reproducing the 'social humanity' appear.

Role of Class Struggle

Where is class struggle in all of this? Class struggle is secondaryto the contradiction between the relations and forces of production. This is not to say that it is unimportant but it appears at the level of "main events of that course (of history) and the surface relief of society"and not the "fundamental explanation of the course of history and the structure of society" (Cohen 1988, p. 14). Let us explore this point before we proceed to formulate its exact role in the epochal stage of historical materialism.

To begin with, Cohen distinguishes the revolutionary and the reactionary class on the basis of *Development Thesis*. That class is revolutionary which has the potential to develop productive forces more effectively, and this force emerges, as per the logic of historical materialism, the winner from the epochal conflict. One can see that the rationality principle finds its expression in the collective manifestation of divided classes and that too in relation to the epochal contradiction between the forces and relations of production. This is important for it distinguishes Cohen from some of his comrades in the Analytical Marxist group (using the game theory) who conceptualize class struggle as a continual battle going on in terms of strategic behaviour. Cohen criticizes this approach for its inability to situate class wars in the historical plane of epochal shift, that is, the location where class struggle become class wars (as opposed to battles) in the sense that they are instrumental in producing historical changes of the kind demanded by historical materialism. Cohen interprets Marx and Engels' claim that, "The history of all hitherto existing society is the history of class struggles" to be implying that, "major historical changes are brought about by class struggle." (1988, p. 14) Unlike continuous class battles, Cohen locates the source in Marx of why the class wars are settled in one way or another not in strategic behaviour but in the 'character of the forces of production.' This explains the importance of class struggle qua class war in Marx's theory of history, but its secondary presence to that of contradiction between the forces and relations of production derived from the assumed inevitability of the development of the productive forces must be kept in mind.

In historical materialism, if the condition for transition lies in the contradiction between the forces and relations of production, its medium is class struggle. Each society is divided into two opposed classes. The relations of groups of people organized with respect to the power describe the class character of the relations of production within a society. Class divisions are germane to the slave, feudal and capitalist modes of production. As the relations of production become fetter to the development of the forces of production, class conflict intensifies. Since classes (defined in terms of property or power) embodies diverging groups' locations vis-a-vis the creation and appropriation of surplus, the conflict expresses itself in the inability of the ruling class to extract its desired surplus from within the existing relations of production. It also means that the fulfilment of wants of the mass of people becomes increasingly difficult to attain. That is, a crisis in reproducing the necessary surplus leads to an extreme form of social antagonism between the two existing classes erupting into a class war. The existing class relations of production are thus no longer conducive to the development of the forces of production which, given the Development Thesis, must develop which in turn means that the crisis must be resolved through class wars. The scenario is made murkier by the entry of the new class force that is attempting to usurp the economic power from the hands of the old ruling class. As we exemplified earlier, the sharpening of the conflict between the lord and the serf during the crisis of feudalism saw the rise of nascent capitalist class intent on usurping power. The conflict erupts into and disrupts the reproduction of the superstructure as well making its institutionalized socio-political order difficult to sustain. Under the growing challenges, the ruling order or the its representative state is no longer seen as capable of securing the existing class relations of production; the conflict is resolved through a change in economic power that takes the form of a new revolutionary class ultimately defeating the existing ruling class. Therefore, Marxian theory describes how the bourgeoisie appears as revolutionary class under feudalism to defeat the feudal ruling class of lords. In turn, such a resolution of the crisis leads to new class relations of production (again, specified in terms of new set of economic powers over the forces of production) that will provide ample space for the arrested forces of production to develop freely once again and thus allow the new ruling class to achieve a desirable level of surplus extraction. As an example, the previous revolutionary class of capitalists becomes now the ruling class under capitalism and the working class the newly formed ruled class. A new class differentiation and conflict between the two classes emerge. Thus, as the forces of production change, so does the class relationships of production and so do the new elements of superstructure conducive to the new class relations of production, leading to new class struggle and a conflict in the new society born out of the womb of the old. And so history is made and unmade.

Imperialism as a Pioneer of History

Cohen's thesis that history is essentially moved by the development of productive powers has had its adherents among other Marxists since the 1890s onward when the linkage between the Western countries and the 'backward nations' became an important topic of analysis among Western European as well as Eastern European Marxists, including the Russian Marxists. Despite other significant differences, Engels, Kautsky, Hilferding, Plekhanov, Lenin, Trotsky, Bukharin and Luxemberg seem to agree that imperialism (which most of them identified with monopoly capitalism) distinguished by the domination of finance capital, export of capital, centralization of capital, formation of cartels and territorial division of the world amongst the advanced countries, produced an all-round development of capitalism serving not only the imperialist countries but also carried the possibility of the colonized countries to break the shackles of pre-capitalist formations. Theorists like Lenin and Bukharin however expressed doubt that imperialism might have run out of its progressive impetus and could be, in this historical juncture, seen as merely an instrument for plundering the resources of backward nations for the benefit of imperial power represented by monopoly capitalism. That is, imperialism in the early twentieth century might have become a cause of underdevelopment of imperialized nations by preventing the development of the forces of production there. Therefore, the progressive journey that capitalism was supposed to personify through its application at a global level jerked to a halt implying that it had become a barrier to the development of history; to recall, this was one of the justifications given for initiating a socialist revolution in 'backward' Russia. This implied under-development thesis in Lenin and others of that time was picked up, developed and popularized later by scholars like Paul Baran, Paul Sweezy, A.G. Frank and others during the 1950s-70s period. In doing so, it drew Bill Warren's ire who in contrast upheld imperialism as progressive and argued his thesis as the only plausible outcome of the historical materialist model. Let us briefly revisit Warren's argument in order to establish the connection of imperialism to the development of the forces of production.

Warren (1980) in a provocative book declared imperialism and its modern version in neocolonialism (post-independent status of the peripheral countries) to be the pioneer of capitalism. Justifying the capitalist penetration of Third World countries through imperialism, Warren argues that imperialism helps to develop the forces of production and set up advanced society in these countries. He asserts that even if one accepts the argument of underdevelopment theorists about international bondage, the satellites are still better off as compared to the counterfactual situation where foreign investment and international exchange relations are absent, a solution that was argued for fiercely by the underdevelopment theorists in opposition to the bondage. Following Warren, gains from trade far outweigh the gains from autarky and trade helps in the *development of the forces of production* by enabling the satellites to stay on the cutting edge of global competition. If trade takes the form of imperialism or neo-imperialism, so be it. It is self-evident that Warren's defence of imperialism was a logical culmination of the deterministic role of forces of production in his rendition of historical materialism and the self-fulfilling rational and progressive connotation in its theory of history. The transition of society was to take place as per the logic of 'industrialization through capital accumulation' which is the other name of industrialization through growth of productive powers (for capital accumulation in Marxian sense is the growth of sum total of labour power and means of production) and that too by whatever means possible. This too was Hariss' (1986) point, which expands on Warren's proposition with the aid of wide-ranging data from the development process of the 'newly industrializing countries' such as those of East Asia. It must be remembered though that, unlike Marx and Engels (for example, they opposed British occupation of Ireland), who differentiated between the imperialisms, Warren seems to produced a one-dimensional representation of imperialism by arguing that all imperialisms are valuable for the colonized countries.

Transition Model II—Dialectical Materialism

For most Marxists of classical variety, historical materialism refers to the 'scientific theory of history' while dialectical materialism refers to 'Marxist philosophy'. Dialectical materialism underlines the functioning logic of transition in historical materialism. Cohen of course did not use dialectical materialism which he considered as lazy epistemology. Instead, he replaced the logic of historical materialism by functional explanation that he contended serves as the central logic of explaining the primacy of the forces of production over relations of production, production relations as providing real foundation to the superstructure and of *why* epochal shifts in history take place. He considered the parts of society as independent and autonomous of one another. Once having posed them, he then used the functional explanation to explore their roles and basis of transition. In contrast, Marxists following dialectical materialism reject the fact of autonomous and independent existence of the parts and emphasize instead interdependence and inter-penetrability. Let us explain.

Unlike Cohen who adopts Hegel's image of history encapsulating the sketch of sequence of stages, dialectical materialism adopts the methodology of Hegelian dialectic. In Hegel, dialectics presumes that mind/world spirit is primary while matter is secondary. Idealism and not materialism is Hegel's foundational basis. Marxist theory changes the content of the model by taking the forces of production—the material basis of society—as the fundamental bedrock of society and its transition. It replaces idealism by materialism. The philosophy of dialectical materialism is based on certain assumptions.

The central assumption of dialectical materialism deployed in historical materialism says that, given that matter is the central objective reality in Nature, Man's relation with the material world, his material conditions of life, forms the fundamental objective reality in society. There are some fallouts of this assumption, at least in the overwhelming approaches that follow dialectical materialism. To begin with, *matter is primary* and man's social experiences and activities secondary. Man must first fulfil his need to produce his livelihood before he can devote time for other activities like family, religion, art, etc. This introduces a temporal sequence whereby man's reproduction of livelihood from the material resources of nature must come before the development of other aspects of society. Another aspect that follows from the above would refer to the cause and effect of society, that is, what determines society, its reproduction and transition. Man's practical relations with the material world would in turn be constituted by a basic set of *property relations* which in turn would determine the existence and type of other social institutions such as government, law, politics, religion, education, etc. The latter exists to serve the former. This entails that dialectical materialism introduces a *essentialist/deterministic* structure of causality (relation between cause and effect) in which man's practical relations with the material world (inclusive of man's encounter with material resources of nature and property relations) is the primary, objective reality—the material basis—that would determine the existence, nature and functioning of all other social institutions, the super-structure.

Given this preliminary set up, the philosophy of dialectical materialism is characterized, among others, by a few features. First, the components in the world do not exist as independent and autonomous of one another but as mutually interpenetrating and interdependent parts of one vast, continuous process. Objects can only be understood in relation to other objects and are in a state of change. Every object is a process, interactive and changing. Therefore, the components of the forces of production, relations of production and of super-structure are related and changing, and their manner of relation too undergo change. Secondly, it considers the process of change in a special way. Sequences of additive, quantitative change give rise to qualitative shifts. This is *lawlike* and derived from natural science (properties of atoms, molecules and cells) which then was applied to analysis of society by Marxian theory. The point at which the quantitative accumulation of change produces a qualitative alteration of reality is known as the nodal point. This centrality of process is not acceptable to Cohen who says, "In seeing dialectic in a process, we discern its contour in an intellectually satisfying manner, but the explanation of why it does is not thereby disclosed to us." (1988, p. 185)

Anyway, these two points give rise to a third feature of dialectical materialism, that of a materialistically based theory of evolution. That is, since at the nodal point, the cumulative quantitative change gives rise to qualitative changes, old society must be giving way to new society. It signals a juncture where the present society, say, with feudal property relations, has become inconsistent with the developed material forces of production as a result of the change from the quantitative to the qualitative. Hence, new relations of production must arrive so as to facilitate the development of the material forces of production. The character of process of change means that the society must be in a state of evolution, moving from one qualitative shift to another. The movement from primitive communism to slavery to feudalism to capitalism to communism is reflective of this nodal point shift signifying the shift from the quantitative to the qualitative.

The dialectic from beginning to end is the development of the same essence (say, forces of production) that represents itself from the lower to the higher moments via the alienation of the original simple totality. This simple totality driving the complex totality develops by alienating (negating) itself to represent an ever-increasing complex totality. Thus essence always has its negative within itself. This is what is understood as the contradiction in historical materialism. As one can see, this contradiction is simple, defined as the negativity of the essence. The contradiction does not lead to the destruction of the complex society but rather to its supersession to a higher stage. This happens due to the presence of the progressive movement from cumulative quantitative change to qualitative shift in society as asserted by dialectical materialism. Driven by the inexorable development of the material forces of production, each stage in history is negated by the next one through a change in property relations of class and consequently the superstructure—signalling the eruption of the nodal point qua the shift from the quantitative to the qualitative. Driven by this law of motion, this auto-development of the simple original totality, as Althusser (1969) calls it, represented in each successive stage as an ever-increasing complex totality is the core of Hegelian dialectics and one that was embraced by dialectical materialism in describing historical materialism.[7]The determinism at the heart of dialectical materialism reduces the complex society into a simple essence and of its transition into an auto journey of the same essence; its explanation of society and history thus simplifies what is otherwise complex, straightens in a somewhat Euclidean fashion what is otherwise full of curves, breaks and new articulations; renders transparent and certain what is otherwise uncertain, murky and contingent.

While the same set of criticisms against material/economic/class/structural/teleological determinism/essentialism can be launched against Cohen's rendition, one must be careful not to reduce Cohen explanatory device to dialectical materialism. As explained earlier, Cohen debunks the idea of process, inter-penetrability and laws of motion as asserted by dialectical materialism. He theorizes the components (forces of production, relations of production, superstructure and consciousness) as levels that must be defined independent and autonomous of one another and whose relations and roles are explained by the functional explanation. Interpenetration will only make the definitions murky and their roles unclear; he faults Marxists for undertaking such a sloppy theorization. Not surprisingly, Cohen quibbles over definitions of each of the components and their roles which turn out not to be quite the same as in most other theories of historical materialism. As an explanatory device, functional explanation replaces the laws of dialectical materialism to answer the question of why certain components rise and then fall and in the process help locate and differentiate one epoch/stage from another. Taking off from this perspective, Cohen would dismiss the above described theory of dialectical materialism for delivering a philosophy of history and not a *theory* of history. The Hegelian dialect of 'Negation of Negation' is a powerful picture to relay the trope of history but has no explanatory import. A theory of history must explain the mechanism through which the epochs appear and disappear (this is the question of 'why' an epoch appears and disappears), and on this issue dialectical materialism has a sloppy answer, if at all. Its claim of being an explanatory device of history is in this case spurious.

Finally, the very aspect of the law of cumulative quantitative changing to the qualitative shift at the nodal point has been subjected to numerous criticisms, including from non-Marxist thinkers. First, this feature is taken from the field of natural science. Even there, it is difficult to identify the exact point—the nodal point—at which the cumulative quantitative changes lead to qualitative shift. In fact, evidence shows that such shifts can be arbitrary and at times even inadequate for survival. Secondly, it is not clear why the addition or change should not be treated as simultaneously quantitative and qualitative. To say that some change is quantitative and others qualitative seem to be more of an assertion rather than a well worked out claim. The third criticism points to the application of dialectical materialism to historical materialism. How can the assumption and findings of material aspects of nature be so clearly transported to serve as the logic for material basis serving society? It will be an error to think that what applies in nature should also apply to society and its transition. Therefore, transferring the feature of cumulative quantitative addition leading to qualitative shift into an explanation of societal evolution is an unjustified theoretical leap that seems to place historical materialism in a murky pitch.

Class Once Again: Economic and Political

Having unpacked Karl Marx's theory of history in Classical Marxism, we now raise some issues related to class that while latent in the theorization are nevertheless critical.

Let us begin by marking a contrast. In historical materialism, class whether in its economic or its political form always signifies a group of people. People who occupy structurally given positions within the relations of production are referred to as classes and people who can act as a homogeneous force at the level of superstructure are also adjudged as classes. That is, whether in its economic or political dimension, *class is fundamentally understood as a noun* or a group of people. Such a notion of class is in sharp contrast to the idea of *class as an adjective*, that is, *process.*

The deterministic rendition involving economism is very important in historical materialism and has major implications for class analysis. There are two moments that must be considered. To start with, take the relation between the superstructure and economic structure. The economy remains the primary force explaining the existence of the superstructural elements. Consequently, any concept of class must capture this primacy of the economy over the superstructure. Class relations that arise to constitute the economic structure capture the economic dimension of class; it comprises economic subjects defined by the structural location in the relations of production.

The second moment follows from the identification of an economic contradiction between the forces of production and relations of production, which is presumed to be the objective condition for introducing social change, including changes within superstructural strata. That is, which superstructure elements come to exist at a time in history is ultimately reduced to the economy. However, at the same time, it is claimed that the superstructure elements, including the political, influence the economic elements. That is, the economy is prior and more fundamental as compared to the political but the political also influences the economy. Change in society is produced through social struggle between contending forces, which is seen to resolve the objective contradiction posed as the fundamental contradiction of society. Historical change needed to resolve the contradiction then requires conflict and its resolution at the level of superstructure. The existence and role of social actors who will produce the desired changes are in line with the laid down historical trajectory. These social actors are seen to be linked with the structurally defined classes in the relations of production and are, as such, class actors. Class division and class conflict cannot be separated. Transition of the structure of economy and society then calls for a political definition of class. Classes are also social forces or social actors and are as such political subjects.

We then come across a close association of determinism and historicism with the dual definitions of class – economic and political. Determinism necessitates the economic definition of class, while historicism necessitates the political definition of class. Historical materialism demands that, at different levels of social analysis, the political dimension of class must be reconciled with the economic dimension of class. Another association related to this dual definition of class is that regarding the structure and social actor where the social actor is regulated by the structure (defined by the existing superstructure) and serves to produce structural changes (acting as social force to change the relations of production). For example, the working class is at one and the same time structurally defined as an economic entity and politically defined as a social actor.

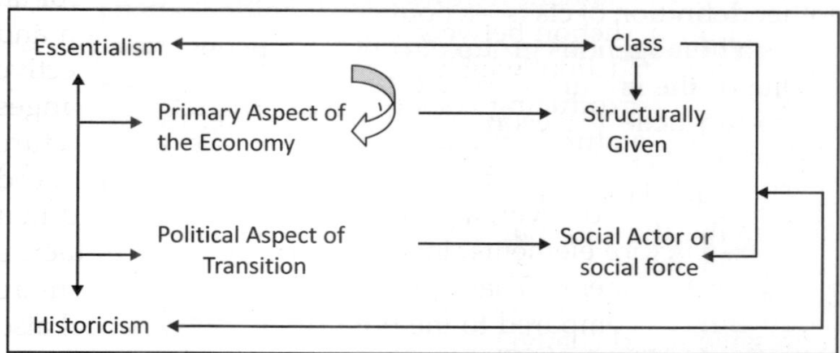

The above diagram indicates that the root of the specific definitions of class and the relations between the differing definitions flow from the determinist and historicist logic that underlie the portrayal of society and its transition in historical materialism. Much of what has followed in the history of Marxian politics has been on how to resolve the two domains of class.

Dual Definitions of Class and Class Formation

As explained, there are two definitions of class that function within historical materialism. The first notion pertains to a structurally given position within the relations of production. For example, take the power specific definition of class. Suppose that one group of people have complete power over the means of production and none over labour power and the other group complete power over labour power but none over the means of production. We name the former as capitalist class and the latter as working class. Those who belong to these classes belong because of their structurally given position within the relations of production. Because this definition of class encapsulates the relations of production, this is often referred to as an economic definition of class. But this class does not have any mechanism or explanation concerning why and how such a class will act. And if class cannot operate as a social actor then there cannot be any class struggle and consequently transition of society does not materialize. Therefore for transition to transpire, class must also be a social actor, a social force that can act and which must be related to this structurally defined class position. There is then another definition of class—a political definition—that refers to class as a homogenous group of conscious people who can act.

One of the enduring puzzles in conventional Marxism is how to reconcile the economic definition (i.e. the structural definition) of class with the political definition (i.e. the subjective definition) of class, that is, make consistent the two claims or rather make the singular claim: those who are occupying a structurally given class position will also be ones who will form themselves as a social actors in order to struggle for or against progressive social change.

Class positions are those structurally defined (economic) positions that individuals occupy in the relations of production. Roughly, class positions are often referred to by the term, *class in itself. Class formation* refers to the transformation of class *in* itself to class *for* itself, where *class for itself* is the consciousness demanded of a class, that is, where class truly becomes a social actor at the political level. This in turn requires that the individuals belonging to the class must have similar consciousness about their political role. In terms of historical materialism, the issue of class formation is nothing but the matter of reconciling the two definitions of class to realize the transition of society. The missing element in this apparent gap between the economic and the political concept of class is 'interest'.

The historical materialist model takes interest as given, as already embodied in the structurally produced economic definition of class. Say, the working class, defined in terms of the relations of production, by virtue of that definition, always already embodies interest consistent with its role in society and history as assigned by the model of historical materialism. Thus, the working class is imbued with the possibility of arriving at an objectively defined intelligibility about its role in society and knowledge of what it needs to do to forward the historical evolution of society. This is argued as transpiring because the benefit of working class and the benefit of society merge; resultantly, the interest of society gets telescoped in the interest of the working class. This given interest embodied within the economic concept of class is then carried over to the political concept of class. That is, once interest becomes embodied in (the economic definition of) working class, then that class is presumed to have a clear reason as to why it should organize itself as a social actor or social force and struggle in order to fulfil its assigned goal and role. The concept of interest provides therefore an explanatory link between structurally defined class and class as a social actor. It also means that the individual must personify the 'interest' of the social actor; or, the individual is subsumed or immersed within the social actor. In the end, both working class and working class individual are thus defined and regulated by the overarching structure in historical materialism. The structure in the first instance (as in Cohen) or last instance (as in Althusser of 'For Marx') determines working class and class subjectivity; the ultimate explanation of decision-action-interest-consciousness must then be traced to structure. What is true for the working class is true for all classes regarding the relationship between structural position, interest and class action.

The basic contour of class in historical materialism is in the following:

Structurally Given Class Position → Pre-Given Interest → Class as Social Actors → Class Struggle.

In the above, it is presumed that ideally working class consciousness would automatically translate into the consciousness of individuals holding that class position. This is the concept of 'imputed consciousness' that refers to consciousness embodied in true or real interest that is in turn structurally given. Because the concept of working class arises from a structural disposition, this imputed consciousness is regulated by the knowledge and intelligibility flowing from the totality – the working class. Interest is said to have an objective or structural basis but which may not be necessarily recognized by those whose interests they are presumed to be. The actual consciousness, however, may be completely different. The individuals holding working class positions and consequently belonging to the working class may not know the 'truth' about their social and historical role. They may not realize their true interest, that is, their true identity. And if they are in sufficient numbers, the formation of class as a social actor or class in itself has not yet materialized.

Marxist practitioners have recognized that individuals holding class positions may not be aware of their real or true interest and hence of their historical mission. However, *they do not question the existence of a pre-given true interest*. Taking interest as objectively and structurally given and hence as true, they then proceeded to analyse the apparent problem of reconciling imputed consciousness with actual consciousness. If the worker does not act as prescribed by his given structural position then he or she does not fully know his identity, does not know the truth about his role in history. This is the cause of false consciousness. To put it in another way, he is not yet a political subject and false consciousness a measure of this lack. In order to supplant and transcend false consciousness, one needs a *vanguard party* of the working class that educates those individuals holding the working class position about their true interests and historical role. In the erstwhile socialist countries, vanguard parties embodied the very basis of so-called working class domination.[8] Conventionally, the members of vanguard party are deemed as educationists. In short, the central goal of the party is to mediate between the workers as individuals and working class as a social actor so that the real interests engraved in the latter would be realized; what is given, lying in the depth of the subject, would have to be stirred and activated. Forging class interests and class identity become the said goal of vanguard party.

The following diagram presents our arguments schematically:

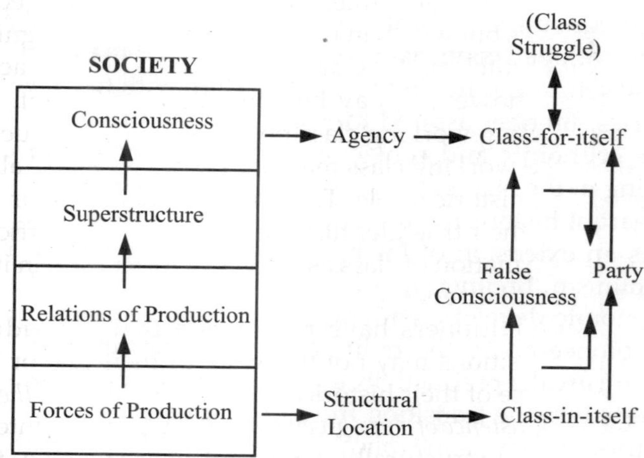

Having laid down the basic structure of historical materialism, we now highlight some debates within it and some which are targeted at it. This set of critical engagements is basic and representative. It complements the criticisms of determinism in Classical Marxism made by Post-classical Marxists in another chapter in this volume.

Robert Brenner's Critique of Cohen's Primacy Thesis and Functional Explanation

Intervening essentially in the debates on transition from feudalism to capitalism in Western Europe and particularly England, Brenner (1977, 1985) pointed out that the motor of change was not any economic element per se but the political aspect of class struggle. Given a level of forces of production, the outcome of crisis in a society would depend on the resolution of class struggle. Intervening in the Dobb-Sweezy debate on transition (see Hilton 1978), Brenner turned his criticism against the economic essentialism in Dobb (development of forces of production as the prime mover, Dobb 1978a, 1978b) and Sweezy (external trade as the prime mover, Sweezy 1978a, 1978b) into a full-fledged attack on the underdevelopment theories proposed by Paul Baran, Paul Sweezy, A.G. Frank, Immanuel Wallerstein, Samir Amin, etc. Brenner averred that advanced countries were not dependent on the underdeveloped countries for growth or luxury consumption and that the economic plight of the underdeveloped countries should be identified in their internal class structure and not in their relationship with the developed countries. Brenner aspired to overthrow the privileged status of the economic and replace it with class struggle thereby bringing in the element of political as the prime mover within the heart of historical materialism.

As an extension of his basic argument against economic determinism, Brenner also attacked the Smithian explanation of economic development encapsulated by economic growth to be pioneered by the individual economic actors trying to achieve a greater productivity and hence efficiency. This solution depended on the transition from pre-capitalism to capitalism. "But this outcome is inexplicable in terms of the rationally self-interested actions of pre-capitalist individual economic actors or classes; it must be understood as an *unintended* consequence of the actions of individual pre-capitalist actors and especially the conflicts between pre-capitalist classes". (Brenner 1986, p. 26) Thus, going against the current of the Smithian perspective, Brenner emphasizes the political qua class struggle and the contingency of it; actual historical outcomes (say, from pre-capitalism to capitalism) are the result of unpredictable resolution of class struggle out of many possible solutions that could be achievable.

Along similar lines, Brenner (1986) takes up Cohen's assumption that says that, "because the new productive forces increase productive efficiency, some economic actors will, sooner or later, find it in their rational self-interest to adopt them and will find a way to transform the property relations to make this possible" (Brenner 1986, p. 47)[9]. Brenner argues that this assumption is spurious. He contends that under pre-capitalist property relations, "economic actors simply cannot be assumed to find it in their self-interest to adopt, new, more effective techniques and, above all, that they cannot be assumed to find it in their self-interest or their capacity to make the necessary changes in the property relations required to adopt the new techniques. But, even, more to the point, if one believes, as I have contended, that the unprecedented productiveness of capitalism derives not from any productive force or technique, but is a consequence of the property relations themselves, it becomes just about impossible to see how the sort of argument Cohen makes for the primacy of the productive forces can be sustained." (Brenner 1986, p. 47) Brenner replaces the primacy of forces of production with property relations where the essential motor of transition is now class struggle over property relations rather than the forces of production and its presumed development. But then, some questions may be asked: is Brenner lapsing into political qua class essentialism as the major driver of historical change? Is the problem resolved by simply moving the emphasis from the economy to the political? By equating the political to class struggle and because class is located in relations of production, isn't he reducing class to the economy? Moreover, critics have argued that Brenner's emphasis on class struggle is only a short-term measure; in the long run, even if one accounts for Brenner's theory, the development of society and the specific form of class struggle and, subsequently, its outcome will depend on the level of development of the forces of production. Thus, in the last instance, Brenner's political emphasis of class struggle depends on the economic, thereby undercutting his critique of economic essentialism.

Articulation of the Mode of Production Approach: An Innovation that Failed

This section refers to a particular approach popularized by early Althusserians and which came to be known as the articulation of modes of production school. Its central question is: what explains underdevelopment? If Brenner's approach was principally addressing the feudalism to capitalism transition debate in England and Western Europe, this intervention arises as a response to the underdevelopment theories of the 1950s-1970s that tried to answer the question by demoting the class structure and mode of production. But this attempt by Althusserians also reflects the acceptance of the fact that the stricter form of historical materialism may not be adequate to capture the complexities of the 'underdeveloped' society and its transition. This then calls for a modification of the analytics of historical materialism somewhat without changing its basic thrust. The following is a brief account of this innovation and of its ultimate failure.[10]

Pierre-Philippe Rey (1978), one of the most famous of the articulation theorists, claimed that capitalism is innately dynamic and cannot be blamed for underdevelopment. Underdevelopment in the peripheries arises because of the precapitalist relations of production that act as a barrier to the development of capitalism. So the cause of underdevelopment resides in the social formation in the peripheral countries. Following Althusser and Balibar's (1975) adaption in a Structuralist Marxian frame, Rey distinguishes between social formation and modes of production. Mode of production or infrastructure is composed by the real appropriation (the relation of the labourer to the means of production by which the transformation of nature is undertaken) which constitutes the forces of production and property relations (that harbours the class structure) which determine the relations of production enabling the appropriation of surplus labour. In the Athusser and Balibar frame, it is the relations of production that is more important. One must be careful that the usage of these categories (forces and relations of production) or of their explanatory device does not exactly follow Cohen or other versions of historical materialism. In Rey, mode of production is an analytical concept and the articulatory existence of the different modes of production at a concrete historical stage makes up the social formation. He stresses three types of precapitalist modes of production—feudal, traditional and colonial—but also declares that most underdeveloped countries are constituted by either the colonial or traditional modes of production in addition to the capitalist mode. According to Rey, the transition from precapitalism to capitalism gets divided into three stages. The first stage is when the precapitalist mode of production is dominant compared to the capitalist mode of production. The second stage is when the capitalist mode of production is dominant but it is still dependent on the precapitalist mode of production for food and labour power. Here, the capitalist form of exploitation is supplemented by the precapitalist form of exploitation. Most underdeveloped countries are in this stage of transition. In the third stage, precapitalist modes of production are fully supplanted by capitalist modes of production. According to Rey, transitional countries will move toward a socialist revolution before they reach this stage, since the transition process from the second to the third stage is painful and sluggish due to the considerable influence and the reactionary nature of nonfeudal precapitalist mode of production to which the capitalist mode of production is articulated.

Capitalism is not to blame for this slow and painful transition because by definition capitalism is dynamic and hence cannot be held accountable for any hindrance. Given the state of history, its unfolding is progress. Violence is the only way out of this gridlock. Capitalism will have to eliminate these nonfeudal modes of production through force by expelling the peasants from the land. This violence will be counterproductive and will stir up the conditions for a socialist revolution.

After the post-structuralist criticism against structuralism and its inherent determinism, the so-called 'structuralism' of Althusser was put to sword. Logical problems were raised followed up by its inadequacy in explaining, among others, the transition problem of postcolonial nations. The underlying teleology (for the assumption of progression from capitalism to socialism is embedded in this frame) that seems to be secured and alive in treatments such as that of Rey came under fire. Moreover, even leaving aside questions of epistemology as also of the renditions generated out of its deterministic logic, there are other deep problems internal to the treatment of transition in the articulation of mode of production approach. To take a case, Bradby (1975) and Foster-Carter (1978) criticize the centrality of violence in Rey by arguing that capitalism does not necessarily require violence for its development. If violence is ruled out then Rey's explanation of capitalist development collapses, since in Rey there are no other ways for capitalism to advance. Also, Rey is criticized for taking a unidimensional view of capitalism by assuming that capitalism works in the same way everywhere and the differences in the social formations are only due to the types of precapitalist modes of production to which capitalism is articulated. Pre-capitalist modes of production are blamed for underdevelopment and the particular nature of capitalism is absolved from any role in it. This reductionism in identifying the root of underdevelopment was criticized by Foster-Carter, who also expressed doubt about the validity of the concept of traditional mode of production and colonial mode of production. Because a country has been colonized does not mean that its mode of production can be called colonial. The definition of 'modes' as expressed in Rey and other theorists of this school lacks clarity and rigour. They do not face questions such as, "What are the relations of production and class structures in the colonial mode of production?" and "How and why is it different from other modes of production"?

From a Cohenian perspective, this school stumbles because of the failure to rigorously define and analyze components and their relations, precisely the quality for which Cohen praised Althusser's *For Marx* and for generating his interest in *Capital* and its history. In contrast, he criticizes Althusser and Balibar's *Reading Capital* for its failure to maintain that standard, and especially for the fact that it failed to crown the 'growth of human productive power' (forces of production) as the centre of history. Since the articulation of mode of production approach is based on *Reading Capital* where the centrality of forces of production as a motor of history is abandoned, Cohen would consider it sloppy theorization and inconsequential for explaining history. While we may be more reticent in embracing Cohen's centrality of 'growth of human productive power' as against relations of production in Althusser and Balibar, what is certain is that the usage of Althusserian frame in the context of transitional economies creates all kinds of intractable difficulties in definitions and in analysis of relation of various levels that are posited analytically.

All the different kinds of problems had an adverse impact on the articulation of modes of production school. By the early 1980s, the influence of this Althusserian school had waned.

Caste: A Problem of Historical Materialism

As an example of how new elements can pose definitional difficulties for the frame of historical materialism, we consider very briefly and roughly the debate over the location of caste in Indian Marxism. What we intend to highlight through this example is what some argue as the rigidity of the frame of historical materialism that makes it difficult for it to incorporate aspects, such as caste, that were not present in its original framing which was constructed in the backdrop of Western European societies and their transition. Because it seeks to represent other societies through the lens of this basic Western European derived model so as to make the former fit into the latter, charges have been levelled against historical materialism for being Eurocentric.

It is not that caste has not been studied in the Marxian context (for example, D.D. Kosambi, R.S. Sharma and Irfan Habib's Marxist historiography remains a formidable intervention) where the debate, whether among the intellectuals or party organization, remained primarily over (i) is caste an economic, political or cultural aspect? and (ii) if so, what is its role in the context of the historical transition of Indian economy, especially in relation to capitalism?

A section of Marxists has treated caste as an element of the superstructure consistent with a feudal base or going back to the ancient past, some even seemingly equating caste and class. Whatever it is, it is held that caste can only be explained in terms of its economic foundations and more specifically, class relations of production. In the order of explanation and importance, class relations are privileged and to which caste relations are ultimately reduced. As the capitalist relations of production overtake feudal relations, it is expected that caste as a relic institution of the past will wither away. The argument being that caste by definition is an unequal institution and is fundamentally different from the modern formal (Western) notions of equality and freedom that are the basis of the superstructure consistent with capitalism. Resultantly, caste relations, despite being frozen thus far, cannot be sustained by capitalism and will face its gradual dissolution. This is akin to what Marx and Engels had forwarded as the effect of capitalism on the past institutions in *The Communist Manifesto*:

> Constant revolutionizing of production, uninterrupted disturbance of all social conditions, everlasting uncertainty and agitation distinguish the bourgeois epoch from all earlier ones. All fixed, fast-frozen relations, with their train of ancient and venerable prejudices and opinions, are swept away, all new-formed ones become antiquated before they can ossify. All that is solid melts into air, all that is holy is profaned, and man is at last compelled to face with sober senses, his real conditions of life, and his relations with his kind.

It is a logically corollary that the central category and struggle over which progressive journey of society (against capitalism and for socialism) is going to be enacted is class and not caste.

The other Marxian position (Omvedt 1982) has challenged the above reading of caste and argued that in the context of India, class constitutes the material form of the base in Indian society. That is, caste must be located in the infrastructure or economic base comprising of forces and relations of production. It was argued that the pre-British period relations of production were based on caste so much so that, "it was impossible to speak of a 'caste system' and a 'class structure' as a separate concrete phenomenon" (Omvedt 1982, p. 14). Only with capitalism does class start taking a pure economic form as distinct from political and cultural forms where caste is to be ideally located. This separation was formally attempted by the British colonial rule but it took a distorted form. The British rule abolished the caste based access to land and introduced changes in tenancy, landownership and property rights structure by delinking it from caste. But then instead of bringing capitalism in Indian agriculture, it brought in a version of feudalism. Feudal relations in agriculture were reconstituted to favor the landlords and merchants in a manner that served to reproduce capitalism in Britain. But, did caste really disappear from the economic domain? Omvedt disagrees by arguing that the changes introduced by colonial administration meant that the ownership of resources and division of labour in the relations of production continued to be heavily influenced by caste considerations; those who owned capital and appropriated surplus became the landlords and merchants while the sellers of labour power and artisans came from lower castes. Over time, as capitalist relations of production started to appear in India, the caste division inflected it along similar lines; the owners of capital, appropriators of surplus and their immediate cohorts came from upper caste while the working class came primarily from lower caste. Summarizing Omvedt pithily, it can be said that while caste was class in the pre-British period, in the post-British period they became separated but highly correlated. The formal separation between caste and class falters in the concrete scenario of India. Rather, caste comes to occupy the material base of economy.

Critics have taken to task both these Marxian representations of caste. For example, take the subaltern school with its self-proclaimed Marxian stance in its earlier phase (Guha 1982). Partha Chatterjee representing the then subaltern school rejects the Marxian structure of base-superstructure as a framework for explaining the phenomenon of caste relations in India by arguing out that (i) caste does not necessarily follow from the economic, the base, and (ii) the linear stage view of history associated with the mode of production narrative is dubious in the background of the recent critiques of such teleological understanding of history (Chatterjee 1989, pp. 174–178). Concerning the other claim that class takes the form of caste at the material base, Chatterjee avers that caste and class are dual structures, one internal (caste) to India and the other external (class), external since it was first implanted in Indian soil via colonial rule. As the current form of capitalist production structure was imposed by the British independently of the relations of castes, the duality between the internal and external cannot be reconciled at the level of the production relations of the base, where the duality of the structures cannot be identified and resolved. Faulting this as theoretical inconsistency in Omvedt's position, Chatterjee contends that,

> the question then becomes one of identifying the appropriate level where the dual structures exist as part of a whole. Disregarding the validity of the base/superstructure formula, it is our argument

> that this level cannot be found either in determinate productive structures or in determinate legal-political institutions. As a point of access, this level of unification, its historical effectiveness and its contradictory character need to be sought in social consciousness. (Chatterjee 1989, pp. 178–179)

The social consciousness materializes at the level of community; the essentials of politics related to caste thus come to be situated on community. This demotion of caste in infrastructure or superstructure provides another reason for the subaltern studies school to abandon the Classical Marxian frame which they see as reducing caste to some other aspects. It must be noted that Chatterjee's formulation and the subaltern school in general were taken to task by Classical Marxists and others for ignoring the relations of production and the related superstructure into which caste is considered by them as integrated or enmeshed; the centrality of social consciousness and the political based on it as separate from economic relations is considered to be a return to de-materialized idealism which some even allege is a variant of Brahmanical ideology, an ironical end if one recalls the chief goal of subaltern studies is to enact the end of elitist historiography (Singh 2014).

From superstructure to infrastructure to social consciousness, the location of class seems to be moving in a cycle thereby spelling trouble for the theoretical framework of historical materialism and for other versions of Marxism such as the subaltern school. Our brief foray was not to provide an exhaustive account of the Marxian treatment and debate on caste but to highlight the vexed problem of accounting for caste in historical materialism and beyond. It must be said though that attempts to theorize caste from a Marxian perspective have since continued in the older and newer directions. Limitations and failures from previous efforts have raised questions as to whether the chief problem is one of fitting in caste in historical materialism or is it more fundamentally that of deterministic epistemology itself. Is it then apt to have a non-deterministic epistemology that will be more habitable to incorporate caste within the economic-political-cultural complex?

One line of intervention along this direction is the growing call to expand upon the newly developed theories of class and caste so as to open a field in which caste and class could be dealt with in their relation. Does it give way to a new unified theory, something like 'relational theories' of caste and class, theories of the *hyphen* of class-caste? How to theorize this 'hyphen' is a task in its own right. While we shall not pursue the problem any longer, we would deal in the next chapter with the epistemology of overdetermination that can be taken as a precursor to producing such a theory of hypen from a Marxian perspective.

Marx versus Marx: Revisiting the Question of History

Historical materialism such as that espoused by Cohen take their main source from *Capital*, the book. Now whether a deterministic reading proposing historical inevitability in terms of the sequence of stages is compatible with the 'scientific' *Capital* is a different question. By proposing a non-deterministic reading, the post-classical Marxian approach, as explicated in the next chapter, would certainly not agree to this. But, suppose for argument's sake we take the traditional interpretation of Marx'streatment *ala* Cohen as valid in this section.Having accepted that, we now contend that an*other* Marx, Late Marx, when faced with the 'Russian Road/Question' (a correspondence with Russian Marxists that began from 1870s onwards continuing till his death) regarding the route of its transition ended up challenging the very idea of 'historical inevitability' and with it the stagist theory of history(Marx 1970, pp. 75, 83, 89; Bailey and Llobera 1981, Shanin 1983, Dhar 2003, Chakrabarti and Dhar 2010, Chapter 6 and 7). This 'Late Marx' challenges and critiques 'Scientific Marx' and generally historical materialism of Classical Marxian variety such as that of Cohen. The details are presented in the above references; here we only disclose the outline of a critique of historical inevitability that raises questions concerning the validity of historical materialism.

To begin with, what was Marx's position regarding the translation of the genesis of capitalism in Western Europe into a general historico-philosophical theory of transition and development, imposed by fate on all people? After all, it was precisely the question of transition of non-Western, so-called backward, nations such as Russia and whether they should follow the path of their Western counterparts that set off the whole series of correspondence. It is worth recalling the exuberance of the triumph of global capitalism that Marx and Engels had forwarded earlier in *The Communist Manifesto*:

> The bourgeoisie...compels all nations, on pain of extinction, to adopt the bourgeois mode of production; it compels them to introduce what it calls civilisation into their midst, i.e., to become bourgeois themselves. In one word, it creates a world after its own image.

From today's vantage point, even if we agree that the bourgeoisie does attempt to create a world in its own image it is still an open question as to whether that image creation actually transpires and that too as the bourgeoisie wants it to be. Looking back at history, while Marx's description of capitalism going global is truly of the contemporary, there is enough reason to cast doubt (given the contradictions of capitalism and resistance to it) on the ability of the bourgeoisie to impose its stamp over the entire world, in all relationships and in all spaces as described in the *Manifesto.* One can even have doubts regarding whether the bourgeoisie wants to do it at all so long as the capitalist organization of exploitation is secured from challenges. Also notably, in this universal picture of the bourgeoisie as described in Marx: is the Western European bourgeoisie attempting to impose its will of capitalism across the globe in the name of introducing civilisation shift of a higher order? There is certainly a triumphant inevitability attributed to this imperial venture of capitalism in this Marx and in which he argues that the (White Western) bourgeoisie encapsulating this historicist logic at this stage of history plays a 'revolutionary' role. This seems to substantiate the claim of historical inevitability in the stage based sequence in Cohen's rendition and in fact generally of historical materialism as forwarded in various versions of Classical Marxism. As we observed, Cohen further suggests that the same underlying stagist/epochal logic of history as teleological get integrated in Marx's *Capital*.

When quizzed over the question of transition in Russia, Late

Marx starts becoming doubtful about the above theory of history. Whether he was doubtful to begin with or whether it is a doubt that appeared when confronted with the Russian Question is a matter that need not bother us here. The pertinent issue is Marx's response to the question of whether or not Russia should inevitably take the path of capitalist development as it had unfolded in England and other Western European countries. If we are to pose the question within the evaluative space of *The Communist Manifesto* and *Capital* as presented by Cohen then the matter ends there. However, it made Marx doubtful and after long deliberations he started responding. His reply is tabled in a series of detailed letters and responses over a decade till the end of his life. In between he starts studying the Russian language and society in details. We simply produce below a few instances of that response to make our case. Reacting against an admirer who emphasized the aspect of teleology in his work, Marx hits back:

> It is absolutely necessary for him to metamorphose our historical sketch of the genesis of capitalism in Western Europe into a *historico-philosophical theory of general development, imposed by fate on all peoples, whatever the historical circumstances in which they are placed*, in order to eventually attain this economic formation which, with a tremendous leap of the productive forces of social labour, assures the most integral development of every industrial producer. But we beg his pardon. This does us too much honor and yet puts us to shame at the same time. . .Thus events strikingly analogous, but occurring in different historical milieu, led to quite disparate results. By *studying each of these evolutions on its own, then comparing them*, one can easily discover the key to the phenomenon, but it will never be arrived at by employing the all-purpose formula of a general historico-philosophical theory whose supreme virtue consists in being *supra-historical*. (Marx 1975, pp. 293–4)

Claims of a general historico-philosophical theory with 'supra-historical' feature (another name of teleology governing historical inevitability) is dismissed by Marx as sloppy theorization and certainly not one that he proposed. Taking up the specific case of historical inevitability for 'backward' Russia he says,

> ...I expressly limited the "historical inevitability" of this process to the countries of Western Europe. Why so?...we are dealing here with the *transformation of one form of private property into another form of private property*. The land tilled by the Russian peasants never having been their *private property*, how is this to be applied in their case? (1970, p. 152)

> ...does this mean that the development of the "land commune" (in Russia – emphasis ours) must necessarily follow the same lines under all circumstances? Certainly not. Its constitutive form allows the following alternative: either the element of private property implied in it gains the upper hand over the collective element, or vice versa. Everything depends upon the historical background in which it finds itself...Both these solutions are possible *a priori*, but both obviously require entirely different historical environments. (1970, p. 156)

Through this Marx opens the space for contingency in history which has to be accommodated in any Marxian theory of history; the theories of history we have presented in this chapter do not leave room for such contingencies. Notably, Chernyshevskii's *Essays on Communal Ownership of Land* has had a profound influence on Late Marx. He questioned the requirement of a stage based history to break the (existing) back-bone of village societies and argued instead that greater wholes with existing network of relationalities were not always backward. Reacting against the logic of 'historical inevitability,' Chernyshevskii warned:

> History is like a grandmother; it loves the younger grandchildren. To the latecomers it gives not the bones but the marrow of the bones, while Western Europe has hurt her fingers badly in her attempts to break the bones.

This clearly casts doubt on the idea of teleology, of sequence, as highlighted by Cohen. It also points to the astronomical costs of following blindly a supra-historical logic. But then what about the 'progressiveness' of capital as it strives to "put an end to all feudal, patriarchal, idyllic relations" deemed as backward that Marx averred to in *The Communist Manifesto*? What about the revolutionary role of the bourgeoisie that both Marx earlier and Cohen make a case for? Again making a case for the Russian commune that existed then, Marx writes in the following remarkable passage:

> At the same time as the commune is being bled and tortured and its land made barren and poor, the literary lackeys of the "new pillars of society" refer ironically to the wounds which have been inflicted on the commune as symptoms of its spontaneous decrepitude. They claim that it is dying a natural death and the kindest thing would be to put an end to its agony. Here we are no longer dealing with a problem to be solved, but quite simply with an enemy who must be defeated. In order to save the Russian commune there must be a Russian revolution. And the Russian government and the "new pillars of society" are doing their best to prepare the masses for such a catastrophe. If the revolution takes place at the right time, if it concentrates all its forces to ensure the free development of the village commune, the latter will soon emerge as the regenerative force in Russian society and as something superior to those countries which are still enslaved by the capitalist regime. (Marx 1970, p. 161)

Through his passage Marx can be interpreted as deconstructing the idea of inescapable historicity and scientific inevitability tied to the origin and evolution of capitalism and industrial society. He is also unveiling in the process the 'masked political character' of capitalism and the 'hidden hostility' of the modern West to Other Worlds and possibilities that can be derived from it. The character of 'torn asunder' deemed as revolutionary in the *Manifesto* is here projected as violent, retrograde and catastrophic, the same as Chernyshevskii has mentioned. When faced with the issue of surrendering to the logic of historical inevitability of capitalism, Marx is veering towards a clear 'no'. He thus turns what was supposed to be an inevitable historic event into a critical political possibility of an alternative.

This reversal/modification in Marx is part and parcel of an unambiguously critical position vis-a-vis capitalism. The Marxian understanding of transition cannot be held prisoner to teleology and whose accounting must foreground the political (the struggle for non-exploitative arrangement) above the historical (in the sense we are describing here). The faith of historical inevitability as a defence of capitalism is accordingly shelved here. Interestingly, this turn in Marx receives a stamp of approval in the preface to the Russian edition of the

Communist Manifesto where he writes: "...present Russian communal land ownership can serve as a point of departure for a communist development". Preparing the second German edition of *Capital*, Volume I, that was published in 1873 Marx made the following important corrections in this edition: (i) the deletion of the exclamation mark (!), from a passage in the preface— 'The country that is more developed industrially only shows, to the less developed, the image of its own future!' (ii) the deletion of Footnote 9 at the end of the volume in which Marx, earlier, had scoffed at Herzen's Populism[11] and his 'Russian Communism' and (iii) in the 'Postscript to the Second Edition' Marx paid a glowing tribute to Chernyshevskii. The 'Chronological Notes', a massive volume of notes written in 1880–82 (comparable to the Grundrisse, the notes that Marx wrote down while working on *Capital*), which also included a chapter on a Bengal village, highlight Marx's new attention to the issue of 'uneven development'—to *non-capitalist* societies and their complex historical predicaments (Dhar, 2003).

The implication of our point is crystal clear. Once we break away from the teleological theory of history there is no need to be enslaved to capitalism in thinking about the paths of development. Rather, the *path* itself becomes open to thinking, especially for transitional economies such as that of India. And that opens the field for alternative constructions and deviations from the current one. In the process, it opens up the very question of transition and of history as a theoretical category. What then *is* transition in a Marxian frame is a question that needs to be asked once again? Our analysis though makes one thing clear. Cohen's certitude about his developed 'Marx's theory of history' appears to wilt away in the face of this turn in Late Marx.

Criticisms against Class as Noun and Class in Historical Materialism

There are some fundamental criticisms against the noun based theory of class. While this would take us to a more advanced level, here we simply put down the basic thrust of the critique without giving any further explanations.

(i) Class, as a homogenous group of people, does not fulfil the minimum requirement of an actor which, as defined by Hindess, is, "a locus of decision and action, where the action is in some sense a consequence of the actor's decisions" (Hindess 1988, p. 45); there is no class actor qua social actor; organizations (trade unions, political parties, etc.) are social actors who can act in the name of class or otherwise but that is not the same as class per se deciding-acting (Hindess 1987, 1988).

(ii) The assumption of real or true interest (say, class interest) as given or as reflecting some structural location within the social is logically non-sustainable; "Interests are not fixed or given properties of individuals or groups, and they should not be regarded as structurally determined." (Hindess 1987, pp. 112-113); 'interest' must be contextual, specified in terms of cluster of effects that produce it and be related to action in a particular juncture. There is no *a priori* interest, pre-existing core, outside of a context that can operate like a law attached to the subjects who can then be taken as behaving (or not behaving) according to that engraved interest (Hindess 1987, 1988). If there is no pre-given interest, then the connection between class in itself and class for itself is broken; there is no longer a necessary one to one correspondence between class position and class politics; the basis of existence of class identity and politics as theorized in historical materialism is thereby rendered spurious.

(iii) Even if we accept that the above two conditions hold, the process of class formation, that is, the transition from class in itself to class for itself or, to say the same, the reconciliation between the economic and political definition of class is impossible; false consciousness is no explanation of actual consciousness and, and if one accepts that no theory of actual consciousness exists then the argument of consciousness deficit made for the existence of vanguard party (in so far as it is traceable to false consciousness) is rendered invalid (Laclau 1988; Chakrabarti and Cullenberg 2003).

If one accepts these criticisms then, no matter how it is bent, historical materialism comes to the verge of collapsing since its associated agency theory required to produce the transition of society becomes untenable. It is for theoreticians and proponents of historical materialism to answer and account for these and other limitations and failures if they want to retain it as an evaluative space for initiating action for social change. On the other hand, this set of problems in turn is taken as one of the reasons for abandoning class theory in terms of noun (homogenous group of people) thereby providing a legitimate reason to move to an alternative class theory where class is treated as a process which in turn undercuts/overcomes all the mentioned criticisms (Chakrabarti and Cullenberg 2003; Chakrabarti, Cullenberg and Dhar 2007).

Conclusion

At a theoretical level, historical materialism, notwithstanding its varieties and innovations, seems to stumble on questions regarding its treatment of epistemology where it embraces determinism at all levels and its definition and analysis of class which it takes as a noun rather than a process. The demotion of surplus labour and hence of exploitation in many variants of historical materialism which Marx seems to make the centrepiece of his analysis of economy and capitalism in the book *Capital* is also troubling. Can we conceptualize a Marxian theory that is non-deterministic and non-teleological, which takes class as a process and that too in relation to surplus labour, delivering in the process a class focused approach without lapsing into class or economic determinism or a teleological theory of history? To this end, Resnick and Wolff pioneered a new approach to Marxian theory based on a novel interpretation of Marx and it is to this Post-Classical Marxism we move next.

Questions for further Discussion

1. Forces of production are material while relations of production are social. How and why?
2. What are Primacy Thesis and Development Thesis?
3. What is the role of functional explanation in Historical

Materialism? How does it ensure Primacy Thesis and Development Thesis?

4. Why do you think functional explanation is a better option than the laws of dialectical materialism?
5. Point out the various layers of determinism in Cohen's historical materialism.
6. Use the examples of China and East Asia to examine Cohen's historical materialism. What would be Brenner's contention regarding this?
7. If you agree to historical materialism, how should you then look at imperialism and why? What do you think is the problem with this rendition?
8. (i) When might not the change from class in itself to class for itself happen? What kind of problem is responsible for this?
   (ii) What should be the solution if the transformation from class in itself to class for itself does not happen?
   (iii) Do you think that the solution resolves the problem?
   (iv) Do you think that class defined as a homogenous group of people can act?
   (v) Do you think that class as an embodiment of given interest is conceptually valid?
9. What is the problem of historical inevitability that Late Marx raised? Do you think that it undercuts historical materialism?
10. Caste is a phenomenon peculiar to India. What would be its place and role in historical materialism? Go into the various theories and debates on Marxian rendition of caste and analyse them critically. Do you think that accounting for caste dilutes the importance of historical materialism as a frame?

REFERENCES

Althusser, L., 1969 (1965). *For Marx.* trans. Ben Brewster – Allen Lane. The Penguin Press.

Althusser, L., 2002 (1978). 'Ideology and Ideological State Apparatuses: Notes Towards an Investigation' in *Marxism: Approaches in Literary Theory* ed. Anand Prakash Worldview: New Delhi.

Bailey, A.M. and J.P. Llobera (1981). *The Asiatic Mode of Production: Science and Politics*. Georgetown Routledge: Chapman and Hall.

Bradby, B. 1975. 'The Destruction of Natural Economy.' *Economy and Society*, Vol. IV (2).

Brenner, R. (1977). *The Origins of Capitalist Development: A Critique of Neo-Smithian Marxism* in *New Left Review*, No. 104.

Brenner, R. (1985). *Agrarian Class Structure and Economic Development in The Brenner Debate*, ed. T.H. Ashton and C.H.E. Philpin, Cambridge University Press.

Brenner, R. (1986). 'The Social Basis of Economic Development' in *Analytical Marxism*by J.E. Roemer (ed). Cambridge University Press: Cambridge.

Chakrabarti, A. and S. Cullenberg (2003). *Transition and Development in India* (with). Routledge.

Chakrabarti, A. and A. Dhar (2010). *Dislocation and Resettlement in Development: From Third World to World of the Third* (with). Routledge.

Chakrabarti, A., S. Cullenberg and A. Dhar (2007). *Class Trouble*. Sanhati.

Chatterjee, P. (1989). 'Caste and Subaltern Consciousness'. In *Subaltern studies VI*, ed. R.Guha. Delhi: Oxford University Press.

Cohen, G.A. (1978). *Karl Marx's Theory of History: A Defence*. Oxford: Oxford University Press.

Cohen, G.A. (1986a). 'Forces of Production and Relations of Production' in *Analytical Marxism*by J.E. Roemer (ed). Cambridge University Press: Cambridge.

Cohen, G.A. (1986b). 'Marxism and Functional Explanation' in *Analytical Marxism*by J.E. Roemer (ed). Cambridge University Press: Cambridge.

Cohen, G.A. (1988). *History, Labor and Freedom*. Oxford: Oxford University Press.

Dhar, A. (2003). 'Other Marx: Marx's Other,' in *Other Voice* Kolkata, 47–66.

Dobb, M. (1978a). 'A Reply' in *The Transition from Feudalism to Capitalism*, ed. R, Hilton, London:Verso.

Dobb, M. (1978b). 'A Further Comment'in *The Transition from Feudalism to Capitalism*, ed. R, Hilton, London: Verso.

Foster-Carter, A. (1978). 'The Modes of Production Controversy.' *New Left Review* no.107 (January/February): 47–77.

Guha, R. (1982). 'On Some Aspects of the Historiography of Colonial India.' In *Subaltern Studies I*, ed. R. Guha. Delhi: Oxford University Press.

Harris, N. (1986). *The End of the Third World.* Harmondsworth, Penguin.
Hilton, R. (1978). *Introduction* in *The Transition from Feudalism to Capitalism*, ed. R, Hilton, London:Verso.
Hindess, B. (1986). 'Actors and Social Relations'" *in Sociological Theory in Transition*, S.P. Turner and M. Wardell (eds.). London: George Allen and Unwin.
Hindess, B. (1987). *Politics and Class Analysis.* Oxford: Blackwell.
Hindess, B. (1988). *Choice, Rationality, and Social Theory.* London: Unwin Hyman.
Laclau, E. (1988). 'Metaphor and Social Antagonism.' In *Marxism and Interpretation ofCulture*, ed. C. Nelson and L. Grossberg. Urbana and Chicago: University of IllinoisPress.
Marx, K. (1970). 'First Draft of the Reply to V.I. Zasulich's Letter' in Karl Marx and Fredrick Engels, *Selected Works*, volume three. Progress publishers: Moscow.
Marx, K. (1975). 'Letter to OtechestvenniyeZapiski.' In Marx-Engels Selected Correspondence.ed. S. Ryazanskaya.Moscow: Progress Publishers.
Marx, K. (1983). 'Marx-Zasulich Correspondence: Letters and Drafts.' In *Late Road and the Russian Road: Marx and 'the Peripheries of Capitalism'*, ed. T. Shanin. New York.Monthly Review Press.
Marx, K. (1989). *In Pre-Capitalist Economic Formations.* Trans. J.Cohen. New York: International Publishers.
Omvedt, G. (1982). 'An Introductory Essay.' In *Land, Caste and Politics in Indian States.* ed. G.Omvedt. Delhi: Authors Guild Publications.
Roemer, J.E. 'Should Marxists be interested in Exploitation' in *Analytical Marxism*by J.E. Roemer (ed). Cambridge University Press: Cambridge.
Shanin, T. (1983). *Late Marx and the Russian Road; Marx and 'the peripheries of capitalism'*, London, Melbourne and Henley: Routledge and Kegan.
Singh, H. (2014). *Recasting Caste: From the Sacred to the Profane.* Sage Publications Ltd.
Rey. O.P. (1978). *Les Alliances De Classes.* Paris:Maspero.
Roemer, J.E. (1986). *Analytical Marxism.* Cambridge University Press: Cambridge.
Warren, B. (1980). *Imperialism, Pioneer of Capitalism*, London:Verso.
Wright Erik Olin, Levine Andrew and Sober, Elliot (1992). *Reconstructing Marxism.* Verso: London and New York.

Additional Reading List

Amariglio, J.L., Callari, A. and Cullenberg, S. (1989). 'Analytical

Marxism: A Critical Overview.' *Review of Social Economy* 47 (4).
Chakrabarti, A. and Cullenberg, S. (2003). *Transition and Development in India*. Routledge: London and New York. Chapters 1-3.
Roemer, J.E. (1986). *Analytical Marxism*. Cambridge University Press: Cambridge.

NOTES

1. There are other claimants of Political Economy. Therefore, taking off from one of the pillars of Classical Political Economists, David Ricardo, some scholars following Piero Sraffa have developed another version of surplus approach (Roberts 1987); this Cambridge or Neo-Ricardian School is different from the other mainstream approaches that appeared through the lineage of Adam Smith, David Ricardo (as they interpret it) and John Stuart Mill as well as from Marxian ones. Thus, the offshoot from classical political economy are varied. In our treatment here, we concentrate mainly on the neoclassical version that, additionally integrating the marginalist revolution, seems to encapsulate the basic thrust and theme pioneered by Smith, Ricardo and Mill.
2. Foreclosure is a psychoanalytical concept popularized by the Lacanians. Roughly, it captures the purging of a sign or concept from language entailing that it does not appear in the system of representation. Foreclosure is then a necessary step through which a specific system of representation about economy and capitalism appears. As I contend here and elsewhere, in the economic representation proposed by Classical Political Economy, class process of surplus labour stands as foreclosed.
3. For a critically engaging detailed work on Cohen's framework from a historical materialist perspective, see Wright Erik Olin, Levine Andrew and Sober, Elliot (1992).
4. Teleological implies that there is a given purpose underlying history (of anything that is analyzed). This purpose is guiding the trajectory of history, defining and sorting out its stages. The implication is that, typically, there is a beginning point and an end point of history and the journey is, as per the logic of telos, the rational, ordered and progressive movement from the origin point to the destined end point.
5. Interestingly, this puzzle is also acknowledged at the level of mode of production and superstructure by Althusser (1969, 2002) who tries to resolve the primacy of the former and the important role of the latter through concepts such as 'determination in the

last instance' of the economic, 'effectivity', 'relative autonomy' and 'reciprocal action.' Cohen, of course, remains unfazed by this theorization which, for him, is inadequate and inconsistent insofar as resolving the fundamental puzzle of historical materialism is concerned.

6. There is a controversy within Marxism regarding the validity of Asiatic as a mode of production but we shelve that issue for the moment.
7. Later we shall see that Althusser (1969) gave rise to a new idea of dialectics aka overdetermination that he claims is theorized from Marx. The concept of dialectics discussed here in this chapter is a far cry from that used by the Post-Althusserians.
8. The vanguard party was assumed to uphold the pure interest of the working class. As a result, the interests of the working class and the vanguard party became synonymous. Since the totality of the subject directly translates the objective interest of the working class (the whole/totality), the interest of an individual holding a working class position should coincide with that of the working class as a whole and the vanguard party. The subject is represented by a working class that, in turn, is represented by the vanguard party. Any dissent or revolt against the vanguard party is considered a revolt against the working class and its true interests.
9. Brenner takes property as the basis of capturing the relations of production. This is unlike Cohen who defines relations of production by economic powers; Brenner seems to be reducing economic power to that of property relations thereby proposing a property theory of class.
10. Some of the most innovative writings in historical materialism in the context of underdeveloped nations transpired in India during the 1960s and 1970s. It came to be known as the Indian modes of production debate. For a critical assessment of that debate, see Chakrabarti and Cullenberg (2003, Chapters 2 and 3).
11. In appended Footnote 9 at the end of the first German edition of *Capital,* Marx ridicules Herzen's idea that the Russian village commune was unique to the Slavic world. Marx contended that it was universal, and was no different from what had already been dissolved in Western Europe.

2

Post-Classical Marxian Critique of Political Economy

Anjan Chakrabarti and Anup Dhar

In this chapter, we shall lay down the basic contours of Post-Classical Marxian theory so as to deliver a critique of political economy. Before proceeding further, let us distil the basic thrust of Post-Classical Marxian theory that is proclaimed as emanating from Marx's *Capital* and other works. We isolate four points in particular to this end.

(i) No approach exists in the history of knowledge that posits surplus labour as its entry point and then analyse economy and society with reference to it. This is the 'what' of Marxian theory, the focus that was opened by Marx in *Capital*. Putting it in another way, process of surplus labour represents its *entry point* in comprehending the world. The question of 'how' surplus labour is situated and functions at the level of explanation of 'social' takes us to the question of its connection/relationship with other processes. But then how do we conceptualize the idea of 'relationship'? It is done through the *logical structure* of Marxian theory—dialectics qua *overdetermination*. In terms of both 'what' (the entry point) and 'how' (the logical structure) of society, this approach claims that Marxism has no parallel.

(ii) Insofar as the name *class* stands for *process* of *surplus labour*, it also renders the Marxian category of class unique. As this theory claims, before and after Marx, class has been defined in terms of groups of people and that too predicated on power, property, income, status, etc. While these categories of class are important and relevant and which at times even Marx refers to, they do not serve the purpose in isolating his unique contribution to the theorization of class. Nor do they specify the exact location of the source of class division in Marx which, as will be made clear, lies at the point of production which in turn is attached to the category of surplus labour. Thus, defining class as process of surplus labour enables us to examine class organization of surplus labour and exploitation which is what makes Marxian theory's definition, description and critique of society, especially its form of capitalism, special. For reasons that will become clearer in the course of our presentation, we call this Marxian theory comprising the entry point of process of surplus labour and epistemological standpoint of overdetermination as 'class-focused.'

(iii) 'Marxism'—class-focused analysis based on overdetermination—opens the route to posit the critique of Political Economy of Capitalism. It develops further the context and content of Marx's *Capital: Critique of Political Economy*. Roughly, the connection of this Marxian theory to Marx's *Capital* is the following. Beginning from commodity, market and homo economicus founded on the liberal political principle of equality, freedom, property and independent self that form the substance of Political Economy, Marx soon entered into the 'hidden adobe' of production through the entry point of surplus labour (whose process is defined as class) which can be identified as the secret crypt of the Political Economy of Capitalism. Having done that in Vol. 1, Marx connected his class-focused analysis of production to circulation and distribution in later volumes.[1] As the book proceeds, the complexity of the mutual constitution between the three becomes apparent as well. The same is elaborated in the volumes of 'The Theories of Surplus Value' though the emphasis there is more on theories of distribution of surplus labour. Marx thus recasted capitalism by producing a connection of commodity, market, individualism, private property, income distribution and other aspects with the entry point of class process of surplus labour. Not only did he unpack class organization of exploitation in due course but he further showed capitalism as exhibiting inherent properties of instabilities governed by cycles of boom and bust. Such a rendition is in sharp contrast to the Political Economy in which class as process of surplus labor is absent and which essentially looks at production and the rest of economy and society without any reference to class. A critique of the Political Economy can therefore be seen as integrating and expanding on the class-focused framework by making the occult, the invisible, and the repudiated component of surplus labour visible so as to enable an alternative viewing of the economy and society as also to produce a guide in rethinking socio-economic formations beyond capitalism (Roberts 1996). In this way, the class-focused approach is a version of Marxian theory that expands and develops further Marx's epistemology, contents and insights, and attempts to give it a clearer shape and direction. It is also a framework that tries to account for and undercut much of the criticisms of economism, class determinism and teleology made against Marx and Marxism. To ensure consistency and robustness in Marxian theory, it gives up and even disapproves certain aspects such as the ones mentioned, that tend to be at times present in Marx and certainly in Classical Marxian theories. We refer to this approach as post-Classical Marxism since it criticizes and gives up completely economism, class determinism and teleology that are, notwithstanding their varieties, considered the hallmark of Classical Marxism. Insofar as Classical Marxism builds its framework from an interpretation of Marx's thought which are supposed to justify this approach, the Post-classical Marxian class-focused approach rejects those strands of thought in Marx and/or interprets them in different ways. While seeking progress in thought from the basic methodology, contents and insights in Marx and other subsequent Marxian thinkers and the practices that have evolved since, it thus demands and retains a certain self-reflexivity and criticality of the space of Marx and Marxism, including that of its own created one.

(iv) Moreover, Marx's analysis does not merely lay down a unique rendition of capitalism but the class-focused approach that is developed through the interpretation of Marx enabled us to theorize the economy as distinct from capitalism. It does so by showing the other kinds of organization of surplus labour and associated economic forms of society—feudal, slave, communist, communitic, and independent—that may co-exist alongside capitalism. This turns 'economy' and 'society' into concepts distinct from and in excess of capitalism; as also 'history' and 'transition' in excess of and beyond capitalism. That in turn took Marx to the question of origin of capitalism, of how it historically appears as a result of dissolution of other socio-economic forms. For example, by emphasizing on the 'blood and dirt' involved in this process of original/primitive accumulation of capitalism, Marx differs sharply from the Political Economy wherein, in contrast, the transition to capitalism is an extension of bloodless natural journey driven by human traits and correct incentive structure (seen through the lens of market and competition) in which these traits may find fruition. It also turned the attention to the question of movement beyond capitalism, of how such a transition can be thought of and what it involves. Should transition be seen as a movement from one form of exploitation to another (say, from feudalism to capitalism or from private capitalism to state capitalism and vice versa) or should a movement beyond capitalism be construed as a movement beyond exploitation per se? What then is to be the nature of this post-capitalist society? While his immediate object of analysis was capitalism, Marx's attempt to open a new approach to examine it in turn paved the way for a general framework that led the way for unparalleled ways of categorizing and analysing economy, society, history and transition. Taking a cue from this opening provided from Marx, the Post-Classical Marxian theory very strongly rehabilitates class as a category and forwards an analytical structure that they argue not only opens a historical account of the past (including that of Marxism) in an innovative way but is also suitable to address the problems and demands of the twenty-first century world through a progressive account and practice. Having sketched the main thrust of post-classical Marxian theory, let us now begin our analysis by defining surplus labour, class and overdetermination.

The Category of Surplus Labor

As a precursor to defining surplus labour, we need to refer to labour process. Labor process is defined as the process of using labour power (which is the embodied mental and physical capacity to labour of the labourers) to transform the elements of nature (taking the form of material means of production) into final goods or services or what are known as use values (material or immaterial). The elements of labour power and means of production available in a society are at times clubbed together as *forces of production*. In a labour process, there is realization or consumption of labour power, that is, performed labour (the actual work effort) in it. The labour time exerted through consumption of labour power in the labour process is embodied in the use value/value and can be divided into *necessary labour* and *surplus labour*. What are necessary labour and surplus labour?

Following Marx, necessary labour captures the amount of labour performed to produce the socially necessary subsistence basket of goods and services required to reproduce the labourer's capacity to labour that is, his labour-power. It captures what is needed to replenish the labour power of the worker and his/her family so that the labour process can begin anew and be inter-generationally continued (Marx 1990, ch 6). Surplus labour, on the other hand, is defined as labour performed over and above necessary labour. Total labour time exerted by a labourer in any labour process to produce goods or services would contain a certain portion of labour time spent on reproducing the necessary labour and another portion as surplus labour. The necessary labour equivalent of basket of goods and services is returned to the labourer in the form of money wage or in kind. In contrast, the surplus labour is unpaid or unremunerated. The relation and exact division between necessary and surplus labour are contingent and vary across time and space. Take for instance necessary labour. Rather than being merely biologically determined, it is subjected to specific constellation of elements spanning the economic, political, natural and cultural domains that constitute the meaning and substance of what is 'socially necessary'. This means, among others, being open to constitutive effects of the changes in the process of surplus labour that in turn results from various cause-effect factors to which it is related (as we shall discuss later). It may also be the case that, in a concrete situation, the necessary labour equivalent of socially necessary basket of goods and services may not be provided to the workers which, evidently, could even force the workers into a state of poverty; the case of working poor or precariat labour is much discussed in the present time. Having clarified the constitution and relation between necessary and surplus labour, let us now examine the content of surplus labour.

Consider a simple example. Suppose that an individual is employed for a wage of Rs 400 per day by a person (employer) to produce tables by using the existing material means of production that the employer has bought from the market. In that labour process, let the employee—call him the *direct producer or worker*—labour for eight hours for each day to produce four tables, that is, his per hour productivity is half a table.

Necessary Labor	Surplus Labor
Four Hours (2 Tables)	Four Hours (2 tables)

The table is the *use value* produced by the worker which when sold in the market for a price acquires an *exchange value*. We then say that the produced use value obtains a commodity form. Suppose that the price or exchange value of a table is Rs 200. If the daily real wages of the worker—the value of labour power—are Rs 400 worth of goods and services then two tables would account for the socially determined basket of goods and services needed to reproduce the direct producer. The labour time of 4 hours embodied in the production of two tables is the *necessary labour*. Rs 400 is the monetary equivalent of performed necessary labour or value of labour power. The contract of direct producer/worker and the employer to the tune of agreed upon value of labour power (real wage of Rs 400) based on the social necessary basket of goods and services is thus equivalent to the necessary labour (4 hours) or its equivalent value form (Rs 400 worth of 2 tables). That is, what is agreed upon, contracted in market, to replenish the worker is derived from a portion of the value created in the domain of production. It is however pertinent to note that the direct producer/worker does not rest after four hours of necessary labour but goes on to exert another four hours. This is surplus labour. The extra two tables are *surplus produce* which results from the additional four hours of *surplus labour* performed beyond the necessary labour of four hours. The extra quantum of Rs 400 worth of goods and services that is fetched as a result of the *performance of surplus labour* are its value equivalent, that is, *surplus value*. As forms of *surplus labour, surplus produce and surplus value are thus two expressions of surplus*. This surplus labour or its forms in surplus value or surplus produce is appropriated by someone, the employer in our example. Therefore, two processes come to be associated with surplus labour—its *performance* and *appropriation*. Marx thus opened for us a special theory of surplus.

Based on this preliminary definition of surplus labour we now clarify some questions that pinpoint Marx's unique contribution with the intention to particularly foreground his critique of political economy.

(i) Is surplus labour necessary? How is class connected to surplus?

> The origin of surplus-value ... (is) *unpaid* labour, that constitutes the share of the capitalist, or more accurately, of the capitalist class... In general it is unpaid labour which maintains all the non-working members of society. The state and municipal taxes, as far as they affect the capitalist class, the rent of the landowners, etc., are paid from it. On it rests the whole social system. (Engels 1974, p. 16)

Must the direct producer, as in our table example, deliver surplus labour merely because he is asked to do so by his employer? This is especially the case when it seems to have no direct bearing on his socio-economic reproduction as a worker which is guaranteed by 4 hours of work. Why should he work more? To push the matter further, supposing that we have an independent (self-employing) organizational form in which the direct producer is the only entity (both as performer and appropriator of surplus), we may wonder as to why surplus still needs to be produced. As long as we restrict our discussion to surplus producing society[2], no matter its type, this is indeed the case.

In our prototype example, the employer might have acquired the money capital for purchasing the various material forces of production needed for making tables through credit from banks for which he is required to pay an interest rate. Similarly, he might have to pay taxes to the state in order to get legal sanction and political protection for securing his business activities; he might have leased in land for producing tables for which he needs to pay rent to the landlord; he might have to pay the merchants a fee for facilitating the sale of his tables and so on. For providing the diverse *conditions of existence* to reproduce the performance and appropriation of surplus labour, the condition providers—banker, state ministry/bureaucracy, merchant, shareholder, merchant, etc.—must be paid, which can only be sourced through surplus value. Thus, as Engels argued, distribution in society is a claim on a portion of surplus value. This indicates then the presence of two more processes associated with surplus labour—*distribution of surplus labour* and *receipt of surplus labour*.

Notwithstanding the variegated organizational structures of surplus production and appropriation, the point remains that all of them have to account for their specific and distinct conditions of existence and by default the claims (financial or in kind) the condition providers make on the enterprise as part of the contract that may have preceded production. This claim is by default a claim on the produced surplus now in the hands of the appropriators. In short, surplus is necessary since the existence of enterprise and that of employer and worker can only be procreated in connection with the sets of conditions laid down by providers. Without the latter the former cannot exist and vice versa.

Continuing with our table example, for the employer to distribute the surplus and for others to receive a portion of it, he must acquire *possession* over the surplus created by the direct producers. Typically, *those who appropriate the surplus also distribute it*. The point of distribution thus will remain in the hands of employer since he is also the appropriator of surplus; even as the direct producer is excluded from it. At least in the example we are forwarding, there is a division/schism between the person who appropriates the surplus labour and the one who performs it. As we shall see, other kinds of institutional arrangements will generate more diverse organizations of surplus performance, appropriation, distribution and receipt.

Two quick points can be summed up. First, of the total wealth created by the workers in an economy, a portion is paid back to him while the rest is unpaid. This unpaid labour is appropriated and distributed to maintain the rest of society. Second, why is appropriation socially important? The surplus literally is the discretionary funds of society and which connects the appropriators of surplus with the rest of society who are not its producers. Surplus is thus a location of enormous wealth, prestige and power, both within the enterprise and across society; more so in a formation such as capitalism where one of the purposes of organizing economy and society is to pump out the maximum quantum of surplus value from the workers. Evidently, the possession of this discretionary wealth gives extraordinary social leverage to the appropriators as they can create, influence and shape the minds and public opinion through investment and control in education, health, media, political establishment, etc. Therefore, organization of surplus labour regarding how and who performs and appropriates the surplus is central to the question of what kind of society will emerge.

Clearly, performance, appropriation, distribution and receipt of surplus labour are caught in a mutually constitutive embrace. For example, how much of surplus is to be distributed and for whom it is to be distributed will induce pressure on the process of performance and appropriation of surplus labour. Suppose that the banks announce a hike in interest rate. To meet the extra payment, our employer might have to either increase the amount of appropriated surplus labour, say, by increasing the working time of his employed direct producers or, instead, lower the distributive payments to some other conditions of existence (say, through renegotiation on their terms and contracts or simply quitting those conditions); or, he might have to do both or more. This puts the appropriators and enterprise they head in a state of tense relation, if not in permanent crisis, with a multitude of stakeholders. The reverse is also true. If, say, due to some effects, the amount of appropriated surplus drops then the inability to pay back the contracted amount of surplus might truncate the ability of the condition providing enterprise (say a bank) to perform its task (say, provide loan). For example, the airline Kingfisher India's inability to pay back its loan has had the effect of cutting down banks' condition providing ability to advance credit; indeed, many condition providing enterprises end up in crisis due to such failures of surplus producing enterprises.

Generalizing, any labour process comprising necessary labour and surplus labour *will have four processes in terms of which surplus labour can be organized—performance, appropriation, distribution and receipt.* Following Resnick and Wolff (1987, Chapter 3 & 4) we name these processes as *class*. In such instance, labour process is associated with class process.[3] Class thus is an adjective/name to a verb—process of surplus labour; it is not fundamentally to be treated as a noun-in-action—a homogenous group of people who can act. The latter is the way Classical Marxism and non-Marxian approaches (see Max Weber, for example) have understood class. The rest—economic and non-economic—are non-class processes. Those who personify the class processes take up *class positions* while the rest of processes in which the same population and others are involved are *non-class positions*. Individuals personifying these class and non-class processes are accorded distinct names, for example 'productive workers' and 'productive capitalists' (to be explained later) when the organization of surplus is capitalist in nature. In line with its class-focused approach, Marxism thus produces a distinctly different language (a class-focused language) of conceptualizing the organization of individuals and groups in society. Finally, class struggle is conceptualized as fundamentally a struggle *over* class *processes* of surplus labour (performance, appropriation, distribution and receipt) that is conducted by contingently situated actors (individuals and collective); unlike non-class struggle (over non-class processes such as gender, caste and race), class struggle is a struggle over the object of class *process* with the intent to eliminate, modify or maintain it. Like in case of class and non-class process, class and non-class struggles too are mutually constitutive of one another. One cannot reduce one struggle to another or make one primary and the others secondary.

These four class processes, while distinct, cannot exist independently and autonomously of one another. Each is simultaneously the cause and effect of the other. So is the case for class and non-class processes, class and non-class positions and class and non-class struggles. This idea of relation points to the logic underlying the conceptualization of 'relationship' between processes in Marxian theory. This logic which can be called dialectics takes the name of overdetermination for reasons we will explain soon.

Departure from Political Economy: Political Economy considers production as backed by given technology, endowment and technical division of labour (founded on the principle of comparative advantage) while return to the resources (labour-time/effort and capital advanced in production) are what agents contribute in production (marginal productivity) times the price of the product fetched in the market. In a competitive market economy, as each gets back what they contribute in production, the return to the resources (labour, capital) would exhaust the value of total produce. Critically, since distribution is payment for their contribution in production there is *no unpaid labour*. In short, its distribution theory is disconnected from class process of surplus labour or for that matter any conception of surplus. Therefore, the signifier of class entailing the process of surplus labour is foreclosed or occulted in Political Economy with the additional implication that its interpretation of income inequality is disconnected from the question of mode of appropriation of surplus or of its form, say, exploitation. Instead, inequality is seen as an outcome of natural traits of individuals (work, thrift and entrepreneurship), technology (say, how much machines allow individuals to produce) and unequal ownership of resources/assets (endowment) which though is legitimized legally as private property since they are seen as rightfully acquired through hard work, thrift and talent.

Moreover, the idea of class in our presented theory is very different from the conventional Marxian and non-Marxian theories. Unlike the other treatments of class, here, class is distinguished in two fundamental ways: (i) it is defined as a process and not a noun-in-action and (ii) it is predicated on surplus labour and not on power, property or income. Consequently, its proposed class theory is irreducible to other theories of class and their interpretations. To take one example of Political Economy to show why separate definitions of class matters, one needs to consider the Marxian and Ricardian interpretations of class; the latter's interpretation of class has nothing to do with process of surplus labour and is instead based on distributional groups and their struggle. Glossing over this difference has had deleterious effects on Marxian theory including its value theory and class politics. Due to this conflation, Marx's understanding of value was wrongly reduced to that of Ricardo and rendered redundant/incorrect; again, class and exploitation in surplus labour sense stood occulted and gets purged out of the language of economy and its transition; Marx was reduced to a minor Ricardian (Wolff, Callari and Roberts 1982, Chaudhury 1998). On the other hand, class struggle as *struggle over processes of surplus labour* by contingently formed groups is very different from struggles between homogenous groups of pre-determined classes to change property, power or income. The object (of what to change) and subject (who are the agents of change) of class struggle are different in the two cases. Reduction of one to the other has serious consequences for class politics, including that of displacing the meaning and thrust of class struggle as we are defining it here.

(ii) Is there a logical structure in Marxian Theory? How is class connected to non-class process?

We have learnt that class, the entry point of Marxian theory, is fundamentally not a noun-in-action but a process and that too premised not on power, property or income but on surplus labour. The processes of surplus labour arise in connection with the production of goods and services and, as such, are economic processes. Class as a process of surplus labour is an economic process and, consequently, the Marxian entry point of class is an economic entry point. However, the class process as such is an abstract category on its own; it is a hollowed-out void. Only in *concrete/social setting* when a class process (thesis) is connected to a non-class process (anti-thesis) in a relation of mutual constitutiveness (where each effect literally brings into existence the other) does class get socially 'placed', acquires content, and class effect emerges in meaning and substance.[4] Let us recede and figure out the logical structure underlying this special framing and treatment.

Dialectics has been used in two ways: deterministic and non-deterministic. Post 1960s, the deterministic rendition of dialectics was rendered controversial and heavily criticized. Following Althusser (1969) and Resnick and Wolff (1987, Chapters 1 and 2), overdetermination is the name for non-deterministic dialectics and informs the epistemology of Marxian theory. I will now explicate why dialectics qua overdetermination can be used to interpret the framing of 'Capital' in a non-deterministic way and in the process avoid the logical pitfalls of determinism that have been the object of criticisms within and outside Marxism.

Using a broad brush, four properties of *overdetermination* can be forwarded: (i) processes (economic, political, cultural and natural) mutually constitute one another that is bring one another into existence, (ii) every process is the combined effect of an infinite number of processes that constitute it; the constituting processes form its conditions of existence, (iii) each of the constituting processes brings its distinctly different/contradictory effects to bear in the event of constitution, therefore making every process a site/bundle of contradictions, (iv) resultantly, as one process changes, so do all the other processes meaning that every process is in a state of change, or is in a flux (Resnick and Wolff 2006, Chapters 1-4 and Chakrabarti, Cullenberg and Dhar 2012, Chapter 2 for details).

Following the overdeterminist logic, no definite forecast or projection can be made since there is no way to know all the results of the constituting effects (some even unknown) and the effects that constitute the constituting effects and so on.

Therefore, reality is a cluster of an infinite number of mutually constituting processes. Reality is not fixed, transparent or definite. It cannot be traced to one or a few processes or to laws of motion underlying them; to do so would be to *reduce* the overdetermined complexity of reality to the effects of the chosen/privileged processes as against others. It misleadingly simplifies what is otherwise a complex phenomenon. Non-determinist dialectics banishes the property of reductionism inherent in deterministic dialectics. For example, an individual is to be analysed as the combined effect of an infinite number of processes that constitute him or her; because these changing constituting processes pull and push him in contradictory directions, the individual moves. An individual is thus constituted as decentred, disaggregated and in a state of flux. That is true for everything—relationships, events, institutions, practices, etc. Finally, overdetermination leads to another way of interpreting society. Suppose society is defined by the complexity of relationships. Then clearly, it is dialectically constituted, that is, by the combined effects of an infinite number of overdetermined and contradictory processes. Society thus cannot be reduced to one aspect, say, an economic aspect; the two are related but without being reducible to one another.

From the above we observe that *change* is central to Marxian theory, integrated in every way to its understanding of the world (the ontological imperative) and its functioning. That is why we take every aspect in reality as a *process*—an entity in a state of change. But a question surfaces at this point. How do we produce knowledge, say, Marxian theory, from this mess where reality is infinite, and where everything constitutes everything else? Where to begin and where to end? To get around this problem, Resnick and Wolff argue that all theories choose one or a few processes to identify the spotlight of their theory. They call it the *entry point*.

Entry point is one or a subset of process of reality that is only chosen for the sake of constructing knowledge. The choice of entry point is overdetermined by numerous processes as is the case with everything else. It also helps us to produce a particular/partial understanding of our world (the ontological imperative). How?

Take Marxian theory. The chosen entry point concept of Marxian theory—say, class process of surplus labour – is to be seen as connected to the rest of its constituting non-class process. All relations (between processes) then are to be conceptualized as mutually constituting, where each process is both the cause and effect; in any site, the entry point concept (say, class) causes other processes just as it is caused by the combined effects of other processes. As per overdetermination, the entry point of class process of surplus labour has no logical priority/privilege in the order of explanation. It has no priority in explaining our understanding of the world and therefore does not designate an ontological privilege since every relation/connection in any concrete/social scenario is a result of the combined effects of overdetermined and contradictory processes that constitute it. As combined effects of infinite number of processes, no relationship can therefore be regressed to one or a few core points taken as the entry point of the theory; that follows from the definition of overdetermination; if that were to happen, we would have fallen into the deterministic trap of reductionism (with its variants of empiricism, rationalism, Cartesian totality, and Hegelian totality). In case of the latter, the chosen entry point becomes the *essence*, an underlying core that is operationalized as the driving rationale of everything else. This essentialism with its reductionist property is ruled out under overdetermination. In short, the epistemological imperative of dialectics is always in operation in any explanation of society.

Following the described nature of dialectics, in Marxian theory, economy and non-economy, class and non-class mutually constitute one another, that is, bring each other into existence; none can exist without the other, none can be explained without the other; none can be considered *a priori* or primary in the order of explanation. Economism (where economy is taken as the primary determining variable of non-economic aspects) or class essentialism—class existing a priori and exclusively in an order of determination—cannot be accommodated in this Marxian theory. This contrasts sharply with most approaches in Classical Marxism which follow deterministic logic by taking class or economy as the core/ essence. Unlike in deterministic approaches where A/cause is separated out from B/effect such that what is the cause is never the site of effect in a singular logical structure, under overdetermination, what is the cause is also being affected in a relation of mutual constitution. Thus, overdetermination entails that class process and non-class process affects each other, and bring each other to existence in any concrete social setting; explanation, relationship, practices, events, etc., are thereby class-focused but not class-specific. There is no way non-class processes, its concrete existence, explanation or change, can be reduced to class process and vice versa; no way, for example, caste/gender/race process can be reduced to class process and vice versa. Rather, caste/gender/race and class processes bring each other into existence; to reduce one to the other (as has happened many times) is to forego dialectical analysis. Caste/ gender/race process is constituted by the effects of numerous other processes, including class. To reduce caste/gender/race process to class as a means to explain the existence and function of caste/gender/race would be tantamount to class essentialism/determinism which has the problem of simplifying what is otherwise a complex phenomenon. It would truncate the actual explanation of caste/gender/race process by a spurious one reducible singularly or primarily to class; the same is true if class process is reduced to caste/gender/race process. In any concrete setting, Marxian analysis will distinguish itself from other approaches by this non-reductionism, encapsulated in its non-deterministic logic of overdetermination. Along with the entry point/focus of class process, the dialectics qua overdetermination—the 'how' of theory—distinguish class focused Marxian theory from other theories of Marxian and non-Marxian varieties which will have a different set of entry points and epistemologies (Resnick and Wolff 2012).

Departure from Political Economy: *Marxian theory* is

distinguished from Political Economy or for that matter all other theories by its focus (class) and logical structure (non-deterministic dialectics of overdetermination). In *what* it looks at and *how* it looks at it, Marxian theory is incomparable. It is able to interpret and explain the same event, institution, action, etc., differently. The first step in Marxian politics is to accept and be sensitive to the *difference* of Marxian explanation/interpretation from other competing ones. It is also important to note that Marxian theory understands difference in a certain way. It does not claim to be the singularly true theory, as other deterministic theories do. That would happen if the entry point becomes the essence, the core causal factor of explaining the social. By falling in the trap of determinism, certain variants of Marxism have not always kept this lesson in mind which in turn has had damaging practical implications for politics and societal transformation. In contrast, under our framework, Marxism is seen as competing with other theories regarding how it sees society, what it sees in it and why it wants the kind of society it seeks. It is competitive without the additional claim of being absolutist, overarching and all powerful. In short, the political stake of what we mean by Marxian theory cannot be underestimated.

To see the importance of its difference with Political Economy, we need to only turn our attention to the entry point (preference structure of individuals, endowment (private property) and technology) and epistemology (determinism qua methodological individualism) of neoclassical economics (Resnick and Wolff 2012, Chapter 2). It generates a different idea of economy than what is economy and society in Marxian theory, a difference traceable to their diverse and contesting entry points and epistemologies. The consequences become marked in the way interpretations, insights and outcomes clash with one another generating in the process two very different ways to think of economy, society and transition. Therefore, as explained previously, neoclassical economics does not acknowledge the presence of process of surplus labour and hence exploitation which is central to Marxian theory. Moreover, it reduces all explanations of economy to its chosen entry points which is axiomatically non-changing in the course of explanation; in the order of explanation, the cause (epitomized by its entry point) is separated sequentially from the effects it produces. This determinism is rejected by Marxian epistemology of overdetermination wherein its entry point of class process is both the cause and effect of other non-class processes. Not only are the focuses of these theories different but the manner in which they explain things or events also differs.

(iii) What is Class Enterprise and Institution?

As per our focus, it is important to define enterprise in general and capitalist enterprise in particular. Cluster of processes and the practices, activities and relationships they contain occurs together in conceptual locations called sites. We define an enterprise as a conceptual site comprising of a specific cluster of class and non-class processes that bring it into existence. Constituted by a unique set of class and non-class processes, each enterprise is distinct. As any of these constituting processes changes so does the enterprise and that too each in its particular way. Moreover, in this approach, enterprise is no longer an economic entity reducible to class process but is rather an overdetermined and contradictory site of class process and its constitutive economic, cultural, political and natural processes. The enterprise is in this sense a social institution.

Departure from Political Economy: In neoclassical economics, enterprises are seen as maximizers of some wants (profit, sales, etc.) subject to constraints (like given costs and technology). The processes connected to an enterprise, internal or external to it, are seen through the lens of such a pre-defined goal. Especially popular is the goal of profit maximizing which entails that an enterprise is an embodiment of profit and since the capitalists are appropriators and keepers of profit, they are positioned as natural leaders of enterprises. In contrast, no such reductionism marks the Marxian understanding of enterprise since it is seen as an embodiment of class and non-class processes caught up in an overdetermined and contradictory embrace. It is interesting to note that the criticisms of neoclassical theory of enterprise are not only forthcoming from such a Marxian approach but also from frontline scholars of management who have questioned the theory of enterprise as emanating from the self-driven, inexorable, will of the capitalists (Teece and Winter 1984).

(iv) Does surplus labour signify economic forms of society?

> What distinguishes the various economic formations of society —the distinction between for example a society based on slave-labour and a society based on wage-labour—is the form in which this surplus labour is in each case extorted from the immediate producer, the worker. (Marx 1990, vol. I, 325)

Performance and appropriation of surplus labour is central in the way Marx distinguishes economic forms and analyzes societal specificities. Three basic possibilities arise in relation to *the mode in which this surplus labour is in each case extracted from the actual producer*. The process of appropriation can be *exploitative* if the direct producers of surplus are excluded from the process of appropriation. Slave, feudal and capitalist class processes are three classic forms of the exploitative mode. We shall define capitalist class process and its specific difference with other exploitative arrangements such as feudal and slave in a later section. The class process is *non-exploitative* if the direct producers are not excluded from the process of appropriation; instead, in some commonly decided manner, they participate in the process of appropriation. Communism is a form of non-exploitative class process. In contrast to these, communitic class process can be both exploitative and non-exploitative[5]. Finally, the process of appropriation is *self-appropriating* if both the performance and appropriation of surplus labour is done by one and the same individual. Ancient or independent class process is the classic form of self-appropriating mode.

Following Marx, the adjective we put before an enterprise —capitalist or feudal or communist and so on—would crucially depend upon the manner of performance and appropriation of surplus labour. Enterprises of exploitative, non-exploitative and self-appropriating varieties exist across the social terrain spanning sites in industry, agriculture, state, household and even the unlikely sites of temples, schools, universities, brothels, etc. Class enterprises are thus socially dispersed. While the name before an enterprise, 'capitalist' or 'communist', would follow the specific mode of performance and appropriation of surplus labour, their concrete existence would be dependent on the constellation of class and non-class processes.

In a society, such as that of India, these different forms could co-exist meaning that the economy is disaggregated (many class types co-exist) and decentered (one cannot reduce the economy to one class form such as capitalist) (Chakrabarti and Cullenberg 2003). It also delivers a very important lesson: the concept of economy is not the same as that of capitalism; capitalism is only a component of the economy. Such a lesson is missed in Political Economy in which the only relevant economy is capitalist, that is, there is a tendency to reduce economy to capitalism. This lesson is also overlooked in many other versions of Marxian theories that tend to reduce economy to a singular mode of production, say, capitalism (Gibson-Graham 1996, 2006).

In our presented version of Marxian theory, questions may and do remain as to which economic organization is dominant and even more so in what sense is it dominant. Is, say, the capitalist mode of appropriation, dominant because its mode is really in the majority? Is capitalism, dominant here because we may have started to think of and analyse economy, society and transition by making it the *centre* of economic/social examination? Is it legitimate to reduce the conception of economy and society to that of the centre of capitalism? Is it dominant because it has achieved a hegemonic form (where the part—capitalism—starts to acquire as if the proportion is of the whole) even though it may be comparatively less numerically? These have led to some of the important debates in Marxism.

Finally, a slight digression on the question of individual. Depending upon the class and non-class processes they personify, individuals take different class and non-class positions and are assigned names accordingly for identification and classification. For example, under the exploitative arrangement, the master-slave, lord-serf, capitalist-worker represent the individuals occupying exploiting-exploited class positions in slave, feudal and capitalist class processes respectively. Moreover, an individual may be the occupying various class positions. For example, he might be exploiter in office while exploiting at home in two different kinds of class processes—capitalist at office and feudal at home. Moreover, the same individual would definitely occupy many more class and non-class process by being embedded in various class and non-class processes and even at times both of these in the same institution. To exemplify the latter, the individual may be a worker performing surplus labour (for which he receives a wage payment equivalent to necessary labour) but he might also be asked to supervise his co-workers which is a non-class process against which he might receive a portion of the surplus value and in that role occupies another class position; here the individual personifies two class (performance and receipt of surplus labour) and one non-class (supervision) position. Our example reveals that, like all aspects, an individual too is a result of the effects of infinite number of class and non-class processes (which includes also the psyche, unconscious, education, etc.) just as the individuals in turn constitute the other processes. Overdetermination gets us beyond the subject-structure dichotomy or for that matter any dichotomy (human-nature, whole-part and so on). Unlike deterministic theories, an individual/subject cannot be traced back to some inner logic or depth—nature, class location, etc.; an individual is, like everything else, pulled and pushed into numerous directions by the multiplicity of mutually overlapping and constituting processes. An individual is in a state of becoming, relocation and flux. In short, one cannot take the subjectivity of the individual for granted, not least in politics.

There are a priori no subjects of revolution; there are revolutionary subjects as shaped in a specific time-space context. Unlike many Marxists, more incisive ones like Lenin, Gramsci and Althusser understood this point well. This realization though has subsequently produced one of the important questions of recent times: how do the individuals acquire a disposition? How does he become a subject—both as in 'subjected by' and 'subject of'? What is subjectivity? What is the role of mind-psyche, culture and of institutions such as schools? And, indeed if Marxian politics cannot find a way to answer these questions, what then becomes of the politics of unveiling the grand delusion that Political Economy and conventional institutions prop up at a mass level? Because of its previous historical demotions, this remains one of the thrusts of Marxists in the present time.

Departure from Political Economy: In Political Economy, because surplus labour is non-existent, so too is exploitation. Consequently, its manner of conceptualizing the socio-economic system cannot replicate the Marxian frame. Rather, its conception of economy is based on market exchange, private property and pursuit of gains which replicate the capitalist form of economy (also see problem 18 at the end). That is, economy is reduced to capitalism; non-capitalist moments are conceived of as idiosyncratic existences, outliers, and abnormal existences in relation to capitalism. They are what are not capitalist; they are represented in terms of their relationship to capitalism – as the same as, the opposite to, a complement of, or contained within capitalism (Gibson-Graham 1996). That is, the otherwise decentered and disaggregated economy is seen and analyzed through the lens of capitalism. This was what Gibson-Graham referred to as capitalocentrism which is similar to that of androcentrism where the complex space of gender/sexuality is reduced to the centricity of man/hetero.

Moreover, in Political Economy, the individuals are conceptualized as reducible to some inner nature that can be dubbed as rational implying that their behaviour embodies intentionality, reason and is goal-driven; whether as a person of exchange, a calculating subject of cost-benefit, entrepreneurial self or maximizer of gain. From among all possible alternatives, the individuals would select the best/optimal possible outcome. This idea of pure rationality has been challenged and advanced by another version of rationality named as 'bounded rationality.' This was pioneered by Herbert Simon in a series of writings. He argued that because the decision-making acts of individuals are *bound* by incomplete information and limited number of alternatives at any point in time, the individuals try to make the best of this situation. They cannot make the optimal choice they would have made if the feature of boundedness was not there. That is, the assumption of pure rationality is impractical and does not govern the behaviour of individuals. In contrast, decision rationality is limited by the bounds it confronts in any given situation; this truncated practice of rationality is what Simon called 'bounded rationality'. Notwithstanding the fact whether we construe the individuals as grounded on pure rationality or bounded rationality, what is common to both is that Political Economy takes its conception of individual or subject as an embodiment of some notion of rationality; moreover, it turns its theory of individual into the subject as ontologically true, that is, what he is supposed to be (or behave) into what he is. This maps the comprehension of what we mean and to understand and do as individuals to fixed points—say, work with the assumption that to rationally calculate, whether bounded or pure, is our inner pre-given human nature. There are, in conjunction, attempts at creating and governing the social institutions through a frame/structure that rewards such behavioural patterns and punishes other patterns it sees as breaking away from the ideal state. Those fixed points then become our norms we take as given to organize our life. For instance, Political Economy tells us that what we get in return are what we contribute in production; our wages/income/wealth is traceable to what we as individuals choose and make ourselves to be; and what we as individuals choose is, what we, depending upon our pre-given human nature and ability, consider apt to choose. Irrespective of the fact that the processes of surplus labour, exploitation, inequality, etc., are shaping the processes in which we are embedded, the cultural process organized in part by the knowledge production of Political Economy tries to render these as ineffective and irrelevant and in fact to occult them altogether from the language-logic-experiencing-ethos of the hegemonic delusional cosmology which it engenders. This attempt to define and transform the subject is the very task of the hegemonic, the unconscious consent generation necessary for the production of delusional cosmology. The point is to produce subjects of consensus, subjects who recognize and live on the surface cleaned by the Political Economy which is now to be the only surface available to be traversed. After cleaning, this argument is put forward: we are by virtue of what we choose to be and make ourselves to be; the good and bad times are all a result of our human nature or at most bad luck. Of course, many think that way; it would have to be for the hegemonic accrual to materialize. But our analysis also refers to other ways of constructing meanings, that is, other cultural processes that might work in a reverse direction, and that do challenge the delusional cosmology thereby pulling and pushing the subject in a reverse direction. Marxist theory, among other things, is also one such countereffect and it internalizes this feature of the individual as socially constructed, as decentred and disaggregated, into its theory of individual and of its role as subjects in society. The hegemonic is thus precariously placed when such subjects challenge and see through the delusional cosmology; the hegemonic breaks down; that is why the hegemonic formation must be founded on a continual process of procreation of delusional cosmology of capitalism, at least for a sufficient number of its subjects.

(v) Is Mode of Appropriation and Exploitation the same?

To begin with, one needs to make a distinction between surplus, appropriation and exploitation. This distinction is conceptually important in order to see the multiple ways in which they could appear in any concrete situation. As we have seen, organizations of surplus are diverse; in turn modes of appropriation of surplus must be distinguished from the aspect of *exploitation* which is a *particular manner* of appropriation of surplus labour encapsulating the exclusion of the direct producers/workers from the fruits of their labour. Otherwise, there is non-exploitation. These three—surplus, appropriation and exploitation—would occur in diverse sets of groupings under variegated situations. Rather than beginning from any predetermined position/judgment, it is worthwhile to contextually analyze the 'situation' in order to comment on a particular relation between surplus creation and its mode of appropriation. Two qualifications are important here.

First, it is notable that the definition of Marxian exploitation does not fundamentally refer to high or low income/wages, more or less power, more or less property, high or low wealth, more or less advantage, normalcy or marginality. It has nothing per se to do either with violence or non-violence. In any concrete situation, exploitation can co-exist with all, some or any of these. It is, of course, a different question as to whether specific forms of exploitation or non-exploitation can produce serious impacts on how we as individuals live, how our family life and workplace are shaped, how our community life is formed and what kind of state and public institutions emerge. Indeed insofar as these occur in conjunction, effects of exploitation/non-exploitation matter in the production of meanings, conflicts, violence, love, care, masculinity, sharing, marginality, morality, property, environment, inequality and corruption just as these in turn would also affect the form of exploitation/non-exploitation. One of the purposes of Marxian theory is to demonstrate such effects of exploitation/non-exploitation on these diverse social practices, activities and relationships and, in turn, to see the reverse effects of these in the making or unmaking of exploitation/non-exploitation. Much of the recent literature in Marxian theory has drawn attention to this incessant relation of their being mutually constitutive. However, this relation should not take our minds off the critical point that exploitation as a category is conceptually distinct from and irreducible to those on which it impacts or which impacts it. If such reductionism transpires then they would have, as they did, fatal consequences for Marxian theory and the practices it harbours.

Second, it is important to appreciate that since appropriation and exploitation are related to surplus labour and hence their definition is derived from class, reducing class to some other entity and then claiming to be explaining mechanisms of exploitation through it can be debilitating for Marxian theory (Chakrabarti and Cullenberg 2003, Chapters 2-5). For example, reducing class to relations of domination-subordination is problematical; when this happens, statements such as that the power relation mirrors exploitation and hence the two are equivalent become commonplace. Therefore, without accounting for and analyzing exploitation per se claims are made on relations of exploitation by reducing them to mechanisms of power. In that case, one does not produce a surplus labour theory of class but a power theory of class. Similarly, it is misplaced to reduce capitalist exploitation to unequal prior distribution of productive assets. In that case, the latter becomes the point of interest and exploitation secondary and even redundant. On this ground, many radicals such as from Analytical Marxian School reject labour theory of value because for them the concern is distributive justice per se; by defining class in terms of property (note: its existence transpires fundamentally outside the domain of production) they would either reject exploitation or consider it redundant (since exploitation follows from unequal endowment in a causal sequence). But, that is tantamount to displacing Marx's focus on class and particularly exploitation if we pay heed to the warning of Bruce Roberts, "Wait a minute, many Marxists who use labour theory are not concerned with distributive justice in the first instance" (Roberts 1996). Class, exploitation and in the specific case of capitalism, labour theory of value are central to Marx's frame and any idea of distributive justice that is derived must be located in relation to this frame; the frame itself cannot be reduced to the aspects of distribution and distributive justice per se. Therefore, in Marxian framework, the question of distribution must be seen in conjunction with class and mode of appropriation; value theory (a theory that describes the concept and role of socially necessary abstract labour time) makes it possible for us to see this connection in the context of the system of capitalism. Power and property are very important and they occur in conjunction with class process in a concrete setting but that is no excuse to reduce class to them. Class, power and property, in any concrete situations, materialize in various assortments and that too in specific overdetermined and contradictory relations (Resnick and Wolff 2006, Chapter 6).

(vi) Does organization of exploitation produce a class division? Does this class division correspond to social division?

The event of exploitation entails the schism or division between performers of surplus labour and its appropriators; they are constitutionally separated. Organizations of exploitation as in capitalism produce a specific kind of division: class division. In short, class exploitation institutionalizes class division; class division co-exists with income, wealth, caste, gender, and ethnic divisions; its source is unique that makes it irreducible to the other divisions even though they would, in any concrete situation, be related in a mutually constitutive relation. Indeed, much work in Marxism is currently ongoing on the question of intersectionality between class, income, gender, caste, race, etc.

Under capitalism, Marx further held that the social position and status of workers and their children would somewhat mirror the class division. Social division perpetuating differential opportunities/abilities and class division perpetuating differential income and wealth would correspond to one another. This provokes many questions. For example, is there a correspondence between the stratified school system (which teaches different things to different groups of people for different roles in society) and the exploitative relations of production? Exploitation and class division generated in capitalist production stemming from the peculiarity of labour market and labour process can be said to be the cause and effect of the stratified school system in which one group (the future workforce) learns by rote and following rules (what takes the form of learning 'market' skills and values [work ethics] in human capital theory) and the other group learns how to be creative and independent (the future capitalists, managers and experts). Not only is there a correspondence between the division in the labour process that one witnesses (with capitalists, managers and special experts on one side and workers on the other) and the division in terms of those who are buyers (the same capitalists helped by the cohort managers and experts) and sellers (the workers) of labour power as Marx has pointed out, but that one must also contend with the correspondence of these economic divisions with social divisions, such as in schools and the process of schooling. The same holds for access to health and other public resources that, previously considered as commons, are in a continual process of being privatized in favour of capitalists and their cohorts. The correspondence principle can be extended to argue in favour of this systemic connection. Is capitalism an intergenerational system that socially produces in tandem, in the same spatial-temporal plane, the *potential* mass of exploited and exploiters through social institutions (family, school, etc.) and the *actual* exploiters and exploited embedded in organizations? Is it also the system that continually secures the differences in access to public resources by virtue of facilitating control over the discretionary wealth that the capitalists and their cohorts enjoy?

Departure from Political Economy: For a theory that pledges on 'Freedom, Equality, Property and Bentham', Political Economy will refuse to accept capitalism as a source of class and social division. It says that there is no systemic aspect traceable to capitalism that can be related to these sets of division. Instead, by refusing to acknowledge the class division, it would consider the social division as a natural outcome, a result of individual choices concerning hard work, thrift and entrepreneurship. It thereby defends social division in capitalism on this basis and would argue in favour of social mobility as a feature of capitalism as against the above Marxian critique that points to systemic social hierarchy and immobility arising from the correspondence thesis.

(vii) What is the relation between Class, Commodity and Value Theory? (A Technical Note)[6]

Marx sought an understanding of commodity in relation to his chosen focus of analysis—class. Depending upon the relation of commodity with processes of performance, appropriation, distribution and receipt of surplus labour, the meaning of commodity would undergo a change. Capitalist commodity would be conceived differently from, say, a slave commodity, a communist commodity or a feudal commodity. Our focus here is on 'capitalist' commodity.

To capture the specificity of capitalist commodity, we must first focus on the special relation of commodity with value and value form and then move on to examine the relation of value and commodity to class process. A specific relation between commodity and class process produces the notion of 'capitalist' commodity and 'capitalist' class process; each takes shape in terms of the other. Marxian representation of the capitalist class process builds on this intimate and inalienable relation between value, commodity and class.

In relating commodity to class process Marx identified two moments within his rendition of commodity—production and circulation. Both production and circulation not only mutually constitute one another but each remains overdetermined by other economic and non-economic processes. Given the overdetermination of production and circulation, by economic and non-economic processes, the pertinent questions for Marx were the following: what sense can we make of the *given* world of commodities? What sense can we make of the world of *appearances*? How are we to deconstruct the metaphysic of money, money as the *general equivalent*, money as *the* standard measure which by making things commensurable, renders it possible to make them equal? How are we to move away from the, "hegemonic logic of general equivalents" (Goux, 1990, p. 5); move to the "secret hidden away beneath the manifest fluctuations in the relative value of commodities" (Marx, Capital Vol. 1)? How are we to move to the, "site of the unconscious of commercial circulation" (Goux, 1990, p. 53)? How are we to move from *idealism of general equivalents* to the *materialism of labour*? How are we to locate processes of performance, appropriation, distribution and receipt of surplus labour in the commodity form?

To unveil the secret of social relations, of class processes embodied in commodity that is expressed through the figure of money, Marx needed a common standard related to labour time—an abstract unit—that would enable him to open up the monetary expression and relate it to class processes of performance, appropriation, distribution and receipt of surplus labour. That common standard or unit is social necessary abstract labour time or SNALT. "Socially necessary labour-time is the labour time required to produce any use-value under the conditions of production normal for a given society and with the average degree of skill and intensity of labour prevalent in that society" (Marx 1990, Vol. 1, p. 129). SNALT thus abstracts away from the concrete property of labour that produces a particular use value. It is a social estimation of an average, something that is expressed through market; unlike use values and concrete labours that entail heterogeneity, market equalize the different use values (4 chairs = 1 table) through the act of exchange; in the transformation of use values into exchange values, what are thus equalized are units of SNALT embodied in each produce. As exchange values materializing in market relation, the products of labour abstract away from their use values and the labours specific to them (heterogeneous concrete labours); they are left only with the SNALT meaning what is central at the point of exchange is the, "congealed quantities of homogenous human labour, i.e. of human labour power expended without regard to the form of its expenditure" (Marx 1990, Vol. 1, p. 128). SNALT seen from the site of production is called value while SNALT when viewed from the site of circulation is defined as value form.

A commodity comprises elements of value and value form, both expressed in SNALT. Value is simply socially necessary abstract labour time (SNALT), the average amount of labour expenditure needed to produce one unit of a commodity. Value has its corresponding value form, which can be described as use value in exchange.[7] Value form is the form value takes at the level of exchange, which under 'capitalist' existence, is expressed in money price. That is, exchange of use values is indeed (also) an exchange of SNALT. Value—SNALT—and exchange value—price as expression of SMALT—are thus not independent and autonomous of one another. Exchange value or price is the form of value. Because exchange value involves money and since value expresses itself through exchange value, there is an intimate connection of SNALT (value) with money (value form).[8] Each unit of money embodies some amount of SNALT. As an embodiment of value, money under Marxist theory is not simply a thing but reflects a social relationship. While we have been, like Marx, focusing on individual commodity, it should be evident that, "the wealth of societies in which the capitalist mode of production prevails appears as an 'immense collection of commodities' " (Marx 1990, Vol. 1, p. 125) and where, "as exchange-values, all commodities are merely definite quantities of congealed labour-time" (Marx 1990, Vol. 1, p. 130).

The money price attached to the commodity embodies SNALT attributable to paid labour (representing necessary labour) and unpaid labour (representing surplus labour). The unpaid labour measured by SNALT is called the surplus value. Surplus value is then the value expression of surplus labour. The payments out of the total appropriated surplus value are routed through the process of circulation, that is, the process of commodity exchange. Consequently, the movement of commodity from production (value) to circulation (value form) generates the revenue/income flow across the various agents in the economy. The double structure theory of value is necessary because of the need to capture the class process in which the unremunerated surplus labour (measured by SNALT) as distinguished from paid labour (again measured in SNALT) is appropriated, distributed and received as payments and revenue flows (Roberts, 1987). The latter set of processes materializes through the circuits of circulation and takes the form of exchange value capturing the social flow of SNALT.[9]

To take a step back, we have seen that every commodity has two inescapable encounters with performed labour. First, every commodity contains performed labour under specific material and social conditions. Second, every commodity (with embodied labour) is a market claim on other commodities (that is, claim on performed labour embodied in these commodities). Since the commodities are sold, incomes are generated. There is then a social relation between labour performed and income generated, and the associated relation between the portions of unremunerated labour time contained in the total performed labour time or surplus labour and the resulting revenues that gets created and distributed. Revenues then are numerical expressions of distribution and receipt of surplus labour, or, more specifically, in the context of value representation, surplus value.

The above understanding means that there are two distinct but related ways in which commodities are counted. Value as embodied SNALT counts the flows of 'doing' (of the total value and the surplus value). Value form counts the payments (income and revenue flows) expressed in SNALT. Value of a commodity with its value form of price, and surplus value and its value form of revenues are counted in two different but related ways even as both the value and value form are expressed in SNALT. This way of counting, of putting down numbers or signs to commodities, is a method of expressing the performance of surplus labour (the doing) and the process of appropriation, distribution and receipt of surplus labour (the payments or forms the unpaid part of the doing takes).

Value theory then provides us with a method of expressing the performance of surplus labour (the doing) and the process of appropriation, distribution and receipt of surplus value (the payments or forms the unpaid or surplus part of the doing takes). Without the categories of value, one cannot decipher the components of paid and unpaid labour embedded within commodity nor can surplus value as a form of unpaid labour that is appropriated, distributed and received be accessed. It is obvious that commodity must be related to the specific kind of class process. As per our focus on capitalism, we remain concerned with the social form of commodity that is connected to the performance, appropriation, distribution and receipt of unpaid surplus value performed by productive labourers and appropriated by productive capitalists. Such commodities are defined as capitalist commodities and such class processes referred to as capitalist. Having specified the relation between commodity and class through value theory, we are now in a position to precisely define capital and capitalist class process.

(viii) What is the secret of capitalist-exploitative mode of appropriation? What is capitalist class process?

As a way of prefiguring the definition of 'capitalist' mode of performance and appropriation, Marx foregrounds and distinguishes between labourer, labour power and labour. The labourer (the individual/subject) personifies labour power which he is free to sell to a buyer ideally specified by a contract (written or unwritten) that in turn is sanctioned by, to use Friedrich Hayek, the Rule of Law. According to Marx: "We mean by labour-power or labour-capacity, the aggregate of those mental and physical capabilities existing in the physical form, the living personality of a human being, capabilities which he sets in motion whenever he produces a use-value of any description" (Marx 1990, p. 270). The realization of labour power—in its activated state involving a definite quantity of expended human muscle, nerve, brain, etc.—is *labour* which materializes in the process of transformation of the elements of nature into final goods and services. This process of transformation of labour power into labour in production—what Marx calls the consumption of labour power—is called the labour process. What makes a labour process 'capitalist' (as against feudal or communist) is its connection to the specific mode of performance and appropriation of surplus labour or class process. Let us explain.

The point is that the relationships sanctified by the Rule of Law in the two domains—market/exchange and production—are dramatically different, albeit related. In the domain of exchange, as Marx argued, the so-called 'Freedom, Equality, Property and Bentham' rules since individuals (as buyers and sellers) do contract to buy and sell labour power as free persons, that is, equal before the Law; each has his gain to consider in this transaction that involves recognition and transfer of private property of labour power from seller to the buyer through a price rule (the essence of labour market). In this set-up, the labourer under the capitalist form is epitomized by the fact that he cannot be bought and sold (as in slave form); nor can he be held under control and be accountable by personalized ties and attachment related to nature and community (as in feudal form). Under capitalism, once the labourer follows the capitalist into the production domain, their market relationship undergoes an alteration and so does the physiognomy of the individuals.

> While we leave this sphere of simple circulation or the exchange of commodities, which provides the 'free-trader vulgaris' with his views, his concepts and the standard by which he judges the society of capital and wage-labour, certain changes take place, or so it appears, in the physiognomy of our dramatis personae. He who was previously the money-owner now strides out in front as a capitalist; the possessor of labour-power follows as his worker. The one smirks self-importantly and is intent on business; the other is timid and holds back, like someone who has brought his own hide to the market and now has nothing else to expect but—a tanning (Marx 1990, p. 280).

It is notable that what transpires in the domain of exchange gives capitalists the key to control the consumption of labour power in the labour process; here consumption of labour power embodies, along with necessary labour, the performance of surplus labour. Together, they form one of the essential conditions in instituting the subjugation of workers as a group. Of course, the workers may not recognize their subjection and could instead deliver surplus labour of their free will and joy just as housewives may deliver surplus labour out of love for her husband. Louis Althusser through his concept of ideological apparatus and interpellation theorized this moment of subjectification (where the workers govern themselves according to the given norms and rules of capitalism that they have come to accept as natural) and subjection (where workers are subjugated by capitalists and their cohorts) under capitalism; later Marxists using Gramscian, Foucauldian or Lacanian approach have been focusing on the aspect of subjection and subjectification even further.

Anyway, getting the right of labour power by purchasing it is one thing and the actual effort or work in production is quite another; that is why labour power/labour market and labour/labour process must be conceptually distinguished. The domain of production involves the process of consumption of labour power wherein the labour power is activated i.e. actual work extracted; it is the domain of performance of surplus labour without which capitalists cannot access surplus value and profit. The labourers who perform surplus labour are known as *productive labourers* and the employers who appropriate unpaid portion of surplus labour or what is surplus value (capital) are known as *productive capitalists;* productive workers and capitalists are personification of class processes. Their relation , along with those concerning property, market and power is also one of exploitation; productive capitalists' exploits and productive workers are exploited in a labour process in which their performed surplus labour is appropriated and distributed as surplus value.

Let us summarize what happens in the process of consumption of labour power. It is captured by the manner in which the labour power (bought at its value, say, V from the market) is activated over the material forces of production or constant capital (also bought at its value, say, C) in order to produce goods and services. The use value born out of it is sold/ exchanged in the market and hence appears in a commodity/ value form (its value being, say, W). It is notable that out of the total performed labour embedded in the commodity, a part is paid back to the labourers (the mentioned V) which is the necessary labour equivalent of the value of labour power or real wage and the other part is the unpaid surplus value (SV) appropriated by productive capitalists by excluding the productive workers from the fruits of surplus labour (the moment of exploitation). To put it succinctly,

Value of the commodity = W = C + V + SV .

The value contained in constant capital C would be transferred via market exchange from its previous owner to the existing capitalist who then uses it in the current labour process as material forces of production. New values, V + SV, are created by activating labour power in that labour process. Labor power and not constant capital create/add new value in the labour process. That is why labour power is the 'golden goose' capitalists would like to get control of. Of this newly created value, only a part is returned to its direct producers (the productive labourers) as wage and the rest SV (the value equivalent of surplus labour) is the unpaid portion that is appropriated by the capitalists. SV expressed in monetary form is capital; as personification of appropriation through the process of M (C + V) – C′ (produced commodity) – M′ (M + M″

— where M″ is surplus value), the adjective 'productive' applies before the capitalist. In turn, depending upon different kinds of organizational structure that are legally validated (sole proprietorship, partnership and corporation), one comes across various kinds of productive capitalists (single capitalist, partners, board of directors and big shareholders).

Definition: *Capitalist class process* is defined as the process of appropriation of surplus value by productive capitalists materializing through a formation of capitalist commodity that contains a combination of values comprising of the value form of labour power (V), value form of the means of production (C) and value form of surplus labour (SV).

From the above, we can identify capitalist surplus value appropriation and capitalist commodity as the two *defining signifiers* of capitalist class process. These two signifiers then emerge in our analysis as the master signifiers in the sense that the name of capital in any form (whether private or state capitalist, global or national capitalist and so on) must, by definition, be connected to these signifiers.

Moreover, unlike Political Economy, Marxian theory does not consider capital as a thing, as a product simply tied with investment. In Marxian theory, capital is fundamentally a social relation. Capital is a product of capitalist class process. Take away capitalist class process and there is no capital. Or, to put it in another way, since the relation between productive labourers and productive capitalist is one of exploitation, capital is founded on the relationship of exploitation. We thus cannot have capital without (relations of) exploitation either.

This 'capital', unlike surplus value or capital procured in circulation such as through banking and trading (advancing money/value to get more money/value; generating extra value/money by buying and selling of commodities), is ultimately a form of unpaid surplus labour created through commodity production. As personification of capital the productive capitalists are distinguished from unproductive capitalists (bank capitalists, merchant capitalists and big shareholding capitalists) who generate surplus value through circulation and not commodity production per se.

The distinction of productive capitalist from unproductive capitalists enables Marxian theory to clearly point out that exploitation as a form of appropriation of surplus labour/value is associated with productive capitalists and not with capitalists generally; unproductive capitalists such as merchant capitalists or moneylender neither appropriate and distribute surplus labour nor exploit. A capitalist becomes a *productive* capitalist not simply because he personifies capital (so do unproductive capitalists). Rather, he gets this name for his role in personifying the process of appropriation and distribution of surplus value/capital created by the productive labourers. Productive and unproductive capitalists are clearly related since they provide each other's condition of existence. Surplus value that is appropriated by the productive capitalists is distributed to other members of society, including the unproductive capitalists for providing various conditions of existence.

> The capitalist who produces surplus value, i.e., who extracts unpaid labour directly from the workers and fixes it in commodities, is admittedly the first appropriator of this surplus-value, but he is by no means its ultimate proprietor. He has to share it afterwards with capitalists who fulfil other functions in social production taken as a whole, with the owner of the land, and with yet other people. Surplus value is therefore split up into various parts. Its fragments fall to various categories of persons, and take on various mutually independent forms, such as profit, interest, dividends, gains made through trade, ground rent, etc. We shall be able to deal with these modified forms of surplus value only in Volume 3. (Marx 1990, Vol. 1, p. 709)

Landlords, moneylenders or banks, merchants or traders, shareholders, managers, state and so on are paid off from the surplus value because they are all providing critical conditions of existence to the processes of performance and appropriation of surplus value in a capitalist class process.[10] They are first hand receivers of surplus value. To secure their role as receivers of surplus value these condition providers employ another set of workers—'unproductive' labourers (for they do not exert surplus labour)—to do work on their behalf, and who are paid by the unproductive capitalists (and others such as state and landlords) from the already distributed surplus value that has fallen in their lap against the contracted condition providing roles. Thus, while unproductive capitalists do not directly distribute surplus value created in class process, they do redistribute surplus value further amongst members of society. Unproductive labourers are thus essential for unproductive capitalists as also for indirectly being responsible for reproducing the class positions of the direct performers and appropriators of surplus value, that is productive labourers and capitalists. To capture the systemic character of capitalism, Marx defined, classified and arranged the positions and roles of the different kinds of capitalists and the workers. But this must not be an excuse for privileging one set (say, productive) over the other (as unproductive) as many Marxists have unfortunately done. This intention is certainly not one that Marx had in mind:

> He [the unproductive laborer] performs a necessary function, because the process of reproduction itself includes unproductive functions. (Marx, 1992 Vol. 2, p. 209)
>
> The reproduction process includes both functions of capital, and thus also the need for these functions to be represented, either by the capitalist himself, or by salaried workers, his agents. But this is just as little a reason for confusing the circulation agents with the production agents as it is a reason for confusing the functions of commodity capital and money capital with those of productive capital. (Marx 1992, Vol. 2, p. 205)

In any social setting, capitalist class process and non-class processes would mutually constitute one another. They can be, as explained earlier, grouped into enterprises and can possibly occur in any site, even seemingly unusual ones. Such capitalist enterprises could also be subjected to changes. Consider a brothel where sex is bought and sold as a commodity. A host of personnel would typically be working in various processes that constitute a concrete brothel in any social setting. Therefore, suppose that a group of sex workers provide the service with the help of already purchased means of production or constant capital, C (buildings, rooms, condoms, sex instruments, etc.). Against providing the commodity of sex service whose value received is W (paid by the customer), the value added by the sex worker is the portion in the form of wages of sex workers which is their socially determined necessary labour equivalent (V) and the surplus value (SV) that is appropriated in money form (capital) by non-performing individual or groups (capitalists). Once having appropriated the SV, the capitalists go on to distribute it to various condition providers (those who supervise and manage the sex workers, dalals who bring in customers and new sex workers, those who keep law and order problem away from brothels, etc.), keeping the remaining for themselves as profit. As the sex workers are exploited in value form, this brothel resembles a capitalist enterprise. Clearly, as our example suggests, the class process of surplus labour in the specific form they take cannot appear without the combined effects of various non-class processes (regarding managing and disciplining, supply of sex workers and customers, law and order, etc.); the latter in turn facilitate the specific form taken by performance, appropriation, distribution and receipt of surplus labour. In contrast, in case, the sex workers themselves form a collective by agreeing to perform and appropriate the SV without excluding anybody from participating in them (that is, there is no exploitation), the brothel is transformed into a communist enterprise. In case, the sex workers are bought and kept as slaves in perpetuity, the brothel becomes a slave enterprise. The questions of whether sex work is right or wrong, liberating or degrading, etc. are conceptually different from the question of class; one can proceed to produce an analysis of their complex relations in a particular scenario (and they may indeed be related) but to reduce one to another would be fatal for developing an understanding and politics of sex work. To sum up, as is true for all institutions, the brothel can actually and possibly take various forms, and these are open to being subjected to class politics and class transformation.

SV/V (epitomizing the ratio of surplus labour to necessary labour) is the rate of exploitation or the rate at which surplus value is pumped out of the workers for each unit of exerted necessary labour, V. The rate of exploitation could be increased by extension of working hours (say, from 8 to 9 hours per day) that enables an expansion of surplus value without changing V or it could be increased by introducing technical changes and hence rise in productivity that, with existing labour time expended (that is, say, the same 8 hours), reduce the (necessary) labour time required to produce the socially necessary V, thereby leaving more as SV. The former is known as absolute surplus value production and the latter relative surplus value production.

There is one final point. The three aspects—labour market, labour process and organization of exploitation—get intertwined in a dialectical relation. The appropriation of surplus value by the productive capitalists would depend on numerous factors, labour process being one. Hence, given other things as they are, control over the labour process—place, time, intensity, technology, type of work, etc.—is seen as providing flexibility to the productive capitalists with the purpose to pump out the maximum amount of surplus value from the labourers; rate of exploitation thus becomes critical from the perspectives of both capitalists and workers. It is pertinent to note in this regard that the capitalists may give more or less space for the creativity of labourers in the labour process depending upon which is suitable to produce the greater surplus, but the point is that the decision to do so rests solely with the capitalists and remains their prerogative. *Unless challenged*, good or bad work conditions remains in the final instance the license of capitalists.

Departure from Political Economy: An exclusive focus on the market system (of analyzing capitalism) said to epitomize 'Freedom, Equality, Property and Bentham' without a focus on the social relations inside the production system will make invisible the effect of market system on class relations and the economy at large and vice versa. It will fail to reveal the underlying source of class exploitation and how it is procreated. Political Economy thus fails to account for the role of class exploitation in the capitalist organization of economy and society. Class politics and class transformation in the specific Marxian way are accordingly excluded from the realm of possible domain of undertaking social change.

(ix) What is the Working Class?

From a Marxian perspective, the workers are disaggregated and broadly clubbed into two types: productive and unproductive. The term 'productive' labour refers to the direct producers who create surplus value through the capitalist class process in order for it to be appropriated by 'productive' capitalists. "The worker who performs productive work is productive and the work he performs is productive if it directly creates surplus value, i.e. if it valorizes capital." (Marx 1990, Vol. 1, p. 1039) In contrast, unproductive labourers are those who do not directly produce surplus value for the productive capitalist. At an elementary level, the unproductive labourers can be divided into five types. The first group is the 'internal' unproductive workers employed by the capitalist enterprises and includes the clerks, managers, supervisors, sales and marketing agents, etc., who provide direct conditions of existence for the production of surplus value by 'productive labourers' and its subsequent appropriation by 'productive capitalists'. Second, we have already explained that part of the surplus value created by the capitalist enterprises is distributed to other 'unproductive capitalists' such as the merchant capitalists, the bank capitalists, the shareholder capitalists as also other agents/institutions such as the landlord and state for providing various external conditions of existence for capitalist class process to procreate. The 'unproductive capitalists', landlords and state employ a host of workers—the second group of 'external' unproductive labourers—such as clerks, accountants, managers, supervisors, state bureaucracy and staffs, etc.—to ensure that the guaranteed conditions (such as the processes of buying and selling commodities, lending money or lending ownership capital, political and legal support) are completed against which they receive wages as part of the surplus value already distributed to the 'unproductive capitalists', state and landlord. Thirdly, unproductive labourers include those direct producers who exert surplus labour in other non-capitalist types of enterprises. Fourth, there are multiple labouring activities providing those conditions of existence that enable direct producers engaged in non-capitalist enterprises to produce and appropriate surplus labour. Finally, there are labouring activities that have nothing to do with any class process, capitalist or non-capitalist, either as direct producers of surplus or working for fulfilling conditions of existence to secure the former processes. Marx gives the example of a singer to draw this contrast. "A singer who sings like a bird is an unproductive worker. If she sells her song for money, she is to that extent a wage-labourer or merchant. But if the same singer is engaged by an entrepreneur who makes her sing to make money, then she becomes a productive worker, since she produces capital directly". (Marx 1990, Vol. 1, p. 1044)

Generally, through this distinction between productive and unproductive labour, and between various types of unproductive labour, Marxian theory is able to capture the diversity of labouring activities and their relations with one another as well as the varied capitalist and non-capitalist employers and employees. The analysis of the disaggregated working force that is produced through this differentiation between the 'productive' and 'unproductive' helps us conceptualize the multiple positions occupied by the workers in concrete reality, sometimes even in conflict with one another. Take the case of singing. The worker can be doing both productive and unproductive work in the same or different sites. The singer can be singing at home for herself or for her friends (unproductive work), she can sing at a hotel, party or event for a specified wage contract with the capitalist (productive work in capitalist class process), she can well be singing on her own in a local train or in streets to earn her living (unproductive work in independent class process) and so on. Let us leave aside the first case out from our analysis. Accordingly, the category of 'working class' as consisting of all those labourers who perform labour and receive remuneration (monetary or in kind) resembles what Laclau called the "kaleidoscopic movement of differences". Just as the capitalist is disaggregated so is the worker. The term 'capitalist' before 'class' captures those people who personify the custody of surplus value, that is, the difference from the process of M-M', whether they get it through commodity production process (as in case of productive capitalists) or through process of circulation (as in case of unproductive capitalists like financial capitalists, merchant capitalists and shareholding/ownership capitalists). The term 'working' before 'class' refers to all kinds of productive and unproductive workers who work on behalf of and under the capitalist class, non-capitalist class, state, landlord, etc. or their appointed personnel hired and delegated cohorts (top management, bureaucracy, etc.).

We may choose to insist on usage of the term 'working class' in the sense of noun or group of people, but it is clear now that its disaggregated nature tells us nothing about the politics and subjectivity that would arise on the social plane. That is, the political articulation, actual and possible, cannot be traced to structurally defined capitalist class and working class; not the least because even the structure, whether of economy or of capitalism, is disaggregated. Moreover, on the question of class struggle and class transformation (that is, here, struggle *over* process of surplus labour), one cannot a priori infer anything from the capitalist and worker positions to claim any natural alignment or relation to the struggle and change. That is, who struggles and how and why the struggle is conceived and articulated is the contingent and articulatory play of politics. This means that interest, subjectivity and politics must be conceived as problems in themselves rather than being singularly or primarily reduced to or derived from the economy or structure or its assumed inner depth.

While the Marxian discussion on the critique of exploitation in general and capitalism in particular and the question of injustice (as discussed later) is connected to Marxian politics, it cannot be taken as the singular determinant of the anatomy of theory, conduct and strategy of Marxian politics. The latter needs to be thought of distinctly as some major exponents of Marxian politics like Lenin, Gramsci, Mao Zedong, Althusser and Laclau understood very well. An example helps put my point sharply. Led by Lenin, the chief slogan of the Bolshevik revolution was 'bread and peace'. It did not relate directly to working class politics or capture of factories and so on. In the context of Russia these are what the Russian people desperately wanted then and the Bolsheviks recreated the Russian political scenario by reconnecting that demand with the objective as encapsulated in the slogan. The genius of Lenin and the Bolsheviks was to ignite this possibility into political praxis, something that did not exist then in Russia. What was seemingly impossible was articulated and shaped into a political possibility. What happened thereafter, including the capture of state power, land reforms, building up of initial Soviets through takeover of factories and their later replacement by state capitalism is a different history.

(x) What is the Secret of Profit?

It is notable that in Political Economy, the distinction between labour power and labour is absent; no surplus labour or its form in surplus value is present. Therefore, the origin of profit gets disconnected from surplus labour or class; it is, in contrast, at best, projected as return on advanced capital. Rather than being an explanation of 'profit', this is really a name given to the return on capital. In short, value/price of commodity in effect is exhausted through return to capital and labour; to put it another way, under competitive market economy, per unit value must be equal to per unit cost leaving no surplus. For profit in the sense of something surplus/additional to emerge in Political Economy, competitive market economy must be violated in some fundamental way such that commodities cannot trade at their desired competitive value/price. One example of such violation is mark-up pricing under monopoly condition in which the concept of 'mark-up' over the competitive price stands for economic power that allows monopolists to garner extra value (profit) above the competitive value; this really is not extra value created in the labor process but a form of redistribution of value to the monopolist. While the political economists are not particularly fond of such extra economic power that violate rules of perfect competition, the point to be noted is that these violations are incidental and arbitrary and are no way critique of the idealized form of capitalism qua competitive market economy, namely, that there is no profit when commodities trade at their values. For Political Economy, it is the latter which is sacrosanct and 'reforms' are nothing but attempts to take the economy towards the competitive market economy; that is, there is always scope for improvement from imperfect capitalism to a more perfect capitalism. What is called into question is undue market power rather than capitalism per se; it needs to be dismantled or curbed. Capitalism cannot be called into question because by rendering profit qua surplus absent in the ideal competitive market economy, the origin of profit is obfuscated and made into a secret by Political Economy. Marx called this 'fairness' one of central components of the delusionary cosmology of capitalism Political Economy forwards and defends.

> To explain, therefore, the general nature of profits, you must start from the theorem that, on an average, commodities are sold at their real values, and that profits are derived from selling them at their values, that is, in proportion to the quantity of labour realized in them. If you cannot explain profit upon this supposition, you cannot explain it at all. This seems paradoxical and contrary to every-day observation. It is also a paradox that the earth moves round the sun, and that water consists of two highly inflammable gases. *Scientific truth is always a paradox, if judged by everyday experience, which catches only the delusive appearance of things.* Karl Marx in Value, Price and Profit (1969, pp. 77-78)

From our analysis of Marxian theory it is clear that profit is one distributed form of surplus value. In other words, profit under capitalist arrangement is founded on the social theft of labour. To begin with, profit is *not* definitionally equivalent to surplus value nor is it the fundamental category. That is, if the appropriated surplus value is exhausted through a distribution of the surplus value to all the constituent elements that provide the conditions of existence for the performance and appropriation of surplus labour—the moneylenders, managers/ supervisors, capital accumulation, banks, landlords, state, etc. —then profit is the residual payment to a subset of another group of people (say, as in a corporation, funds as dividends to shareholders and investment fund given to managers for capital accumulation). Profit in Marxian approach is a name given to a specific form of the distribution of surplus value. It highlights a certain kind of distribution of the quantum of the loot signifying exploitative appropriation of surplus labour. Unlike Political Economy, profit is then a portion of unpaid labour. Evidently, 'profit maximization' stands for valorization of a subset of distribution towards social groups such as shareholders who incidentally, as the owners of capital, can forward claim, as per the Rule of Law, to be the residual claimant of any surplus; the other profit claimants have varied historically, such as the present emphasis being on distribution of a portion of surplus value for the process of capital accumulation. Not surprisingly, profit maximization is a particularly striking slogan in a scenario of shareholder capitalism (especially where big shareholders form the bulk of ownership of the capitalist enterprise) and competitive capitalism.

(xi) The forms of Injustice

1. Appropriative Injustice

Exploitation is by definition based on the social theft of surplus labour; legalizing this theft does not change the fact that it is theft. Exploitation is wrong by virtue of what it is; one does not need any additional arguments to bolster this position. By extension, as a form of exploitation, capitalist appropriation is unjust because it is exclusionary whereas, in contrast, collective surplus appropriation as in case of the communist form is *just* precisely because it does not exclude the direct producers from it (Cullenberg 1992, 1998; Wolff 2012). As a system of organization of surplus value, capitalism is therefore founded on injustice.

Ending exploitation is to end capitalism. In fact, if exploitation per se is unjust as Marx makes the case, ending exploitation would be tantamount to ending all kinds of exploitation, capitalist, feudal, slave and CA communitic. We exemplify the problem of exploitation through an interrogation of capitalism. Our focus in this Marx's critique of capitalism should thus be seen as an argument not merely for ending capitalist exploitation, but exploitation per se. It entails ending the division between performers and appropriators/distributors of surplus labour. There are two alternative arrangements to think about. First, exploitative arrangement of surplus labour could be replaced by non-exploitative arrangement of surplus, say, communist class process; this is as long as the category of surplus labour exists. Here, communism materializes in the presence of class i.e. where the division between necessary and surplus labour is still present, but there is no schism between the performers and appropriators of surplus. Second, achievement of communism would be the same as terminating the existence of surplus labour or class; the object of this struggle over class process—class struggle—is to achieve a classless society, a paradoxical politics indeed as the purpose of struggle becomes the elimination of the object of struggle—class (Resnick and Wolff 2006, Chapter 16; Chakrabarti and Cullenberg 2003, Chapter 7). Since the time of Marx, there has been a huge debate within Marxism regarding which one is true communism; how to achieve it; what, if any, are the stages in it and what would such societies look like and so on.

Departure from Political Economy: Because it does not recognize the existence of class or process of surplus labour, Political Economy dismisses injustice of class exploitation and the politics of ending it. In contrast, no matter how it is bended, Political Economy defends capitalism. It considers capitalism as *just* for it gives everybody rightful return against what they have contributed. In its scheme, capitalism is the *end of history*. *Transition* means transition to and within capitalism and nothing more. For Marx, transition is a struggle over the crypt of capitalism—class exploitation—which can take two forms: one, a change from one form of exploitation to another and two, a change that strives to eliminate exploitation per se. Marx argued in favour of the latter. To eliminate fundamentally the process of class exploitation and not the people who exploit so that we do not replace one set of exploiters with another is the key corrective measure for Marx and Marxian theory.

2. Distributional Injustice

Because the appropriators are also in charge of distribution, exploitation entails that workers are excluded from distributional decisions. The control over distribution of surplus rests in the hand of the few appropriators or their chosen cohorts. Take the case of capitalism. Typically, the initial class distribution of surplus tends to flow to those who are immediately connected to the capitalists (merchant capitalists, bank capitalists, shareholder capitalists, landlords, top managers, etc.). Therefore, distribution tends to be tilted against the direct producers of surplus labour also known as workers by virtue of this structural inequality imposed through the separation of producers of surplus and appropriators/ distributers of surplus. A similar kind of depressing wage pressure is imposed on the unproductive mass of labourers who are employed by the unproductive capitalists, state etc. This raises the question of what should be 'fair' distribution pertaining to distribution of surplus, a question that is important in itself but which also cannot be detached from the mode of appropriation, particularly its exploitative form.

The source of the inequality of income/assets seen at the social level can be traced to the systemic feature of capitalist exploitation that divides the few appropriators of surplus from the rest of the population including its producers. One must here make a distinction between capitalism's systemic properties (what it sows by its very procreation) and the modifications that transpire in it due to a constellation of forces that oppose this inequality. In various phases of capitalism, in different countries, social movements, public institutions and opinion, left wing politics have brought their influence to bear upon the state forcing its intervention in order to make inequality under capitalism tolerable. Exploitative organization of surplus is here combined with a state policy of *redistributing* a portion of that surplus; this redistribution is on top of distribution of the surplus to the condition providers of capitalist enterprises (Chakrabarti, Cullenberg and Dhar 2008, Chakrabarti 2013).

Notable instances of such welfare capitalism have been the Western European countries which for decades after post Second World War were ruled by social democratic parties. Under welfare capitalism, the conduit of state was used to heavily tax corporations and high income individuals to ameliorate the systemic inequality of capitalism; decades of generous redistributive policies concerning unemployment benefits, education, health, pension, etc., followed. In our own country, welfare programs such as MGNREGA and Food Security are important acts that would require tapping into the surplus value for its functioning. Putting it in our frame, the aspect of non-exclusion in the functioning of the capitalist system is being recognized here and following which attempts are made to fix the problem with state led redistribution. Mitigating inequality makes the system of capitalism palatable.

On the other hand, neo-liberal philosophy that pioneered globalization in the last three decades built opinion and agreement in the other direction by forcing the state to cut down on such expenditures; taxes on corporations and rich individuals were trimmed which allowed a higher surplus to be retained by the capitalists and their cohorts than what would have been without the tax cut. Resultantly, income/wealth division in these erstwhile welfare capitalist economies started to mirror more and more the exclusionary face of capitalism. State-led expenditure on education, health, other social security services were savaged and many state enterprises and schemes privatized. An exemplification of this growing income, wealth and resource divide is the income gap between rich and poor in the OECD countries that has widened over the last two decades; the situation is particularly glaring for the USA (www.oecd.org/els/social inequality.october 2008: Are we growing unequal?) The phenomenon of income/wealth inequality is also true for developing countries as well which are transiting to matured capitalism. India's inequality and other BRICs countries are no exception (OECD Secretariat. 2012. Growth, Employment and Inequality in Brazil, China, India and South Africa: An Overview. www.oecd.org/employment/emp/45282661.pdf). Our point is that the capitalist organization of exploitation explains the cause of inequality. If exploitation is the disease of inequality then its solution requires a systemic transformation by way of the end of exploitation and hence of capitalism; instead of trying to humanize the organization of exploitation through redistribution which while important is always in danger of being undermined and undone as history has shown. In fact, as Thomas Pickety (2014), by surfing centuries of data has shown, except for the brief post-war period we referred to, capitalism always was associated with high inequality.

Departure from Political Economy: Political economy views distribution of income as a return to what one has contributed in production. In contrast, we have unpacked the need to link income distribution to mode of performance, appropriation and distribution of paid and unpaid labour. It is necessary to link income distribution with the class division in which one group of people labour and get partially paid for it while another group appropriates and distributes the fruits of surplus labour. Other than themselves, the latter is distributed to their employed cohorts and other condition providers who employing a host of other kinds of labourers ensure the reproduction of the cycle of performance, appropriation and distribution of paid and unpaid labour and through that constitute not only the produced wealth of the nation but also the system of who gets what and why. Income distribution is thus related to the systemic reproduction of the class organization of paid and unpaid labour. In a situation where the system is attempted to be organized (with the help of various conditions of existence) to produce and protect the class division, the presence of income and social inequality is hardly surprising. While re-distribution of surplus value to the state and international agencies (World Bank, etc.) to meet socially demanded needs does somewhat ameliorate the distributive injustice, it is not a sustainable solution to the problem of structural inequality of capitalism. Any policy put in place is always already vulnerable to being dismantled by the capitalists and their cohorts as and when they become powerful enough to do so.

3. *Democratic Injustice*

Exploitative organization of surplus is associated with democratic injustice (Wolff 2012). This critique stems from absence of economic democracy in the workplace and in participating in vital decisions-actions pertaining to it.

The decision regarding what, when, where and how to produce remains the prerogative of the appropriators or their appointed cohorts; the workers are in general excluded from these decisions that have an important bearing on their life/ well-being, environment and society in which they live. Therefore, for example, workers are excluded from the decisions of whether to outsource jobs, something that will have an impact on their own employment and surrounding social life. The source of this exclusion from participation in the functioning of the enterprise lies in the following: to ensure the scenario where those who perform surplus labour can be excluded from decision-making over its appropriation, all rights (unless challenged or amended) in the domain of production and what transpires there must be made the prerogative of the exploiters such as the capitalists. Without disconnecting the workers from the right of participation per se, it will be difficult if not impossible for the capitalists to exploit, that is, to be capitalists. Even if some rights relating to labour process are granted inside the production process, they remain the license of the capitalists; they are 'gifts' by exploiters such as capitalists and hence arbitrary.

Next, consider distribution. The decision-making process regarding distribution of surplus is inherently undemocratic whereby the rest of society including the workers are excluded from it even if they are greatly affected by it; the prerogative of distribution and who gets what remains with the appropriators and their coterie or appointee. If democracy (in the sense of equal participation of all) has any value then it is not clear as to why one should accept such an undemocratic arrangement when the same is increasingly considered as unacceptable elsewhere in society.

Finally, to answer the question of why collective appropriation, we will turn around and ask why not? If one rejects collective appropriation, one also rejects the right of individuals to participate on an equal footing in making decisions concerning issues that are of central importance to their lives and that affect the better part of their waking hours. Ruling out 'exclusion' of direct producers from the decision-action pertaining to the process of performance and appropriation of surplus value foregrounds the importance of workers' participation in all decision-making in enterprises. A case could be made that not all members are equally informed and skilled enough to make decisions on the allocation of resources, techniques of investment, financial management, and any number of other specialized and highly skilled decisions. This is a misrepresentation of the idea of 'non-exclusion' and of what we mean by participation. When we talk about 'non-exclusion' in performance or appropriation, we do not necessarily mean that all are part of every labouring activity and every decision with respect to appropriation and distribution must be taken together in absolute agreement. What is being suggested is that all must, at least, be participating in the decision-making process of what to produce, who will produce, where to produce and what to do with the produce by some common and collective agreement that everybody accepts and that they must, in the least, be participants in the process of any decision (in agreement or disagreement) pertaining to appropriation and distribution of surplus labour (Cullenberg 1992, 1998). In this context, the collective/community may decide to delegate many allocative, financial, or investment decisions to highly skilled personnel of their choice, who then might insist on an array of interventions, which in turn would require ratification by those who have delegated the authority in the first place. Again, the point is that the delegation and ratification of such decisions is collectively made and is thus democratic. It is evident that different social arrangements would arise in this regard, depending upon the site, context and configuration of constituting processes.

Departure from Political Economy: Political Economy has little to say regarding economic democracy or democracy inside the enterprise. It connects enterprise to market consideration, competition, strategy, human capital, etc., and democracy to state-centric political democracy. It would argue: isn't it the case that ownership of a capital input necessarily implies the right to appropriate the output of production process as well? On this premise, capital owners are presumed to have the right to alienate (sell/rent) their capital for whatever price the market will bear and to appropriate the full fruits of any production to which their capital contributes, including any residual, profit/ surplus.

This is a critically important myth to explode because it opens up the question of who should be the appropriator, whether of the whole product or of surplus labour. The counter-argument of Marxians could be this: private ownership confers special rights and privileges on owners but not necessarily on appropriation of surplus or residual clemency (Cullenberg 1992, 1998). This distinction separates, analytically and juridically, the right to alienate one's private property from the right to appropriate the fruits of production that one's property helps produce. Alienation and appropriation are simply two distinct attributes of ownership that have no 'natural' relationship to each other. Their reduction, as and when it happens, has been referred to by David Ellerman as the *Fundamental Myth of Private Property*; this myth sustains the 'great capitalist deceit' that those who *own property* must *appropriate* the surplus labour by natural (and by extension juridical) right. Clearly, the myth applies not merely to ownership of material-capital but also to the ownership of labour power. That is, the myth would uphold the view that workers have no natural or inalienable rights either to the residual or surplus that their labour-power helps to produce. By virtue of the fact that the golden goose of labour power is now owned by capitalists any return from it is rightfully theirs. Even Marxists at times have been taken in by this great capitalist deceit entailing a recurring confusion between capital-ownership and appropriation, and the reduction of the question of appropriation to the control of ownership. The inability to keep these aspects distinct means that the social gaze remains interpellated to the questions of property or productive assets while the issues concerning class and exploitation get displaced, demoted and ultimately occulted from the discursive terrain. The political consequence of this confusion emanating from the distinct task of socializing property and socializing appropriation can have devastating consequences for politics and socio-economic transformation. For example, in the erstwhile Soviet Union, socialism was rendered akin to socialized/nationalized control of ownership even as the right to appropriation of surplus value passed from the hands of private capitalists/landlords to state appointed board of directors; the workers continued to be excluded from the process of appropriation and distribution of surplus even as the form of exploitation changed from private capitalism to state capitalism; therefore, from a Marxian perspective, Soviet 'socialism' took the paradoxical form of state capitalism (Resnick and Wolff, 2002).

These three negative features that are particularly glaring under capitalism have also been argued to have contributed, in combination with other processes, to the scenarios of systemic instability, unemployment, alienation, marginalization, inequality, poverty, stratification, violence, ecological imbalance and environmental degradation. These effects materialize because of the manner in which organization of exploitation, via cause and effect, appears in conjunction with other social processes. That is, the scope and span of the effects of exploitation far exceeds its immediate mandate and tend to give shape to, in conjunction with other processes, a systemic form. Interesting, the critique of the three axes of injustices of capitalism paves the way for rethinking the political space towards non-exploitative modes of being.

(xii) Is capitalism inherently unstable? Does a market system of capitalism create its own condition of crisis-collapse?

Marx shows that the functioning of the capitalist enterprises in a competitive market environment can produce a systemic crisis in capitalism; we found out later, as in case of the Soviet Union, that state capitalism too can produce its quota of systemic crisises. Let us focus on the former, the most well-known type of capitalism. Capitalism contains the mechanism of business cycle, producing booms and busts. Booms typify growing investment optimism leading to overproduction while busts capture periods of destruction of constant capital (machines, plants, buildings, etc.) leaving a large number of people unemployed. Excess capacity and huge unemployment (who could put the idle machines, buildings, etc. to work) appear that also show the waste of capitalism and its hypocritical call to maintain economic efficiency (another name for avoiding waste) at the micro level functioning of decision units (individuals, business enterprises). Thus, capitalism is inherently unstable, wasteful and contains seeds of a crisis (Resnick and Wolff, 2010). While this insight of capitalist business cycle in Marx has stood the test of time, there is a debate, within and outside Marxism, whether the exact theory he propounded of business cycles is correct or not. In this regard, one of the central debates in Marxian theory has been over the falling rate of profit (Cullenberg, 1994). In its simplest form, it has been argued that growing capital accumulation (capturing expansion in C and V), rising organic composition of capital (C/V) fuelled by investment optimism would lead to a consequent fall in the rate of profit. However, in connection to business cycle, it has also been argued both by Marx and later Marxists that there exist counter-veiling tendencies that mitigate and can reverse the falling rate of profit. Therefore, when, how and whether business cycle of capitalism will lead to a fall in the rate of profit remains somewhat ambiguous and hence contingent on contradictory pulls and pushes of mutually constituting processes.

Finally, instability of capitalism points to the potential presence of a crisis *in* capitalism. But whether the crisis in capitalism will turn to a crisis *of* capitalism will depend upon whether the point of addressing the crisis involves transforming the exploitative mode of appropriation or not. In case the politics/policy of surmounting the crisis (as and when it appears) leaves the exploitative mode of appropriation intact, the crisis in capitalism does not give way to a crisis of capitalism. This is because capitalism remains intact even as its form may have changed following its rectification from its previous crisis. It is therefore wrong to think that capitalism will inevitably collapse from its crisis. The presence of the current global economic crisis has demonstrated the problem with the crisis-collapse hypothesis; the crisis in capitalism did not automatically lead to its collapse. It also demonstrates the importance of the cultural process of the hegemonic in ensuring that the crisis in capitalism does not translate into a crisis of capitalism.

Departure from Political Economy: This inherent property of instability in capitalism (its business cycle) is contrary to the strict classical/neoclassical dictum of Political Economy which theorises a picture of a spontaneous and harmonious system or macro economy emanating from microeconomics of choices made by consumers and firms. Political Economy would further hold that such an economic system rules out systemic failures such as depression; good and bad times are the consequences of individuals' decision making. Any state interference here will produce an inferior outcome or worse. If evidence is any proof (and economists revel in it), then we can conclude that there must be something fundamentally wrong with this claim of a depression free system. Just in the last 100 years, the two great crises and many intermittent ones in between have demonstrated the falsity of this claim.

There is another point to note. An economic crisis is not a wound but reflects the spreading of the wound into gangrene; markets are the conduit that enables this spread-effect as we are witnessing under the present global economic crisis. Far from being self-regulating, markets may produce, as it has, self-annihilation leaving people, regions and even nations struggling to survive. Therefore, not only do we get the insufficiency of the classical/neoclassical framework in locating and explaining depression but find its chief logical conduit of explaining the functioning of economic system faltering. Surely, there is something fundamentally wrong with this kind of crisis-prone, wasteful and unstable environment which in turn calls for a rethinking of the basic economic system itself, that is, in the way production, distribution and consumption of goods and services materialize under capitalism.

This was exactly the point argued for by Marx whereby he related the crisis of capitalism to the contradictions, convulsions and failures of the competitive market economy functioning through capitalist organization of surplus and suggested the abortion of capitalism as a recipe for resolving the macro crisis. By connecting the capitalist business cycle to class exploitation to demonstrate its inherent possibility of instability, he argued in favour of a systemic transformation involving a fundamental shift in the very model of appropriation from exploitation to non-exploitation. This is in contrast to John Maynard Keynes who suggested the role of the state in overcoming depression and ensuring smoothening of capitalist business cycles by actively intervening in and influencing the market economic outcomes. The difference between the two is revealing. Marx argued that systemic economic instability and social disaster cannot be solved except by replacing capitalism as a system while Keynes suggested that the same can be averted, that is, capitalism saved with the active role of state preventing business cycles from turning into possible depressions. From a Marxian perspective, this Keynesian solution is akin to (i) addressing the symptom of the crisis rather than the disease, and (ii) protecting class exploitation. Hence, instead of resolving the problem it pushes the source of the problem away; in doing so it adds another delusionary cloud cover to capitalism. Keynesian solution is therefore never enough from a Marxian perspective which calls for an end to the disease called capitalism itself by eliminating its source of exploitation. The crisis in capitalism becomes a crisis of capitalism only when the latter is foregrounded and becomes the object of politics.

REFERENCES

Chakrabarti, Anjan and Dhar, Anup (2010) *Dislocation and Resettlement in Development: From Third World to World of the Third*. Routledge: London.

Chakrabarti, Anjan, Dhar, Anup and Cullenberg, Stephen (2012) *World of the Third and Global Capitalism*. World View Press. Chapter 2.

Chakrabarti, Anjan and Cullenberg, Stephen (2003) *Transition and Development in India*. Routledge: London.

Gibson-Graham, J.K. (2006) *A Postcapitalist Politics*, University of Minnesota Press: Minneapolis.

Gibson-Graham, J.K. (1996) *The End of Capitalism (As We Knew It): A Feminist Critique of Political Economy*. Blackwell: Oxford.

Marx, Karl (1969-1976) *Theories of Surplus Value*, Parts I, II and III, Progress Publishers: Moscow.

Marx, Karl (1990-93) *'Capital: Critique of Political Economy.'* Vol 1, 2 and 3. Penguin: London.

Resnick, Stephen and Wolff, Richard (1987) *Knowledge and Class*.

University of Chicago Press: Chicago.

Resnick, Stephen and Wolff, Richard (2006) *New Departures in Marxian Theory*. Routledge: London and New York.

Resnick, Stephen and Wolff, Richard (2012) *'Contending Economic Theories: Neoclassical, Keynesian and Marxian'*. Chapters 1 and 4. MIT Press: Mass.

Additional References

1. Ajit Chaudhury. 1998, Toward Closing a Century-Old Debate: Transformation of Values into Prices in a World of Heterogeneous Labors, *Rethinking Marxism*, Volume 10, Issue 1.
2. Anjan Chakrabarti, 2013. Class and Need: Social Surplus and Marxian Theorization of Development. Philosophers for Change. http://philosophersforchange.org/2013/11/05/class-and-need-social-surplus-and-marxian-theorization-of-development.
3. Anjan Chakrabarti, Stephen Cullenberg and Anup Dhar. 2008. 'Rethinking Poverty Beyond Non-Surplus Theories: Class and Ethical Dimensions of Poverty Eradication.' *Rethinking Marxism* 20 (4), 673 – 687.
4. Stephen Cullenberg. 1994. *The Falling Rate of Profit: Recasting the Marxian Debate*. Pluto Press: London.
5. Bruce Roberts, B. 1987. "Marx after Steedman: Separating Marxism from 'Surplus Theory.'" In *Capital and Class* 32 (fall).
6. Bruce Roberts. 1996 "The Visible and the Measurable: Althusser and the Marxian Theory of Value" in *Post-Modern Materialism and the Future of Marxist Theory: Essays in the Althusserian Tradition*, ed. Callari, A. and Ruccio, Wesleyan University Press: D.F. Hanover and London.
7. Evald Ilyenkov. (1982) (1960). *The Dialectics of the Abstract and the Concrete in Marx's Capital*, translated by Sergei Kuzyakov, Progress Publishers: Moscow.
8. F., Engels. 1974. *Engels on Capital*, 2nd ed., International: New York.
9. J-J. Goux. 1990. *Symbolic Economics: After Marx and Freud*. Trans by Jennifer Curtiss Gage. Cornell University Press: Ithaca, New York.
10. Karl Marx. 1973. *Grundrisse*. Trans. M. Nicolaus. Vintage: New York. Pp 81-112.
11. Louis Althusser. 1969. *For Marx*. Chapters on 'Contradiction and Overdetermination' and 'On the Materialistic Dialectics', Verso: London.
12. Louis Althusser and Etienne Balibar. 1975. *Reading Capital*. Verso:

London.

13. Richard Wolf. 2012. *Democracy at Work: A Cure for Capitalism*. Haymarket: New York.
14. Richard Wolff, Bruce Roberts, and Antonino Callari. 1982. "Marx.s (not Ricardo.s) transformation problem: a radical reconceptualization", *History of Political Economy* 14 (4) 564-582.
15. Stephen Cullenberg. 1992. "Socialism's Burden: Toward a "Thin" Definition of Socialism." *Rethinking Marxism* 5 (2).
16. Stephen Cullenberg. 1998. "Exploitation, Appropriation, and Exclusion: Locating Capitalist Injustice" in *Rethinking Marxism* 10 (2).
17. Stephen Resnick and Richard Wolff. 1988. "Communism: Between Class and Classless." *Rethinking Marxism 1 (1).*
18. Stephen Resnick and Richard Wolff. 2002. *Class Theory and History: Capitalism and Communism in the USSR*. Routledge: London & New York.
19. Stephen Resnick and Richard Wolff. 2010. "The Economic Crisis: A Marxian Interpretation", *Rethinking Marxism*, 22: 2, 170 — 186.
20. Stephen Resnick and Richard Wolff. 2012. *'Marxism'* in Rethinking Marxism. 25:2, 152-162.
21. Thomas Pickety. 2014. *Capital in the Twenty-First Century*. Harvard University Press: Mass.
22. Teece, David J & Winter, Sidney G, 1984. "The Limits of Neoclassical Theory in Management Education," *American Economic Review*, American Economic Association, vol. 74(2), pages 116-21, May.

QUESTIONS FOR FURTHER DISCUSSION

Q1. What is the entry point of Marxism and how does it connect with the dialectics of overdetermination? What then is Marxian theory? Is reductionism (economic, class, etc.) consistent with this theory?

Q2. What is the status of truth claim in Marxian theory (absolute, partial)? How does it compare with other theories, say, historical materialism and (neo) classical political economy?

Q3. How is class defined? What is the basic criterion in terms of which economic forms of society are distinguished in Marxian theory? Define and explain these forms? How do they relate to produce a class-focused conception of economy? How is this economy related to society? Can you have class and economic essentialism in this Marxian theory?

04. What is a class subject? What is class struggle? What is non-class struggle? What is the relation between class and non-class struggles? Can the non-class struggles be reduced or made secondary to class struggles? What then is Marxian politics? Can it be reduced to class politics?

Q5. Mode of appropriation per se is a problem. Do you agree with this thesis?

Q6. What is the distinction between mode of appropriation and exploitation? Can you have communism with mode of appropriation of surplus? What then is the minimum/thinnest criterion that differentiates communism from capitalism (as also feudalism, slavery)?

Q7. Why is exploitation a fundamental justice question raised by Marxian theory? How is it related to Marxian politics?

Q8. Distinguish between labourers, labour power and labour. Use these categories to differentiate between slave, feudal and capitalist forms?

Q9. Why do we need value theory to unpack surplus labor and exploitation in capitalism?

Q10. Define a commodity. Exploitation is contained in commodity form under capitalism. Explain. What is the rate of exploitation and how is it connected to class?

Q11. Why is labour power a golden goose for capitalism? In neoclassical economics there is no difference between labour and labour power. What does it imply?

Q12. Explain very briefly how Marxian theory differs from (Neo)classical Political Economy in terms of (i) epistemology (ii) entry point (iii) structure of causality (iv) economy (v) subject (vi) income distribution and profit.

Advanced Questions

Q13. What is the distinction between Marxian definition of class and a Weberian definition of class? (hint: read Max Weber, "Class, Status and Party" in *From Max Weber: Essays in Sociology*, ed. and translated by H.H. Gerth and C. Wright

Mills, Oxford University Press, New York, 1946).

Q14. Use the contrasting ideas of class in this Marxian theory (treats class as a process of surplus labour) and historical materialism (treats class as a homogenous group of social actors based on power/property) to critically analyze the understanding of politics of communist parties of India? Do your think that these parties maintain the methodology, focus and objects of Marxism being referred to here? What are the consequences?

Q15. What would be the basic idea of relation of caste, gender and race with class in this Marxian theory? In what ways would it be different from historical materialism?

Q16. Can you have an inner law of motion (like capital accumulation) to define and describe capitalism in the class-focused Marxian theory? What are the problems with this kind of reductionism?

Q17. Austerity in Greece and other European nations redistributed assets, including public goods, in favour of the rich capitalists. Explain how this redistribution can be related to the organization of capitalist exploitation.

Q18. This is how Amartya Sen defines 'capitalism':

What are the special characteristics that make a system indubitably capitalist—old or new?...It seems to be generally assumed that relying on *markets* for economic transactions is a necessary condition for an economy to be identified as capitalist. In a similar way, dependence on the *profit motive* and on *individual* rewards based on *private ownership* are seen as archetypal features of capitalism. (2009, pp. 2-3)

What are the essential ingredients of this definition of capitalism? Critically engage with it from a Marxian perspective. (Reference: Sen, A. February 25, 2009. 'Capitalism beyond the Crisis' in *The New York Review of Book)*.

Common Questions from both Chapters

Q19. Does reducing surplus labour/exploitation to power or property, which is given an a priori explanatory privilege, obscure the complex nature of the social existence of surplus labour and explain away the effects produced on and by the processes related to the social phenomena of performance, appropriation, distribution, and receipt of surplus labour? Give an example to substantiate your answer.

Q20. The 'socialist' nature of Soviet Union was explained in terms of socialization of property; it was considered to have, as if, put under erasure class (for property based division was considered absent). However, socialization of property does not necessarily imply socialization of the processes of performance and appropriation of surplus labour, that is, an end to exploitation. In the case of Soviet Union, it was the ministries or their appointed bureaucrats who appropriated the surplus value produced by the workers. While property relations did change in the Soviet Union and these produced a change in the organization of surplus (for now it was state appointed bureaucrats and not private capitalists who were in charge of appropriation of surplus), the change in property did not lead to the desirable change in the organization of surplus labour along the lines to end class exploitation. Rather, the change helped transplant one form of exploitation with another form of exploitation.

By what criterion are the Soviet enterprises socialist? Are they socialist if you analyse Soviet enterprises from a surplus labour based class perspective?

NOTES

1. For a detailed analysis on the making of Marx's Capital, see Roman Rosdolsky, *The Making of Marx's 'Capital'*, trans. Pete Burgess, Pluto Press, 1977.
2. In this paper we desist from the matter of classlessness and society based on it. For a detailed treatment on these, see Resnick and Wolff (2006, ch 7)) and Chakrabarti and Cullenberg (2003, Chapter 7).
3. Not all labour processes would be associated with class process. Therefore, somebody mowing his own lawn is participating in a labour process but not a class process. On the other hand, if that somebody is a worker of a company which takes up contract to mow lawns of its customers then the labour process in which

the worker is participating has an associated class process; he performs necessary labour against which he is paid wages while the surplus labour is expropriated as surplus value by the capitalist of the company.

4. Evald Ilyenkov (1982) on the relation between the abstract and the concrete.
5. CA communitic class process signifies a situation where labour is performed collectively (C) in the sense of being shared, but one member (A) of the collective appropriates the accumulated or total surplus labour of all the labourers including his own. An example from the rural Indian context would be a family farm where the entire family (head of the family, brothers, sisters, children, wife, cousins etc.) takes part in the production process collectively, but only one performer, say, the 'male head' of the family, is the sole appropriator of surplus. Here, many direct producers are excluded from the process of appropriation. AC labour class process is a situation where performance of surplus labor is done individually (A), while appropriation is collective (C). Suppose, in a rural set-up, agricultural producers produce a particular crop individually in their respective land, but decide to collectively pool together their produce in a marketing cooperative in order to sell the produce and appropriate the surplus collectively. No exclusion of direct producers occurs here. Unlike capitalist class process, some (as in CA) or all (as in AC) the appropriators of surplus labour are performers of surplus labour in communitic class process; on the other, unlike communist class process, there is exclusion whether in performance (as in AC) or in appropriation (as in CA).
6. This section follows *World of the Third and Global Capitalism* by Anjan Chakrabarti, Anup Dhar and Stephen Cullenberg, Worldview Press, New Delhi. 2012.
7. The aspect of 'socially necessary' in the definition of value captures the point that value is a sign – a socially determined number capturing the worth of a product; socially determined in the sense that it results from the overdetermined web of economic, cultural, political and natural processes. Economic processes related to the presence or absence of market or planning, technical conditions of production, strategies of appropriators, of managers, of workers, role of buyers and sellers; political processes and cultural processes related to trade union activities, corporate groups, state, gender, race, caste and even desire; natural processes such as weather, etc. are only some of

the factors that go in the determination of value of a commodity.

8. While values are contained in commodities, it is obvious that the price—the form of value—remains regulated by value magnitude, and, as such, by the latter's constitutive processes. In terms of our class analysis, the exact manner and amount of performance of surplus labour will have an important effect on its appropriation, distribution and receipt. Value constitutes the price. Interestingly, the value form capturing the conditions of exchange too constitutes value. This is because production require purchase of means of production. The purchase is made at the prevailing price. Thus, the conditions of production and of the process of value creation are affected by the changing price, and to take the argument further, by all those conditions of existence in the realm of circulation that affect the price of the means of production. Thus, value too remains regulated by the value form.
9. Value and value form may not be identical because (i) though overdetermined, the realm of production is different from the realm of circulation, (ii) since production and circulation are differently determined, SNALT as value and SNALT as the expression of value form are counted differently and, (iii) because they are counted differently, they will have different numbers. This means that, value and value form may not be the same and, in fact, are usually not the same.

As the conditions of production and circulation vary. Value form can no longer be taken as numerically the same as value. Not only that, the value form because of the changing conditions of existence of circulation is placed on a continuous state of transit. These include, to name a only a few processes, the presence or absence of monopoly power, the turnover time, productivity differences, wholesale/retail price differentials and capital mobility across industries. The same is true for value which changes with the changing conditions of existence of production. This means that for each commodity, value (capturing the doing measured in SNALT) and price (capturing the flow of revenues measured in SNALT) will diverge. This will have an immediate impact on the distribution and receipt of unpaid surplus labour or surplus value. Changes in value and value form capture the changing dynamics of organization of surplus value.

To exemplify the difference between the value form and exchange value or price (which is equal to value), Marx forwarded the concept of price of production. Suppose that the rate of profit differs between industries due to say different techniques of production. Competition between capitalists would ensure that value form or price change in order to equalize the rate of profit on capital across industries. Changes in price move the profit rate to an average. Price of production is then the price that will reproduce the capital in every industry with a profit rate the same as the other industries. Price of production as the new form of value becomes different from the exchange value.

Yet the point remains that no matter how much the individual commodities may diverge due to the two counts (value and value form), that is, no matter what the difference between the amount done (labour time involved in production) and the amount paid (the labour time expression for the revenues generated by its sales) is, no matter how many layers of distribution the unpaid labour passes through, the sum total of the doings and payments, expressed in labour time, must be definitionally equal. The redistribution of performed labor time captures the flow of labour time between agents holding different class and non-class positions and, as such, does not change the sum total amount of labour performed (expressed in SNALT) and the payments they receive (expressed in SNALT). As an identity, sum of values must be equal to the sum of prices. Moreover, take the total amount of labour time performed and subtract the labour time which is remunerated (that is, the paid labour). This is the unremunerated or unpaid labor or surplus value expressing the surplus labor. On the other hand, take the total income expressed in SNALT and subtract the remuneration or income (again, in SNALT) received by the labourers who are doers. This is then the total revenue or the bundled profit for which no payment to the labourers is made. The unpaid labour or surplus value expressed in SNALT, by definition, must be equal to the total revenue or bundled profit, expressed in SNALT. It is clear then that sum of values = sum of prices, and sum of surplus values = sum of profit (or revenues) are accounting identities. For details on the complexity of the relation between value and value form as also the accounting identity, see Wolff, Roberts and Callari (1982), Roberts (1987, 1996) and Chaudhury (1998).

10. Part of the surplus value could go even to the workers—productive as well as unproductive. Other than the wages, they could get bonuses, perks and other benefits that would only come from a distributed amount of surplus value.

3

Commodity Value Money and Capital

Pranab Kanti Basu

As Marxists we are all concerned with conceiving and striving towards an exploitationless world. While there is no disagreement on this score, there is a wide range of conceptions among Marxists both about the precise nature of the exploitationless society as well as about the nature of appropriate transformational practice. My focus will be on these two issues. Through this lecture—on commodity, value, money and capital—I will try to present how far Marxian political economy (particularly value theory) is helpful in understanding of these issues. My position is that taken alone, as is done in the 'orthodox reading', Marxian political economy (MPE) does not further practice and in fact may act as a hindrance. But Marx (even purely of *Capital*) did not present MPE as a standalone theory. The primary proof of this is that many more pages of *Capital* are devoted to history than to political economy (PE). Just as the intellectual position of Marx is *supplemented*[1] by his position as an organiser of working class movements, the logical or epistemological position is *supplemented* by the ontological (historical) position.

Whatever the details of the revolutionary project of the Indian communist parties, there is commonality in the faith in the stages of revolution. And hence of history as a sequence of MOPs: primitive communism – slavery – feudalism – capitalism – communism. This interpretation is confirmed by the orthodox reading of *Capital*. Kautsky and, following him, Lenin in *What is to be done,* and *Three Sources and Three Component Parts of Marxism* presented a theory of the sources of Marx. They present Marx as a bourgeois intellectual who condensed and reformulated the ideas of German philosophy, French socialism and English political economy[2]. The idea that history is a fated succession of MOPs progressively arranged according to the development of the 'forces of production' flows from this specific reading of Marx's *Capital* as well as of other tracts including the *Communist Manifesto*. This is what we are referring to as the 'orthodox reading' of Marx. This presents Marxism as a *logical science,* the core of which or the *essence* is Marxian Political Economy. MPE's critique of Political Economy (PE) also sometimes referred to as Classical Political Economy (CPE), therefore, is also a logical critique. This critique establishes that contrary to the various explanations of profit provided by PE, like reward for abstinence, profit is a species of exploitative extraction. That is just like feudal rent profit is sourced by the surplus labour of the labouring people. Here the extraction takes a particular form: surplus value (which we will presently elaborate). It also claims that the exploitative character of the capitalist system cannot be seen if one analyses the sphere of exchange alone, as PE does. The hidden abode of capitalist exploitation is the sphere of production. Equality prevails outside the factory gates and the master-servant relation within.

There are other readings of Marx that are more open ended belong to the genre that generally claims lineage from a non-reductionist or overdeterministic[3] tradition. They are critical of the tendency of the traditional reading to assign a sole determining role to economic interaction of society and therefore to MPE. This, they claim, is a form of reductionism or essentialism.[4] Rejection of essentialism also entails rejection of teleology or the claim that history is logical.[5] These interpretations have emerged since the birth of post structuralism/postmodernism. These other readings also confound the claim that Marx was just a bourgeois intellectual, which is the basis of the 'logical', scientistic or epistemological reading of Marx. Rather these new readings tend to corroborate our understanding that Marxism is as much the result of the ontological position of its author as an organiser of workers' movements as it is an epistemological exercise to construct a different logical structure of capitalism. Just to avoid confusion: whenever I talk of a *logical, scientistic, etc.* reading of Marx I will be referring to the *linear logical* or *dialectical method of Hegel*, which Marx deploys most consistently in his critique of political economy. On the other hand, when I talk of *illogic, ontological position, historical narrative, etc.* I shall be referring to what we shall elaborate as *overdeterministic logic*.

I will elaborate the genesis and meaning of the structure of capitalism through this lecture using the logical or scientistic reading of *Capital*. In another lecture, 'What is Capitalism?' I will examine the alternative readings as also the mutual dependence of the two readings. I will then attempt to see the possibilities and problems of using these different readings for revolutionary practice in India.

Let me, at the outset, put down my understanding of what can constitute a reading of Marx that can motivate transformational left politics in India. There is no disagreement that Marx was constructing a critique of Political Economy (PE) as an analysis of existing social order. The question was what kind of a critique did he write? There are two conflicting answers. Both are implicitly provided by Marx in *Introduction to the Critique of Political Economy, Grundrisse* and *Capital*. One, Marx wrote a *logical* critique of political economy. He pointed out the logical fallacies of the abstract system of PE and proposed a more logical abstract model—the capitalist MOP—as a counterposition. This is the interpretation that informs Lenin's *What is to be done, Three Sources and Three Component parts of Marxism*. Two, Marx wrote an *ontological* critique of PE. There are two interpretations of this second position. One that this *ontological position* resides within capitalist MOP i.e. he criticised PE from a particular position situated *within* the existing society—the working class or proletarian position elaborated within the theoretical structure of capital. This is a critique to which Althusser of *Reading Capital* subscribes[6]. Two, Marx wrote his *ontological* critique from a position situated *outside* the capitalist social totality. This is the position taken by Enrique

Dussel (2001) and also tallies with the writings on the Indian scenario by Kalyan Sanyal, Rajesh Bhattacharyya, etc. This is also the position that Althusser takes in *Marx in his Limits* and *The Underground Current of Materialism of the Encounter*. I propose that it is a condensation of the two interpretations of Marx as *ontological critique* and epistemological critique that could provide useful insights for activists in India. There are also certain problems, which I will try to touch upon.

I will argue that the two positions supplement each other—the epistemological reading position and the ontological reading position. While appreciating the need for less rigid interpretations (i.e. for ontological position) in order to forge authentic alliances between different groups of *exploited* people, it is also necessary to stress the role of the logical or epistemological reading in order to choose between ethical positions.

1.1 Simple Commodity Production: Exchange Value, Use Value, Value

Marx starts his logical critique from simple commodity production. *Capital* begins thus "The wealth of those societies in which the capitalist mode of production prevails, presents itself as "an immense accumulation of commodities," its unit being a single commodity. Our investigation must therefore begin with the analysis of a commodity." (C1, p. 26)

We have to be a bit more specific: we have to indicate the organisational form under which these commodities with which we begin our discussion are produced. "The mode of production in which the *product takes the form of a commodity*, or is produced directly for exchange, *is the most general and most embryonic form of bourgeois production*." (C1, 51, emphasis added). The product, not the labour power used in production, takes the form of commodities. The commodities are produced by what are termed 'petty producers' with own tools and with own or family labour. Importantly, they do not employ wage labour. This is like a cottage industry. This mode of production has also been called 'Simple Commodity Production' (SCP).

We will later discuss the cultural connotations of this

starting point in greater detail when we discuss commodity fetishism. But for the time being we will remark that Marx thinks SCP is the 'most embryonic form of bourgeois production'. This implies that its coming into being entails the production of some of the fundamental conditions of bourgeois production.

But what is a commodity? It is simply anything one unit of which is bought and sold in the market against fixed quantities of other commodities. We are here talking of the simplest kind of exchange—barter exchange. You produce and sell one table and get two shirts in exchange. Two questions immediately follow: what induced you to sell the table? What determined that you would get two shirts in exchange?

You sold the table because you had produced it but did not need it and because you needed the shirts and did not produce them. Converse is true for the buyer of table and seller of shirt.

So there must be quite a developed *social division of labour*. Some people specialise in the production of this thing and some others in the production of that thing. But this too is not sufficient ground for exchange. Social division of labour among the members of a society demands economic interaction. But this does not have to take the form of exchange. For one, the producers may not be free to exchange. The lord may take their produce and distribute some of it at will among the producers and enrich himself with the rest. Alternately, there could be common rights over all products, which may then be distributed according to some community norms.

> Trading nations, properly so called, exist in the ancient world only in its interstices... Those ancient social organisms of production are, as compared with bourgeois society, extremely simple and transparent. But they are founded either on the immature development of man individually, who has not yet severed the umbilical cord that unites him with his fellowmen in a primitive tribal community, or upon direct relations of subjection. (ibid, p. 58).

In contrast to this situation, it is necessary that the simple commodity producers independently take their decisions. And this implies a host of cultural changes and changes in psyche or subjectivity are necessary for this to be feasible. We will elaborate this during our discussions of commodity fetishism:

> In order that these objects may enter into relation with each other as commodities, their guardians must place themselves in relation to one another, as persons whose will resides in those object, and must behave in such a way that each does not appropriate the commodity of the other, and part with his own, except by means of an act done by mutual consent. They must therefore, mutually recognise in each other the rights of private proprietors. (C1, p. 59)

But how do these independent producers decide what amounts of goods to produce i.e. the allocation of social labour? This was not a problem in a command or community economy. In the former case the authority decides the allocation of social labour; in the latter the division is decided by consensus.

Humans were initially hunters and food gatherers. They led nomadic, tribal lives. There was social division of labour, generally based on gender or age. Those who hunted did not have any special claim on the hunted animals. Similarly, the food gatherers did not have any particular claim on the fruit that was gathered. The tribe as a whole was the proprietor of all that was hunted and gathered. In fact, there was no sense of property. The social produce was distributed according to some socially agreed norms. Maybe those in the working age got more because they needed to replenish their energy and spent muscles and sinews. Maybe the hunters got more. In any case the distribution was not discriminatory as the tribe, by some form of consensus, agreed upon the subsistence requirement of each group within the tribe. Social labour was allocated by agreement according to the overall subsistence requirement. There was no surplus production so there was no question of anyone living on the surplus produced by others.

With the evolution of agriculture, the production of surplus became technically necessary. If all the agricultural crop is consumed in a season then there will not be any seed crop for next season's cultivation. With the production of surplus, conflict and inequality emerged: one group of people, the priests generally, took control of the surplus. Two things need to be pointed out here. First, there was quantitative inequality previously also: probably the hunter got more than the gatherer. But there was qualitative equality: the product was divided among all according to the socially agreed subsistence requirement of each group. This had to be so because society did not produce more than its subsistence requirement. So if some got more than their subsistence requirement then some would get less; the latter would not survive. Secondly, the priest or magician, existed before the evolution of agriculture i.e. before surplus was produced. They made the cave paintings of animals which the tribe believed implied the capture of the animal, as the idea that reality and representation were different had not been born. Part of social output was voluntarily given because the members of the tribe believed that the special craft of cave drawing (which was magic or ancient religion) was essential for the success of their hunt. So the services of the priest-magician i.e. the cave painter were thought to be as necessary for the survival of the tribe as the services of the hunter. Gradually, with the evolution of agriculture, unexplained natural elements were personified as gods—fire, lightning, winds, etc. The priest established his exclusive 'right' of mediating between the gods and the rest of the tribes. For his prayers he claimed surplus. Power over producers also emerged in other ways as one tribe conquered another. So emerged the master-slave relation.

Once the division between surplus producers and surplus appropriators emerged, social division of labour was decided by the masters or the appropriators of surplus.

Social division of labour was directly decided in both these forms of decision making: by agreement in tribal society; by command in surplus producing societies like the slave societies.

In the modern societies, like the one we live in, social division of labour is not decided directly by any individual or group of individuals, but is indirectly decided through the working of the market. In the market economy it is decided by the *law of value*. The law that demands that prices be equal to *Abstract Labour* (AL) values.

1.2 Abstract Labour/Concrete Labour: Exchange Value/Use

Value

Prices or *exchange values* are common to all commodities. They should, therefore, be explained by something else that is also common to all commodities. Marx argues that there are two other attributes common to commodities: they all have *use values* and they are all products of labour. "As use values, commodities are, above all, of different qualities, but as exchange values they are merely different quantities, and consequently do not contain an atom of use value. If then we leave out of consideration the use value of commodities, they have only one common property left, that of being products of labour." (C1, p. 27). That is if one table exchanges for two shirts, the reason cannot be that one table and two shirts have the same utility or serve the same purpose. This because the use values are qualitatively different and hence cannot be quantitatively compared. But if the usefulness of tables and shirts cannot be compared, so also the labour of the weaver and that of the carpenter cannot be compared. They are qualitatively different. There is also another qualitative difference between the labours of different labourers: they have various degrees of skill and intensity (some lazier than the others, some working on more automated machines, etc.). So exchange values are determined by the *socially necessary abstract labour* (AL) value of a commodity.

But what is AL? It is labour that has been shorn of all concrete or specific attributes: neither productive of particular commodities; nor possessing differences in skill or intensity. The latter is implied by the term 'socially necessary': if one carpenter is lazy and takes two days to produce a table, which is produced on the average by one day's labour it does not mean that the lazy carpenter's table will contain twice as much AL and so have twice as much price. Time will be a day's labour (say, eight or ten hours or whatever is the length of the working day). But these are the negative attributes, what is its positive content? That it is labour that produces private (*not common*) property. "As a general rule, articles of utility become commodities, only because they are products of the labour of private individuals or groups of individuals who carry on their work independently of each other" (C1, p. 47). In other words

AL is private property producing labour. Is AL measurable? No, because it is *essence* and is *manifested* in exchange value or price. A religious person does not see God. But that does not make his belief false. God is the *essence* and so not physically manifest. But the believer sees him in his *manifestations*—the whole world. One can work back from equilibrium prices and wages to value. Heterogeneity caused by the fact that different labours produce different goods can be evened out by using the price differentials between different goods; the heterogeneity caused by skill or intensity differences is ironed out through market wage differentials. This is the famous solution to the 'transformation problem' offered by Wolff, Calari and Roberts (1984). "[E]xpression of equivalence between different sorts of commodities that alone brings into relief the specific character of value-creating labour, and this it does by actually reducing the different varieties of labour embodied in the different kinds of commodities to their common quality of human labour in the abstract" (C1, p. 34). So AL is worked back from prices but one cannot independently measure AL. Again we mention in passing that that the emergence of the concept of AL is not the result of just a logical economic process but is overdetermined by the socio-cultural history of the emergence of capitalism. AL is not an abstract concept in the usual sense but is *affective* in the sense that for barter exchange to be the dominant form of economic coordination among those who produce (unlike in the command or consent economy) the SCP agents must perceive what are different kinds of labour to be equal in terms of some general form of labour without any specificity. This is a point that has been discussed by Amaraglio and Callari (1989) in the context of CF. We will talk of this later.

1.3 Law of value: Allocation of Social Labour

So we know what is AL and that AL values, which is simply called 'values' by Marx determine exchange values or prices. But how does this solve the problem of allocating social labour? The equality between the exchange value ratio of two commodities and their value ratios ensure this. If $P_S/P_T > Ws/W_T$ (where W, P stand for values and exchange values or prices, respectively; subscripts T and S for 'table' and 'shirt', respectively) shirt production will increase and the production of tables will decline. If the inequality is the other way round then shirt production will decrease while that of tables will increase. To understand this intuitively, let us assume that all labour is homogeneous. That is the carpenter can move to weaving and the weaver can move to carpentry. Also there is no skill or intensity variation within an activity. It requires a day's labour to produce one table and one day's labour is also necessary to produce two shirts. On account of our simplifying assumptions $Ws/W_T = 1/2$. Suppose $P_S/P_T = 1$, i.e. in the market you get one table in exchange for one shirt. The carpenter sees that by labouring for 1 day he/she can produce 1 table and exchange it in the market for 1 shirt only, whereas with one day's labour he/she can produce two shirts. Obviously the carpenter will relocate. If the inequality is the other way round the weaver will relocate. So the proper allocation of social labour between the various activities according to the social requirements is achieved when the law of value operates. This, Rubin (2008) says, is the material basis of *Commodity Fetishism*.

2 Commodity Fetishism

> "Whence, then, arises the enigmatical character of the product of labour, so soon as it assumes the form of commodities? Clearly from this form itself. The equality of all sorts of human labour is expressed objectively by their products all being equally values; the measure of the expenditure of labour power by the duration of that expenditure, takes the form of the quantity of value of the products of labour; and finally the mutual relations of the producers, within which the social character of their labour affirms itself, take the form of a social relation between the products.
>
> A commodity is therefore a mysterious thing, simply because in it the social character of men's labour appears to them as an objective character stamped upon the product of that labour; because the relation of the producers to the sum total of their own labour is presented to them as a social relation, existing not between themselves, but between the products of their labour." (C1, p. 46)

First, labour is equal only when their products have equal

exchange value. Secondly, AL is not measured in hours but in terms of commodities (or by the money worth)—this we have already discussed. Thirdly the allocation of social labour between the various productive activities is not carried out directly as under a community system or under a command economy, but indirectly through the law of value: through the relation between the products of social labour. This is what Rubin calls the material basis of commodity fetishism. "There it is a definite social relation between men, that assumes, in their eyes, the fantastic form of a relation between things... This I call the Fetishism which attaches itself to the products of labour, so soon as they are produced as commodities, and which is therefore inseparable from the production of commodities." (C1, p. 47) There is striking similarity between Marx's theory of commodity fetishism (CF) and Feuerbach's ideas on religion. Feuerbach, who was an atheist and later on joined the German Social Democratic Party under the influence of Marx, contended that God was simply the outward projection of man's nature. Having created God, man now thinks that he is ruled by God. In a similar vein Marx argues that commodities are produced with human labour and man then believes that his social, man-man relation (Marx is here thinking of a limited range of social relations—the social division of labour) is determined by the exchange value relation between things. Rubin (ibid, chap 7) contends that it is wrong to claim on this basis that Marx simply transferred Feuerbach's theory of religion to commodity exchange. This, because as we have explained, there is a material basis for the claim that the value and exchange value relation between commodities determines the social division of labour under SCP (and then under Capitalist Commodity Production). The relation between the gods does not result in any material effect.

CF has another significance that has been brought out by Amaraglio and Callari (1989). We normally take CF as a kind of *false consciousness*[7] which commodity production breeds. Amaraglio and Callari have argued that CF is the product of a cultural political process which is a *precondition* for an exchange system. The products of different kinds of labour are equated in the market. This is only possible under the condition that the labourers see the different kinds of labour as being quantitatively comparable. A particular kind of subjectivity (that of individual property owners) has to be produced. This is not just a logical effect. It is, among other things, the product of dissolution of community ties. We will come back to this in another essay in which we discuss Primitive Accumulation in detail.

The idea of CF has particular significance in today's world. It is an important weapon in the arsenal of the *ideological state apparatus*. This idea, which was mooted by Althusser in a book of the same name, shows how the state operates at the cultural level to create meanings that work in the service of the existing order. When Marx talked of the relation between men appearing as the relation between commodities, he was talking of a particular set of relations—the relation of social division of labour. But he was almost prescient of the great field of CF as it exists today. He had, of course, remarked that under SCP men see each other as owners of commodities only. We measure ourselves and others not in terms of ethics, morality, humaneness or some such attribute, but in terms of the relation of each with commodities. There are two such relations that mark our position in the social order: property—what we own; 'productivity'—what we earn. This is the basis of self-centredness, on which the entire edifice of mainstream economics stands. From this follows a host of effects, some of which have strong regressive impact on workers' movements. For example, the IT sector workers, because of their vastly greater income, and therefore wealth, compared to manufacturing sector workers feel no class affinity with the rest of the working class. This is also true of other highly paid workers. We will later see that the within the communist movement (the working class position is built up *logically* or through a *logical* critique of PE. As a result, it is flawed with the marks of CF, with self-centredness. I have argued this position in detail elsewhere (Basu, 2012).

CF has taken on a totally new dimension in the current global context. Rubin had correctly contested the claim that

Marx simply transferred Feuerbach's analysis of religious mystification to the mystification by commodities. His point was that there was a material basis of commodity fetishism which is absent in fetishism of religion. The material basis was that the law of value ensured the proper social division of labour without any man-man interaction. In the current context it appears that commodity fetishism has severed its ties with the material base. The subprime crisis is perhaps a reflection of this: exchange values of securities were bloating without any connection with values of material production. People were chasing constantly bloating exchange value, which had no connection with values and in fact had no connection with any material product, which could be discerned by the buyers of these securities. Securitisation and increasing leverage led to a situation where the relation between material goods and securities in which major speculation was occurring was being mystified by the financial system. This, of course is just a suggestion on which Marxist scholarship could perhaps concentrate.

3 Commodity Circuits and Money: The *Logical Genesis* of Capital

3.1 Commodity-Commodity (C-C)

This is the first commodity circuit: commodity—commodity. The carpenter has made a table that he/she has no personal use for. That is it has been made purely for sale. The table has *exchange value* but no *use value* for the carpenter. The carpenter wishes to buy two shirts with this table. He obviously knows the normal relative price P_S/P_T $(=Ws/W_T)$ i.e. that he should be able to procure 2 shirts for his table. Our carpenter has the good fortune of meeting another who wants a table and offers shirts in exchange. That is there is another petty producer who has exchange value for shirts and use value for tables. There is no glut or shortage in the market for either community. In other words, social labour has been properly allocated through the operation of the law of value. This exchange has occurred because the pattern of exchange value and use value was reciprocal for the two petty producers: one had exchange value for the table and use value for the shirt, the other had use value for table and exchange value for the shirt. The two ends of the circuit are qualitatively different, looked at from either the point of view of the carpenter or the weaver. They are different commodities and the 'C' at the beginning has exchange value while the C at the end has use value.

3.2 Commodity-Money-Commodity (C-M-C)

It is fortuitous that the carpenter and the weaver have a mutually consistent pattern of demand and supply. If that does not happen then the carpenter may have to sell the table for paddy, paddy for wheat and ultimately wheat for shirts. Or the chain could be even longer.

There is another related problem. What is the exchange value of a table? You would say 2, if you were selling shirts. If you were selling paddy (given 1 table = 15 kg paddy) you would say 15, and so on. From this disagreement or what philosophers prefer to call 'dialectical contradiction', emerged a general form of exchange value – money. Before its emergence you would have to say 1 table = 15 kg paddy = 20 kg wheat = 2 shirts = ... Now you simply had to say 1 table = Rs 400 and this would be sufficient to express all the other equivalences, because, similarly, 15 kg paddy = Rs 400, 20 kg wheat = Rs 400, 2 shirts = Rs 400. In technical jargon we would say that Rs 400 is the general[8] (*universal*) form of value of 1 table, which synthesises the *particular* forms: 15 kg paddy, 20 kg wheat, 2 shirts. This form of reasoning is called dialectics. We will not go into the theoretical discussion of this. We have just given this example because this is the form of reasoning that Marx borrowed from Hegel and this forms the basis of his *logical critique* of Political Economy.

Mind, that money, as yet, is simply a *unit of account* i.e. it is a unit of measurement of a particular attribute that is common to all commodities: market price. A unit of measurement does not exist physically: litres, metres, kilograms, etc. We have a measuring tape on which is marked out distances in metres; we have a weight (of iron) that is equal to one kilogram etc. But it would be nonsensical to ask a person, 'how many kilos or metres do you have?'. Similarly money as simply the unit of measuring prices does not exist. For example, if the price of a text book is marked in dollars it makes perfect sense, though the vast majority of us have never seen a dollar. We simply convert it to rupee terms. But rupees do exist! So what is this nonsense about money not existing physically like kilograms and litres? That is because rupees have a role beyond just being a unit of measurement: it is also a *medium of exchange*. If the price of a ball-pen is Rs 10 it means that if you give Rs 10 to the shopkeeper the latter would give you a ball-pen. But if the size of a flat is 1000 sq ft it would be nonsensical to say that if you give 1000 sq ft to the seller you would get the flat.

This, in Marx's narrative is the genesis of money—as unit of accounting prices and as medium of exchange. But of course money comes only with the trader. The carpenter sells the table to the furniture trader against money, goes with the money to another specialised trader and buys shirts. Thus money is not just a unit of account, but also exists physically as a means of payment. So the circuits, for the carpenter and the weaver becomes C-M-C. The mediation of money in what was a barter exchange does not change the objective of the exchange as viewed by the weaver or the carpenter: both want to give an exchange value to procure a use value (that has equal exchange value) at the end of the circuit.

3.3 M-C-M to M-C-M$'$, M$'$>M

For the trader it is a different story. First, let us clear a possible doubt. Without the advent of the trader the introduction of money would not have reduced the cumbersome chain of exchanges that the carpenter (and also the weaver) have to undertake to get what they want through the exchange. The carpenter must know of a trader who specializes in trading furniture (though not necessarily only furniture) and also one who sells garments. The weaver, similarly, must be aware of a trader of clothes and a trader of furniture. Now, the trader of furniture spends money to buy the table and later sells it to someone who has use value for the table. So his circuit of exchange can be represented as: M-C-M unlike the carpenter's and weaver's circuits—C-M-C. See the difference in the two circuits: the former begins and ends with money, which is qualitatively the same at the end as at the beginning. The latter circuits begin and end with qualitatively different objects. For the carpenter the circuit begins with table and ends with shirt and the opposite is true for the weaver. The purpose of exchange for both carpenter and weaver is to obtain a use value, which they do not have. But the trader starts and ends his circuit with the same thing—money. So his objective cannot be the same. If it is not to get something qualitatively different from what one took to the market, then it must be to get more of the same thing—money. So to the circuit it is not M-C-M but M-C- M', where $M' > M$. Obviously this is not possible if normal prices prevail everywhere. The trader can make a profit only on condition that either the seller gets less price than the value of the commodity sold to the trader or the buyer pays a price greater than value. In the former case for the seller and in the latter case for the buyer the circuit will be: C-M-C', where $C' < C$.

Whenever some agent starts a circuit with a sum of money to end with a larger sum, the agent is a capitalist. The trading capitalist, the only type with whom we are familiar so far, no doubt makes a profit as $M' > M$ but this does not lead to any general expansion of value. It cannot happen if all commodities sell at their value.

3.4 M-C- C'- M', $C'>C$ '! $M'>M$

"The conversion of money into capital has to be explained on the basis of the laws that regulate the exchange of commodities, in such a way that the starting-point is the exchange of equivalents. Our friend, Moneybags, who as yet is only an embryo capitalist, must buy his commodities at their value, must sell them at their value, and yet at the end of the process must withdraw more value from circulation than he threw into it at starting. His development into a full-grown capitalist must take place, both within the sphere of circulation and without it." (C1, p. 114)

> We are, therefore, forced to the conclusion that the change originates in the use-value, as such, of the commodity [that is purchased in the first act of circulation], i.e., in its consumption. In order to be able to extract value from the consumption of a commodity, our friend, Moneybags, must be so lucky as to find, within the sphere of circulation, in the market, a commodity, whose use-value possesses the peculiar property of being a source of value, whose actual consumption, therefore, is itself an embodiment of labour, and, consequently, a creation of value. The possessor of money does find on the market such a special commodity in capacity for labour or labour-power. (C1, p. 117)

In order that labour power appears as a commodity two conditions must be fulfilled:

1. The labourer must be the free owner of the commodity. "In order that he may be able to do this, he must have it at his disposal, must be the untrammelled owner of his capacity for labour, i.e., of his person. He and the owner of money meet in the market, and deal with each other as on the basis of equal rights, with this difference alone, that one is buyer, the other seller; both, therefore, equal in the eyes of the law. The continuance of this relation demands that the owner of the labour-power should sell it only for a definite period, for if he were to sell it rump and stump, once for all, he would be selling himself, converting himself from a free man into a slave, from an owner of a commodity into a commodity." (C1, p. 117).
2. "[T]he labourer instead of being in the position to sell commodities in which his labour is incorporated, must be obliged to offer for sale as a commodity that very labour-power, which exists only in his living self." (C1, p. 117-118). For this it is essential that the labourer does not have ownership of the means of production, apart from his power to labour that will allow him to produce commodities with his own labour and means of production.

To summarizing his position: "For the conversion of his money into capital, therefore, the owner of money must meet in the market with the free labourer, free in the double sense, that as a free man he can dispose of his labour-power as his own commodity, and that on the other hand he has no other commodity for sale, is short of everything necessary for the realization of his labour-power." (C1, p. 118)

The labourer in a free exchange sells labour power (according to the agreed number of hours) against its value. But in its consumption in the course of production it embodies more value than its own value. This is surplus value that augments the capital invested. Labour power, like every other commodity, sells at its value i.e. the AL embodied in the wage basket socially deemed necessary to produce that labour power. For simplicity of exposition let us forget the difference between concrete and abstract labour. Since labour power is considered homogeneous, it does not have to be homogenised through exchange values (commodity prices and money wages). So we can measure it in hours. Suppose the work-day is 10 hrs. To reproduce 10 hrs' labour power or one life day (the wage basket that is conventionally considered to be necessary is produced with 6 hrs of labour. The value of 10 hrs of labour power is 6 hrs. The value that is embedded through the consumption of the purchased labour power (in the course of production) is 10 hrs. So *surplus value* of 4 hrs is produced. So within a system where all exchanges take place at value the capitalist is able to expand his capital. The *productive capitalist* i.e. one who extracts surplus value, unlike the trading capitalist we discussed earlier, is not making profit by robbing someone of value.

Let us see the process of expansion of productive capital schematically:

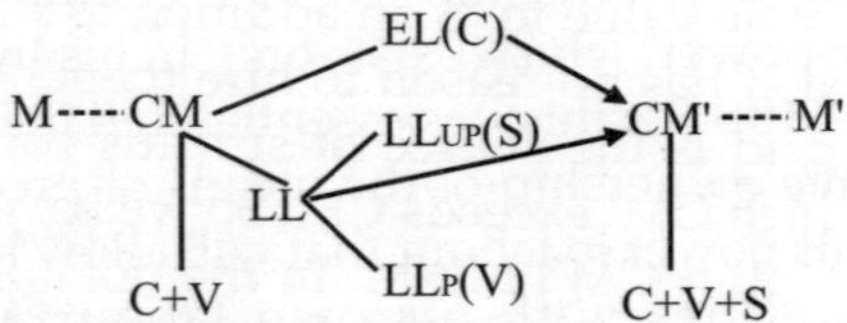

EL (C) : Embodied Labour(Constant Capital)
LL : Live Labour
LL_{UP}(S) : Live Labour which is unpaid (Surplus Value)

LL_P (V) : Live Labour which is paid back to the labourer as wage (Variable Capital)
—— : Free exchange.
→ : Production Process/labour process.

The productive capitalist invests M to buy inputs or commodities, CM. Note that we are using CM instead of the familiar C, which we have previously used. This is to differentiate this from constant capital for which also Marx uses the symbol 'C'. CM contains two components: *embodied labour* or *constant capital* and *live labour*. The former contains the non-labour inputs like fuel, raw materials, wear and tear of machinery, etc. Labour has already been spent in their production and therefore the value that this component adds to the products is constant and equal to its own value (C). Live labour, i.e. the labour power actively engaged in this factory in transforming the raw materials into finished products with the aid of machinery, fuel, etc. is purchased at its value (V). This investment is called investment in *variable capital*, because its contribution to the value of the finished product CM! is not given before hand, unlike in the case of EL, which has already been rendered and is therefore given. The capitalist has contracted with the labourer that against a wage payment whose value is V that labour will work for a day. Now the length of the working day is liable to variation for various political reasons. Besides, the workers render *alienated labour*, a point which we will elaborate presently, and therefore are averse to work diligently in the factory. They have to be coerced. So how successfully they can be made to work for the agreed time is variable. Hence the term 'variable capital'. In any case they have to contribute some value to 'S' in addition to their own value. Else the capitalist has no reason to hire them. This additional value is LL_{UP} and is the source of surplus value—the value addition by which CM! exceeds CM. So we have the circuit M-CM-CM!-M!, CM! > CM'! M!>M. In the notations of Vol. I of Capital we have: M-C-C!-M!, C!>C'! M!>M

4. Equality and Master-Servant relation

What is *alienated labour*? And why does the labour want to dodge work? The labourer has already advanced his labour power (LL) to the capitalist against promise of payment LL_p (i.e. V). He enters the factory to perform labour the control over which has already been taken over by the capitalist. The labourer, in this sense performs *alienated labour* – labour in which he/she has no interest. Human labour is performed twice – once in the mind and then materially when the plan in the mind is executed. Once the freedom to plan is taken away there is no self realisation in work. "A spider conducts operations that resemble those of a weaver, and a bee puts to shame many an architect in the construction of her cells. But what distinguishes the worst architect from the best of bees is this, that the architect raises his structure in imagination before he erects it in reality. He not only effects a change of form in the material on which he works, but he also realises a purpose of his own that gives the law to his modus operandi, and to which he must subordinate his will... The less he is attracted by the nature of the work, and the mode in which it is carried on, and the less, therefore, he enjoys it as something which gives play to his bodily and mental powers, the more close his attention is forced to be." (C1, p. 124). The labourer, rather, has every incentive to dodge the contract and convert some of the labour time sold to the capitalist into life time or leisure time. So the labourer has to be coerced within the factory. Of course, with improvement of technology in the developed countries such coercion is built into the mechanical processes and does not require direct policing.

So the master-servant relation prevails within the factory, in the production process, while equality rules in the exchange relations outside. "This sphere [of exchange] that we are deserting, within whose boundaries the sale and purchase of labour-power goes on, is in fact a very Eden of the innate rights of man. There alone rule Freedom, Equality, Property and Bentham. Freedom, because both buyer and seller of a commodity, say of labour-power, are constrained only by their own free will. They contract as free agents, and the agreement they come to, is but the form in which they give legal expression to their common will. Equality, because each enters into relation with the other, as with a simple owner of commodities, and they exchange equivalent for equivalent. Property, because each disposes only of what is his own. And Bentham, because each looks only to himself. The only force that brings them together and puts them in relation with each other, is the selfishness, the gain and the private interests of each. Each looks to himself only, and no one troubles himself about the rest, and just because they do so, do they all, in accordance with the pre-established harmony of things, or under the auspices of an all-shrewd providence, work together to their mutual advantage, for the common weal and in the interest of all.

> On leaving this sphere of simple circulation or of exchange of commodities, which furnishes the "Free-trader Vulgaris" with his views and ideas, and with the standard by which he judges a society based on capital and wages, we think we can perceive a change in the physiognomy of our dramatis personae. He, who before was the money-owner, now strides in front as capitalist; the possessor of labour-power follows as his labourer. The one with an air of importance, smirking, intent on business; the other, timid and holding back, like one who is bringing his own hide to market and has nothing to expect but – a hiding. (C1, p. 121)

5. Critique as Abstract Logic

We have analysed Marx's dialectical or abstract logical journey from SCP to Capitalist Commodity Production (CCP). There are other classes of income earners, apart from the worker and the capitalist that Marx mentions in Vol. II and Vol. III: the landlord, the moneylender, the trader. Their activities are essential for the reproduction of productive capital. Therefore, the productive capitalist pays their income out of the surplus value appropriated by him. For the same reason capital is willing to give a share of surplus value to the state for the necessary aid it provides for the reproduction Capitalist MOP through judiciary, armed forces, etc. Of course, capital tries to shift the burden of such cost to other groups through indirect taxes, etc. Because they are payments after the receipt of surplus value by the productive capitalist such payments have been named *subsumed class payment* by some. Vol. III also discusses the logic of the law of expanded reproduction of capital or the laws of motion of the capitalist system. However we will not analyse the subsumed payments or the dynamics of the capitalist system. Our concern is with the implications of this logical critique and whether it is meaningful to construct both an understanding of capitalism and a strategy of revolutionary practice based on this reading.

The logic is Hegelian dialectics. It moves from lower levels of generality to higher, more universal levels. We gave an example of this in the movement from exchange value expressed in this and that commodity to a general form of value expressed in money. This logic is reflected in the constant movement from more complicated class arrangements to more and more simplified. "The modern bourgeois society that has sprouted from the ruins of feudal society has not done away with class antagonisms. It has but established new classes, new conditions of oppression, new forms of struggle in place of the old ones.

Our epoch, the epoch of the bourgeoisie, possesses, however, this distinct feature: it has simplified class antagonisms. Society as a whole is more and more splitting up into two great hostile camps, into two great classes directly facing each other—Bourgeoisie and Proletariat." (Marx, 1848). The last revolution, according to this reading, will cause the end of class contradiction as only one of the two classes—the proletarian—will remain and without classes (in the plural) you cannot have class conflict.

The movement through the sequence of MOPs culminating in the classless communist MOP is a fated journey, logically derived by application of the method of Hegelian dialectics in totality to society.

The concept of the capitalist mode of production is built through an essentialist Hegelian logic which is unavoidable in the *logical* critique of Political Economy. You start from a SCP MOP. The *essence* of this is value. Through the *self development* of this essence through money capital and *self expansion* of capital you come to surplus value. So capitalism becomes *generalised commodity production.* The extraction of surplus value by the capitalist is but a logical outcome of this generalised commodity production.

This logical scientific structure and its laws of motion or dynamics of the capitalist economy (which we are not discussing) could only have been constructed on the basis of the knowledge of German philosophy (Hegelian dialectics), English political economy and French socialism. The experience of struggles of the working class (and that includes the experience of Marx) matters not a bit. It is the only bourgeois intellectual who has this specialised knowledge who can grasp this. Understandably Marx is appropriated to this group, ignoring his years of struggle and association with the workers' organisations.

This interpretation of capitalism and the philosophy of this interpretation have major implications for activism. First, knowledge is scientific-deductive and vests with those who are trained in its method. This leads to the unquestionable authority of the party leadership. Secondly, the experience of working class struggles is irrelevant for revolutionary practice.

In another lecture chapter we will contest these positions through other constructions of the meaning of capitalism which can also be read out of Marx.

Note: C1 stands for Capital Vol. 1

REFERENCES

Lenin, V. (1977) *Three Sources and Three Component Parts of Marxism* available at www.marxists.org/archive/lenin/works/1913/mar/x01.htm (accessed on 10th January 2014).

Lenin, V. What is to be Done? (1902) available at https://www.marxists.org/archive/lenin/works/download/what-itd.pdf. (accessed on 11th November 2013).

Marx, K. (1887) *Capital, Vol. I,*available athttps://www.marxists.org/archive/marx/works/download/pdf/Capital-Volume-I.pdf (accessed on 12th May 2013).

Marx, K. (1970) *Critique of the Gotha Programme* available at https://www.marxists.org/archive/marx/works/1875/gotha/ (accessed on 10th January 2010).

Marx, K. and Engels, F. (1987) *Manifesto of the Communist Party,* available at https://www.marxists.org/archive/marx/works/1848/communist-manifesto/(accessed on 10th Jan 2010).

Rubin, I.I. (2008). Essays on Marx's theory of value. Trans. M. Samardzija and F. Perlman. Aakar Books: Delhi.

Wolff, R.D., Callari, A. and Roberts, B. (1984) 'A Marxian Alternative to the Traditional "Transformation Problem"' *Review of Radical Political Economics* Summer & Fall, Vol. 16 no. 2-3: 115-135.

NOTES

1. This is used in the Derridian sense. In this context what it means is that thoughts of Marx the logician were not and could not have been self-contained. There were inevitable gaps in the structure of logic. This, the postmoderns like Derrida argue, is not on account of the personal failure of the logician but is inevitable in any logical text. The gaps in the logical narrative of Marx are filled with the experience of Marx the organiser of working people's movements. This is an act of *supplementation.* The supplement, like the words in the supplement of a dictionary also modify the meanings in the initial text, in this case the logical narrative of Marx.
2. This, in spite of Lenin's disavowal of this position in the 1907 Preface to the Collection *Twelve Years* quoted by Althusser in 'Limits in Marx' in *Philosophy of the Encounter*: "What Is To Be Done? is a controversial correction of Economist [spontaneist] distortions and it would be wrong to regard the pamphlet in any other light.... The basic mistake made by those who now [1907] criticise What Is To Be Done? [1902] is to treat the pamphlet apart from its connection with the concrete historical situation of a definite, and now long past, period in the development of our Party .... To maintain today that Iskra exaggerated (in 1901 and 1902.0 the idea of an organisation of professional revolutionaries, is like reproaching the Japanese, after the Russo-Japanese War, or having exaggerated the strength of Russia's armed forces .... To win victory the Japanese had to marshal all their forces against the probable maximum of Russian forces".
3. This is a term borrowed from Freudian psychoanalysis. In the context of the social sciences this term was first deployed by Althusser and popularised by the *Rethinking Marxism* School and refers to the interdependence or mutual constitutivity of the various spheres of human interaction – economic, political, religious, etc. Because of the continuous interaction between all these spheres, the impact of an initial cause is never complete and the temporal (over time) course of a social formation does

not follow a simple, one dimensional or linear course.

4. This is a philosophical term and cannot be dealt with in a footnote. However within this restricted context it means that the nature of all social activity or relation is determined solely by the nature of economic relations prevalent. i.e. by the Mode of Production.
5. If society can be reduced to its mode of production (constituted by forces and relations of production that are themselves connected *dialectically* by contradiction and synthesis) then the logical transition from one MOP to another, generated by the internal conflict between the forces and relations of production, is also the logical course of history. Rejection of such reductionism implies that no event is purely economic, religious, political, etc. All kinds of social interaction *overdetermine* each other. The italicized term is much favoured by those who reject essentialist reading of Marx and is used to indicate mutual constitution. If this is so then economic, polity, etc are not compartmentalized. Analysis of society cannot proceed in the rarefied level of closed categorical spaces. Knowledge is never complete and knowledge gathering has to constantly mingle with practice or experience. That is epistemology and ontology buttress each other.
6. He changed his position completely in his *Later Philosophical Writings*.
7. A kind of myth that the ruling order breeds in order to hide its true exploitative or oppressive character.
8. Technically (in philosophical terms) this is called the *singular* i.e. the expression of the *essential universal*.

4

What is Capitalism? *Capital*: Another Reading

Pranab Kanti Basu

1. A Logical Definition

From our previous discussion it follows that *generalized commodity production is the logical definition of capitalism*. The *essence* of commodities—value—*manifests* itself in all commodities, including labour power, in capitalism. The logical critique of Political Economy also establishes that the self development of the *essence* of commodities (i.e. value) is completed at this, the highest stage of commodity production. **The wage labour-capital relation is itself a *particular* of the *universal* law of value.**

Considering the centrality of the theme of exploitation in Marxism the wage labour-capital relation assumes special significance. How does this construction of the capitalist economic present exploitation? As the most generalized or developed mode of commodity production everything becomes a particular *manifestation* of the *essence*—value. Surplus exploited by the capitalist class, too, takes the form of a manifestation of value as *surplus value*. And mind you, for the elaboration of the concept of surplus value one does not need the master-servant relation that exists in the interior of the factory, according to Marx. Conceptually, the ground of 'equality, property and Bentham' that rules the marketplace are sufficient to explain the *appropriation* of surplus value. And this is precisely the sense in which surplus value is the result of the logical self-development of the concept of value. Of course, 'consumption of use value' of labour power in the course of production *generates* surplus value, in this narrative. But this (consumption of use value) is the end of all commodities. That this process of consumption of (use value of) labour power entails the master-servant relation is a conclusion generated by an extraneous idea not belonging to the logical story—that of alienated labour.[1]

But how does this philosophic knowledge—that the capitalist exploits them by appropriating surplus value, which can be conceived but not measured—enlighten the revolutionary path of the working class?

In the first place this analysis takes us to the 'hidden abode' of capitalist exploitation. It shows (of course with the induction of the specificity of labour power commodity through the concept of alienation) that while equality reigns in the world of exchange—which is the only world that concerned PE—it is in the sphere of production, in spite of apparent equality, that capitalist exploitation occurs. To my mind this is its major strength: in the domain of discourse. But this also gives it a certain rhetorical strength. As some commentators forcefully put it: 'Despite Marx's strong disavowals, *Capital is* indebted for much of its potency and resonance to ideas he disavowed, including most notably an Enlightenment humanist understanding of labo[u]r as the origin of all wealth and a discourse of rights in which man's entitlement to the fruits of his labo[u]r is naturally ordained. This ambient discourse of rights (to property in labo[u]r and its fruits) was a volatile source of the political energies circulating around Marx's project. Even today, whatever frisson of outrage we may feel in the presence of exploitation derives, to some undecidable extent, from a politically charged discourse of natural property rights that renders the exploitative relation fundamentally "unjust." (Gibson-Graham, Resnick, S.A., Wolff, R. 2000) *Class and its Other*. This feeling of injustice done by the system is evident in other systems but is masked by the market in the capitalist system. This unmasking was the work of the critique of political economy that the logical reading of capital produces.

However, as I have pointed out elsewhere (Basu, 2012) that the image of the worker that emerges from the value theoretic analysis of capital may pose problems for working class movements. I am quoting at some length:

"The point is that the working people's—those who produce with their labour—position, as elaborated by MPE [Marxist Political Economy], at its moment of institution, i.e. at the moment of institution of AL, is already worked through and through by the notion of private property. It is of course property in one's own labour. But without eclectically bringing in questions of morality and theft that are quite out of character with Marx's analysis we have just the property relation as the inherent attribute of the definition of the working class position. We find corroboration of this position in The Critique of the Gotha Programme. Elaborating on the nature of the economy that Marx thought should emerge in the immediate post-socialist situation he says:

> What we have to deal with here is a communist society, not as it has *developed* on its own foundations, but, on the contrary, just as it *emerges* from capitalist society... The same amount of labour which he [the labourer] has given to society in one form, he receives back in another.
>
> Here, obviously, the same principle prevails as that which regulates the exchange of commodities, as far as this is exchange of equal values. (Marx 1875, p. 4)

And further on:

> Hence, *equal right* here is still in principle — *bourgeois right*... **this equal right is still constantly stigmatized by a bourgeois limitation**. The right of the producers is *proportional* to the labour they supply; the equality consists in the fact that measurement is made with an *equal standard*, labour. (Marx, 1875, p. 5) (Basu, 2012, p. 229)

Thus, even the working class person, is self-centred with no community feeling and is united only through the mediation of the party. On the one hand this conceptualization of the working class places the party leadership in a hierarchically and morally superior position. On the other, it raises the question: through what concrete practice will the *community of the working class* (as opposed to the class for itself) emerge so that at the next stage of development of society (under communism) the workers are not motivated by the propriety of property but by fellow feeling so that the law can be: from each according to his ability and to each according to his *need* (not work). In an age when atomism, individualism and hedonism are ruling there is the material basis for Marx's view regarding consciousness: "Each looks to himself only, and no one troubles himself about the rest, and just because they do so, do they all, in accordance with the pre-established harmony of things, or under the auspices of an all-shrewd providence, work together to their mutual advantage, for the common weal and in the interest of all." (C1, p. 121) But the communist activists will still have to think of concrete practice through which working class consciousness can elevate itself from its self-centredness to a community consciousness.

What then is the specific use of this concept of surplus value, (which implies the logical definition of capitalism) which Engels and much later Althusser were to liken to the discovery of Oxygen displacing Phlogiston in chemistry? Precisely in the way they elaborated: *surplus value* is to *political economy* what *oxygen* was to *chemistry*. Its worth is immense in the field of the academic discourse of economics, which was then called political economy. To take an example with which those belonging to the discipline of economics will be familiar: it demolishes the Marginal Productivity Theory of distribution as so much nonsense. The Marginal Productivity theory says that all *factors of production* are paid according to what the last unit of the factor produces and all product is exhausted in the process, hence there is no exploitation in a competitive market system. The theory of surplus value shows, on the other hand, that exploitation occurs through the extraction of surplus value within a perfectly competitive market framework.

Contestation of the mainstream position within the discipline does have its worth. Mainstream economics, as all social sciences, is a part of the *ideological state apparatus*. Students of economics, particularly, learn that all individuals are on an equal footing as owners of means of production: capitalist owns capital, labourer owns labour, etc. Each factor owner is paid according to the contribution of the factors of production each owns. This story which we build through increasing degrees of sophistication at various stages of academic training within the discipline wipes clean the story of the exploiter-exploited relation. Hence, it is important to demolish its edifice. And mainstream economics is well aware of this potential of Marxist political economy. Consider, for example, how a standard primer of economics, *Principles of Economics* by Lipsey and Chrystal begins. The opening section 'proves' that 'Smith was right and Marx was wrong' because the experience of the last half of the 20th century has shown that planning, which was proposed as desirable for developed economies by Marx has failed, while free market has prospered!

But even in this restricted domain, the theory of surplus value has limitations in today's world. True it provides an excellent set of propositions to counter vicious mainstream economic theorems like 'the poor are poor because they so deserve'. Succinctly, the proof of this theorem runs on these lines: whether you are frugal and choose not to consume or you eat up what you earn is your personal decision. If you choose the former then you accumulate capital and later earn 'rental'. If you choose the latter course then all you have in the future is wage income and you will probably end up in poverty. There are other variants of this 'proof'. The common theme is that poverty is a matter of choice! The theory of surplus value, on the other hand, shows with precision that the riches of the rich are the surplus value generated by the workers and extracted by the capitalist. So it demonstrates conclusively that to pose the questions of distribution in the realm of choice is just premeditated propaganda. But the theory of surplus value fails to attack the most effective weapon in the arsenal of mainstream economics today: the myth of competition and invisible hand of the market. The oppressed, within and without the working class, have been by and large forced into docility through a variety of instruments. A potent means of persuasion is the propaganda that the impersonal forces of the market determine all economic outcomes like wages, unemployment, etc. The oppressed are persuaded that their misery is fated by the impersonal forces of the market. Even the left in power accepts this tacitly. This is an aspect of commodity fetishism that Marx's theory of value fails to expose. The theory of surplus value, which teaches that equality, among other things, rules the market, corroborates this faith.

When Marx was writing his *Critique of Political Economy* (i.e. *Capital*), this was probably true. But in this age of global capital, little is left to the market. All is decided by global capital: what will be produced where, to what degree labour mobility will be allowed so that desirable wage differentials may exist. Of course, I am 'bending the stick' perhaps a bit too much backward, but that is only a matter of degree not of substance. The point is that the forces of the free market simply do not operate any longer. So basing a theory of exploitation on such a presumption may not be appropriate for theoretical discourse from the exploited classes' position at this juncture of history. The significance of an expanded concept of rent, which I will elaborate in a later lecture, is now immense and considering it as a species of subsumed class payment is problematic.

2. Another Marx

There is another Marx who has in fact written more pages of *Capital* than the 'logical' Marx or Marx the dialectician. This is the Marx who wrote the 'ontological' critiques that we have referred to in our previous lecture. This Marx, the historian of class violence, of cultural change, of uncertainty emanating from the mutual constitutivity among the various spheres of social interaction is intertwined with the dialectician Marx. It is this Marx who provides many pointers to the revolutionary path that are still relevant. Beside this the non-reductionist Marx of class violence has made a signal contribution to the critique of PE also. This follows from the articulation or mutual support that the dialectician Marx and the Marx of ontological overdetermination render each other. As a result history or experience unavoidably complements the logic of the critique of PE. Thus, for the first time, the discourse of PE recognizes the role of class violence[2] and non-economic factors in structuring production and distribution of social output.

We will try to establish the connection between the dialectician Marx and the Marx of class violence and overdetermination. We will then see how capitalism can be redefined through the latter reading of Marx and finally we will pose the question of the probable connotations of this reading for activism.

But, first, in what sense is the organizer, historian or ontological Marx necessary to the logician Marx and vice versa? See, every logical or theoretically conceived structure of society has gaps. These are filled up with propositions or historical moments that are not derived from the logic of the structure. On the other hand, these moments together do not make up a structure. The method of logic weaves them into a structure. Of course, because of the autonomy of the moments, the structure is always provisional and incomplete. We have to determine how these separate moments can actually reinforce each other and become parts of a coherent structure. Let us see a few of the instances where Marx fills up the gaps in the logical critique of PE with historical moments.

The reading of Marx, particularly of parts of *Capital* that we have presented so far is explicitly, by its own claim, a *logical* critique of political economy. It claims logical rigour derived from the application of the method of Hegelian dialectic. This logic is ruptured at several points. These necessitate the other parts of *Capital* that cover the gaps in logic—the parts narrating the violence of class and non-class struggles. Let us take up some of these instances.

2.1 Primitive Accumulation

Marx is here talking of the encounter of the dispossessed or the pauperized with capital and so of the genesis of the capital-wage labour relation. "Nature does not produce on the one side owners of money or commodities, and on the other men possessing nothing but their own labour-power. *This relation has no natural basis*, neither is its social basis one that is common to all historical periods. *It is clearly the result of a past historical development, the product of many economic revolutions, of the extinction of a whole series of older forms of social production.*

So, too, the *economic categories*, already discussed by us, *bear the stamp of history*. Definite *historical conditions* are necessary that a product may become a commodity. It must not be produced as the immediate means of subsistence of the producer himself. Had we gone further, and inquired under what circumstances all, or even the majority of products take the form of commodities, we should have found that this can only happen with production of a very specific kind, capitalist production. *Such an inquiry, however, would have been foreign to the analysis of commodities*." (C1, p. 118, emphasis added)

This passage occurs in the course of Marx's narrative of the self-development of the concept of value. We are here on the threshold of the final stage of this self-development (which is the same thing as the logical development) of capital, i.e. on the threshold of capitalism. But you find you cannot proceed further. There is a deep crevice which has to be bridged with the *history* of the dispossession (and its complement—accumulation of wealth in the hands of a few) and the encounter between the owners of monetary wealth and the dispossessed. Look closely at what Marx is saying here: "Had we gone further, and inquired under what circumstances all, or even the majority of products take the form of commodities, we should have found that *this can only happen with production of a very specific kind, capitalist production*." So what was meant to be the starting point of the logical genesis (Simple Commodity Production or petty production) turns out to be itself the product of capitalist class violence or of all the violent moments that culminated in the development of capitalism. This story of violent dispossession belongs both to the interior of the logical narrative and outside. It is inside, because the story of self-development of value to surplus value (i.e. of money to productive capital) will come to an abrupt halt before its final moment unless this moment of violence is introduced. It is also outside because **dispossession** is the narrative of raw *violence* (and violence is elementally illogical) and the **encounter** of capital with the dispossessed pauper is a chance factor, and violence and chance violate

Hegelian logic and are therefore removed from the gaze of the reader who is concerned with the logical story alone. For "**such an inquiry, however, would have been foreign to the analysis of commodities.**" But it has to be pointed out that in Vol. I itself Marx devotes more space to the violence of this *primitive accumulation* than he does to the logical story.

Let us look at another aspect of this same quote. Marx is saying that if one were to enquire under what circumstances all or even most of the products of a society were to become commodities, we would find that '*this can only happen with production of a very specific kind, capitalist production*'. That is the conditions for commodity production to prevail in the main is the same as those necessary for capitalist production. In other words, the class violence that was deemed necessary to complete the journey of self-development of value is actually a precondition for what was taken as the logical starting point of the journey of self-development of value that culminates in capitalist production: thus we have a situation of mutual dependence of the logical and the historical narrative of chance and violence. And Marx is saying clearly 'and such an enquiry would have been foreign to the analysis of commodities'. What he implies is that commodity has to be a starting point of the logical journey so we cannot let the discussion of capital precede this entry point.

2.2 Commodity Fetishism

There is another moment of illogic or of overdetermination that precedes the entry point into the discourse of commodities. I am talking of Commodity Fetishism. Within the community economy *differences* among the different *concrete labour*s was the basis of their social aspect—their interdependence. Now the *indifferent* character or their *abstract labour* content becomes the basis of their social aspect. This is a point we touched upon in our previous lecture, following Amaraglio and Callari (1989). A great cultural transformation is necessary for society to think in these terms. This is related to the breakup of community, the attendant loss of commons and emergence of the concept of private property. The exchange relation that we are discussing is not a natural law—not going into the question of whether there can be a 'natural' law that does not require the authority and violence of ruling culture for its establishment. Let us extend a quotation from Vol. I that I have used in our previous chapter:

> Trading nations, properly so-called, exist in the ancient world only in its interstices, like the gods of Epicurus in the Intermundia, or like Jews in the pores of Polish society. Those ancient social organisms of production are, as compared with bourgeois society, extremely simple and transparent. But they are founded either on the immature development of man individually, who has not yet severed the umbilical cord that unites him with his fellowmen in a primitive tribal community, or upon direct relations of subjection. They can arise and exist only when the development of the productive power of labour has not risen beyond a low stage, and when, therefore, the social relations within the sphere of material life, between man and man, and between man and Nature, are correspondingly narrow. This narrowness is reflected in the ancient worship of Nature, and in the other elements of the popular religions. (C1, p. 51)

Obviously, belonging to Part I of *Capital*, the view is tainted with some scientistic or linear view of historical development. But 'severing the umbilical cord' is an act of violence. The kind of social formation that must be suppressed to give birth to the proposed beginning of the journey of commodity-capital is also indicated, of course in a pejorative way from a modern perspective: "the development of the productive power of labour has not risen beyond a low stage, and when, therefore, the social relations within the sphere of material life, between man and man, and between man and Nature, are correspondingly narrow. This narrowness is reflected in the ancient worship of Nature, and in the other elements of the popular religions." This is unequivocally the community life where there is direct communion between not just man and man but also between man and nature. What we have, then, is a moment of violence closing a gap that occurs at the moment of entry into the logical journey.

This has a very serious implication for the development of the category of exchange value and the dropping out of the category of use value from further determinations of the journey of the MOP. At this moment use value as a social category drops out. Use value as a social category is banished from social communication. It becomes purely private or subjective. Hence it cannot be communicated, unlike the socially agreed use values of a community: the table of our previous lecture has use value only for the seller of shirt, the shirt has use value only for seller of table. Being purely private use value, it is not communicable, it is not like language, say, which belongs to a community of speakers. So it cannot form the basis of the language of commerce—exchange value. Though, as we have seen from the quote, Marx does talk of the historical violence dislodging the man-man and man-nature community, he does not devote much space to this species of violence. I feel, however, that this is a crucial moment the importance of which has to be grasped for practice. The re-invention of a new community among the working people and of working people with their environment has to be imagined. This can also provide a thread to tie up the diverse environmental movements with the working people's movements. It is such a communion that can transform the working class steeped in the culture of private property, imagining the end of exploitation to mean 'from each according to his ability and to each according to his work', to a community of working people imagining a world where the rule of work and distribution is 'from each according to his ability and to each according to his need'.

2.3 *Variable Capital*

Another instance: Marx differentiates between *constant* and *variable* capitals. The former, made up of fuel, raw material, wear and tear of machinery in the course of transformation of the given raw materials. These are called 'constant capital' because there is no possibility of variation in the amount of value that this capital passes on to the produce. It must be identical to its own embodied value. On the other hand the wage expenditure is termed 'variable capital'. It is called variable because the value that the labour power (purchased with this wage) will add to the produce is not pre-given. This variability occurs for two reasons. First, the wage good basket socially necessary for a day's labour is not predetermined. Secondly, the value that the labourer will add to the produce in the course of a day's work is also not predetermined. To take the second reason first: the number of work hours in a working day is also indeterminate. The worker enters the factory with the promise of working for a day, a week, a month. But a host of conflicting factors determine how many average work hours they will contribute to the produce in that time: conflict over the length of the working day, conflict between the supervisors and workers, the introduction of labour displacing machinery, development of machinery such that control over the labour process vests in the machine, etc. So the addition is variable. Again we have the story of conflict, which logic abhors but which is necessary to close a gap in the story where logic fails. How much work the labourer will perform is not logically decided. It is determined by the particular history of struggle. It is region-specific, depends on the relative cohesion of the contending parties—the workers and capitalists and is also influenced by the reading of the state regarding the outcome and hence its pre-emptive actions. Again one must point out that Marx devoted approximately 200 pages in Vol. I of *Capital* to the historical analysis of these conflicts, while he devoted some 124 pages to the logical structure elaborated in Parts I and II of the same volume. Together with the variability of hours of work Marx also discusses the 'intensification of labour' (C1, p. 275) by the application of machinery and by imposition of stricter discipline. When the hours could not be lengthened, because of legislation that the parliament was forced to adopt on account of labour movement, labour was intensified.

As we have mentioned, another aspect of the variability of this component of capital arises because what is deemed to be necessary for the reproduction of a working day's labour power is itself variable, hence the surplus value that it adds to the product is also variable. Marx cites various reasons for this variability of the value of labour power. For example, as long as a worker is the only earning member in his family, his wage must be sufficient to reproduce not only his personal labour power but must be sufficient to maintain an average family for a day. The moment that the women and children enter the work force this component of necessary labour is reduced.

Introduction of new machinery also leads to an as if lengthening of the working day through increase in 'relative surplus value'. On the other hand, actual lengthening of the working day is called increase in 'absolute surplus'. Relative surplus value can be increased by an innovating firm before the innovation has been replicated by competitors.

> During this transition period, when the use of machinery is a sort of monopoly, the profits are therefore exceptional, and the capitalist endeavours to exploit thoroughly—the sunny time of this his first love, by prolonging the working day as much as possible... As the use of machinery becomes more general in a particular industry, the social value of the product sinks down to its individual value, and the law that surplus value does not arise from the labour-power that has been replaced by the machinery, but from the labour-power actually employed in working with the machinery, asserts itself. Surplus value arises from variable capital alone, and we saw that the amount of surplus value depends on two factors, viz. the rate of surplus value and the number of the workmen simultaneously employed. Given the length of the working day, the rate of surplus value is determined by the relative duration of the necessary labour and of the surplus labour in a day. (C1, pp. 273-274)

Let us bring together the moments of violence, of illogic or logic of a different kind (i.e. overdetrministic) that supplement the logical critique of PE in *Capital*. We bring them together in the logical order in which they appear in the logical story of development of commodity. First, the violence necessary to cut the umbilical cord that binds man to some community of fellowmen and nature in order to create man that acknowledges the propriety of property. Second, the violence of dispossession that, as Dussel (2001) points out, breeds the pauper—one who has lost all extraneous means of production (or all means of production other than labour power)—and has no means of purchasing his subsistence. Third, the violence that the labourer (ex-pauper who had the good fortune of meeting a capitalist willing to buy his labour power) faces within the factory.

3. Capitalism: Another Definition

So what is the answer to the question: what is capitalism? There seems to be two possible routes through which we can seek the answer. First: the logical route that suggests that capitalism is simply the highest stage of commodity production. This we have already spelt out in some detail. The second path, which we may call ontological or historical (in the sense that it is a path where analytical, categorical logic fails and the 'logic' of overdetermination takes over), would consist of simply bringing together the various effects of violence that Marx's discussion shows to be necessary for the birth of capitalism. I would go along with the second option.

Of course, a simple argument in support of this position is just the small number of pages Marx devotes to the logical critique compared to the vast description of violence within the factory and the violence of Primitive Accumulation (whereby the working people are dispossessed of all means of production which can be seized from them). But that is a rather simplistic argument. The point is that just as violence is not logical, the sequence of the violent moments is also not logically determined. That they occurred in the sequence narrated is purely accidental. That they all even occurred in some social formations giving birth to what we call the capitalist MOP is also accidental. Thus the birth, structure and stability of the capitalist formation is not logical and therefore not ordained or predetermined. So a general definition should take into account the potential for variations. Therefore the answer to the question 'what is capitalism?' is that it is a coming together of a large number of elementary moments at some historical time. These moments would include generalized commodity production, pauperization of large segments of population, concentration of money capital in the hands of a small segment, the investment of money capital to employ the paupers (now the working class) in factories under the supervision of capitalist. And all these moments are moments of violence.

So what I am proposing, not at all originally, is a rather untidy definition or rather a taxonomy of elements that together constitute what we know as capitalism. This definition is bound to be untidy because as we have read Marx the development of capitalism is itself not a logical journey. On a broader canvas this implies that the sequence of modes of production should also be challenged.

4. Implications for Practice

This has important connotations for the Marxist activists in India today. To bring out the relevance I will, very sketchily, argue that the three broad divisions of communist revolutionaries in India—leaving aside the question of the frequent violent condemnation of each other as non-Marxist—argue for different revolutionary paths based on the Marxist stage theory. Whatever the details of the revolutionary project of the various communist parties of India, there is commonality in the faith in the stages of revolution. And hence of history as a sequence of MOPs: primitive communism—slavery—feudalism—capitalism—communism. This also implies that they all subscribe to Marxism as science. By implication they support the position that Marx developed an entirely logical critique of PE—a position against which we have argued.

The principal difference between the CPI and CPI(M) appears to be on the question of whether the 'big bourgeoisie' is nationalist. Apparently, this will determine the course of the strategy/tactics of the 'democratic' revolution, which both believe is the immediate task. The principal enemy is the feudal class. That is both believe that the task of transforming the MOP/social formation to capitalism remains to be completed and this cannot be left to the bourgeoisie. In other words, the transition to capitalism has to be completed before a socialist revolution. The principal opponent to such 'progress' is landlordism which has not been abolished completely. The point of discord is whether the revolutionary alliance should include the big bourgeoisie or not. The CPI did not differentiate between the different groups of industrial capitalists and subscribed to the view that the bourgeoisie as a whole should be part of the revolutionary alliance. Hence they were not averse to sharing state power with the capitalist class as a whole. The CPI(M) believes that the 'big bourgeoisie' or monopoly capital shares state power with big landlords. Hence the task of the democratic revolution had to be completed by an alliance of workers, poor and middle farmers, petty bourgeoisie, and small national capital. The CPI(ML) believes that the principal enemies are imperialism and feudalism. It believes that the capitalist class as a whole is 'comprador', though the meaning of the term has become increasingly nuanced over the years. But it also subscribes to the stage theoretic programme of revolution. The first stage will establish 'New Democracy' where the economic programme is to complete the transition to capitalism under the leadership of the working class whose stable ally will be the landless and poor farmers, unstable allies: the petty bourgeoisie.

Clearly the Marxist parties are arguing for a) transformation through stages; b) some sort of 'democratic revolution' as the first stage of establishment of socialism. Let us try to see the implications of how these positions relate to the second or non-scientistic reading of Marx.

We are just sketching some points for discussion. First, the moments of violence that constituted capitalism in the West may not obtain in other parts of the globe. So we can have other combinations of elements with varying degrees of stability. This is how Kalyan Sanyal, Partha Chatterjee, Rajesh Bhattacharya and others have seen the emergence of the vast informal sector in India. This would mean that activists have to think of new alliances, new objectives and forms of movement. This also challenges the belief in the stages of revolution. It may be pointed out that, in spite of the differences in terms of the revolutionary alliances that the CPI, CPI(M) and CPI(ML) espouse, they all subscribe to some two-stage theory of revolutionary transformation to socialism. Another fallout of admitting the possibility of various stable articulations of modes of being and performance of labour is that activism has to accommodate a diverse array of aspirations and experiences. It also has to formulate its course of action on the basis of such diversity. Perhaps, the absence of recognition of diversity (let alone accommodating these within the transformatory project) is a major reason for the stunted growth of leftist politics. Also, if societies are simply relatively stable combinations of certain elementary processes born out of the particular history of the region, it is quite possible that certain elements of the Western state and superstructure may prevail in a country whose economic base is vastly different. Such is true of India—it has adopted a democratic form of government with an economic base that is not capitalist in the Western sense. This seems to go formally unrecognized in the party programmes. The establishment of democracy is important to activism in a positive and negative sense. Positive: there is some degree of freedom of expression and association that can be utilized. Negative: the ideological state apparatus, in a very direct sense, has to reach out even to the remote parts of the country in the process of electioneering. In any case the political formation and their modes of operation have to be different within a formal democratic set up compared to those under dictatorial or, say, feudal regimes.

Secondly, if you abandon the idea of Marxism as a logical totality you give space to the experience of the exploited people in the construction of a revolutionary path. The unquestionable authority of the party leadership, *which knows the truth,* is no longer valid. This would require new organizational forms.

Thirdly, if you recognize the importance of violent dissolution of community for the development of capitalism, you also recognize the importance of reconstructing a community of working people in the course of struggles. That is a community which is more than an association of individualistic workers whose community feeling is mediated through the party alone.

Conclusion

Any revolutionary practice based on Marxism must dream of an exploitationless world. This is the fountainhead of passion that has and must continue to motivate left activists. But activism has to be more nuanced. It has to think of constructing a community of working people. I do not say 'working class', as the conventional definition is narrow and excludes very large segments of the exploited people who would be reliable friends of any transformative practice. When one talks of community two things stand out: one, restitution of the idea of *use value* as a social concept. (Within the global order of capitalism it has been reduced to a private value dominated by newer forms of commodity fetishism) this will also help in allying with serious environmental movements and perhaps also with movements based on identities like gender and ethinicity. Two, the working people's party must concern itself with the life time and not with just the labour time of the working people alone. I am not saying that this is not done, but it needs to be much more generalized in practice and not confined to the lives of party comrades only and the practice needs to be sensitive.

The experience of the working people has to enrich party programmes and strategies. It must be realized that there is no *scientific* path known to the intellectuals who continue to head the party organizations. The activists will have to think of ways in which the conventional hierarchy and structure of commands can be suitably modified. The TU organizations must learn and educate the workers about the changes that are occurring on the shop floor. The workers must understand the violence on the shop floor in concrete terms. I see the 'Gurgaon Workers' News' is doing good work in this field. There must be others too, of whom I am not informed.

Not being an activist I have probably overstepped the ethical boundary of what I should have said. Put it down to age and years of talking too much in classrooms!

REFERENCES

Amariglio, J. and Callari, A. (1989) "Marxian value theory and the problem of the subject: The role of commodity fetishism." *Rethinking Marxism* 2.3: 31-60.

Dussel, E. (2001) *Towards an Unknown Marx: A Commentary on the Manuscripts of 1861–63*, tr. Yolanda Angulo, Routledge: London.

Gibson-Graham, Resnick, S.A., Wolff, R. 2000. 'Introduction' in Gibson-Graham, Resnick and Wolff(ed.) *Class and its Others*, University of Minnesota Press: Minnesota.

Marx, K. (1887) *Capital, Vol. I,* available athttps://www.marxists.org/archive/marx/works/download/pdf/Capital-Volume-I.pdf (accessed on 12th May 2013).

Marx, K. (1970) *Critique of the Gotha Programme* available at https://

www.marxists.org/archive/marx/works/1875/gotha/ (accessed on 10th January 2010).

Sanyal, K., Bhattacharyya, R., (May 30, 2009) 'Beyond the Factory: Globalisation, Informalisation of Production and the New Locations of Labour', *Economic & Political Weekly (Review of Labour).*

Sanyal, Kalyan K. (2007) *Rethinking Capitalist Development: Primitive Accumulation, Governmentality and Post-Capitalism* Routledge: New Delhi.

NOTES

1. I say this is extraneous in the sense that it is not logically derived. It is derived from the particular kind of relation that the labouring person has with one's labour (planning and execution, realizing oneself in labour, etc.). These are not derived from the general relation of a commodity owner with the commodity owned. And it is this general relation and the exchange of commodities on the basis of value that generates surplus value.
2. 'Violence' is a concept that I use frequently in this lecture. I use it in a broad sense of an event that defies the system of categorical logic. There is therefore an imposition as the event, which is the outcome of a process, does not evolve from a linear Hegelian dialectical process.

5

Land in Marxian Theory

Pranab Kanti Basu[1]

Introduction

Land is important in Marxian theory not only by itself but also because it serves as a metaphor of various other categories of inputs that have the same specifics as land (which specifics we will elaborate presently). The list of such inputs is ever open to supplementation. Thus the question of land remains a field that has a lot of potency for analyzing contemporary globalized capital. Within the binary scheme of reading Marx (linear logical/Hegelian dialectical/essentialist/epistemological reading based, on the one hand, and overdeterministic/defying Hegelian dialectical logic/historical reading, on the other) that I have tried to elaborate through the initial chapters, the discussion of land in Marx fits the latter scheme.

I have touched most of the issues that we will discuss today in the earlier chapters. To my mind *there are two major aspects of the discussion of land in Marx, the process of it becoming a commodity or the genealogy of land as commodity and its peculiarity as a commodity. The process of becoming commodity again has two aspects, the violent abrogation of common rights of peasants and the attendant cultural impact which is, largely, the genesis of commodity fetishism (CF). As a commodity it is peculiar for two reasons, at least: it is a commodity that commands price without having value; it is immobile; in fact it defines spatial specificity.*

1.1 Becoming commodity of land: Primitive Accumulation (PA)

The first aspect of the process of becoming commodity of land (abrogation of common rights) has been termed Primitive Accumulation by Marx.[2] This entails dispossession through legal and extra-legal measures comprising what is called the enclosure movement—a process discussed in great detail by Marx (C1, Part 8) in the context of Britain. As Gibson-Graham and others have pointed out (and we have quoted this in previous chapter) there was an enlightenment discourse, which Marx took over, that asserted labour was the source of all wealth and, therefore the labourer was naturally entitled to the fruits of his labour. This ethical notion was sufficient ground for the entry point into the discourse of commodities through SCP. I do not subscribe to this idea of wholesale borrowing, because I think that this was rather the result of his ethical entry point of exploitation, given his involvement with working class movement that committed him to the position that the labouring people had both the right to the produce as well as to the right of decision making with respect to production. My assertion of course begs the question: did he derive his ethical position from his experience alone? Or was it not influenced by the enlightenment discourse? However that may be, this *ethical* position was insufficient to establish any proprietary rights over nonproduced resources like land. Nonproduced resources (in the sense that labour is not involved in their production or reproduction) or what are generally termed 'natural' resources together with resources whose reproduction is costless, like knowledge, were traditionally treated as common property. Once feudal exploitation penetrated the community mode of being and producing, the right of the feudal authority over all land was enforced. The manorial lord forcibly took over parts of arable lands called the demesne. Peasants were allotted own plots with various degrees of freedom and a large part of the village territory remained as commons or common property accessible to all villagers—waterbodies, pastures, forest lands. The commons were 'enclosed' through the fifteenth and sixteenth centuries. That is the rights of the peasants to these lands and their products were abrogated through part legal, part extra-legal coercive means and sole proprietary rights were conferred on/ceased by the manorial lords. As long as the commons existed, the peasant plots were only nominally personal, because of the dependence of peasants' life and peasant plot cultivation on the commons: the animals engaged on a farm had to be fed on the common pastures; a considerable part of the peasants' food basket was procured from the commons—fish from the rivers and ponds, venison and other animal meat from the forests, etc. Thus, in spite of existence of peasant plots, individualism and private property in land had not come into being. As Perry Anderson (1996) has argued, the feudal system was a combination of traits of the slave and the community modes of production. The various kinds of unfreedoms and economic impositions on the peasantry were the legacies of the slave system, while the continuance of community production and culture among the peasantry was a legacy of the ancient communities.

The Enclosure Movement brought land into the realm of the market. Even the peasant plots were commercialized as in the absence of the commons, the peasants were forced to give up cultivating their own plots also. This happened because of the dependence of the peasantry on the commons for their livelihood which we have already mentioned.

1.2 Becoming Commodity of Land: Culture

The second aspect of the genealogy of land as a commodity is the cultural impact of this process. Commoditisation of land caused immense cultural changes without which the logical journey of self-development of capital could not have started as Marx remarks in C1 (as we have pointed out in an earlier chapter). This also ties up with our discussion of commodity fetishism (CF) in an earlier chapter. Following Amaraglio and Callari we had said that CF is the product of a cultural political-process which is a *precondition* for a stable exchange system. The products of different kinds of labours are equated in the market. This is only possible under the condition that the labourers see the different kinds of labour as being quantitatively comparable. A particularly kind of subjectivity (that of individual property owners) has to be produced. This is not just a logical effect. It is, among other things, the product of dissolution of community ties. What is the relation of CF with the becoming commodity of land? Have we not remarked that land is a peculiar commodity that commands price but has no value? Then where is the comparability with the general form of commodities that command price because they have values? We will come to the question of pricing of land presently, but for the time being we are concerned with the question of subjectivity that is necessary for the functioning of the capital-commodity system. To see the relation of the emergence of this subjectivity with the genealogy of land as commodity let us recall a passage from C1.

> [T]he *economic categories*, already discussed by us, *bear the stamp of history*. Definite *historical conditions* are necessary that a product may become a commodity. It must not be produced as the immediate means of subsistence of the producer himself. Had we gone further, and inquired under what circumstances all, or even the majority of products take the form of commodities, we should have found that this can only happen with production of a very specific kind, capitalist production. *Such an inquiry, however, would have been foreign to the analysis of commodities.*" (C1, p. 118, emphasis added)

The 'definite historical circumstances' that Marx is referring to, include the culturally conditioned specific subjectivity necessary for commodity exchange to attain acceptability, and hence stability. Marx is then saying that these conditions can 'only happen with production of a very specific kind, capitalist production.' What this means, as pointed out earlier, is that PA must be already completed. This implies that though simple commodity production is the entry point of the *logical* discussion of self-development of commodities to capital, this is simply an entry point into the discourse and not ontologically prior: without the particular subjectivity characterised by sense of private property as ethically justified, commodity exchange cannot stabilise as a rule. And this can happen only under capitalist production for which PA is a precondition. Let us elaborate why Marx takes this seemingly paradoxical position: the journey of self-development of commodities to commodity capital starts from the premise of petty production or the simple commodity producing economy, which Marx calls the most embryonic form of bourgeois production. The journey ends in self-expanding capitalist production. At the last moment of this journey, labour power commodity is born through PA and we have an all pervasive commodity producing economy, which is the capitalist economy. But then Marx makes this paradoxical statement that the journey could not have started if the capitalist form of production had not been *historically* extant. What is the reason behind this seeming paradox?

PA as discussed in *Capital* involved dispossession of land converting it from common property to private property. The break-up of the commons meant that the economic foundation of the village community ceased to exist. This is a precondition for the emergence of a kind of subjectivity or consciousness that thinks that private property is justified. The violence of PA is not just the violence of enclosure but also the attendant violence of the break-up of community culture and its replacement with the culture of individualism whose economic basis is the notion of private property. The dispossessed pauper migrated to the towns in search of industrial employment. Clueless about the new life, torn from the solace of their village community they were thrown into the cesspool of cities lacking any civic amenities (rather like our migrants inhabiting Dharavi or Pilkhana). Vivid descriptions of the trauma of loss of community abound in *Capital* and in greater details in the works of historians like Thompson (Thompson, 1963.), Hobsbawm (1968, 1962), Christopher Hill (1969). Tremendous increase in alcohol intake, dissolution of families, increase in prostitution are some of the indicators of an overarching depression that engulfed the working class.

The violent erasure of community culture forced the multitudes to try and make sense of the world in terms that were different from those of the community with which they had always looked at the world and fellow humans. *A fundamental aspect of this erasure of community values, which has a special significance in Marxian Political economy, is the erasure of use value as a communicable category and the common perception of Abstract Labour (AL) value.* We will not spend time on this as we have already elaborated this in an earlier chapter. The large scale eviction of peasants was, therefore, an essential ingredient of the historical transition from community culture to commodity culture. And commodity exchange cannot become the staple form of economic intercourse without this huge cultural transformation. So we have the seeming paradox in Marx's statement. In fact it is not a paradox but a manifestation of Marx's overall overdeterministic world view that we have been trying to argue throughout: every sphere of social interaction affects every other. The method of presentation however, constrained as it is by language and predominant culture, has to be sequential. Look, we are not saying that Marx was consciously trying to break free of these constraints that he clearly perceived (in other words, we are not claiming that he was a postmodern!). After all every man is a prisoner of his time. But this is an obvious instance where Marx realised the deficiency of his mode of reasoning and was critiquing his own 'dialectical' reason.

It is necessary to remark at this point that that the resistance of *Adivasis* against land acquisition, mainly for mining and mega projects like dams and highway construction is a reflection of this clash of civilisations.

2.1 The Being of Land as Commodity: Rent and Price

The first specificity of land as commodity within Marxian Political economy is that it is a commodity that commands price without having any value. Recollect that we had discussed in an earlier chapter that within Marxian Political economy AL values are the basis of price. AL is not manifest. Yet as Amaraglio and Callari argue, it is affective in the sense that for exchange to become a staple form of economic interaction within a culture that recognised labour as the source of wealth, it was necessary that economic agents should conceive of some form of generalised labour embodied in the products that make them quantitatively comparable.

Let us consider the peculiarities of land as a commodity. We have said that part of its peculiarity resides in the fact that it does not have value but commands a price[3]. How can we explain this? Land is a condition for capitalist production. Not only is it necessary for agricultural production but it is necessary for locating factories. We are currently acutely aware of the conflict between these two uses of land because of the movements against the new land acquisition bill. Marx argues that because it is a necessary condition for capitalist production, the capitalist is willing to pay a part of the appropriated surplus value in the form of rent. This redistribution of appropriated surplus value has been termed subsumed class payment. This is treated in much the same way that payment to merchant capital, money lender and state by the capitalist is treated.

It is understandable that the capitalist is willing to make 'subsidiary class payment', called rent, for the use of land, which is a necessary condition for his production. But how is the landlord able to claim this payment? It is on the basis of the property right over land which he has personally seized or which was seized by the state and conferred on him.

Rent is earned on the basis of monopoly of rights over resources that are not replicable. Marx discusses this in Volume III of *Capital* (C III). Primitive Accumulation (PA) has already occurred. This is discussed in Volume I of *Capital*. There are now three classes of economic functionaries. There are the landlords who have dispossessed the traditional right holders of their rights and established sole proprietary rights over land. There are the capitalists who take this land on lease against payment of rent to the landlord to use the land for profit. And there are of course the labourers who work on payment of wages.

Discussing the basis of the ability to extract rent, Marx says, "...the monopoly of the so-called landed proprietor of a portion of our planet, enables him to levy such a tribute" (C III, p. 625). Marx then goes on to divide rent into two analytical parts: differential rent (that is generated by the extra productivity of some plots, which causes the product to fetch more revenue than is sufficient to cover normal wage charge, material cost, other charges and profit at the normal rate); and absolute rent (that is generated by diminishing wage and/or rate of profit on capital invested on such plots). This latter is rendered possible because such capital or labour has no alternative field of employment. Marx cites the case of the small farmers who cannot hire large plots of land because of the paucity of funds. Because of the large numbers of such farmers in comparison to the number of such plots available, the owners of such plots were able to depress the profit on capital of the small farmer and so extract absolute rent.

To my mind, the key factors that allow rent extraction are barriers to the ability to replicate (produce or reproduce) some resource, necessary for commodity production— this aspect also Marx mentions explicitly (C III, p. 633)—and monopoly of ownership over this resource. The planet earth is not replicable and so monopoly over fractions of this earth allow the owners of these titles to extract a payment, called rent, from the capitalist who would employ this resource.

At this point I will recall an assertion that I had made at the beginning of this lecture: Land is important in Marxian theory not only by itself but because it serves as a metaphor of various other categories of inputs that have the same specifics (the specifics we will elaborate presently) as land, the list of such inputs being ever open to supplementation. If the specific attributes of land that we have mentioned exist or are created in other fields then rent could be extracted from these fields too.

If land is valueless then what determines its price? The price of land is anticipated ground rent capitalized at some 'notional' rate of interest. The purchase of land 'merely secures for the buyer a claim to receive annual rent' What is bought and sold is the title to the ground-rent yielded by it.

Any stream of revenue (such as an annual rent) can be considered as the interest on some imaginary, fictitious capital. For the buyer, the rent figures in his accounts as the interest on the money laid out on land purchase, and is in principle no different from similar investments in government debt, stocks and shares of enterprises, consumer debt and so on. The money laid out is interest-bearing capital in every case. The land becomes a form of fictitious capital, and the land market functions simply as a particular branch—albeit with some special characteristics—of the circulation of interest-bearing capital. Under such conditions the land is treated as a pure financial asset which is bought and sold according to the rent it yields. Like all such forms of fictitious capital, what is traded it is a claim upon future revenues, which means a claim upon future profits from the use of the land or, more directly, a claim upon future labour. (Harvey, 1982, p. 347).

Capital circulates through land markets promoting activities on the land that conform to the production of highest anticipated (surplus) value. Anticipation being an act of speculation, land emerges as an instrument of financial speculation.

By perpetually striving to put land to its 'highest and best use', landowners create a sorting device which sifts land uses and forces allocations of capital and labour that might not otherwise occur. By looking to the future, they also inject a fluidity and dynamism into the use of land that would otherwise be hard to generate. The more vigorous landowners are in this regard, the more active the land market and the more adjustable does the use of the land become in relation to social requirements - in the present instance, the accumulation of capital.

> .... But by the same token, the more open the land market is, the more recklessly can surplus money capital build pyramids of debt claims and seek to realize its excessive hopes through the pillaging and destruction of production on the land itself. Speculation in land may be necessary to capitalism, but speculative orgies periodically become a quagmire of destruction for capital itself. (Harvey 1982, pp. 368-369)

Note this was at the root of the latest financial crisis out of which the global economy has yet to recover.

2.2 Being of Land as Commodity: Absence of Spatiality

Commoditisation of land erases specificity of space in Marxian PE and this has significant political consequences. Commodity (so prices and values) becomes the focus of Marxian PE. To grasp the significance of commodities in this particular context one must appreciate that property is prior to commodity. The laws of property and contract are the prerequisites of exchange, which is the becoming of commodity. I feel that the proper place to start an analysis of the significance of commoditiness of products of labour is Hegel because Marx's method of analysing commodities is largely similar to Hegel's method. I am telescoping the discussions in Hegel's *Philosophy of Right*. The journey starts from *individual will* as *pure subjectivity*.

Free will (technically 'proposition', 'thesis') is posited as 'pure abstraction'. At this stage, personality is only subjective. Self-consciousness is one sided—purely reflexive (i.e. inward looking). The 'negation' or antithesis of free will as pure abstraction is the external world as 'pure externality'. To personality, as inherently infinite and universal, the restriction of being only subjective is nullity and contradiction. Self becomes conscious of its nullity, of its finitude. The 'negation of negation' or 'synthesis' is free will as right to property. What was immediately pure externality now becomes a particular of free will as receptacle of free will; it is just property of free will. Self-consciousness is now lifted to its universality: he, free will, takes possession of himself and becomes his own property. The lower moments of logical development (thesis/proposition and antithesis/negation) are uplifted and completely contained in this higher moment of dialectical development or synthesis. This is also called 'dialectical sublimation'.

> "Man pursuant to his immediate existence within himself, is something natural, external to his concept. It is only through the development of own body and mind, essentially through his self-consciousness' apprehension of itself as free, that he takes possession of himself and becomes his own property." (Hegel, 2001, Para. 57)

In this journey of constitution of self-consciousness, the highest moment of self-consciousness is attained when "he takes possession of himself and becomes his own property and no one else's". But the property of one, one's properties are only potentially so. They are actualised in exchange. This is there in Marx, but is also there in Hegel.

Let us pursue the rest of the journey of 'right' as it occurs in

Hegel. The next proposition/thesis or the next step of triadic argument of right is self's right to property. Its negation/antithesis, the next step, is another's right to property. The negation of negation/synthesis is contract.

> This relation of will to will [in exchange] is the true and proper ground in which freedom is existent—the sphere of contract is made up of this mediation whereby I hold property not merely by means of a thing and my subjective will, but by means of another's will as well and so hold it in virtue of my participation in a common will. (Ibid, Para 74)

In Hegel's discussion one can read the concept of value, of exchange and simple commodity production.

> Since in real contract each party retains the same property with which he enters the contract and which at the same time he surrenders, what thus remains identical throughout as the property implicit in the contract is distinct from the external things whose owners alter when the exchange is made. What remains identical is the value, in respect of which the subjects of the contract are equal to one another whatever the qualitative differences of the things exchanged. Value is the universal in which the subjects of the contract participate. (Ibid, Para. 77).

While Hegel deduced that the universal being of property lies in contract and value from the triadic formula, this formula does not generate the question of what constitutes value.

The epistemology employed by Marx to construct the commodity economic is the same as that employed by Hegel. Hence the result is, predictably, the same. Instead of the emphasis on the binary 'subjective/objective' or 'will/externality' (used by Hegel) we have, in Marx, other binaries that focus on the same difference. Prominently we have 'use value/exchange value' and 'concrete labour/abstract labour'.

There is, I think, one fundamental difference of the transition from the subjective to the objective form of property as schematised by Marx from the transition in the Hegelian scheme. While the transition in Hegel is clearly a *dialectical sublimation* (a term that we have just elaborated), in Marx the subjective form—the use value—drops out of the exchange circuit, or is *occluded*. Utilities, or use values, are concrete or specific in the sense of being purely subjective and not comparable in a world inhabited by *individuals*. Marx treats it as an occlusion or something that drops out in the process of comparison of values, which is the stuff of exchange. This 'dropping out' is not a theoretical transition; it is forced through PA breaking up the community and constituting the individual. This is, therefore a closure of a gap in logic that can be prised open with force—counter—hegemonic force. *The political implication of this is the counter hegemonic potential of community.*

The Hegelian (idealist) journey starts from the premise of pure subjectivity—from free will. There is no connection between the material world and man that is prior posited. In the course of triadic expansion of the discursive universe the material world is appropriated or absorbed in thought through the property relation. In the Marxian (materialist) narration, however, there is a prior link between the material world and humans—the relation of use value. This is a concrete relation that is part of the identity of local community based existence that exists prior to the beginning of the journey of becoming of commodity of land. This relation is argued to be inconsistent with commoditiness—whose genesis lies in humans putting labour into matter and making it their private property. Thus there is a sharply drawn boundary that excludes use value from the discursive universe within which commodity and capital are constituted. Force has to be employed to cement this exclusion or dropping out of use value. Use value then becomes, as we have argued, a purely individual or subjective category without any social consequence.

This cutting loose from spatial moorings is not a logical process. Force is of the essence and an important connotation of this coercive process is the exclusion of use values in the process of constituting commodities. This is inevitable, as I have been arguing, because the anchoring signifier—commoditiness or prices—robs spatiality of any discursive significance. The antithetical position is that taken by those who can be broadly referred to as radical environmentalists. To them 'nature' has a pristine originality. It is the Garden of Eden. Space is the basis of this natural community. Man-in-harmony-with-nature within a bounded space is the utopia the radical environmentalists crave for. On the one hand, there is the erasure of spatiality in the discourse of exploitation within political economy. On the other, there is the erasure of economic exploitation from the discourse of spatiality in the discourse of the radical environmentalists.

Thus, an effect of being commodity of land is the erasure of spatial specificity and, consequently, erasure of community from the Marxian discourse of political economy. Once 'space' has been detached from its association with a particular geographical territory it is free to be (mis)used without any theoretical liability. Two things stand out if we look at the problem of spatiality in this light. First the process of dispossession of the peasant through the process of PA is simultaneously the process of freeing 'space' from any real mooring (in the sense of association with a geographically specific locality), and of occlusion of use value. Secondly, one can perhaps better understand the reasons behind the acrimony between various groups of the left-in-opposition on the question of forming an unconditional front with rightist opposition parties in the aftermath of state violence for acquisition of farm land for non-agricultural use: There remains no specific Marxist approach to issues concerning land. It is part of the excluded or marginalised. So one is free to take any approach that appears to be suitable to the (subjective) morality of the individual or group. Hence, the acrimony.

In conclusion, in continuity with the last point it can be argued that the occlusion—community—can be resurrected as some form of working peoples' community to sustain counter-hegemonic imagination. This is something that has been tried by the Zapatistas, by Shankar Guha Neogi (with temporary success) and in disjoint ways by various commune experiments. There is a lot of potential for such movements, particularly for integrating with various non-class movements like environment, gender, etc.

Note: C1 stands for Capital Vol. 1, C 3 stands for Capital III.

REFERENCES

Amariglio, J. and Callari, A. (1989) "Marxian value theory and the problem of the subject: The role of commodity fetishism." *Rethinking Marxism* 2.3: 31-60.

Anderson, P. (1996) *Passages from Antiquity to Feudalism*. Verso: London, NewYork.

Harvey. D. (1982) *The Limits of Capital*, Basil Blackwell Publisher Limited, UK.

Hegel, GWF (2001) *Philosophy of Right*, Batoche Books Limited, Canada.

Hill, C. (1969) *From Reformation to Industrial Revolution*, Penguin Books, UK.

Hobsbawm, E. (1968) *Industry and Empire: From 1750 to the Present*, Penguin Books: London.

Hobsbawm, E. (1962) *The Age of Revolution*, Vintage Books: New York

Marx, K. (1999) *Capital Vol. III* available at https://www.marxists.org/archive/marx/works/.../Capital-Volume-III.pdf (accessed on 12th June 2014)

NOTES

1. I am heavily indebted to Rajesh Bhattacharya for comment on this chapter note and have borrowed large chunks from his lecture on the same topic in 2014.
2. I will just touch upon it to tie it up with the rest of the discussion.
3. This facet has been encapsulated in the term 'fictitious commodity' by Polyani—a term with which I am not at all comfortable.

6

Primitive Accumulation: Concepts and Debates

Rajesh Bhattacharya

Introduction: Primitive Accumulation and Marx's Critique of Political Economy

Marx engaged with the notion of primitive accumulation to contest the dominant "bourgeois" history of his times, which sought to naturalize, eternalize and legitimize the emerging capitalist economy. Marx argued that the historic transition from pre-capitalism to capitalism involved the reorganization of society which required violence—including wars, robbery and coercion by the state to undermine existing pre-capitalist modes of production.

In classical political economy, there are vague references in Smith (1776) to a prior accumulation of stock that enabled capitalists to employ workers in production.

> As soon as stock has accumulated in the hands of particular persons, some of them will naturally employ it in setting to work industrious people, whom they will supply with materials and subsistence, in order to make a profit by the sale of their work, or by what their labour adds to the value of the materials. In exchanging the complete manufacture either for money, for

* This chapter is based on Bhattacharya, Rajesh. (2010). "Capitalism in Post-Colonial India: Primitive Accumulation Under Dirigiste and Laissez Faire Regimes". Unpublished PhD dissertation, University of Massachusetts, Amherst.

> labour, or for other goods, over and above what may be sufficient to pay the price of the materials, and the wages of the workmen, something must be given for the profits of the undertaker of the work who hazards his stock in this adventure. (Smith, 1776, p. 48)

Marx ridiculed the bourgeois view in the following words.

> This primitive accumulation plays in Political Economy about the same part as original sin in theology. Adam bit the apple, and thereupon sin fell on the human race. Its origin is supposed to be explained when it is told as an anecdote of the past. In times long gone by there were two sorts of people; one, the diligent, intelligent, and, above all, frugal elite; the other, lazy rascals, spending their substance, and more, in riotous living. The legend of theological original sin tells us certainly how man came to be condemned to eat his bread in the sweat of his brow; but the history of economic original sin reveals to us that there are people to whom this is by no means essential. Never mind! Thus it came to pass that the former sort accumulated wealth, and the latter sort had at last nothing to sell except their own skins. And from this original sin dates the poverty of the great majority that, despite all its labour, has up to now nothing to sell but itself, and the wealth of the few that increases constantly although they have long ceased to work. Such insipid childishness is every day preached to us in the defence of property (Marx, 1912, pp. 784-785).

At the abstract-theoretical level, Marx criticized this view for failing to understand the distinctive class nature of capitalism.

Marx argued that primitive accumulation must be understood as a process that produces conditions of existence of the productive capitalist class relations, in which the capitalists' profit originates in the sphere of production through appropriation of the surplus value produced by wage-labourers. One of the conditions of existence of the productive capitalist class structure is therefore the presence of dispossessed labourers who are compelled to sell their labour-power as a commodity in return for wages. Marx therefore emphasized the forceful dispossession and proletarianization of the peasants and artisans as the central moment of primitive accumulation.

At the concrete-historical level, Marx also contested the view that hoarding, saving or abstinence explain the original accumulation of the capitalists. He argued that a whole range of economic processes were responsible for the emergence of the capitalists. Colonial plunder, the national debt, international credit system, taxation policies and the protectionist trade policies were all instrumental in "manufacturing the manufacturers" (Marx, 1912, p. 830). Marx places emphasis on "enclosures" in accounting for the creation of free wage-labourers. "Enclosures" refer to forcible private or state acts of expropriation of the agricultural producers from their land, which was also their chief means of production. The dispossessed labourers were then whipped into factories through "bloody legislations" against vagabonds, beggars and robbers. Eradication of holidays, game laws that closed hunting grounds to people for self-provisioning, the attack on the "sloths" and wage-legislations were pressed into service for the consolidation of the capitalist class-structure[1]. The nation-states played a crucial role in the so-called primitive accumulation by adopting policies that facilitated the destruction of non-capitalist production units[2] and consequent proletarianization of independent producers and by helping the ascendant bourgeois amass massive wealth. Thus, Marx located *violence* right at the heart of the historic process by which capitalism emerged.[3]

Marx's critique of the bourgeois notion of primitive accumulation is centred on the notion of "dispossession"—i.e. separation of direct producers from any property or control over means of production. For Marx, this rupture of the unity of direct producers with means of production, under certain conditions, precipitates an encounter between owners of capital on the one hand and dispossessed, i.e. "free" labourers—"freed" of means of production and of non-capitalist class relations—on the other hand. This encounter is crucial for the emergence of the capitalist fundamental class relation.[4]

Primitive Accumulation and the Teleology of Historical Materialism

In historicizing primitive accumulation, Marx unfortunately also prepared the ground for the subsumption of primitive accumulation to the Marxian *theory* of transition. The latter is a product of essentialist Marxian historiography—which we know as "historical materialism"—that periodizes history in terms of the dominant mode of production of a society. In its most essentialist version, historical materialism claims that auto-development of the forces of production provides the motor force of history, forcing those changes in relations of production and corresponding changes in the superstructure that are best suited to the development of the forces of production. In its most teleological version, historical materialism presents a certain law of linear succession of modes of production culminating in communism—each succeeding mode of production being more technologically advanced than the one before.

The dominant understanding of Marx's notion of primitive accumulation, grounded in historical materialism, runs as follows. Primitive accumulation precipitates an encounter between owners of capital on the one hand and dispossessed labourers on the other hand. Once created, capital reproduces this separation/dispossession on an expanded scale. The teleology inherent in the historical materialist framework leads to the conclusion that primitive accumulation has a singular, irreversible outcome—it prepares the path for the emergence of capitalism and the inevitable destruction of non-capitalist production based on petty private property as well as communal property[5]. With the development of capitalist production based on exploitation of wage-labour, with the *real subsumption of labour*, the radical transformation of the labour process in capitalist production and introduction of machinery, capitalist production creates the conditions for its final victory.

The assumption of continuous and irreversible development of forces of production dictates that *lower* forms of production must yield to *higher* forms.[6] Unlike an open-ended history of capital—which must recognize the contingency of any social conjuncture—historical materialism presents a *logical* history of capital in which a) the capitalist mode of production is superior to pre-capitalist modes in terms of the development of the forces of production and therefore b) history is fated to unfold in favour of capitalism so long as it supports the continuous development of the forces of production. The historical journey through modes of production—rationally ordered by developing forces of production—endows capital with a *universal* face. As a higher form of production, capital is pre-destined to enfold the entire space of production by dissolving the pre-capitalist "outside".

If and whenever non-capitalist production appears within a capitalist social formation, the dominant tendency within the Marxian tradition has been to treat it as a i) resilient pre-capitalist residue (in a conjuncture of 'blocked' transition), ii) a transitional feature or iii) a non-capitalist articulation of the circuit of productive capital (for example, non-capital as source of cheap labour-power and raw materials). Historical materialism does not recognize radical *differences* at the level of the economic, or in other words, does not admit any intrinsic *limits* of capital.

In the scheme of historical materialism, primitive accumulation plays a very distinct role. Primitive accumulation refers to those processes *within a non-capitalist social formation* that produced the conditions of existence of the capitalist mode of production and thus belongs to the pre-history of capital, or in Marx's words, forms "the prelude to the history of capital". In so far as primitive accumulation is the condition of the *arising* or *becoming* of capital, i.e. the historic *presupposition* of the capitalist class relation, it ceases to exist once that relation has arisen.[7]

> The conditions and presuppositions of the *becoming*, of the *arising*, of capital presupposes precisely that it is not yet in being but merely in *becoming*; they therefore disappear as real capital arises, capital which itself, on the basis of its own reality, posits the conditions for its realization. (Marx, 1973, p. 459)

According to this Hegelian understanding, primitive accumulation is the *becoming* of the capitalist mode of production, which, once become, can secure its conditions of existence by itself, in accordance with its immanent laws. That is, *capital-as-being* is *self-positing* (the profits of capital constitute new funds for investment), *self-reproducing* (expanded reproduction is possible based on mutual interaction between Departments I and II) and *self-subsisting* (its natural, economic, political and cultural conditions of existence are secured through payments out of the expanded surplus value possible in capitalist production). Marx's treatment of primitive accumulation is thus fraught with what Cullenberg and Chakrabarty calls the "metaphysics of full presence", i.e. a notion of capital as a "closed totality" fully comprehensible in and by itself. Capital can exist and reproduce itself independent of its "outside"—i.e. non-capital has no constitutive determination on capital.

Salience of Primitive Accumulation: Contemporary Departures from the Classical Concept

The contemporary literature on primitive accumulation makes two 'departures' from the classical Marxist account of primitive accumulation—namely, the understanding of primitive accumulation as an ongoing process and the recognition of an "outside" of capital.

The first departure has freed the concept of primitive accumulation from its confinement to the discourse on third world capitalist development, where, it had so far been argued, primitive accumulation is an ongoing process because the transition to capitalism is yet to be "completed". In contrast, contemporary critics argue that primitive accumulation takes place even in social formations where the capitalist class process has long been dominant.[8] To substantiate their view, these authors draw from Marx's rich analysis of primitive accumulation in *Capital* Vol. I. In particular they draw attention to the many different processes Marx referred to as moments of primitive accumulation and conclude that '[a]ll the features of primitive accumulation that Marx mentions have remained powerfully present within capitalism's historical geography up to now' (Harvey, 2003, p. 145).

According to these authors, privatization—which has been vigorously unleashed in developed as well as developing countries in the last three decades of "neoliberal" capitalism—is considered an outstanding example of primitive accumulation. The significant presence of the state in production and distribution of economic goods and services, supported by particular political institutions and cultural norms that were erected in welfare-states of richer countries, had created social "commons" that are now being destroyed by commoditization and privatization under what is referred to as "neoliberal capitalism" (De Angelis, 2001; Harvey, 2003, 2006)[9]. Outside the developed world, the integration of former Soviet Bloc countries and China to global capitalist relations constitutes an act of "primitive accumulation" in the classical sense in so far as huge assets are transferred from the state sector to the (global) private capitalist sector (Harvey, 2003). Basu (2007) draws a direct parallel between English enclosures of the 17th and 18th century and forcible acquisition of farmland by the Indian government for setting up of Special Economic Zones in the last decade[10]. However, Harvey (2003, 2006) argues that novel forms of privatization emerged and consolidated under neoliberalism.

> The corporatization, commodification and privatization of hitherto public assets has been a signal feature of the neoliberal project. Its primary aim has been to open up new fields for capital accumulation in domains hitherto regarded off-limits to the calculus of profitability. Public utilities of all kinds (water, telecommunications, transportation), social welfare provision (social housing, education, health care, pensions), public institutions (such as universities, research laboratories, prisons) and even warfare (as illustrated by the 'army' of private contractors operating alongside the armed forces in Iraq) have all been privatized to some degree throughout the capitalist world (Harvey, 2006, p. 153)

Similarly, Andreasson (2006) points to an expanding sphere of dispossession based on an extension of private property regimes not only by traditional means, but also, and increasingly so, by more sophisticated and novel means like "intellectual property rights"[11].

Harvey's influential and provocative account of "accumulation by dispossession"—a term he prefers to "primitive accumulation"— remains at the centre of the contemporary debate. In Harvey's understanding, the operations of "accumulation by dispossession" exceed the sphere of privatization. For example, the operations of financial markets—characterized by speculation, fraud and predation—

facilitate large-scale redistribution of wealth in favour of global corporate capital.

> Stock promotions, ponzi schemes, structured asset destruction through inflation, asset stripping through mergers and acquisitions, the promotion of levels of debt incumbency that reduced whole populations, even in the advanced capitalist countries, to debt peonage, to say nothing of corporate fraud, dispossession of assets (the raiding of pension funds and their decimation by stock and corporate collapses) by credit and stock manipulations—all of these became central features of the capitalist financial system (Harvey, 2006, p. 154)

Further, the "neoliberal" state itself engages in redistributive policies—from lower income to upper income social classes as also from public to private domains—through privatization but also through tax incentives and subsidies to business coupled with a reduction in social expenditure. Internationally, carefully manipulated debt traps (Latin American countries in the 1980s and 1990s) and financial crises (Asian crisis in 1997-1998) have resulted in transfer of wealth from poorer to richer countries. Crises lead to devaluation of assets, which are subsequently seized by corporate capital. Nation-states and international organizations like the World Bank, IMF etc. work in tandem to enable "accumulation of dispossession" through careful management of crises.

These authors, who argue that primitive accumulation is an ongoing process integrated to the processes of accumulation of capitalism, have taken up a variety of theoretical positions. Marx's notion of primitive accumulation combined both the aspects of redistribution (enrichment) and dispossession (separation). However, for Marx, in the context of classical transition, the emphasis was on *enrichment as a means of separation*. Contemporary positions can be distinguished on the basis of relative emphasis placed on either of these two aspects of primitive accumulation. De Angelis (2001), for example, argues that "separation" of the direct producers from the means of production is a central category of Marx's theory and pervades the entire space of capital. According to De Angelis, both capitalist accumulation and primitive accumulation can be understood in terms of the category of separation. Primitive accumulation is the *ex novo* production of the separation while capitalist accumulation is the reproduction of separation on a greater scale. The crucial point De Angelis emphasizes is that capitalist accumulation is, in the final analysis, a reproduction of capital-labour relation itself—on an expanded scale. For capitalist accumulation, it is crucial not only to maintain initial "separation", but also raise it to a higher degree. De Angelis goes on to say that "the difference between accumulation and primitive accumulation, not being a substantive one, is a difference in the conditions and forms in which this *separation* is implemented" (De Angelis, 2001, p. 5).

Harvey's concept of "accumulation by dispossession" focuses more on the "enrichment" aspect than on the "separation" aspect—prompting Brenner (2006) to argue that Harvey's position is closer to Smith's ("enrichment" or previous accumulation of stock) than Marx's ("separation" or creation of "free" labour power). In fact, Harvey seems to focus more on *separation as a means of enrichment*, contrary to Marx.

> If the main achievements of neoliberalism have been redistributive rather than generative, then ways had to be found to transfer assets and redistribute wealth and income either from the mass of the population towards the upper classes or from vulnerable to richer countries. (Harvey, 2006, p. 153)

A position somewhat similar to Harvey's but with a rather distinctive theoretical articulation is found in Basu (2007, 2008). Basu argues that through primitive accumulation, global capital acquires exclusive control over markets, resources of production, etc. By virtue of these exclusive property rights, global capital occupies the position of a landlord (or any monopoly owner of conditions of production) who earns "ground rent" by providing access to such monopolized item. Dispossession does not necessarily imply an expansion of capitalist class structure. Capital might well leave production outside itself while securing ground rent from such a non-capitalist production space by providing access to monopolized means of production used in it.

Sanyal (2007) articulates a third position in the context of postcolonial capitalist development. He argues that capitalist accumulation includes the moment of primitive accumulation. But primitive accumulation may not lead to an exploitative relation—capitalist class exploitation based on appropriation of surplus value from wage-labourers— but to the emergence of a "surplus" labour force dispossessed yet excluded from the capitalist class relations. Political conditions for continued capitalist accumulation then require that the "surplus" population be addressed in terms of welfarist governance—which takes the form of specific interventions to ensure livelihoods for the excluded labour force and requires a flow of surplus from the domain of capital to its outside to re-unite excluded labour with means of production in economic activities for satisfaction of "needs". Thus conditions of existence of capitalist accumulation are secured through two simultaneous and contradictory processes—primitive accumulation, which enables a flow of means of production from the non-capitalist space to the capitalist space, and welfarist governance that necessitates a flow of surplus[12] in the reverse direction. In Sanyal, both the aspects of enrichment and separation are important because together they account for a basic inescapable dualism in the postcolonial economy—the dualism between the capitalist and the non-capitalist sub-economies. However, both enrichment and separation are contradictory moments in Sanyal. Redistribution of means of production in favour of capitalists—the substance of primitive accumulation—is contradicted by the transfer of surplus value from the capitalist to the non-capitalist economy enabling the latter to gain some access to means of production. The dispossession of non-capitalist producers—the effect of primitive accumulation—is contradicted by the subsequent re-unification of dispossessed producers with means of production, within the non-capitalist economy, under welfarist governance.

The dominant[13] tendency in the contemporary literature on primitive accumulation is to emphasize the predatory as opposed to the (class) exploitative face of capital. *Predatory* capital seizes the resources that act as means and conditions of non-capitalist production, whereas *(class) exploitative* capital seizes the dispossessed non-capitalist producers and transform them into wage-labourers in order to pump surplus value out of them. According to the classical Marxian position, primitive accumulation creates the institution of wage-labour market, which is a condition of existence of the capitalist fundamental class process. The contemporary literature points to a new problematic—how primitive accumulation can be understood independent of its labour-market effects.

Let us now turn to the second critique of the traditional notion of primitive accumulation thrown up in the contemporary debate. What emerges in the contemporary debate is recognition of the "limits of capital"—the constraints on the self-reproduction of capital. Central to the contemporary debate on primitive accumulation is the notion of the "outside"[14]. The "outside" is the non-capitalist social space (economy, politics and culture) in a capitalist social formation. There are at least three different notions of the "outside" in the contemporary literature. *First*, there is the *given* "outside" of capital—for example, non-capitalist production spaces based on surviving traditional community rights over means of production and subsistence, the peasants' continued attachment to land, etc. *Second*, there is the "outside" that is a product of resistance to capital. This notion of a *resistant* "outside" includes state welfare institutions created under public pressure to provide direct use-values to the citizens, "commons" created by radical communities, squatter settlements or slums in urban metropolises that are also production hubs of mainly self-employed producers, legal barriers to exploitation achieved through militant workers' movements, etc.[15]

The *third* notion of "outside" is more complicated—since it requires us to recognize that capital may actively produce this outside as a result of its own development. Capital may not be able to secure its conditions of existence internally. Capital may require a facilitative "outside" to stabilize itself, particularly in moments of crisis of reproduction. In this sense, capital may even manufacture it, "create" the "outside" at one point only to destroy it at another point when capital hits its own limits. As Brenner observes, " what makes the primitive accumulation and accumulation by dispossession such essential concepts is precisely the implied recognition that *capital is powerfully limited in the degree to which it can create the conditions for its own expansion*" (Brenner, 2006, pp. 99-100, Italics mine). This "outside" itself provides conditions for capitalist accumulation. According to Harvey (2003),

> capitalism necessarily and always creates its own 'other'. The idea that some sort of 'outside' is necessary therefore has relevance. But capitalism can either make use of some pre-existing outside.......or *it can actively manufacture it*.......capitalism always requires a fund of assets *outside of itself* if it is to confront and circumvent pressures of overaccumulation. If those assets, such as empty land or new raw material sources, do not lie to hand, *then capitalism must somehow produce them* (Harvey (2003, pp. 141, 143), italics mine)

In Harvey's analysis, capitalism in advanced countries has been undergoing a crisis of profitability since the 1970s. The dominant strategy to overcome the crisis, according to Harvey, has been primitive accumulation because "[w]hat accumulation by dispossession does it to release a set of assets (including labour power) at very low (and in some cases zero) cost. Over-accumulated capital can seize hold of such assets and immediately turn them to profitable use" (Harvey, 2003, p. 149). In contrast, Sanyal argues that Marxist theorists have generally located the articulation of capital with its "outside" at the level of the *economic*. Instead, he argues that the "outside" may simply be non-functional for the economic reproduction of the capitalist economy. The logic of the articulation of capital and its "outside", in that case, has to be located at the level of the *political* and the *ideological/cultural*.

There is a long lineage of all three notions of "outside" in Marxist literature.[16] Rosa Luxemburg's under-consumptionist theory of the capitalist mode of production famously argued for the necessity of a non-capitalist space for the realization of the surplus component of the value of a capitalist commodity. Though her theoretical arguments have been challenged and contradicted by later Marxists, her idea that a purely internal reproduction of capital is impossible remains influential. Lenin's theory of imperialism provided another role of the "outside" as the absorber of 'surplus' capital of the imperialist countries—where 'surplus' capital refers to a situation where it is relatively unprofitable to invest within the capitalist economy due to a falling rate of profit, thus necessitating an outward flow of capital to non-capitalist colonies[17]. Some writers like Meillassoux (1972) and Wolpe (1972) argued that a non-capitalist "outside" is required to cheapen the value of labour power in so far as a part of the reproduction costs of labour power is borne by the "outside".

Irrespective of whether the "outside" is resistant, facilitative or both at the same time, the resilience of the "outside" gives primitive accumulation its enduring character. Primitive accumulation is unleashed either i) to overcome the resistance the "outside" poses to the reproduction of capital or ii) to secure the conditions of reproduction and expansion of capitalist class processes by appropriating the space of the "outside", whenever it is impossible to do so internally. It is in this sense that primitive accumulation is crucial not only for the emergence of the capitalist mode of production, but also in securing the conditions of its reproduction. The recognition of a resilient "outside" forces the Marxian theorist to accept the inescapable and indissoluble heterogeneity of the economy. At the same time, the notion of *universal* capital that underpinned classical Marxian ontology of capital makes way for a notion of capital that must negotiate with its "outside" in order to secure its conditions of reproduction. The theoretical challenge before the Marxian tradition is, therefore, to produce an understanding of primitive accumulation that accounts for the reproduction of *both* capital and its "outside".

Primitive Accumulation and the Reproduction of Capital

We will show how productive capital and primitive accumulation mutually constitute each other. Let us revisit the circuit of productive capital.

$$M - C - P\,[LP, MP] - C' - M'$$

Each constituent part of the circuit has natural, economic, political and cultural conditions of existence. Securing such conditions of existence may involve processes that lead to the separation of direct producers from the means of production in non-capitalist class processes.

The capitalist begins the circuit by securing the means of production and labour power. The capitalist may purchase means of production and labour power as commodities in the market. Means of production may be capitalist as well as non-capitalist commodities; in the latter case, the capitalists create a market for and hence provide a condition of existence of non-capitalist production. But capitalists may also acquire such non-capitalist means of production as use-values through extra-economic means—such as forcible acts of expropriation—which lead to a dissolution of non-capitalist production. Primitive accumulation becomes particularly significant when some means of production (land) are presumedly in 'limited' supply to the society as a whole. In such a case, reproduction of productive capital may involve appropriation of non-capitalist means of production. Capitalists may secure supplies of commoditized labour power from the natural increase of the labour force, from labour force retrenched by capital itself or by dispossessing non-capitalist producers. What is essential for productive capital is a supply of labour power without access to means of production; primitive accumulation is only one mode of securing such supply. Further, whenever primitive accumulation is involved, capitalists may secure labour power minus the means of production from which it has been separated or secure means of production minus the labour power separated from them.

Let us now enter the realm of capitalist production. We have already seen how separation is one condition of existence of capitalist surplus value. Separation from means of production forces direct producers to produce surplus value for the capitalists. Conversely, the performance of surplus labour in the capitalist fundamental class process may lead to separation of direct producers from means of production in non-capitalist fundamental class processes. Dispossession is simultaneously the cause and effect of the production of capitalist surplus value and thus they mutually constitute each other. One such mechanism involves "production externalities"—e.g. ecological changes including pollution and depletion of natural resources (De Angelis (2004)). Production of "industrial waste" may lead to devaluation and/or destruction of means of production of direct producers outside the capitalist enterprises. The numerous natural processes (chemical, biological, geological etc.) occurring together with the labour process in the capitalist class process may erode the means of production in non-capitalist class processes. This conceptually amounts to a transfer of means of production from non-capitalist to capitalist class process *to the extent* that capitalist enterprises do not pay non-capitalist enterprises for such "use" of their means of production. The rate of surplus-value may be positively related to the rate of such unrecorded "dispossession".

Further, recognition of the ecological impact of capitalism in the face of a growing environmental movement leads to legislations that legally ban certain methods of production. Many production units have to be shut down if they do not conform to the environmental standards. In the changed situation, many small non-capitalist production units who are unable to make such expensive transformations in the labour process are shut down, even when their net contribution to such ecological damage is insignificant and even when the means of production causing pollution may themselves be capitalist commodities. This has the peculiar effect of "gentrification" of production and consumption—akin to the "clearing of the estates" in 18th century Britain. The point is not to deny the environmental problem, but to add a particular class-perspective to the effects of such desirable environmental legislations. Conservation of forests and wildlife has in fact been one of the biggest instances of primitive accumulation all over the world involving the abrogation of community rights over forest products.[18]

The sale and consumption of capitalist commodities requires certain natural, economic, political and cultural conditions. Advertisement of capitalist products may erode the market of non-capitalist commodities through cultural devaluation of the latter. Similar cultural devaluation of non-capitalist commodities may occur in other ways too. For example, one of the cultural conditions of the existence of capitalism is the exalted status of "science" in popular imagination maintained through the educational system, media and the state. One of the hallmarks of modernism is the idea of a sharp divide between the "age of science" and the "age of faith"—the divide coinciding often with the historic divide between pre-capitalism and capitalism. According to this idea, for example, traditional non-capitalist health commodities are *devalued* because they do not involve "scientific" analysis standardized by modern educational institutions and giant corporate health enterprises. One effect of such a cultural discourse is to destroy the market for non-capitalist health products leading to the progressive devaluation and "erosion" of non-capitalist means of production. It is altogether a different story that traditional non-capitalist products may subsequently reappear as capitalist products—in the wake of a growing criticism of modern medicines and appreciation of traditional solutions to health problems. It is much like the weavers' spindles Marx talks about—the weavers having lost their spindles find the same waiting for them inside a capitalist factory (Marx, 1912)

The consumption of capitalist commodities—the process of consumption itself—may have "consumption externalities" which have similar effects as production externalities. The proliferation of capitalist commodities—whose consumption produces "waste"— has negative ecological outcomes including those that erode the means of production of non-capitalist enterprises. The particular culture of consumption associated with capitalism accelerates the production of such waste. Consider the peculiar cultural process of individuation of entertainment under capitalism—the same TV programme is watched privately by millions of individuals involving millions of separate electrical connections and TV sets, etc. The individuation of consumption—which is the same as expansion of the market for capitalist commodities—also expands the production of consumption-related "waste". Moreover, the multiplication of capitalist commodities require a particular expansion of the *space* for consumption—shopping malls, residential spreads, exclusive private parks and resorts, gated communities, roads for geographically dispersed consumption. All these require infrastructure and power, the expansion of which may lead to expropriation of direct producers from their means of production, most importantly, land.

By recognizing the mutual constitutivity of primitive accumulation and reproduction of capital, the new understanding of primitive accumulation locates violence right at the heart of capitalism, where capital must always face its "outside".

REFERENCES

Althusser, L. (2006) *Philosophy of the Encounter: Later Writings, 1978-1987*. Verso: London and New York.

Andreasson, S. (2006) "Stand and Deliver: Private Property and the Politics of Global Dispossession", *Political Studies*, 54 (1): 3–22.

Basu, P.K. (2008) *Globalisation: An Anti Text; A Local View*. Delhi: Aakar Books.

Basu, P.K. (2007) "Political Economy of Land Grab", *Economic and Political Weekly*, 42 (14): 1281–87.

Boyle, J. (2002) "Fencing Off Ideas: Enclosure and the Disappearance of the Public Domain", *Daedalus*, 131(2): 13-25.

Bradby, B. (1975) "The Destruction of the Natural Economy", *Economy and Society*, 4(2): 127-161.

Brenner, R. (2006) "What Is, and What Is Not, Imperialism?", *Historical Materialism*, 14 (4): 79–105.

Chandra, P. and Dipankar B. (February 7, 2007). "Neoliberalism and Primitive Accumulation in India", *Radical Notes*, available at http://radicalnotes.com/content/view/32/30/ (accessed on 28th January 2014).

De Angelis, M. (September, 2001). "Marx and Primitive Accumulation: The Continuous Character of Capital's Enclosures", *The Commoner*, 2, http://www.commoner.org.uk/02deangelis.pdf (accessed on 2nd 2015).

De Angelis, M. (2006). "Enclosures, Commons and the "Outside."" Paper presented at the annual meeting of the International Studies Association, Town & Country Resort and Convention Centre, San Diego, California. http:// www.allacademic.com/meta/p100277_index.html (accessed on 23rd June 2014).

Government of India (2004). *Foreign Trade Policy 2004-2009*. New Delhi.

Directorate General of Foreign Trade, Ministry of Commerce and Industry, available at http://dgftcom.nic.in/exim/2000/policy/chap-07.htm (accessed January 7, 2010).

Harvey, D. (2003) *The New Imperialism*, Oxford University Press: New York.

Harvey, D. (2006). "Neo-liberalism as Creative Destruction", *Geografiska Annaler*, 88 B (2): 145–158.

Kawashima, K.C. (2005). "Capital's Dice-Box Shaking: The Contingent Commodifications of Labour Power", *Rethinking Marxism*, 17(4): 609-626.

Marx, K. (1912). *Capital*. Vol. I, Chicago. Charles H. Kerr and Company.

Marx, K. (1973). *Grundrisse*. Penguin Books: London.

Meillassoux, C. (1972). "From Reproduction to Production: A Marxist Approach to Economic Anthropology", *Economy and Society*, 1(1): 93-105.

Perelman, M. (2000). *The Invention of Capitalism: Classical Political Economy and the Secret History of Primitive Accumulation*. Duke University Press: Durham.

Perspectives (2008). *Abandoned*. The Perspectives Team: Delhi.

Sanyal, K.K. (2007). *Rethinking Capitalist Development: Primitive Accumulation, Governmentality and The Post-colonial Capitalism*, Routledge: London and New York.

Smith, A. (1776). *The Wealth of Nations*. The Modern Library, 1937: New York,.

Wolpe, H. (1972). "Capitalism and Cheap Labour-Power in South Africa: From Segregation to Apartheid", *Economy & Society*, 1(4): 425-456.

NOTES

1. See Perelman (2000).
2. See Marx (1912).
3. "Force is the midwife of every old society pregnant with a new one" (Marx, 1912, p. 824).
4. "The process, therefore, that clears the way for the capitalist system, can be none other than the process which takes away from the labourer the possession of his means of production; a process that transforms, on the one hand, the social means of subsistence and production into capital, on the other, the immediate producers into wage-labourers. *The so-called primitive accumulation, therefore, is nothing else than the historical process of divorcing the producer from the means of production*." (Marx, 1912, p. 786. Italics mine)

5. According to Marx, at the time of writing of *Capital*, in "Western Europe...the process of primitive accumulation is more or less accomplished. Here the capitalist regime has either directly conquered the whole domain of national production, or, where economic conditions are less developed it, at least, indirectly controls those strata of society which, though belonging to the antiquated mode of production, continue to exist side by side with it in gradual decay." (Marx, 1912, p. 838)
6. "This [petty] mode of production pre-supposes parceling of the soil, and scattering of the other means of production. As it excludes the concentration of these means of production, so also it excludes co-operation, division of labor within each separate process of production, the control over and the productive application of the forces of Nature by society, and the free development of the social productive powers. It is compatible only with a system of production, and a society, moving within narrow and more or less primitive bounds. To perpetuate it would be.... " to decree universal mediocrity". At a certain stage of development it brings forth the material agencies for its own dissolution. ....but the old social organization fetters them and keeps them down. It must be annihilated; *it is annihilated*. Its annihilation, the transformation of the individualized and scattered means of production into socially concentrated ones, of the pigmy property of many into the huge property of the few, the expropriation of the great mass of people from the soil, from the means of subsistence, and from the means of labour, this fearful and painful expropriation of the masses of the people forms *the prelude to the history of capital*." (Marx, 1912, p. 835, italics mine)
7. This Hegelian being-becoming distinction has dominated latter Marxist writings on primitive accumulation. Marxists have generally tended to treat primitive accumulation as a concrete historical process that has no theoretical bearing on the ontology of capital. The concept of "primitive accumulation" has thus long come to be confined to the field of economic history, except occasional application in studies of capitalism in developing economies, and that too only because it is assumed that the history of the rise of capitalism in the West is replicated in the developing countries experiencing capitalist development.
8. "The disadvantage of these assumptions [in the traditional understanding of primitive accumulation] is that they relegate accumulation based on predation, fraud, and violence to an

'original stage' that is considered no longer relevant or, as with Luxemburg, as being somehow 'outside of' capitalism as a closed system." (Harvey, 2003, p. 144)

9. "The rolling back of regulatory frameworks designed to protect labour and the environment from degradation has entailed the loss of rights. The reversion of common property rights won through years of hard class struggle (the right to a state pension, to welfare, to national health care) into the private domain has been one of the most egregious of all policies of dispossession pursued in the name of neoliberal orthodoxy. All of these processes amount to the transfer of assets from the public and popular realms to the private and class-privileged domains". (Harvey, 2006, p. 153)
10. These SEZs are literally described as "foreign territory" outside the purview of the laws of the country. Business enterprises in SEZs are exempt from tax and other financial payments to the state in the same way that owners of enclosed land in England were spared all their obligations to the state. Further, labour laws are relaxed in these SEZs to allow increased exploitation of labour—enhancing coercive power of the capitalists vis-à-vis workers and constituting new versions of "bloody legislations" against labour. According to Foreign Trade Policy (2004-09) of India, 'SEZ is a specifically delineated duty free enclave and shall be deemed to be foreign territory for the purposes of trade operations, duties and tariffs' (Government of India, 2004: §7.1).
11. Also see Harvey (2006), Basu (2008). Boyle (2002) refers to "the enclosure of the intangible commons of the mind" as the "new kind of enclosure movement".
12. From a class-analytic point of view, strictly speaking, there cannot be a flow of *surplus* from one class-structure to another. What Sanyal means is that surplus value appropriated by the capitalists may be taxed by the state to provide some of the conditions of existence of non-capitalist class processes and the non-capitalist appropriators of surplus then receive such benefits from the state as non-class revenues. Alternatively, the capitalists may themselves use a part of the surplus value appropriated within the capitalist fundamental class process to provide certain conditions of existence of non-capitalist enterprises without involving the state.
13. Exceptions are De Angelis (2001), Kawashima (2005), Chandra and Basu (2007), etc.
14. Harvey (2003), De Angelis (2006), Sanyal (2007).

15. "The entitlements and rights guaranteed by the post-war welfare state for example, can be understood as the institutionalisation in particular *forms* of social commons. Together with high growth policies, the implementation of full employment policies and the institutionalization of productivity deals, the welfare state was set to accommodate people's expectations after two world wars, the Soviet revolution, and a growing international union movement. Therefore, the global current neoliberal project, which in various ways targets the social commons created in the post war period set itself as a modern form of enclosure, dubbed by some as "new enclosures" (De Angelis, 2001, p. 19).
16. See Bradby (1975) for a detailed discussion of the various Marxist positions mentioned here.
17. Harvey's use of the notion of "outside" takes as a point of departure the Luxemburg thesis, though he locates the problematic of the "outside" in the context of over-accumulation of capital rather than the under-consumption problem. In this sense Harvey's argument is closer to Lenin's.
18. In India, perhaps the single biggest act of primitive accumulation was not an act of privatization but rather its opposite—the establishment of state control over forests—first in the name of "scientific forestry" during the British rule and later in the name of "wildlife conservation" in independent India. Forests comprise one-fourth of the geographical area of India—and ninety-five per cent of the forest area is legally owned by the state (Perspectives, 2008, p. 37). This act of appropriation of the forest land resulted in the loss of the traditional livelihood of forest dwellers and local communities who were crucially dependent on the forests for their means of subsistence and production.

7

Theorizing the Capitalist State[1]

Surajit Mazumdar

The topic of this chapter is very vast and to cover it comprehensively in such a short space would be impossible. Rather than attempting such a futile task, what we shall try to do is think about the nature of the capitalist state in most basic terms with reference to the capitalist mode of production considered in its simple and pure form. Even this limited exercise, however, would serve the very useful purpose of demonstrating that the capitalist state provides one of the best examples for illustrating the key Marxist proposition that the character of any state has to be discerned from the nature of the society from which that it springs and not the other way around.

The state in Marxist theory is a necessary product of the division of society into antagonistic classes with irreconcilable interests and serves the function of maintaining 'order' (as Engels put it) in such a society through the exercise of the coercive power it commands. Thus it helps to maintain that society and its structure of class dominance even though it might appear to stand above the division. The state is therefore always a class state—an instrument serving the interests of the dominant class (es). It follows that the state in capitalism must be a capitalist state. However, more than in other cases the state in capitalism can *appear* to be otherwise precisely in the process of its functioning as a *capitalist* state. In other words it is only when we place what the capitalist state does against the imperatives created by the capitalist mode of production that its true character of being a capitalist state is revealed.

The Capitalist Mode of Production

Since that is to form the basis for our discussion on the capitalist state, let us begin with briefly setting out what we take to be the capitalist mode of production as it was conceptualized by Marx.

The capitalist mode of production is not simply a system of commodity production but one where labour-power, the innate ability of human beings to work, is also a commodity. Underlying that mode is a pattern of property ownership characterized by the effective concentration of the ownership of the means of production in the hands of one class (capitalists), and the consequent parallel existence of a class (workers) separated from such ownership. The latter class therefore has no alternative for its subsistence save the selling of labour-power in the market for a wage, even if it is under no extra-economic compulsion to do so. It is through the purchase of the labour-power of workers by capitalists that individual concentrations of means of production (which themselves being commodities, are also purchased) get combined with the active agent of production, human labour, in the process of production. Each such production, involving the combining of the labour of many, gives rise to commodities possessing a higher value than the value of the means of production and labour-power expended in their production. The key to this expansion of value, or *surplus value*, lies in the difference in the value of labour-power acquired through exchange and the value created by its use in the process of production—in other words the excess labour undertaken by the workers over and above that which reproduces the value expended by capitalists in purchasing their labour power. It is in this specific way that the surplus labour of workers is appropriated in the capitalist mode of production. Once the commodities produced are sold, a circuit of movement that begins with a certain sum of money is completed—the capitalists receive at the end a larger sum of money than they had initially thrown into the process. Thus through this movement (M-C-

C'-M') is achieved the self-expansion of a certain sum of value. This self-expanding value is *capital,* and the mode of existence of capital associated with the capitalist mode is specifically *industrial capital,* that capital whose motion itself creates the surplus value that underlies its self-expansion.

Capitalism thus is a mode of production where production is subordinated to capital or the self-expansion of value.This self-expansion and its reproduction on a larger and larger scale, is the driving logic of the capitalist mode of production.The capitalist is the personification of capital, whose subjective purpose becomes the pursuit of self-expansion that is inherent in capital. This logic is imposed on each individual sum of value functioning as capital by the process of competition between them, a competition that arises from the division of the aggregate social capital into many separate individual capitals. The self-expansion of value in turn involves capitalists constantly striving to translate the contractual right to control the labour process acquired through the purchase of labour into a *real* control against the resistance offered by workers who have to actually labour and whose interests are diametrically opposite to those of capitalists—the capitalist would seek to make the workers work as longer and with greatest intensity at the lowest possible price while the worker would strive for the opposite. This is the incessant struggle that plays itself out through the very working of the capitalist mode which can only be eliminated by the elimination of the conditions of capitalism.

Capitalism and the State

In understanding the role of the capitalist state, both the basic class divide that characterizes the mode as well as the coercive force of competition acting on capitalists need to be brought into the frame.

Capitalism, like any society based on a division into objectively antagonistic classes, requires a state for its maintenance. Yet, in it the mechanism of exploitation directly relies on economic coercion rather than the direct use of political power or social coercion (extra-economic coercion). However, the underlying condition for the operation of economic coercion is the maintenance of a class monopoly over the means of production—and economic coercion is not sufficient to maintain that condition. In other words, the operation of the capitalist mode necessarily requires an authority to exercise extra-economic coercion to protect the property rights of capitalists. That authority is the capitalist state.

No capitalist is, however, a capitalist on account of his private property alone. It is only when there are other capitalists sharing in the class monopoly over the means of production that labour-power would be a commodity. Thus it is not the property of few individuals but of the class as a whole which needs protection. The very operation of the capitalist mode, however means competition between the constituents of this class of capitalists—which implies in turn that each one's property is constantly threatened not only by the propertyless but also by other capitalists. It follows that the function of protecting their property rights cannot be performed directly by the class as each would tend to deploy any extra-economic power they could command to invade the property of other capitalists. In other words, what is needed is protection of the property rights of all capitalists by an authority which stands apart from all of them. Thus, inbuilt into the nature of the capitalist mode is a state that stands apart from the class whose property rights it protects and which might in the process of protecting these rights exercise its coercive powers against capitalists too. Moreover, since it is a class monopoly it protects, such a protection tends to take the outward form of the state being a protector of property rights *in general* when it actually maintains the property of some to ensure the propertylessness of others.

Protecting the class monopoly in ownership of property (or even creating them) and by extension also of commodities through its coercive apparatus is the fundamental and primary function of the capitalist state. There are, however, additional requirements for sustaining capitalism which the mode of production has no inherent mechanisms of providing. In fact, the purely spontaneous working of the system would generate tendencies which would quickly undermine its own basis, making for a wide role of the capitalist state. Like in the case of property rights, the state is required to generalize other essential rules that capitalists cannot impose on each other through the process of competition and where the unrestrained operation of competition might in fact be detrimental to the survival of the system. Let us consider a few such examples, each of which illustrates the almost spontaneous tendency for the capitalist state's character to be camouflaged.

As Marx emphasized, capitalist competition would always generate tendencies towards lengthening of the working day and depressing of the price of labour power—and forced beyond a point these would eliminate the surplus producers themselves. These tendencies would be reinforced by the existence of a reserve army of unemployed whose members can replace those in active employment. Such a reserve army is essential to the working of the capitalist mode since the existence of a potent threat of the sack is a necessary precondition for the imposition of the capitalist's discipline on workers and also for ensuring that the accumulation process is not impeded by the absence of an elastic supply of workers. However, a reserve army also needs to be maintained. In the absence of restraints on that spontaneity from outside the process, the immediate working of the capitalist mode in such conditions would only generate chaos and mayhem rather than steady expansion—either workers would be physically annihilated by the combination of long hours of work and limited consumption or their increasingly desperate situation would induce desperate actions on their part. A disciplining force capable of disciplining *both* sides of that struggle and ensuring that it stays within bounds is therefore necessary if the capitalist mode is to sustain itself for any duration of time. The capitalist state performs this disciplining function but again its character is camouflaged in the same process. On the one hand, there are elements of this function where the state has to impose a discipline on all capitalists through the application of the coercive force it commands—limits on the working day, minimum wage laws, etc., which each one individually is inclined to violate. The same applies also to things like payment of taxes which the state always needs to perform its functions. On the other had the state may also take measures that have the appearance of 'favouring' labour—like providing unemployment allowance or guaranteeing the right of association or formation of trade unions. In doing all of these, however, it does no more than perform its role as a preserver of the capitalist order. The capitalist state may 'discipline' both capitalists and workers but only to preserve the unequal and exploitative relationship between them—to maintain the power capitalists exercise over workers in the sphere of production.

The State and the 'Autonomous' Sphere of Politics

The discussion so far has indicated that the economic and political role of the state is part and parcel of the normal functioning of capitalism and in that sense there can never be any truly 'free-market' capitalism without state intervention. There are many additional dimensions to the economic role of the capitalist state than have been elaborated here, some of them very important—for instance the state is required to manage money or create a social infrastructure without which the capitalist accumulation process cannot continue. More generally the capitalist state has to play a role in imposing some 'order' on the working of a system whose class antagonisms and inherently anarchic and unstable nature constantly threatens its existence. That such a threat does not always *appear* to exist is in fact partly a measure of the success of the capitalist state.

As mentioned, the capitalist state necessarily appears as a force standing apart from the capitalist class because it has to protect capitalism from capitalists themselves.However, capitalist competition also means that all capitalists would be impelled towards trying to influence the use of the state's powers to serve their individual ends. Indeed, such contradictions between the requirements of the capitalist class as a whole and those of individual capitalists recurrently express themselves in the actual working of the state in capitalism—producing variations among concrete capitalisms across time and space.Thus some states are more effective than others in enforcing regulations and making capitalists pay taxes. The phenomenon of corruption almost always goes hand in hand with capitalism but its degree and nature too can vary. In fact, the state which in appearance is most visibly a state *of* capitalists —that which we associate with the term 'crony capitalism' – may actually not be the most effective *capitalist* state as in its case the tilt may be too far in one direction.

Moreover, the 'interventions' by the capitalist state through which it keeps the anarchic nature of the system within limits are not the product of an a priori plan devised by a state that is 'conscious' of its specific responsibility. They in fact are responses forced by the contradictions of capitalism and the struggles that these gives rise to—which also conditions the specific political form assumed by the state.The capitalist character of the state is expressed not by it always acting overtly in favour of capitalists in an identical determined way and independent of what happens in the sphere of politics but by the content of its actions being always in the interests of preserving capitalism. No matter what happens the capitalist state never goes to the extent of threatening the very foundation of the capitalist order—even in the most advanced capitalist democracy with the most developed welfare state, the formal equality before the law does not translate into a real equality. And it is always welfare measures, labour rights, democracy and such things rather than the class inequality of capitalism that are forced to give way when they become incompatible with that class inequality. In other words, the capitalist state does not and cannot eliminate the contradictions of capitalism which constitute the basis for its existence.

From this follows a conclusion which is very important for Marxists who are ultimately interested in a radical social transformation and the emancipation from exploitation. This conclusion is that while there is an 'autonomous' sphere of politics associated with the capitalist mode which exerts an influence on the actual trajectory of capitalist society, the presence of such 'influence' does not mean that the political struggle to take human society beyond capitalism can succeed without it acknowledging both the power of the capitalist state and the need to demolish it. In other words, the capitalist state cannot be converted into an instrument against capitalism nor turned into a passive spectator—it has to be necessarily destroyed.

The 'National' State

Before concluding this discussion on the capitalist state, let us also note one other feature of the capitalist state—at least insofar as it has existed for most of capitalism's history. This is the feature of it being a *national* state despite the fact that capitalism mode has always been the driving force behind the creation and development of a web of economic connections that stretch across the entire world.

Any capitalist state had to emerge out of a process of transition to capitalism from pre-capitalist society. Its formation had to be initially therefore invariably based on the pre-existing economic, social, and political connections existing within some definite territory which created a capitalist class with a unified identity. Once capitalist states had come into being, they themselves became active instruments for expanding the realm of capital beyond the territory of their direct jurisdiction. Indeed such expansion has been one of the important functions of the capitalist state. However, this only reinforced rather than weakened the national character of capitalist states—their association with a definite territory and with a particular capitalist class— and the splitting up of the economic, social and political processes of capitalism into the internal (national) and the external (international). This contradiction between nationally rooted states and an economic system which tends to brook no boundaries and makes use of the state for that purpose has meant that force and conflict, expressing themselves in different ways, have always been part and parcel of the internationalization of capitalism. Colonialism, imperialism and war have served as the more visible expressions of these in the history of capitalism.

In the current age of globalization, it may appear that the national characters of capitalist states are on the decline and a de facto world state is emerging. However, one has to only think of the important economic phenomena associated with globalization—like the volatility of exchange rates and the proneness towards currency crisis or—to see that this is not quite true. Such phenomena are related to the high international mobility of capital in a world of many different *national* currencies and would not arise if there could be a single world state managing the money of a global capitalist system. On the other hand, the high degree of mobility of capital under globalization co-exists with some of the most severe restrictions seen in the history of capitalism on the movement of people and labour across national boundaries. How does one explain these if states are no longer national?

The Capitalist State in India

In this discussion, we have not directly addressed the specific case of the Indian State. What should, however, be emphasized is that applying any understanding of the *capitalist* state to India must always take into account the fact that the history of capitalism in countries like India—where capitalism itself emerged out of the interaction of pre-capitalist society with capitalist colonialism - has created societies which are far more removed from the pure form of capitalism than others. In other words, these are societies where capitalists and workers are not the only two major classes in society and capitalist mechanisms of exploitation co-exist and are integrated with pre-capitalist ones. This must reflect itself in shaping the nature of the state in India and its working—it is advisable therefore to avoid a mechanical application of the analysis of the capitalist state to the Indian context. The Marxist theory of the state itself suggests that.

NOTES

1. Lecture Notes for the South Asian University - Rosa Luxembourg Stiftung Summer School on Marxism: Ramnagar, July 8-17, 2015.

8

Marxian Theories of Crises

Rohit Azad

1. Introduction

Capitalist crises can be understood as a failure in the process of capitalist accumulation. Since accumulation itself is driven by the expectations of profits, a crisis is intrinsically related to a fall in the *expected* rate of profit. Expectations are an important factor here because it is not known *a priori* to a capitalist what the rate of profit is going to be after the product is sold, if at all, as a commodity. In this context, money as capital plays a central role in Marx's theory. Hoarding of money as capital makes it possible to have an *ex ante* decline in output and, hence, of capital accumulation. But hoarding does not cause the crisis. The source of crisis lies elsewhere in the nature of the accumulation process itself.

A careful reading of Marx tells us that he had in mind two interdependent processes running through a crisis—one which related to the average state of accumulation and another related to the movement around that average state of accumulation. In today's terminology, they correspond to theories relating to the trend rate of growth and business cycles respectively. While his argument on the trend rate of growth was based on some 'normal' capacity output, his story on cycles was based on the interaction between demand, reserve army of labour and scrapping of capital at low rates of accumulation.

Marx's theoretical understanding on crises under capitalism

is spread across different sections in *Capital* as well as *Theories of Surplus Value*, henceforth TSV but it is difficult to find a *complete* treatment of crises in either of these works. However, there are two sections in particular which he exclusively spent on dealing with the subject—one in Vol. III on *Capital* (on the tendency of the falling rate of profit) and another in Vol. II of TSV (on crises arising out of disproportionality and overproduction in response to Ricardo's acceptance of the Say's law). It was later in the writings of Marxist writers of different persuasions that the crises theory *per se* becomes a central matter of discussion. This note will try to present a theoretical overview (by no means exhaustive) of the major strands of Marxian theories of crises.

2. Some Concepts

Before we proceed to discussing his theories of crises, it makes sense to define broadly the variables that will come under discussion. While his labour theory of value in the sphere of production is the underlying benchmark for the system of prices in the sphere of circulation, except under some extreme conditions, these two systems (value and price systems) do not correspond to each other. Since the purpose here is not a discussion on the transformation between the two systems, we will stick to the prices *ultimately* effected when the product is sold both for reasons of tractability and comparability between different sources of crises. That is not to say that his theory of value is of no importance. It is just so that combining his theory of the trend rate and cyclical nature of accumulation is easier in the price system than otherwise.

The process of accumulation is intrinsically related to the *expected* rate of profit. Before we proceed, we need to discuss what we mean by the rate of profit and what are its determinants. The rest of the introduction is devoted to that purpose.

To understand the rate of profit and its origin, it will be useful to draw the distinction that Marx does between simple commodity production and capitalism. Crudely put, in the former, producers own as well as work on their own means of production, whereas under capitalism the set of people who own the means of production (capitalist class) are different from those who work on it (working class).

Commodities have a use value and an exchange value. Use value represents the qualitative (utility generating) aspect of a commodity. It does not matter whether it is used for material or imaginative needs. On the other hand, its exchange value represents the ratio in which it can be exchanged for any other commodity (including money).

When a producer approaches the market under simple commodity production, she does so to acquire some other commodity which has a better use value for her than the one produced by her. One could, therefore, say that the producer comes to the market with a given amount of the commodity (*C*) she has produced in an attempt to acquire another commodity (*C*). To facilitate this, money acts as a medium of exchange. Marx represented this circuit as Commodity-Money-Commodity, i.e. *C*–*M*–*C*. Commodities are the means and the ends in themselves.

On the other hand, under capitalism, a capitalist enters with money capital (*M*), buys commodities (*C*) necessary for production (labour power and machinery, etc.) and sells the produced commodities (*C*′) in exchange for money (*M*′). As opposed to simple commodity production, here the Marxian circuit is *M*–*C*–*C*′–*M*′. It is obvious that since the begining and the end of the process results in the *same* commodity, i.e. money, the only reason why a capitalist will go into this process is if she *expects* *M*′ to be greater than *M*. Now expectation here is important because it is not known *a priori* whether *M*′ will indeed be greater than *M*. It is this expectation which pushes a capitalist into taking the risk of putting her money capital into the process of production. One can, therefore, define the rate of profit *r* as,

$$r = \frac{M' - M}{M}$$

Can we be more specific about *M* and *M*′? It is clear that this difference in value (*M*′ – *M*), which he calls surplus value, is *generated* in the sphere of production, i.e. from the conversion of C–C′. But what generates it? The means of production when they enter the process of production come with *dead* labour which can be measured in terms of the labour time used up in their production, which can be denoted as the capital stock *K*. These means of production are worked on by *living* labour measured by the labour time spent on production. The surplus value is created by the living labour. Out of the total labour time of living labour, a part goes into its reproduction, i.e. workers' wages *W* and the rest is surplus labour time, which corresponds to the volume of profit *P*. So, no surplus will be generated if all the labour time is equivalent to wages.

Now, we can say that the initial capital is $M = K + W$ if the wages are advanced before the production process has begun and $M' - M = P$, so that the expected rate of profit is

$$r = \frac{P}{K+W} \tag{1}$$

Now it is possible that while the capitalist expected *ex ante* to be able to sell all that can be produced by the employment of labour and capital (Let's denote this level of output as O^*), but *ex post*, this expectation is not realized so the actual output sold is *O*. Corresponding to the expected full capacity output, we have W^*, P^*, K^1.

Having defined the rate of profit, we can now discuss the broad contours of Marx's accumulation process. The rate of accumulation, let's call it g, is dependent on the rate of profit. It is obvious that the trend rate of growth g^* will correspond to the trend rate of profit r^* which is average over the cyclical movement of accumulation. The cyclical movement in *r* results from the changes in *P*, *W*, *K* as we go along. So, as mentioned before, there are two stories intertwined into one in Marx, one corresponding to the average rate of accumulation g^*, which is, as we will see, determined by technological considerations in Marx and external markets in Marxists like Rosa Luxemburg, and the other corresponding to the movement in g, i.e. the cyclical movements over this average g^*.

Money plays a central role in Marx's theory of accumulation and crises. In fact, the story of fluctuating *g* and *r* comes from his theory of money and the role of expectations. The fact that money can be held as capital, i.e. withheld from the process of circulation makes the possibility of a crisis into reality. While money facilitates the possibility of a crisis, it does not cause it. The causation lies in the complex process of expectations, bargaining power of workers, technological changes, etc.

In its role as a means of circulation, let's say money circulates at a velocity of V to be able to effect purchase of the current level of nominal output pO. It also acts as a store of wealth, i.e. hoarding H, one could write,

$$\underbrace{M}_{\text{Money supply}} = \underbrace{\frac{pO}{V}}_{\text{means of circulation}} + \underbrace{H}_{\text{store of wealth}}$$

$$M - H = kpO; \qquad k = \frac{1}{V} \tag{2}$$

For a given supply of money, if the output falls as a result of a fall in the rate of accumulation, capitalist hoard the extra money and wait for the future prospects to improve (notice the central role of expectations). On the other hand, if the output increases, either the hoards are depleted or in the extreme case money supply is increased.

3. Trend vs Cycle

We will separately deal with the discussions on the trend rate of accumulation and the cyclical movements around it.

Theory of Cycles:

For the movement of r, g over time, Marx had something like this as a description. Let's take a period under consideration to explain his cyclical movement. At the initial stages of accumulation, with relatively low rates of employment, the working class is quite weak in its bargaining power (presence of a reserve army of labour) so there is a tendency for the profit shares P/O in the rate of profit) to rise pushing up the rate of profit, which pushes up the rate of accumulation (and output) further resulting in an upswing.

Implicit in this process are the seeds of its own destruction since with increasing rate of accumulation, unemployment falls, which increases the bargaining power of the working class, thereby, putting a downward pressure on the rate of profit through a fall in the share of profits. With the fall in the rate of profit, accumulation also falls till we reach a point at which capital starts getting scrapped (a fall in K), which reinvigorates the rate of profit and the cycle starts again. This is broadly the story of cycle of accumulation in Marx. So, there is a *hypothetical* ceiling to the rate of accumulation corresponding to $r_{max} = \frac{O^*}{K}$, which is associated with full capacity output (and zero wages) and floor to it given by the rate of profit below which scrapping starts taking place. In reality the tipping point after an upswing will start much ahead of hitting this ceiling. The average rate of profit is given by the average through a cycle. Corresponding to this rate of profit is the average rate of accumulation.

Theory of the Trend

So much for the cycles around an average. But Marx also focuses on the average itself. Marx himself discussed the upper ceiling having a tendency to decline over time, a proposition given by the famous tendency of the rate of profit to fall. It is obvious from the discussion above that this average rate of accumulation in Marx is positive, i.e. a case of expanded reproduction of the system over time out of its own accord (without the help on any crutches).

This point about expanded reproduction being the average state of affairs in the absence of external crutches was theoretically questioned by later Marxists like Rosa Luxemburg (her argument will be equivalent to a zero trend rate of growth in our case). On the other hand, Marxists like Bukharin argued that there is no threat to expanded reproduction, i.e. a positive average rate of accumulation. At best there can be crises of disproportionality between the consumption-goods and investment-goods producing sectors but never a case of simple reproduction. We will discuss these three possibilities next.

4. Tendency of the Falling Rate of Profit (TFRP)

Marx had argued that intrinsic in the process of capital accumulation is the source of a crisis which might manifest itself as the process continues. Capitalists strive to push the ceiling of the rate of profit up for which they want to increase P^*/W^*. Now this can take place either through increasing the working hours (increases the overall labour time for the same necessary labour time) or increasing the productivity of labour (total labour time remains the same but is divided more in favour of the surplus labour time because the necessary labour time decreases). Given the limitations to which the former can be relied on to increase the rate of profit, the pressure gets shifted on to increasing labour productivity. There is, however, a paradox in this process according to Marx because this process affects both the numerator as well the denominator of the maximum rate of profit defined above. So, while mechanization could increase P^*/W^*, it also decreases the ratio of living to dead labour $(W^* + P^*)/K^*$, i.e. the inverse of Marx's organic composition of capital. Some manipulation for the maximum rate of profit can give us,

$$r_{max} = \frac{P^*}{O^*} \cdot \frac{O^*}{K^*} \cdot \frac{K^*}{K^* + W^*} \qquad (3)$$

If there exists a tendency towards falling $\frac{W^* + P^*}{K^*} = \frac{O^*}{K^*}$ (which we can call the technologically given output-capital ratio), then the r_{max} *eventually* starts falling because there is an upper limit of 1 to the other two components in the above mentioned relationship. In the extreme case, the minimum level of wages is 0, i.e. capitalist appropriate the entire product $P^*=O^*$, which also means that the last term becomes 1. Beyond this point, W^* cannot be suppressed, thereby, making the falling $\frac{O^*}{K^*}$ the dominating factor in the determination of the ceiling rate of profit. This is the paradoxical effect of increasing labour productivity. Since the ceiling keeps falling over time, the average rate of profit over a cycle.

5. Disproportionality Crises

Later Marxist writers like Bukharin elaborated on the case of expanded reproduction in Marx's theory of accumulation. There are two departments of production: department 1 which produces investment goods and department 2 which produces consumption goods. Assuming that workers consume all their wages and capitalists consume only a small proportion 1 – s of their profits, we can lay out the equilibrium condition for the two sectors. Since we are discussing two sectors, all the components can be defined in terms of wage units. Subscripts 1 and 2 represent the two sectors respectively.

The consumption goods demand has to match the production of department 2.

$$\begin{aligned} \overbrace{W_1 + W_2 + (1-s)(P_1 + P_2)}^{\text{C-goods' demand}} &= \overbrace{W_2 + P_2}^{\text{C-goods' production}} \\ W_1 + (1-s)P_1 &= sP_2 \end{aligned} \tag{4}$$

This equilibrium condition shows that in department 2, the surplus left after their capitalists' consumption should match the consumption demand of the workers and capitalists of department 1.

The same result can be arrived at from the other side. Investment goods demand of the economy has to match the production of department 1.

$$\begin{aligned} \overbrace{s(P_1 + P_2)}^{\text{I-goods' demand}} &= \overbrace{W_1 + P_1}^{\text{I-goods' production}} \\ sP_2 &= W_1 + (1-s)P_1 \end{aligned} \tag{5}$$

So, in so far as this proportion between the two departments is maintained, there is no reason why the economy will not move along an expanded reproduction path given by the averages discussed above, i.e. a positive trend rate of growth. The only case in which there is a crisis is if the actual ratios differ from these ratios in which case unplanned inventories would pile up/run down in either of the sectors.

6. Overproduction Crises

Rosa Luxemburg, however, disagreed with this schema of reproduction by arguing that while there is no *logical* problem in it, there is no *plausible* investment behaviour on the part of the capitalists which can explain it. Taking her point of view, one could argue that there is a strong assumption being made that surplus profits left after capitalists' consumption is *necessarily* going to be invested. Now, there is no reason why this should be the case. While they might want to invest it, the actual act of investment is dependent on expectations about the future.

This point becomes clearer if we look at the second relationship above. On the left hand side, one is assuming that all savings are *ipso facto* demand for investment goods. If this were the case, hoarding of money, an act so central to Marx's theory of accumulation, for purposes other than transaction becomes a non-starter. But Marx was correct in assuming that money acts as a store of value as well, which means that if the capitalists of both the sectors decide (based on the bleak expectations about the future) to withhold a part of their profit as money capital, there will be inventories built up in the I-goods sector, thereby creating a realization crisis.

Taking this argument further, she said that there will be a precipitous fall in the rate of accumulation as a result of this initial fall and the system will reach a situation of simple reproduction (zero trend rate). This can be seen from the rate of profit function.

$$r = \frac{P}{O} \cdot \frac{O}{O^*} \cdot \frac{O^*}{K^*} \cdot \frac{K^*}{K^* + W^*} \tag{6}$$

A central role is played by the rate of capacity utilization O/O^* in her argument. According to her theory, a one time fall in the rate of profit would decrease the rate of accumulation which would decrease the level of capacity utilization. Since accumulation itself is dependent on the rate of profit, there is a precipitous fall in the rate of accumulation over time. There is no route internal to the capitalist system which can reverse this trend. Therefore, she argued that capitalism requires external sources of demand to sustain a positive trend rate of accumulation. By arguing this, she brought in the category of imperialism into the theoretical universe of Marxian theory of capitalist accumulation.

She argued further that in the process of encroaching on the pre-capitalist sectors for its own survival, the capitalist sector absorbs its surrounding pre-capitalist periphery gradually till a point is reached where nothing is left to be encroached upon. As this limit approaches, the underlying tendency towards overproduction crises that the capitalist sector is afflicted with rears its head again, thereby, threatening the existence of the system itself.

7. Crises of Underconsumption

Somewhat related to the theory of overproduction is a realization crisis resultii.g from underconsumption. While the jury is still out on whether Marx took the crisis of underconsumption as one of the central themes in his theory of accumulation, there is an entire school of thought broadly Marxian in its outlook called the Monopoly Capital school.

Briefly put, it argues that with centralization of capital, there is a tendency for the profit share to rise. Since the capitalists consume a much smaller proportion of their income than the workers, such a movement brings the share of consumption out of output down. In the absence of a compensating rise in investment (which if anything should fall as a response to a fall in demand), this leads to a fall in the degree of capacity utilization. Since accumulation itself is dependent on the extent to which the current capacity is utilized, any fall in its usage will adversely affect accumulation, thereby, precipitating the downward spiral which stabilizes around a zero trend rate of growth much like the case described by Luxemburg.

NOTES

1. Instead of using a corresponding K^*, we are assuming that the partial usage of capital while the output is less than O^* is captured by the level of capacity utilization.

9

Marxism and the Question of Culture[1]

Paresh Chandra

There are two broad ways in which we can begin to address the question at hand. Either we work towards a theory of what culture is and how it is/has been/can be understood within Marxism, or we can offer ideas about how a human culture suited to a Marxian project, to the needs of the working class revolution can be constructed. Never entirely divorced from each other, I think these approaches can still provisionally be distinguished. I will limit myself to the former. I make no systematic attempt in this lecture to define 'culture'; that would need a separate lecture on basic assumptions and definitions. My attempt to is to introduce certain ways of looking at culture to be found in Marxist literature, to familiarize those listening/reading with important references and finally to indicate what my own preferences are on this question.

I

I will begin with two statements that have come to stand for a kind of Marxian common sense, set pieces that are often used to close debates on politics and on culture.

1) Base determines superstructure. The most famous instance of this statement's occurrence is in Marx's 'Preface to the *Contribution to the Critique of Political Economy*.' There have been some interesting readings of the relevant passages from the Preface that have tried to salvage it from what is seen to be its vulgarization. Raymond Williams, for example, wrote a chapter called 'Base and Superstructure' in his *Marxism and Literature*. Terry Eagleton wrote a commentary on Raymond Williams' take on base and superstructure in which he pointed out that readings of the Preface often conflate the "base determines superstructure" statement with the "social being determines social consciousness" statement, which too occurs in the same passage[2]. The relevance of these interventions notwithstanding, I want to take up precisely the vulgarization they try to correct.

This alleged vulgarization, one could argue, involves an ontologization of the statement. It is seen to be suggesting that the *economic* base (constituted of relations and forces of production) *always*, in all times and all spaces, *determines*, the superstructure that contains *all* of the society's *social-legal-civil-political-cultural institutions and practices*. It is a universal principle that will allow the one who knows it to decode all social signs, ideology, culture, and get to what lies at the bottom of all things —which is, in any case, always the same thing. i.e. the economic base. At the same time, however, this ontologization makes the entire exercise of interpretation futile, not only because the answer will always remain the same, but also because there is nothing left to be done about it. The ontological moorings of the base-superstructure model make change impossible.

2) The history of all hitherto existing society has been a history of class struggles. This statement occurring in Marx's *Manifesto of the Communist Party*, also seems to ontologize—what else can the *all* imply? One can think of the simplest, the most *simplistic* possible version of the narrative that goes around as 'historical materialism'. History starts with primitive communism, moves on to slavery, then to feudalism, then to capitalism, and finally we will have socialism. (The point is not that this narrative is wrong—to say that would be even more simplistic—but that this linearity is merely a pre-theoretical schema, that tends to replace a properly nuanced take on history.) Does this narrative not suggest, willy-nilly, that there may have been many shifts in the history of mankind, but class struggle has *always* been there? Of course, one could argue that the statement still does not mean that class struggle will always continue, and that while class struggle has defined all societies *hitherto*, communism will be its final abolition. However, I don't think this response adequately undoes the effect of such linear narratives—which is that of making the shifts from one society to another seem somewhat programmed, effectively limiting the role of class struggle to being the internal motor responsible for them. If this is all class struggle is, how can it ever take humanity to an egalitarian society? How can something completely synchronized with the internal logic of exploitation ever lead to communism, or how can class struggle ever abolish itself?

I must emphasize at this point, that I am speaking of the effect that certain narrativizations of history can have. I am not suggesting that there is no other way of reading the two statements I have discussed only briefly here. Because this discussion has admittedly verged on parody, allow me to spend a bit of time on what I think to be an important instance that substantiates the ontologizing interpretations of both these statements, and demonstrates, that this is not mere caricaturing.

I am speaking of a portion of the first volume of Marx's *Capital*—the successive sections on the working day and the workers' struggles to shorten it, and the one on relative surplus value[3]. In the working day chapter, Marx details the conditions of work and the struggles of workers for a shorter, less intense working day. But instead of speaking of their victories (when some are won), he immediately moves on to speak of how, in effect, these struggles merely mediate the passage from absolute surplus value accumulation to relative surplus value accumulation. Once again, to return to the question of narrativization, this is the shape of the plot: first capitalists extract absolute surplus value, that is to say, they accumulate unpaid labour by making workers work harder for longer for very little money. They expand surplus by pushing workers' bodies and minds to their physical-biological limit. In response the workers struggle and manage to win a shorter workday. But this victory is merely the passage to a more efficient form of exploitation—relative surplus value accumulation—based on mechanization and more efficient division of labour, in which workers are not pushed quite as hard, but surplus continues to expand at an even better rate. To repeat a phrase I put into circulation earlier, class struggle becomes the *internal motor* of capitalist development.

What better instantiation can we get to demonstrate how class struggle can get reduced to a superstructural element determined by the base of capitalist production? Furthermore, within the narrative of the first volume of *Capital,* does not the contemporaneity of class struggle with the regimes of absolute surplus accumulation *and* relative surplus accumulation (and primitive accumulation?) put an ontologizing spin on the history of class struggle and exploitation? If the workers' struggles are only going to lead to a more advanced, more efficient capitalism, then are they not internal to capitalism. Let me phrase it differently for effect: class struggle is eternal because class struggle cannot offer us a way out of class struggle. Paradoxically, the ontologizing effect is the result of too much historicism, of the attempt i.e., to read a moment in the past as if it were always already leading to a certain present (as if, for example, the struggles of workers were always already going to lead to a new capitalism).[4]

II

The reason why I have spent so much time on something that may seem to have nothing to do with culture, is that the tendency within Marxism that I have outlined above can and is clearly discernible in a lot of Marxist cultural criticism too. Examples:

1) I will begin with a simple example, the kind of which is familiar to most social science students in India. Advertising, or rather, a particular kind of advertising, say of a fairness cream: the advertisement will tell you what you need to do to become fairer, but its main purpose is to persuade you, should you not already be convinced that being fairer is better. There cannot be a simpler example of how an ideology (in this case racism) is used by, or goes along with the needs of industry (in this case with what can broadly be called the body-image industry) and shapes a cultural artifact (the ad) as well as a cultural milieu (India today).

2) A slightly more complicated situation: let us look at the

relation between the liberalization of the Indian economy and the cinema of the mid-nineties. *Dilwaale Dulhaniya Le Jayenge* is the archetypical case, and its popularity allows me to assume familiarity with the plot. What is really interesting about the film, so in tune with the spirit of the 1990s, is not just the NRI life, its desirablity, the freedoms it offers etc. (that too, though!); not even the conflict between the values of the NRI father and the life he invariably ends up giving to his daughter, played out in the form of a love affair (Kajol and Shahrukh Khan), which the father disapproves of. Most interesting is the eventual reconciliation (love marriage with consent of the father). The uprooted NRI desires roots as much as success, and it is only the promise of reconciliation with the roots being left behind ('Indian values') that makes pursuit of success really worth it. You can go abroad and become rich and still remain in touch with a reified notion of what it means to be Indian. One can possibly connect this reading of the film to some known facts: 1) the large donations made to the Akshardham temples by NRIs, 2) NRIs being major funders for the RSS etc.

Once again, in this interpretation, an economic fact (liberalization-globalization) determines a cultural fact (the new cinema of the 1990s).

3) To complicate things still more let us look at still another reading of Hindi cinema. Ajanta Sircar, in a book called *Framing the nation: Languages of "Modernity" in India* argues that the mutations that have come in the form and content of Hindi cinema over the years can be explained in terms of the changes in India's socio-economic reality. The dominant trope in the 1950s was of nation-building, and that through a compromise between the old (feudal) and the new (bourgeois) elite. So, the protagonist could move out of the old feudal folds and those of the joint family, but only to return to it with some modifications (reforms?). The 1970s, the time of the crisis of the welfare state as well as of the 'mixed economy', is also the time of the emergence of the angry young man (the Amitabh Bachchan of *Zanjeer*); frustration with the failed promises of the 1950s gets transmuted into a rebellion against the failed generation of fathers. The move out of this crisis (all over the world) leads us

to what we call neoliberalism—the time of consumerism, co-option and new compromises (and of *Qayamat se Qayamat Tak* and *Tezaab*). So the 1980s bring the 'new man' who realizes that the fathers of the 1950s were not wrong but misunderstood. The rhetoric of socialism (or the 'misunderstood' father) is co-opted; the same language is used in the favor of the free-market and consumerism. The family, as the unit that mediates the individual and the larger collective (the nation) is a very good measure of these changes. The 1950s were the times of the celebration of the joint-family; the 70s the times of its crisis, and the 1980s see the emergence and the celebration of the nuclear family.

Culture (the form and content of cinema, nature of families etc.) is in this narrative shaped by the economic history of the Indian nation.[5]

In all these examples we clearly glean the resemblance with, even the influence of the kind of Marxism we discussed earlier. We are told, in effect, that culture lies; it tries to hide (though it cannot) its problematical roots in a base that is constituted of exploitation. Perhaps the most powerful, if often misunderstood (vulgarized?) version of this approach to culture occurs in the work of the German Marxist Theodor Adorno, especially his formulation of 'the culture industry'. Putting aside many nuances (again!), Adorno and 'culture industry' have become standard incantations for those who try to dig out subliminal messages that cultural products invariably carry to the consumer. And so it should make one pause and wonder, when in a moment of remarkable but also characteristic self-reflexivity, in a passage called 'Baby with the Bathwater' that occurs in *Minima Moralia*, Adorno rues the problems of this kind of 'cultural criticism' which sees the determined relation between the *base* and culture (*superstructure*) to be too direct and too complete. If culture is so completely determined, what really is the use of theory, of cultural criticism, Marxism etc.? Are we not beginning by assuming that all has already been lost? Adorno:

> The fear of the powerlessness of theory yields the pretext of declaring fealty to the almighty production-process and thereby

> fully concedes the powerlessness of theory...That culture has hitherto failed is not a ground for demanding its failure, by strewing the store of milled flour on spilled beer like Katherlieschen [reference to a fairy-tale]. Human beings who belong together should neither be silent about their material interests nor reduce themselves to their lowest common denominator, but should reflectively grasp their relationship and thereby move beyond such.

Seen together with his own 'pessimistic' style of theorization, his exploration of the determinations that shape cultural production, and in the context of the extreme historicism of Marxism-inflected cultural criticism that we have instantiated above, what does this 'moving beyond' mean?

III

Let me highlight another portion of Marx's work (*The Civil War in France*) to act as a bridge between what I have said so far, and the reading of an essay by Walter Benjamin that I want to offer in what will follow.

Although Marx was fairly critical of the leaders of the Paris Commune, his response, when Thiers destroyed the radical experiment would seem jarring in the light of the comments I have made about *Capital Volume I*. Instead of doing a 'told you so' routine, Marx celebrated the experiment and saw in it an image that would allow him and others to imagine what the society of the future could be like. He was interested not in how capitalism co-opted the moment (in this case by destroying it), but in how the working class could continue to use it. I think the difference between his writings on the Paris Commune and the passage from *Capital* I have been speaking about (in the form in which it appears in *Capital*), as much as it *may* derive from the nature of these struggles, also has a lot to do with the mode of narrativization, with the optic used in thinking and writing about the episodes in question. In what follows, I want to offer a second mode of narrativization, and another optic to look at history and culture—one which sidesteps the problem of too much historicism.

IV

I am going to base this part of the lecture largely on a reading of Walter Benjamin's essay 'Theses on a philosophy of history'. I took up this particular essay because it allows some interesting but fairly simple ways of articulating a different version of Marxism that avoids the traps of the kind of historicism we explored (caricatured, I should say) in the previous sections. But instead of moving straightaway to a discussion of historicism I want to take a detour through Benjamin's critique of social democracy. As we will see, Benjamin's essay finds a kind of structural correspondence between the way in which historicist thinking thinks and the way in which social democratic practice works. Beginning with social democracy will also allow us to delineate some political implications of what we have been discussing.

Social Democracy is a strand within working-class politics which holds that the project of the working-class is continuous with capitalism and in harmony with the flow of history; the working class "is moving with the current" (*Illuminations* 258). It is what some Marxist thinkers would call a 'collaborationist' strand, which at its worst completely disavows working class action. In its somewhat more respectable form it is driven by the belief that struggling for economic gains, the working class will *slowly* improve its condition, and a better future will emerge *gradually*, through a process of sustained reform. Such reform is a determinate product of present conditions and composes a progress that is "as irresistible, as something that automatically pursues a straight or spiral course" (*Illuminations*, p. 260).

The Social Democratic version of the history of the working-class, (starkly different, it has to be pointed out, from the kind of historicism we explored above) would suggest that each time the working class asserted itself it won; the past is strewn with victories. We can return to the pessimism of the story I extracted from the first volume of Marx's *Capital* for a corrective. Workers struggled for a shorter working day and better working conditions. Their victory cut down the surplus accumulated by capital, and capital responded by increased mechanization, by the move from 'absolute' to 'relative' surplus value (so, in the first volume of *Capital* 'The Working Day' is followed by the section on the 'Production of Relative Surplus Value')[6]. The workers ended up generalizing the rule of capital and continuing their own existence as workers. Now, the Social Democrat forgets that this continuity does not embody the will of the working-class; the progress of capitalism, which is predicated upon the continuation of wage-slavery, is not the progress of the working-class. The history of the working-class is not a story of victory but one of loss and the attempt to obfuscate this fact is the lie that social democracy is based on. The working-class, as Klee's 'angel of history', is not leading history's charge, but is being swept by the storm blowing from Paradise. The past that it unwillingly stares upon is a gallery of ruins, not monuments.

V

Let us look back at one of those two statements that I began the lecture with. Insofar as all history has been the history of class struggle, for the working-class it is a history of defeat in this struggle. Each time the working-class has asserted itself it has lost and even victories have only meant co-option; the real potential contained in each moment of contention, in each moment of struggle, the potential, one might say, of all history, remains unrealized when seen from the lens of the working-class.

The kind of historicism that Benjamin attacks in his essay seeks to recover the past as it really was. The recovery of the past 'as it really was' is possible only if the past is complete in itself, if all its potential is exhausted. And so, such historicism is the project of the victors of history, of those for whom history is a story of possibility fulfilled. It is based solely upon the "the spoils that fall to the victor" (*Illuminations,* p. 254). Unfortunately, the Social Democrat's construction of progress, and the working-class's alignment with this progress needs the celebration of these spoils, as if they belonged to the working-class.

In fact, it is the co-option of the working-class and the continuity of their loss that gives birth to the Social Democrat;

to be a Social Democrat is to be the worker who identifies with the master. The recovery of the past as past, as not spilling over into the present, as something closed in-itself, that such historicism seeks, is made possible by occupying the position of the ruler, of the structure, a position from where each moment (and all moments are moments of struggle) achieves its closure within itself. Because capitalism continues to exist, from the perspective of capital each of these moments is a moment where capital ascertained its existence, and even generalized itself. So to think of these moments as constituting a continuum of progress (Social Democracy), or to think of them as closed, as recoverable in themselves (historicism), are both symptomatic of the same class position.

Because for the Social Democrat, history is the history of progress, and the progress of the working-class, he sees the working-class as the class which will redeem future generations just by continuing on its merry way. That the past has always fulfilled its potential is implied in the assumption of progress. But when the past is seen in terms of loss, when the debris the angel of history is forced to stare at is recognized as that, history itself begins to seem the story of potential unrealized. Past generations of the working class were unable to fulfil their destiny, they were stopped from fulfilling their destiny, and they could not secure a future for us. The task of the working-class cannot be defined through a secularized version of the old Protestant Work ethic (like in the Gotha Program (*Illuminations*, p. 259)) that ascertains the future of grandchildren; the image of enslaved forefathers must also be remembered.

VI

It is hard to not notice that the historicism that we had discussed in the first part of this lecture is not the same as the one that Benjamin targets. But the two historicisms share an important feature that allows us to club them together. The historicism that Benjamin attacks is that of the ruling class, the one that sees every document of civilization, of culture, as an achievement, and enters working class discourses by aligning the interests of the working class with those of the ruling class.

The historicism that we had spoken about earlier, and the cultural criticism that we saw to be in tune with that historicism, tended to see every such document as a loss, because it saw each moment as being completely determined by capitalism (the base?). One only saw victory and the other only loss, *but in both cases what is left out is the fact that each such document is a site of contestation, not of total determination*. To say that a cultural (arti)fact/a historical moment is an achievement is to conceal the logic of the working class, or in the case of the social democrat, it is to confuse it with that of capital. To say that it is mere loss is, to use Adorno's words, to throw the baby with the water, and leave nothing to struggle over.

In the present of capitalism, the working-class does not receive the fullness of the past (in Benjamin's view this fullness becomes available only on Judgment Day, with a final victory when a complete break with the fallen present is registered (*Illuminations,* p. 254)), but a history of ancestors betrayed, and a culture that covers the lies of history. The past is to be received precisely in the possibilities that were not fulfilled. Instead of being closed, and hence available as a discrete image, the past flows into the present, and at least in part as a memory of loss. In a corresponding manner, it is the gaps in culture that belong to the old struggler, and we find that culture contains only gaps and attempts to cover them up—and so, all of culture belongs to the working class, but it doesn't look the same to them, as it does to those who stand in the position of the ruling class (or the social democrat-historicist).

How do we know that there were possibilities in the past if all that is available to us is a narrative of losses that extends from the present all the way back to the beginning of history? If, as Benjamin says, "the truth that does not run away from us," is the truth of the ruling class, then where is the truth of the working-class? "The true picture of the past flits by," says Benjamin (*Illuminations,* p. 255). On another occasion: "the genuine historical image...flares up briefly" (*Illuminations,* p. 56). The task of the historical materialist is to grasp this flitting picture. The past is co-opted in its recovery as a reified image by the historicist, and the present is co-opted through the jargon of Social Democracy.

> Historical materialism wishes to retain the image of the past which unexpectedly appears to man singled out by history at a moment of danger. The danger affects both the content of the tradition and its receivers. The same threat hangs over both: that of becoming a tool of the ruling class. (*Illuminations*, p. 255)

(While I accept everything Benjamin says here, I think it should be pointed out that what *historical materialism* is to Benjamin, may not be entirely the same for most who speak of it today.) The possibility available to the past was the possibility of breaking with history, of destroying capitalism; it was a possibility available to those who pushed capitalism to crises on so many occasions. It is difficult to affirm these moments in the history of capitalism's continued existence, without at the same time affirming capitalism (Social Democracy). But this is the difficult task of the historical materialist. And much like Benjamin's historical materialist, the task of the Marxist cultural critic is to affirm the gaps in culture, its contested nature, without affirming capitalism, and without affirming the form that capital gives to culture.

VII

The present is the time of action, and failures of the past generations signal that the burden of taking those ventures to their conclusion lies on the shoulders of the present generation. The present, unlike the past, is a site where struggle continues. In fact, the finality of all those victories won by the ruling class come into question the moment the past comes into contact with the present of class-struggle. The present, in this sense, is not the empty time in which the progress of the Social Democratic kind takes place, but the site where the entirety of history can be stopped in its track. Every moment in social life, each aspect, artifact of culture is doubled, keeping in view that it is struggle that constitutes it—on the one hand each moment can seem to perpetuate the sameness of history, the eternity of struggle, and on the other (and that is the shift in optics that Benjamin is calling for) each moment offers a possible end to this eternity. Here is an example that many, including Benjamin, use to explicate Brecht's theatrical method, but which is equally suited to illuminate Benjamin's own theorization: a married, heteronormative couple is fighting in their bedroom. The man, in the heat of the moment, is about to strike the woman. He is completely certain that he *has to* hit her. Such is his certainty that he cannot see any other possibility. He cannot not strike her. Suddenly someone opens the door to the bedroom. The scene ends, the man lowers his hand, and that which had not seemed possible happens—a different course of action till then unimaginable is chosen, and the forces of necessity lose.

Historicism and historicist cultural criticism both have their place in the revolutionist's arsenal, but only when their role is adequately restricted. The attempt to predict a step-by-step path to revolution (the historicism of Benjamin's social democrat) is one trap historicism can fall into. Pessimistic quietism, ('everything is determined', 'capital always wins', 'everything is ideological') is the other. Historicism cannot show us the path to revolution, because that path doesn't already exist as something to be discovered, although in detailing our losses, it can save us from many wrong decisions. The present, though, only moves in the direction of the unknown future, possibly toward a determination-less future. Historicism prepares us for the present of action by studying and explaining determinations, but does not finally predict where the present may go. It convinces us that 'even the dead will not be safe from the enemy if he wins', but our task, Benjamin says, is to fan the spark of hope, with this knowledge.

> A historical materialist cannot do without the notion of a present which is not a transition, but in which time stands still and has come to a stop [Think of the parable of the fighting couple narrated earlier]. For this notion defines the present in which he himself is writing history. Historicism gives the 'eternal' image of the past. The historical materialist leaves it to others to be drained by the whore called 'Once upon a time' in historicism's bordello. He remains in control of his powers, man enough to blast the continuum of history. (*Illuminations*, p. 262)

The present is that which offers the conditions of possibility of unblocking the movement of history, or of fulfilling culture's possibilities, though history does not offer us any instances of unblocking which did not die an early death (Paris Commune?). The belief in real progress, and the belief that the present is the site where this progress will take place continue even as, in fact because we accept that no progress has taken place so far.[7] The present is good and bad at the same, good because it is bad—packed with unrealized possibility. Culture too, as that which constitutes the present is similarly doubled, both co-opted and full of possibility.

Works cited.

Benjamin, Walter (1969). *Illuminations*. New York: Schocken.
Eagleton, Terry (ed. 1989). *Raymond Williams: A Critical Reader*. Polity: London.
Adorno, Theodor (2006). Minima Moralia: Reflections on a Damaged Life. Verso: London.
Marx, Karl (1990). *Capital, Volume I*. Penguin: New York.
Marx, Karl. *Contribution to the Critique of Political Economy*. https://www.marxists.org/archive/marx/works/1859/critique-pol-economy/.
Marx, Karl (2004). *The Communist Manifesto*. Penguin: New York.
Chandra, Paresh (2012). Review of *Framing the Nation: Languages of 'Modernity' in India," Studies in South Asian Film and Media, Volume 3, Issue 1.*

Recommended Reading

'Theses on a Philosophy of History'. In Benjamin, Walter. *Illuminations.* New York: Schocken, 1969.
Jameson, Fredric. *Representing* Capital: *A Reading of* Volume I. London: Verso, 2014.
Lebowitz, Michael. *Beyond* Capital: *Marx's Political Economy of the Working Class*. New York: Palgrave Macmillan, 1992.
Cleaver, Harry. *Reading* Capital *Politically*. New Delhi: Phoneme, 2012.
Federici, Sylvia. *Caliban and the Witch: Woman, the Body and Primitive Accumulation*. New Delhi: Phoneme, 2014.

NOTES

1. This piece is in the most part the transcript of the lecture I delivered at the Marxism School. In some places I have replaced

sections of the lecture with paragraphs written before or after the lecture. Many of its structural shortcomings as a piece of written text—and there are many—come from the fact that I have tried to maintain the structure of the lecture.

2. See Terry Eagleton's essay 'Base and Superstructure in Raymond Williams' in Eagleton (ed.) *Raymond Williams: A Critical Reader*.
3. Here I am depending on pages Fredric Jameson devoted to this question in his *Representing* Capital.
4. See Harry Cleaver's *Reading* Capital *Politically* for a completely different reading of *Capital*. Also see Michael Lebowitz's *Beyond* Capital, paying special attention to his argument about the 'missing book on wage-labour'. Sylvia Federici's *Caliban and the Witch* is an interesting critique of the kind of historicism I have tried to outline till this point.
5. Point 3 is taken entirely from a review of Sircar's book that I wrote after the book was published.
6. This observation plays an important role in establishing Fredric Jameson's thesis that *Capital* is not a book about 'politics'.
7. *To believe in progress is not to believe that progress has already taken place. That would be no belief.* (Kafka quoted in *Illuminations*, p. 130).

10

Twenty-First Century Socialism and a Theory of Practice

Jakob Graf and Anne-Kathrin Krug

I. Today's Left and the Popular Classes

The world has never been to such an extent shaped by capitalist relations as it is today. It is surprising at the first glance that its socialist counterpart has faded into the background at the same time. In various ways the ruling classes managed to convert all the hopes of collective control over the development of our history into isolated self-management.

There was a period in which capital gathered masses of people together in big halls under the stamping rhythms of machines, turning formal into real subsumption of the people under capital. Collective experiences of these workers as a class were mostly common as most of them were living under same conditions, in the same parts of the town and were addressed as a class in political debates. With the exception of some countries as China and branches like the auto industry, new post-Fordist capitalism might today return to formal subsumption. Freelance work, creative jobs under competitive pressure, outsourcing, assignments with small enterprises on the one hand and exploitation by indebtedness of vast parts of societies, big informal sectors, precarity, rising work hours and declining wages on the other hand. The new working class might be, in many countries, still divided between peasants and factory workers. But this division is complemented by a vertical one, into different wage levels, working and living conditions. How can a worker in the IT sector or a creative design worker have the same class consciousness as their maid, who lives far away in the outer part of the city? Or does that just mean that there is a middle class which is lost for a socialist attempt?

The socialist goal, to put an end to domination by the mechanism of profit and competition, has been brought into disrepute by the failure of the Russian Revolution. In the beginning its success fuelled the revolutionary movements all over the world. But its further developments failed to make the state wither away. On the contrary, it turned into a new bureaucratic domination. A today's theory of practice may not ignore this part of its history.

The old questions, concerning how to organise a resistance of the popular classes combined with a socialist world view, are urgent today. This paper refers to the left's main question: how to merge the socialist world view with the popular classes? It jumps into this debate and tries to stress the necessity of a protagonist role of the people. We can't answer the questions just as Lenin, Gramsci, Luxemburg or others did, who struggled in their specific circumstances. A lot has happened after these early years: anti-imperialist struggles from China to Latin America, the 1968 rebellion, the overthrow of military dictatorships in Europe, anti-globalization movements etc. In today's world of Twitter and Facebook there are also new possibilities. New questions have arisen in the meantime: for example gender questions, sexual diversity etc.—new questions that cannot be pushed away just because of a so-called main contradiction.

> Finally, let us speak frankly between ourselves: the mistakes that are made by a truly revolutionary workers' movement are, historically speaking, immeasurably more fruitful and more valuable than the infallibility of the best possible 'Central Committee'. (Luxemburg 1903/04: p. 265)

II. All about Mass Struggle?

When Vladimir Ilyich Lenin wrote *What is to be done?* (*WITBD*) in 1901, he approached the topic of spontaneity and Kautsky's comment, that a bourgeois intelligentsia has to bring the workers their socialist consciousness 'from without'. Lenin's 'scandalous passages' on these two issues—spontaneity and the bourgeois intelligentsia as the worker's avant-garde—might have been a somehow polemical treatise (Lih 2013: p. 613ff.), but it hints at serious questions of a socialist practice. Marta Harnecker notes in her book, called *Rebuilding the Left*, that most of the errors are rooted "[...] in the famous thesis about the need to introduce socialist theory into the labour movement from without because the spontaneous development of this movement can never produce socialism." (Harnecker 2007: p. 56) But before we just reject this famous interpretation of Lenin's passages we have to understand how serious this question is. It is the main puzzle of the relation between theory and practice: How does the connection between the people and the special socialist worldview work?

We can't answer it like the determinist thinkers did: that there is a growing homogenisation of the working class and sharpening of the economic crisis, so the working class will have no choice but to take their historical mission to create a new world. Instead we take Lenin as the starting point here. Of course we could begin earlier, for example with Engels or Lassalle, but we think that Lenin's notes on consciousness and spontaneity are very catchy and still important. This is because leftist activists often see themselves on the one hand in the position of a radical avant-garde which has to guide the masses and at the same time glorify their spontaneity on the other hand. We still struggle with the task to bring these two notions together. In the following quote we can see how Lenin reflects on the 'from without'-problem:

> We have said that *there could not have been* Social-Democratic consciousness among the workers. It could only have been brought to them from without. The history of all countries shows that the working class exclusively by its own effort, is able to develop only trade union consciousness, i.e., the conviction that it is necessary to combine in unions, fight the employers, and strive to compel the government to pass necessary labour legislation, etc. The teachings of socialism, however, grew out of the philosophic,

> historical, and economic theories elaborated by educated representatives of the propertied classes, by the intelligentsia. By their social status, the founders of modern scientific socialism, Marx and Engels, belonged themselves to the bourgeois intelligentsia. (quoted from Lih 2013: p. 614)

We don't want to discuss all the questions concerning this topic in *WITBD* that have been broadly discussed in academic and activist circles[1]. Here it doesn't matter if this appropriately mirrors Lenin's view on this topic. We just want to point out the main puzzles that we think are very important for us in regard to a socialist practice. First, there seems to be a clear division between socialist thinking and the working class common sense. The intellectuals are seen as totally detached from the recipients. Second and as a result, the Social Democracy then has to be the merger of socialism and the working class movement. Third, the political agitation as a pedagogical relation is seen as a completely one-dimensional. One side is shaping the other. Seen like this, the political party is an avant-garde party whose intellectuals are detached from the masses to which they have a one-sided pedagogical relation. In these terms the emancipation of the working classes is not achieved by the working people themselves, which was Marx' claim. The political agent in this sense is only the avant-garde. The leaders have to be incorruptible and impeccable, their thinking would not be a learning process in political practice, as this would mean learning from the masses, what would flip the hierarchical avant-garde model. If the people instead should be an essential part in a socialist strategy, we have to look at these things differently.

The counter-position to the one above could be a complete affirmation of spontaneity. But deosn't history teach us that we have to reject the assumption of a historically necessary development of a revolutionary class consciousness? Rosa Luxemburg is often seen as the advocate of the spontaneity in contrast to Lenin's avant-gardism, what is of course far too one-sided. However, she has an interesting approach to this question. Mass strikes and direct political action are the 'actual school of experience' of the proletariat, she says (Luxemburg

1906: p. 182). The social-democratic party is always seen as a part of these struggles. It helps to preserve and to carry further the experiences of the past. One struggle isn't only born out of the present but is decisively shaped by the past experiences of the masses. If she says that the class struggle is the actual school of the proletariat, then this does not first and foremost mean reading social-democratic pamphlets. Learning then implies a progress in organisation, getting to know each other, emotional bonds etc. Luxemburg sees the overcoming of the division of the economic and the political struggle as a condition for a revolutionary practice. They mutually intensify each other and are thoroughly mixed. (Luxemburg 1906: p. 180f.) "It is impossible to separate the economic and the political factors from one another", she says (ibid.: p. 194). In this process the working class unites itself from below, people recognise themselves as one class in unity confronting domination. Centralism from below falls "[...] to the share of the organized and most enlightened kernel of the proletariat." (ibid.: p. 197)

The role which is played by the Social-Democratic party in this movement is to be part of it. The important agent for Luxemburg is the 'organized and most enlightened kernel of the proletariat'. They are the ones to shape the Social-Democratic party in this context. Of course, Luxemburg would never reject "[...] the mission of Social Democracy to bring the socialist message to the workers as vigorously as possible" (Lih 2013: p. 615). But for her there cannot be a detached avant-garde apart from the movement. The social-democratic party is always part of it. Learning processes can't just be "[...] fulfilled by pamphlets and leaflets, but only by the living political school, by the fight and in the fight [...]" (Luxemburg 1906: p. 182). Political education is thus a complex process in which workers may not be treated as passive objects.

One might say that this point of view is only possible in a period of mass strikes and already rather purposeful workers. That is somehow true, but Luxemburg's view points towards an important approach. The socialist practice always has to target popular protagonism. Parliamentarism in this sense is a big chance but also a pitfall. It has to be used and allows broad agitations, but it tends to detach and corrupt the leaders. The separation of the intellectuals from the proletariat leads to opportunism. This is one reason why Luxemburg considers the non-proletarian inelligentsia sceptically (Luxemburg 1903/04: 258ff.). Thus the pursuit of popular protagonism shifts our view. First, leftist activists have to learn in and from 'the masses'. Second, a division of 'the intellectuals' from 'the plain masses' is a problematic theoretical starting point and if occurring, a dangerous political development, which has to lead to a critique of the actual practice. Third, political and economic struggles cannot be divided as consciousness does not develop according to a schedule defined by the central committee. Still, this approach seems to be attached to a situation in which popular masses are deeply involved in left-wing political activity. Gramsci might give us some answers on the question how we reach there.

> [...] is it better to 'think', without having a critical awareness, in a disjointed and episodic way, to take part in a conception of the world mechanically [...] or is it better to work out consciously and critically one's own conception of the world and thus, in connection with the labours of one's own brain, choose one's sphere of activity, take an active part in the creation of the history of the world, be one's own guide, refusing to accept passively and supinely from outside the moulding of one's personality?
> (Gramsci, Q 11, §12: p. 325)[2]

III. All about the Common Sense?

The period following Luxemburg's assassination would have been a time of the left's failure in her eyes. The Soviet Union converted into Stalinist dominance and Germany into monstrous fascism. It was then Gramsci's starting point to ask, why the revolution took place in Russia and not in Western Europe. His approach revolves around the term *hegemony*. This term stems from the Russian debate of the alliance between the peasants and the proletariat under the latter's leadership. From the usage of the term hegemony as a movement against tsarism it shifted during Gramsci's theoretical journey into a term that points to an analysis of the integration of the people into the structures of the bourgeois state (see Thomas 2013: p. 58ff.). First, the struggles lead to compromises, which give the subaltern classes the feeling of being represented or actual representation in the state as long as these trade-offs do not threaten the fundamental structure of a capitalist society. Second, bourgeois hegemony is a kind of domination which is characterised by the claim that the ruling interests are not bourgeois interests, but universal interests (Q13, §17: p. 205). Through the different positions of the civil society, the ruling class tries to draft a consensus which calms the struggle into compatible tracks. This is the moment when one social group,

> [...] or at least a single combination of them, tends to prevail, to gain the upper hand, to propagate itself over the whole social area – bringing about not only a unison of economic and political aims, but also intellectual and moral unity, posing all the questions around which the struggle rages not on a corporate but on a "universal" plane, and thus creating the hegemony of a fundamental social group over a series of subordinate groups. It is true that the state is seen as the organ of one particular group, destined to create favourable conditions for the latter's maximum expansion. But the development and expansion of the particular group are conceived of, and presented, as being the motor force of a universal expansion, of a development of all the 'national' energies. (Q13, §17: p. 205)

In Gramsci's point of view this is a characterisation of bourgeois domination in Western Europe, where a war of position in the civil society is necessary. In contrast to Russia where there was no intent of tsarism to include the proletariat and the peasants in their rule. This is why Gramsci thinks that in Russia the revolution could have been fulfilled by a war of manoeuvre, a run on the Winter Palace, or a single rupture that just brushes away the repressive state apparatus. The hegemonic type of bourgeois power on the other side works differently. State is political society plus civil society or "[...] in other words hegemony protected by the armour of coercion" (Q6, §88: 235).

As many other leftist thinkers have remarked, resistance is always conditioned by the way the ruling classes organise their dominance. For Gramsci that means that the revolutionary left in the western countries has to struggle in the positions of the civil society. In this context, he leaves us important insights about the emergence of the subaltern subject as a counterhegemonic political force. One of the most important terms in this regard is 'common sense'. Common sense is nothing homogenous; it is a chaotic mixture of different conformisms, of which everyone is always part. Bourgeois hegemony is trying to treat the common sense of the people in a way that includes them in their conformism. This could be a religious movement, an attempt to form an ethnic unit, a nation, racism etc. Some philosophers might in their way build these ideologies in the background or publicly proclaim them in books. The ideological treatment of the people however, is done by intermediate intellectuals. The main task of a political party is to elaborate a social group's own type of organic intellectuals (Q12, §1: p. 309f.). These intellectuals must be organic, in the sense that they are not detached from the social groups but rooted in their social conditions and culture.

The revolutionaries too must begin their struggle over the common sense. As *organic* intellectuals they must be directly attached to a social group, or to its immanent intellectuals. But they may not look at people as empty bottles in which they try to fill their ideology. Gramsci claims that everyone is a philosopher, each man,

> [...] carries on some form of intellectual activity, that is, he is a 'philosopher', an artist, a man of taste, he participates in a particular conception of the world, has a conscious line of moral conduct, and therefore contributes to sustain a conception of the world or to modify it, that is, to bring into being new modes of thought. (Q12, §3: p. 321)

Thus in Gramsci's view: "All men are intellectuals, one could therefore say; but not all men have in society the function of intellectuals [...]" (Q112, §1: p. 304). The function of the new, organic intellectuals is to organize support points of a world view in civil society. They spread awareness of their role in the bourgeois division of labour to a fundamental social group. Thus revolutionary activists try to intensify the notion of the popular classes of the society as a class society and they try to dissolve the universality claim of the ruling class by pointing out another possible way of organizing social relations. It's not about imposing something from without but working with what is already present in the thoughts of the people. In Gramsci's words:

> First of all, therefore, it must be a criticism of 'common sense', basing itself initially, however, on common sense in order to demonstrate that 'everyone' is a philosopher and that is not a question of introducing from scratch a scientific form of thought into everyone's individual life, but a renovating and making 'critical' an already existing activity. (Q11, §12: 332)

Thus an emancipatory approach has to base itself on the common sense, has to fight in the realm of conformisms of which revolutionaries are also part of (e.g. gender, sometimes religion etc.) for their worldview. The aim is not to manipulate but to support critical thoughts, to 'make critical an *already existing* activity'. This is neither a process which develops gradually nor is it only on a cognitive level. Leaps in this process are very characteristic. Many political activists tell their story of politicisation. Of course this is a process and only in retrospect often looks like a single incident. But these leaps shouldn't be underestimated. Luxemburg always emphasises the invaluable importance of mass activity for the leaps of consciousness. These are experiences which are not foremostly cognitive but emotional experiences of class or group solidarity towards the political antagonist. When we quoted above that 'the conviction that it is necessary to combine in unions, fight the employers' was only a 'trade union consciousness' for Lenin, we now have to say, that this combining in unions, workers' solidarity against their employer and direct claims towards better conditions are in most cases shocking ruptures of the bourgeois hegemony and the fertile soils in which socialists move. The separation of political and economic struggles here easily blurs and people become aware of the fact, that the way it is, is not the way things have to be. The struggle in civil society is a struggle about culture. Different social relations, a new culture, ways of thinking and behaviour, must already undermine the old world as a social group must be leading before it comes to power.

Otherwise it will be absorbed by the existing hegemony. Counterhegemony however works in a manner different to hegemony. The former takes class solidarity as a basis for popular protagonism. The aim is to overcome domination. Whereas the latter mobilises the people only to let them participate in a process of affirmation, which ultimately conserves existing class relations, gender inequality etc.

> Eleven years ago I was quite gullible. I even believed in a third way, I thought it was possible to put a human face on capitalism. But I was wrong. The only way to save the world is through socialism, but a socialism that exists within a democracy; there's no dictatorship here. Hugo Chávez 2010

IV. The Venezuelan Experience

If we look at the left in other countries this shouldn't lead us to lean back and disappear in a pessimistic view of our own conditions. Quite the opposite, it should encourage us to look forward in a more optimistic view. Finally, nothing is more conservative as to rule out the possibility of a leap in the development of social conditions concerning leftist world view. On February 27, 1989 could be seen as such a leap in Venezuelan society. What later became known as the Caracazo lasted only something like two days, led to thousands of deaths due to military gunfire, but changed the political conditions entirely. The people of the *barrio*, the surrounding parts of the city where the poorer people use to live, just had enough of a political system that didn't care about them, and at once they gathered and took the city back. Just for some hours, maybe, but hours that gave them the feeling of acting together, the notion that they are the vast majority and they could get control over their lives if they acted together—hours that created the political subject that was named *pueblo*. This is why Luxemburg saw the progress of the left to a great extent dependent on the practical experiences of the masses. The Caracazo was a rupture in the political history of the Venezuelan left which they frequently refer to. The political subject was born which could become the protagonist of a later revolution.

In 1998 Hugo Chávez got elected as president in Venezuela.

He was himself from the *pueblo* and became well known to the people, since in 1992 he attempted a military coup that was set in motion by the Caracazo. This coup failed but made him famous. His sentence that he often used "Los que quieran patria ¡vengan conmigo!" ('Those who want home/fatherland, come with me!'), is not just a slogan. Immediately after his election there was an effort for a new constitution which aimed not only at social rights, but more importantly, at spaces of participation. This constitution was elaborated with a broad grassroot involvement. Goals such as 'self-management, cooperatives of all kinds, democratic planning, and participatory budgets at all levels of society' (quoted from: Harnecker 2007: p. 140). It was not just a usual election but as it reinforced and pushed on a movement of participation and organisation in the *barrios*. It wasn't Chávez and his electoral alliance which seized power, but a movement of indigenous communities, women, workers, peasants, students etc. Agents like guerrilla groups or the communist party of Venezuela have played an important role in Venezuelan history, and sometimes still do. There was an ongoing tradition of cooperatives since the beginning of the twentieth century. It is important to have all that in mind, in order to understand why an electoral success could trigger a process of deep transformation of society. Especially the people of the *barrios* played again and again an important role in this development. Politics had now to adhere to the political subject of the *pueplo*. But politicians didn't only address the pueblo as their followers, but were dependent on it. As for example in 2002, the opposition tried to launch a coup against Chávez and hijacked him, it was only the *pueblo* pouring down from the hills of the *barrios* to the inner city and forcing the Army to hand over their President.

The communal councils were the starting point of a new protagonism of the *pueblo*. Direct democracy, common decisions, decentralisation of responsibility are some of the effects. The *barrios* started to organise themselves and to force politicians to meet their needs. This tendency got more and more important. After the failed coup against Chávez in 2002, the opposition started a strike of the bosses to bring down the economy. As the Venezuelan economy deeply depends on the exports of oil, the lack of production in this sector became a threatening problem. But the situation changed as the workers in the oil sector began to occupy their workplaces and to start production themselves without the engineers in charge. During this time many factories got occupied by their workers and received government support. These developments made Chávez to speak of socialism from 2005 onwards. But socialism can't be implemented by law. One can easily observe in Venezuela how the laws are only followed if the forces in power allow it. Where the rich and powerful are still in charge, progressive laws are treated as a joke.

The *pueblo*'s protagonist role however goes further; workers in ciudad Guayana for example recently wrote a proposal for a new law of workers' education. Without the activity and knowledge of many small leaders in the villages there could never be an implementation of the land reform to increase agricultural production. Cooperatives were founded with government support but by the people. The aim is to organise the economy in cooperatives and product chains instead of selling under conditions of competition on capitalist markets. In this process the government deeply depends on the participation of the people in the political process. Their knowledge of how the local relations work, their activity to throw out corrupt bureaucrats, to handle the local drug dealers, to throw out paramilitary forces, to implement progressive law etc. are the conditions for the progress of the socialist process. Both the state and the basis mutually reinforce each other and create an experimental labouratory of different methods to democratise the economy. Aside from the cooperatives there are different models of workers' control of state-owned enterprises.[3]

Political education of people of the *barrios* takes place as they meet and discuss about Bolivar, gender, socialist economy etc. This is a formation of the basis to organise themselves to make the state wither away. If this will work out in the long run remains to be seen. It will depend on the question if the *pueblo* will be able to organize the economy, which still works in a capitalist way, with big private enterprises and a big informal sector. The events since the death of Chávez only prove that, as there are serious economic problems, which again raise the question of economic power. This is a characteristic of the Venezuelan process; it is constantly pushed forward by the struggles with the opposition.

But these struggles are not only economic ones. Venezuela does not have a long socialist tradition, but a tradition of Americanised consumer culture. This does not necessarily spare the left. Also if the American way of life is more of something the middle classes look up to machismo, corruption and status symbols can be found in all parts of society. Cultural events are increasingly common now, also in Caracas which is known for its criminality. The Chavistas are doing a great job in opening up spaces for public life. People sit together, discuss and read a local newspaper, which is provided for free[4]. You won't be able to organize a cooperative if it's simply about money. It is therefore necessary to build on these public spaces a worldview, which does not primarily focus on maximisation of material wealth. This is the one part of the city, where the *pueblo* gathers. In the eastern part of the city things look different. Here the middle class lives and this is where you find the big malls like, Mc Donald's etc. This is also where the protests against the government take place, which have intensified since February 2014. These classes do not feel as part of the political project. They are often students expecting higher ranks in society. But this group also has leftists who support the project and often play an important role. This is a sign for the struggles in civil society. If the upper classes accuse the Chavistas for having generated a class state, the reaction shouldn't be an attempt to integrate the economic interests of the middle class or even the business interests into their strategy. Compromises might be necessary but concerning the fundamental question of the democratisation of the economy there can't be consent. Either the socialist effort fails because a bureaucratic Boliboergeoisie[5] hands it over or it radicalises itself.

V. A Fragmented Continuity?

Like we have mentioned above, we think, that the left cannot go on addressing the political subject as a homogenous class of workers, since many of the people don't work under circumstances of what are known in theoretical terms as 'classic real subsumption': the surveillance of a boss, a clear hierarchy of a class structure inside the enterprise etc. The collective unionised economic struggles as a class are not the forms in which a freelancer or a precarious temporary worker will spontaneously fight for a better life. In fact, unions have had a hard time in their attempts to organise workers of the liberalised sectors, which often change their employment and always work terms under strong competition. This is why, especially today, the left has to struggle in civil society with a culture of solidarity which is open for everyone and works in a non-commercial way. Squats, bookstores, music, protest marches, rallies, education etc. can be a part of that. Not in Venezuela alone, communal approaches have also been a starting point of collective action. The communal councils in the Venezuelan *barrios* which are one of the most important mainstays of the revolution is a very successful example. This could be a new way of leftist territorialization. We have to look out for new starting points besides the classic factories which in most countries now employ the majority of the popular classes.

Leftist movements of the last decades - such as the anti-globalisation movement and the so-called Arab spring, occupy, *¡democracia real ya!* in Spain, the anti-world cup movement in Brazil and also the Bolivarian revolution in Venezuela - didn't mainly address economic topics in the classical sense. Even if they, like the anti-world cup protest, started because of an increase in the cost of transportation, an always appearing demand is the one for participation. People don't feel represented anymore by the old elites. Parties are usually not very popular if they don't really make a difference, especially in their internal structure. Popular protagonism must be seen as one of the urgent questions of today. Decentralisation instead of centralisation in society's decision-making processes, as Harnecker stresses (2010), might be a new approach. This is not only true for a middle class youth which does not struggle with economic problems. A country like Spain were over fifty per cent of the youth are unemployed and the strongest direct democracy movement took place, is a very good example. The left has to fight for a new way of life, where consumption and wage levels are not the only things that matter but the will to "[...] take an active part in the creation of the history of the world, be one's own guide [...]" like Gramsci expressed it. (Q 11, §12: 325)

A revolution then does not mean a single incident, but an ongoing process of ruptures. We have to reject the view of the revolution as some historical days, after which the new avant-garde replaces the old government. This approach has failed.[6] In his book *State, Power, Socialism* Poulantzas suggested a transformation 'through, against and apart from the state' towards democratic socialism (Poulantzas 2000). This is not reformism. The difference between reform and revolution is not the question of smashing the state, but the question: who is the main agent of the revolutionary process? The revolutionary process in Venezuela illustrates how both the government and the base (the *pueblo*) need to push *each other* forward. Since the democratisation of the economy and the replacement of the old state by the councils is a question of organisation, the revolution takes its time. This doesn't mean that there are no clashes an no leaps etc. of course, still the contradiction between the popular classes and capital is undeniable. This is why the organised peasants and workers, the communal councils and the collectives of the Chavistas have to be strong and always controle the processes in the state apparatus. But revolutionary changes don't only happen after the left seizes power. The left has to organise even before. Otherwise it will just result in an integration of their leaders into bourgeois hegemony. The experiences of the 'fabricas recuperadas' in Argentina are an important example. Of course this movement has had problems, but their struggles do inspire a lot of struggles in other countries. Vio.me a worker controlled factory in Greece for example invited workers from Argentine for an exchange of their experiences. Factories in Venezuela are organising production chains with *fabricas recuperadas*. But we shouldn't look at Venezuela solely; changes happen everywhere; we just have to get involved.

REFERENCES

Chávez, H. 2010: Interview with BBC hardtalk. http://www.theguardian.com/world/2010/jun/13/hugo-chavez- bbc-hardtalk-interview [accessed on May 12, 2014].

Forgacs, D. (ed.) (2014)*The Antonio Gramsci Reader. Selected Writings 1916–1935*. Aakar Books: Delhi.

Harnecker, M. (2007) *Rebuilding the Left*. Daanish Books. Delhi.

—— (2010): Excessive Centralization Creates Inefficiency and Prevents Authentic Popular Protagonism, available at http://mrzine.monthlyreview.org/2010/harnecker200310.html [accessed 15th May 2014]

Lih, Lars, T. (2013) *Lenin Rediscovered: What Is to Be Done? In Context*. Aakar Books. Delhi.

Lenin, V.I. (1922a) *Letter to the Congress*. In: Lenin Collected Works. Vol. 36. Progress Publishers: Moscow. pp. 593–597.

—— (1922b) *The Question of Nationalities or 'Autonomisation'*. In: Lenin Collected Works. Vol. 36. Progress Publishers: Moscow. pp. 605–611.

Luxemburg, R. (1903/04) *Organization Questions of Russian Social Democracy*. In: Hudis, Peter/Anderson, Kevin B.: *The Rosa Luxemburg Reader*. 2005. Cornerstone Publications: Kolkata. pp. 248–265.

—— (1906) *The Mass Strike, the Political Party, and the Trade Unions*. In: Hudis, Peter/Anderson, Kevin B.: *The Rosa Luxemburg Reader*. 2005. Cornerstone Publications: Kolkata. Pp. 168–199.

Malleson, T. (2010) *Cooperatives and the 'Bolivarian Revolution' in Venezuela*. In: Affinities: *A Journal of Radical Theory, Culture, and Action*. Vol. 4, No. 1, 2010, pp. 155-175. http://www.workerscontrol.net/authors/cooperatives-and-%E2%80%9Cbolivarian-revolution%E2%80%9D-venezuela [accessed 12th, may 2014].

Poulantzas, N. (2000) *State, Power, Socialism*. Verso: London.

Thomas, P. D. (2013) *The Gramscian Moment. Philosophy, Hegemony and Marxism*. Aakar Books: Delhi.

NOTES

1. For example the question if this quote really represents Lenin's opinion or if he is out of polemic reasons 'bending the stick too

far'. (see Lih 2013)

2. Here and in the following I quote Gramsci's prison writings by the number of the notebook (Q = quaderno) and the number of the paragraph which are common in collection of the prison notebooks. The page I add refers to David Forgacs' edition (Forgacs 2014).
3. For an overview see Malleson 2010.
4. Referring to CCS http://www.ciudadccs.info/ [May 12th, 2014]
5. Parts of the higher ranks within the socialist party or state bureaucracy that grew rich with the Bolivarian revolution and are only socialist in the sense of wearing a red shirt.
6. Lenin himself admitted, that in effect "[...] they took over the old machinery of the state from the tsar and the bougreoisie" (Lenin 1922: 597) that was just "slightly anointed with Soviet oil" (1922b: 605).

Marxism and the Indian Context

11

The Agrarian Question in India

Amit Basole

PART ONE: THE AGRARIAN QUESTION IN THE MARXIAN TRADITION

What is the Agrarian Question?

The "agrarian question" in Marxian political economy refers to a collection of related problems such as the fate of the peasantry and non-capitalist or pre-capitalist relations of production in general under capitalism, the establishment of capitalism in agriculture, the role of agriculture in sustaining the industrialization process, and the political role of the peasantry and other small capital-holders in the fight against capitalism.

The agrarian question is closely related to the notion of "agrarian transition" or the transformation of a predominantly agrarian society into an industrialized society. A stylized outline of key aspects of the agrarian transition following Bernstein (2004, p. 98) could be as follows:

1. As a result of primitive accumulation and the destruction of pre/non-capitalist land relations (such as sharecropping and independent commodity production) the capital-wage labour relation emerges in agriculture and alongside this class differentiation takes place within the peasantry. On the one hand capitalist farmers emerge and on the other, agricultural wage labourers, replacing both peasants and landlords.

2. Bernstein (ibid, p. 198), following Lenin notes that capitalist relations can emerge by different paths in different

historical circumstances, including through (i) the "internal metamorphosis" of pre-capitalist landed property (in Lenin's phrase the Prussian or Junker path), (ii) the class differentiation of peasants/petty commodity producers, or (iii) some combination of these two dynamics.

The two are also sometimes known as "capitalism from above and capitalism from below" respectively. Where the feudal class does not adopt capitalism, nor does the destruction of feudal or other pre/non-capitalist relations occur endogenously, redistributive land reforms are needed or emerge on the historical platform of Left political parties to "hasten the transition to agrarian capitalism along a 'peasant' path (of subsequent class differentiation; Lenin's American path)."

3. The establishment of capitalist relations means that the logic of competition and accumulation take hold of agriculture previously driven by subsistence, livelihood or consumption motives. This drives productivity growth in agriculture.

4. The resulting increase in surplus (i.e. output in excess of that needed to sustain the agricultural population) can/should be mobilized for industrial accumulation. But, whether this happens or not depends on the balance of forces between agrarian surplus appropriating classes (agrarian capital, landed property and rich peasants) and emergent industrial capital, with the state typically central to the contributions, whether positive or negative, of agriculture to (initial) industrialization. (ibid)

5. The increasing scale of production as well as employment of wage-labour according to the profit calculus rather than subsistence motive imply dispossession of part of the peasantry from the land. These become "doubly free" labour (in Marx's phrase, i.e. "free" from ownership of land and free to move wherever there is work) available for the industrialization process.

6. Productivity growth in agriculture lowers the cost of food thereby lowering reproduction costs of the urban working class and aiding accumulation in industry.

Students of Development Economics will notice the resemblance of this schema to the so-called problem of "structural change." The agrarian question is thus not a question peculiar to Marxism.

This can be schematically depicted as follows:

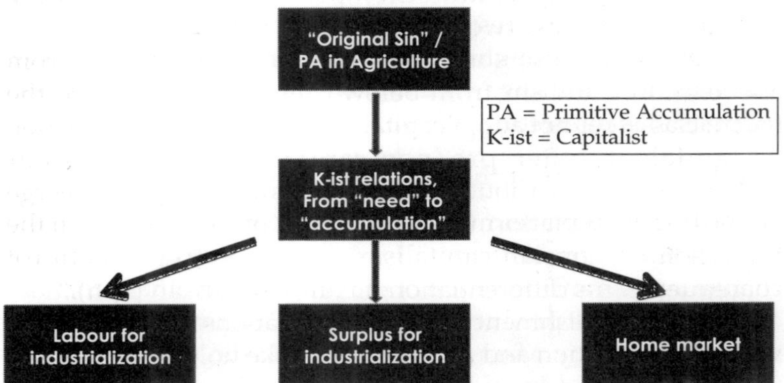

The foregoing also makes clear the importance of "resolving the agrarian question" for the transformation of a pre- or non-capitalist economy into a capitalist economy. Hence Byres (1995, p. 509):

> Unresolved agrarian question is a central characteristic of economic backwardness...a failure of accumulation to proceed adequately in the countryside...failure of class formation in the countryside...failure of the state to mediate successfully those transitions, which we may encapsulate as the agrarian transition.

Immediately the question arises, what has been the Indian experience? Is it a story of successful agrarian transition or a case of delayed or arrested structural change? We will come to this later in the lecture.

Another, more fundamental, question also arises. Is this a *desirable* change? In other words, is there more than one way to resolve the agrarian question? This goes to the heart of the theory of historical materialism and the question of what is progressive and what is reactionary. On this question, at the broad theoretical or paradigmatic level two grand anti-capitalist traditions have locked horns, viz. Marxism and Populism. While Marxists have generally seen anti-capitalist politics of the peasantry and other small-property holders and their efforts to create rural communities as conservative or reactionary and have defended urbanization and the creation of the urban working class as the path to socialism, populists have argued the opposite. In this respect Marx is more theoretically open than commonly thought, especially compared to some later Marxists, and his engagement with the Russian Narodniks (populists) is interesting. We will come to this later.

The Three Aspects of the Agrarian Question

According to Bernstein (2004) the agrarian question is really three different "problematics." First, the question of the agrarian change or the transformation of the peasant and other pre/non-capitalist forms of production into capitalist forms. This question was addressed by Marx, Kautsky, and Lenin (Patnaik, 2007). Second, the problem of accumulation or the extent to which agriculture could/should produce surpluses for sustaining the industrialization process and for structural change more generally. This was the conceptual terrain inhabited by Ricardo and Malthus in the nineteenth century and by Bukharin and Preobrazhensky in the twentieth century, while the figure of Rosa Luxemburg and her idea of unequal exchange looms large in the background also. The third is the question of rural politics and what was the role of the peasantry in anti-capitalist politics. This has been debated by populists and Marxists throughout the late nineteenth and twentieth centuries (Akram-Lodhi and Kay, 2010a, p. 198).

As we shall see in the second half of the lecture, the Indian "mode of production debate" focused primarily on the first and the third: the development of capitalism in agriculture and the role of the peasantry in Left politics. The debate over the New Farmers Movements of the 1980s was about the second and third aspects.

Let us take each of these issues in general before we examine the Indian case.

The Transition to Capitalism in Agriculture

This is the question of the disappearance or lack thereof of the peasant who embodies both the exploiter and the exploited in her person, and her replacement by capitalist relations of production as also the question of the disappearance of feudal relations of production in agriculture.[1] This question begins in the Marxian tradition with Marx himself and was later discussed by writers such as Engels, Kautsky, and Lenin in the European and Russian contexts. In the Indian context, this question formed the centrepiece of the so-called "mode of production debate" that took place in the 1970s between writers such as Utsa Patnaik, Ashok Rudra, Paresh Chattopadhyay, Amit Bhaduri, Pradhan Prasad, Gail Omvedt, and others. The problem facing these authors: is Indian agriculture showing a tendency to move from peasant to capitalist farming (Thorner, 1982).

For Kautsky (1988) generalized commodity production coordinated via the self-regulating market is responsible in part for the state of the peasantry. The peasant has to worry about the prices of output over which he has no control, and possibly no information; this makes him dependent on the merchant. On the other side, he has to worry about the prices of inputs and there he becomes dependent on the usurer for purchase of fertilizers etc. However, even as merchants' and usurers' capital as well as the state continually undermine peasant existence, they also support it by making credit available and by buying their output because alternative livelihoods do not exist.

The common understanding, summarized by Kautsky, is that a petty-producer subordinated to capital survives largely via heroic self-exploitation.

When taking on the inverse size-yield relationship, Kautsky's main point is that higher yield per unit of land on small farms come mainly from overwork and under-consumption on part of the peasant.[2] But he is also careful to notice that overwork and a brutal degraded existence are not intrinsic features of peasant agriculture. Rather they are a result of commodity production and competition via the self-regulating market. The peasant clings to his small property because he values independence when he says, "We work much harder than labourers, in fact like slaves. The only advantage we get is being our own markets." (Kautsky, 1988, p. 113)

Although he is clear that the peasant is doomed to die and that (s)he is not the revolutionary subject (in fact not even capable of collective action), on the question of the transition, Kautsky does present a nuanced view acknowledging that the transition from small-scale and artisanal production to large-scale industry can take a very long time. As capitalist relations develop and class differentiation proceeds, peasants lose land and are forced to first acquire supplementary employment (usually as agricultural wage labourers) before perhaps completely becoming proletarian. However this proletarianization can take a long time since peasants may cling tenaciously to (the illusion of) private property.

Marx too anticipated this "staying power" of the peasant. Speaking about the destruction of domestic industry and its substitution by large-scale capitalist production, Marx notes,

> Still the manufacturing period, properly so called, does not succeed in carrying out this transformation radically and completely...If it destroys these in one form, in particular branches, at certain points, it calls them up again elsewhere, because it needs them for the preparation of raw material up to a certain point...This is one, though not the chief, cause of a phenomenon which, at first, puzzles the student of English history. From the last third of the 15th century he finds continually complaints, only interrupted at certain intervals, about the encroachment of capitalist farming in the country districts, and the progressive destruction of the peasantry. On the other hand, he always finds this peasantry turning up again, although in diminished number, and always under worse conditions.[3]

Githinji and Cullenberg (2003) note that in the chapters on "so-called Primitive Accumulation" in Capital Volume 1, Marx wrote "apocalyptically" regarding the destruction of the peasantry, sometimes leading readers to believe that the transition occurred "overnight" in England when in fact the process he describes took three centuries to develop fully. The above quote also shows that Marx himself was more nuanced on the issue than some later Marxists who continue to be surprised at the persistence of the peasantry and of small capital holders inhabiting the informal sector in developing countries.

What happens to the masses of small producers whose conditions of existence are undermined progressively by capitalism? While the conventional answer has been that they are absorbed into the ranks of the urban proletariat, in fact vagabondage, pauperism and out-migration to the colonies also play an important role. In particular, the idea that Europe has colonies to export its surplus labour to, while the late industrializers do not, has been raised by Third World Marxists. Prabhat Patnaik observes:

> True, empirically, the displaced petty producers in the heartland of capitalism did not linger on as a vast unemployed mass (as happened in the tropical colonies), but this was because of large-scale migration from Western Europe to the temperate regions of white settlement where the "natives" were driven off their land and the immigrants settled upon it. This in turn not only kept the "reservation wage" high in the heartland of capitalism, but, by keeping the unemployment rate restricted, allowed some increase in the wage rate along with the increase in labour productivity, creating the impression that this was an inherent *internal* characteristic of capitalist growth everywhere.[4]

For populous colonies such as India this point is of great importance. This also brings out the point that the first aspect of the Agrarian Question, the disappearance of the peasantry and the emergence of capitalism in agriculture, is fraught with historical contingencies. Lessons drawn from the European experience may need serious modification if not rejection in the case of the rest of the world.

"Terms of Trade Wars"

The second aspect of the agrarian question concerns the relationship between agriculture and industry (or more generally the non-agricultural sector). Recall that viewed from the perspective of the non-agricultural sectors of the economy agriculture performs four important functions:

1. It provides food for the non-agricultural working class and raw materials for industry.
2. It provides labour.

3. Capital accumulated in agriculture can be used to finance the industrialization process.
4. It provides a market for industrial goods.

In all these exchanges, the terms of trade between the agricultural and the non-agricultural sectors are crucial to determine the distribution of produced value between the sectors.[5] Akram-Lodhi and Kay (2010a, p. 194) note that buying farm products at below-market prices and selling industrial products at above-market prices (or in other words unequal exchange) has been one mechanism by which agricultural surplus has been captured for the industrialization process.

The two well-known debates on this issue are the nineteenth century debate between David Ricardo and Thomas Malthus over the English Corn Laws (Kanth 1986) and that between Evgeny Preobrazhensky and Nicolai Bukharin over "socialist primitive accumulation" in the early days of the Soviet Union right after the promulgation of the New Economic Policy in 1921 (Mitra 1977).

The Corn Laws referred to tariffs imposed by Britain on imported wheat (which was then known as corn). Ricardo's class analysis showed him that this tariff resulted in increased domestic prices of grain relative to prices that would prevail without tariffs which in turn meant more expensive food and that capitalists had to pay workers higher wages resulting in lower profits. Surplus was transferred from capitalists to landlords who benefited from the higher price of agricultural commodities. Arguing from the point of view of the capitalist class Ricardo supported the abolishing of this tariff to lower the price of grain so that capitalists could retain a larger proportion of their profits. The rationale was that surplus that stayed with capitalists would be reinvested and the resulting accumulation process would drive economic growth, while surplus that went to landlords would be spent in consumption.

Notice that, while usually told as a story of triumph of free trade over protectionism, in Marxian terms this is a story of class conflict via terms of trade between the capitalist and landlord classes. Of course workers do not figure in this story, neither do the urban nor rural workers benefit in either scenario.

This is because, according to the classical theory to which Ricardo, Malthus (and indeed Marx with some modifications) subscribe, wages are tied to subsistence for both types of workers. Marx makes the point that the "free trade" debate is irrelevant to workers in his characteristically caustic style in a speech given to workers in Brussels, published under the title "On the Question of Free Trade."

More pertinent to the Indian experience, the question of the role of the state in squeezing agriculture to aid the accumulation process in industry emerged again in the aftermath of the Soviet revolution. The debate between Preobrazhensky and Bukharin was over the role of the new socialist state in ensuring accumulation for socialist industry (so-called "socialist primitive accumulation"). In Soviet Russia (and not only there but in most late industrializing countries) the state played a major role in mobilizing resources for and guiding the industrialization process. This is because given minimum efficient scale as well as presence of externalities, private citizens were not willing nor able to carry out investment needed (later developmentalist theories by Rosenstein-Rodan, Nurske, etc. are also along these lines).*

* The following section is derived from the works of Rajesh Bhattacharya with his permission.

Thus the major burden of large-scale investment is on the state. The state has to mobilize capital and since private agents hold capital, it has to either coerce or provide incentives to mobilize privately held capital. In fact, both coercion and incentives were used in most of the cases where state-guided industrialization has been attempted.

The role of agriculture assumes special significance with respect to two issues—

a) size of the agricultural surplus and,

b) transfer of that surplus via terms of trade (or other mechanisms) to finance industries.

Preobrazhensky recognized that, "Large scale industrialization in a peasant country would have to be largely paid for by the peasants" (Nove, p. xii, Introduction to Preobrazhensky, 1926). In the early stages of industrialization in a predominantly rural economy, agriculture is the only significant activity capable of producing the surplus required for industrialization. Preobrazhensky claimed it to be 'economically obvious' in his polemic against Bukharin (ibid) that some form of 'socialist primitive accumulation' is necessary to initiate and sustain industrialization in Soviet Union.

In Russia, the 1863 emancipation of the serfs led to a peasant economy largely dominated by family farming. In Marxian terms, they were self-exploitative independent producers and constituted 80% of the population. In the civil war period after the Russian Revolution, Russia was governed by a system called 'war communism'. "The state nationalized virtually all industry, outlawed private trade, forcibly prevented the peasants from marketing their products, and sought to requisition surpluses" (Nove, p. viii in Introduction to Preobrazhensky, 1926). The peasants responded by reducing production and resisting requisition. Massive public discontent due to the resulting food shortage and subsequent chaos led Lenin to retreat and adopt the New Economic Policy. Private trade and small-scale private enterprise were allowed, and the peasants were free to sell to private traders or market their own produce.

It was in the context of NEP that Preobrazhensky brought up the issue of financing rapid industrialization. To Preobrazhensky, it was obvious that the peasants comprising 80% of the population should supply resources for industry. His famous solution was to achieve this by manipulating the terms of trade against agriculture so as to transfer the agricultural surplus to socialized industrial sector.

As Mitra (1977) notes:

> To accelerate socialist accumulation, the state, maintains Preobrazhensky, should offer the lowest possible price to farm products raised in the private economy and, in return, sell the products of the state sector to the kulaks at the highest possible price. (p. 61)
>
> Relative prices must be made to move uninterruptedly in favour of industrial goods, tuned out by the state, and against the produce of farms, raised by the kulaks. (p. 61)
>
> Rosa Luxemburg is thus turned upside down... What Luxemburg says capitalist industry *does* to primitive agriculture,

> Preobrazhensky says nationalized industry *should do* to pre-socialist, private agriculture. (pp. 61-62)

This led to the 'scissors crisis' in 1923. The terms of trade between agriculture and industry had become so unfavorable for the former that the peasants reduced their marketed surplus. Bukharin and Stalin criticized Preobrazhensky for advocating a policy that exploits peasants, promotes 'internal colonialism' and undermines the alliance between the peasantry and the proletariat. Preobrazhensky replied by reaffirming his belief that some sort of primitive socialist accumulation was indispensable. However, he claimed that agricultural incomes might rise, in the presence of PSA, if industry became more efficient and agriculture more productive.[6]

This question of agriculture-industry relations remains relevant as long as agriculture plays an important role in a country's economy. It was hotly debated in the Indian context in the 1980s, the decade that saw vast numbers of farmers take to the streets protesting unfavorable terms of trade. However, as the contribution of agriculture to GDP declines, it is perhaps no longer as relevant. I return to this later.

Politics

The third aspect of the Agrarian Question, the political function of the peasantry, has an equally grand theoretical tradition behind it. Here the principal fissure is that between anti-capitalist revolutionary populism and Marxism.

We start from the theoretical point that which social struggles are seen as 'progressive' and which as 'conservative' or 'reactionary' depends on the theory of history with which one approaches any actually existing social conflict. Historical Materialism (hereafter HM) is one, though by no means the only, theory of history founded upon the notion of material progress. Even if one discards the strict stagism of Stalin (primitive communism, slavery, feudalism, capitalism, socialism, communism), some type of stagist history continues to inform those working towards socialism. Perhaps least controversially, a sectoral transition, in terms of employment and output, from agriculture to industry, growing importance of wage-labour over self-employment, and increasing scale of production are all taken to be evidence of progress, while the converse would be regarded as regress. Then it follows directly that social movements which aid the former are progressive and those which retard it or aid the latter are reactionary. Incidentally, since the same features are strongly correlated with a rise in per-capita incomes, they are also taken to be evidence of progress in bourgeois economics though for it, history stops with the establishment of capitalism.[7]

The populists, contra the Marxists, thought that the struggles of the small property holders could lead to a new socialist society. It is well known that Marx was dismissive of the type of socialism that valorized peasant and small-proprietor relations. Not only did he think these would disappear in due course being replaced by economies of scale and industrial production methods, but he also thought that to attempt to preserve these social relations was to betray a misunderstanding of the dynamics of capital itself. Thus Marx:

> Hard-won, self-acquired, self-earned property! Do you mean the property of petty artisan and of the small peasant, a form of property that preceded the bourgeois form? There is no need to abolish that; the development of industry has to a great extent already destroyed it, and is still destroying it daily.[8]

And as regards the politics of these classes:

> The lower middle class, the small manufacturer, the shopkeeper, the artisan, the peasant, all these fight against the bourgeoisie, to save from extinction their existence as fractions of the middle class. They are therefore not revolutionary, but conservative. Nay more, they are reactionary, for they try to roll back the wheel of history (ibid).

The above quotes from the Communist Manifesto outline, if polemically, the basic Marxist position regarding petty producers or owners of small capital, including peasants and artisans. Lenin considers peasant production to harbor a, "very sound, deep-rooted basis for capitalism, a basis on which capitalism persists or arises anew in a bitter struggle against communism."[9]

This position has become more nuanced over time as the transition to a capitalist society based on large-scale industry has proved to be less smooth than imagined by both its proponents and its detractors, and the peasant and the artisan have refused to die (see discussion earlier). And Marx himself was more nuanced in his position later in his life as Shanin (1984) has discussed extensively.

Although here we are concerned with the peasantry there are theoretical similarities between peasants, artisans and small traders. They are both, capitalists and workers, or if you prefer, neither. Although the concept of the 'intermediate classes', i.e. social classes that are neither capitalist/bourgeois nor worker/proletariat but display features of both is associated with the Polish economist and contemporary of Keynes, Michal Kalecki, we find it in Marx, as seen below:

> In countries like France, where the peasants constitute far more than half of the population, it was natural that writers who sided with the proletariat against the bourgeoisie should use, in their criticism of the bourgeois régime, the standard of the peasant and petty bourgeois, and *from the standpoint of these intermediate classes*, should take up the cudgels for the working class. Thus arose petty-bourgeois Socialism. Sismondi was the head of this school, not only in France but also in England (ibid).

There exist many trenchant Marxian critiques of the populist position. I will have occasion below to discuss a bit further the critique of Brass (2000). Bernstein (2009, p. 68) elaborates on populism from a Marxian perspective:

> Advocacy of the intrinsic value and interests of the small producer, both artisan and "peasant," as emblematic of "the people," arises time and again as an ideology, and movement, of opposition to the changes wrought by the accumulation of capital.
>
> Agrarian populism, in particular, is the defence of the small "family" farmer (or "peasant") against the pressures exerted by the class agents of a developing capitalism—merchants, banks, larger-scale capitalist landed property and agrarian capital—and indeed, by projects of state-led "national development" in all their capitalist, nationalist and socialist variants, of which the Soviet collectivisation of agriculture was the most potent landmark.

> Not surprisingly, the moral dimension of agrarian populism —as defence of a threatened (and idealised) way of life—often encompasses strong elements of anti-industrialism and anti-urbanism. Such ideologies are often explicitly anti-proletarian too, as new classes of wage labour represent the same threatening urban–industrial milieu as classes of capital and "modernizing" regimes of different political complexions. Much agrarian populist ideology, then, is backward-looking and explicitly reactionary...

Note that it is *by virtue of their position* in the historical materialist theoretical framework that peasants (and other small property holders) cannot engage in progressive politics unless they are willing to be led by the urban proletariat. Kautsky (1988) is explicitly on this point. When discussing the agrarian program of the Social Democrats, Kautsky first refutes the argument that the peasant should be treated as the proletarian of the countryside. He argues that poverty does not define a proletarian, but rather production relations do. It is the means of production that modern wage-workers lack, not the means of consumption. While for the peasant it is the reverse. Further there are other points of conflict between peasants and workers, for instance, the former are sellers of food while the latter are buyers.

According to orthodox Marxist theory, four major obstacles stand in the way of recognizing the peasantry as a revolutionary force. First, the peasantry is itself divided along class lines and does not constitute 'a class'. On this point Marx is contradictory. In the same passage that he famously compares French peasants to potatoes in a sack, he also outlines ways in which they do form a class.

> In so far as millions of families live under economic conditions of existence that separate their mode of life, their interests and their culture from those of the other classes, and put them in hostile opposition to the latter, they form a class. (Marx in Shanin 1987 p. 332)

However being incapable of organization they cannot represent their interests in parliament or elsewhere and hence need to be represented.

Second, in so far as they fight to preserve small property,

they stand in the way of collectivization and the 'march of history'.

Third, as illustrated by the Indian new farmers' movements (see below), if the peasantry as a group raises the issue of exploitation by the state and the urban bourgeoisie, it is placing the town-country contradiction ahead of class contradictions within town and within country. This is unacceptable from a Marxian perspective.

Lastly, more fundamentally, peasants, being rustic and 'uneducated', may even articulate politics outside the ambit of European liberal-radical theory. This automatically makes them suspect. The suspicion of such political discourses and the movements that use them is seen clearly in Brass (2000).

For Brass, the historical revolutionary subject in the era of capitalism, is the doubly-free proletariat. Whether in agriculture, industry or services, wage-workers who possess little or no property and hence have the least vested interest in preserving the institution of private property form the revolutionary subject. However the vast majority of the producers of the world are neither workers nor capitalists, but both, or neither. The enduring puzzle has been how to place them in the current historical conjuncture. Even as the political unity of the proletariat as a class is asserted (at times eliding the many divisions within it), the political unity of the petty-producers (peasants and artisans) is denied by Marxism. However united they may be along the dimensions of ethnicity, nationalism, caste, race etc., they are differentiated along class lines and this is what matters 'in the last instance' as far as socialist revolutionary politics is concerned.

Thus, Brass criticizes the Indian communist parties (in particular the Naxalite or Maoist parties) for utilizing existing tribal, ethnic formations for mobilizing peasants. Speaking of Naxalite tribal organizers he notes that,

> ...guerilla activity mobilized through the kinship system was actually structured by—and thus could not but reflect the interest of- the existing socio-economic order, as embodied in the authority of tribal elders. (p. 107)

The determinism in the phrase "and thus could not but reflect..."

is all too obvious. It is tantamount to arguing that because workers' councils are formed in the context of capitalist class relations, they cannot but reflect the interests of capitalism!

Later, Brass asks how it is possible to advocate socialism when,

> ...no account is taken of the fact that tribals and peasants are not just internally differentiated along class lines, but are willing to mobilize on this basis; when it is implied that the future for which socialists are fighting is no different from an idealized tribal past; and when no attempt is made to create prefigurative socialist forms (choosing instead to lock on to existing ones and operate through these). (p. 107)

Kautsky (1988) demonstrates an early example of this when he asserts, "As with the case of maintaining the handicrafts and the peasantry, it is reactionary utopia to call upon Social Democracy to support the resistance of the indigenous peoples of the colonized countries against their expropriation." (p. 330)

Unfortunately, for those who have interpreted Marx mechanically, as long as a political position can be shown to put any one of myriad contradictions before class, it is suspect. Further if within the discourse of such a 'reactionary politics', class is denounced as a foreign ('western') category which will only sow discord in the harmonious/traditional village community, then the suspicion is confirmed. Whether the attack on Eurocentric politics comes from the left or the right is of no consequence. Brass argues:

> ...the RSS endorses an unambiguously populist/nationalist approach to agrarian change and—again like Gandhi, Charan Singh and Sharad Joshi—not only support the cause of 'the small entrepreneur and the yeoman farmer', advocates the abolition of landlordism, but also promotes the concept of village-based artisan production ('cottage industry'). (p. 119)

Since the Hindu fundamentalists (the RSS) also argue for indigenous revolutionary politics it must be the case that any political position adopting indigenous politics must be Hindu fundamentalist! Here we see a classic reversal of positions. Just as socialism and capitalism are equated in communitarian discourses (such as Gandhism and various types of populisms) for being enamoured of large-scale mass production etc., Brass, the Marxist, equates Gandhi and the RSS (the organization which plotted his murder) because they both champion small-scale industry.

The linearity of the deterministic version of historical materialism has been critiqued from within the Marxian tradition (see lecture notes by Anjan Chakravarti). On a dissenting note, Akram-Lodhi and Kay (2010a, p. 195) note that,

> In the canonical works on the agrarian question, the transformation of pre-capitalist social relations of production into capitalist relations of production sketched out by Marx in *Capital* and analysed in precise detail by Lenin in *The Development of Capitalism in Russia* are too often assumed to be a linear process.

Determinist versions of historical materialism predict the disappearance of the peasant, the artisan and the petty trader during the course of human history both because economies of scale ensure that large-scale agriculture (whether capitalist or socialist) will be more productive (certainly more productive per unit labour if not per unit land) than peasant production and because the profit motive ensures the dispossession of small-property holders via the process of primitive accumulation. Under capitalism this will be achieved via class differentiation within the peasantry as more and small and middle peasants lose their holdings and are forced to work as wage-workers for capitalist farmers. Under socialism this will occur via a less anarchic or spontaneous and more planned programme of collectivization by the socialist state. As Githinji and Cullenberg (2003) point out however, attempts to understand society within such a restrictive framework do violence to the complexity of social relations. Every producer must either be a 'worker' or a 'peasant'. And once (s)he is so labelled their historical roles, their futures are already determined. This circumscribes rather than opens up paths to social emancipation.

Interestingly, Marx's 1881 letter to Vera Zasulich also shows that he was willing to be flexible on the issue of which present-day social relations could be turned to progressive ends. Zasulich was a prominent Russian socialist, a translator of Marx into Russian, and along with Lenin a founder of the revolutionary newspaper Iskra. Her query: Is it "historically necessary for every country in the world to pass through all the phases of capitalist production" (Shanin 1983, 99)? Can relatively technologically 'backward' capitalist societies follow their own distinct path to socialism? Marx considered this question in his reply and came down positively on the second question.[10]

It is worth reproducing the letter Zasulich writes to Marx at length:

> You must be aware that your *Capital* enjoys a great popularity in Russia... But what you are probably unaware of is the role that your *Capital* plays in our discussions on the agrarian question in Russia and on our rural commune...In one way or another, the personal destiny of our revolutionary socialists depends on what you have to say on this question. One of two things: either this rural commune, freed from the inordinate demands of the public treasury, from payments to the lords of the manor and from despotic administration, is capable of developing along the socialist path, that is, of gradually organizing its production and its distribution of the products on collectivist bases. In this case the revolutionary socialist must sacrifice all his strength to the liberation of the commune and to its development.
>
> If, on the contrary, the commune is doomed to perish, there remains nothing for the socialist, as such, to do but devote himself to more or less arbitrary calculations in order to learn in how many decades the land of the Russian peasant will pass out of his hands and into those of the bourgeoisie, in how many centuries, perhaps, capitalism will reach in Russia the development it has attained in Western Europe. They will then have to conduct propaganda only among the workers of the towns who will be continually swamped in the mass of peasants who, as a result o£ the dissolution of the commune, will be thrown on the streets of the big cities in the search of hire.
>
> In recent times we often hear it said that the rural commune is an archaic form which history, scientific socialism, in a word, everything that is beyond dispute, has condemned to doom. The people who preach this call themselves your preeminent disciples: "Marxists." Their strongest argument is often: "Marx says so." "But how do you deduce that from his **Capital**? He does not deal in it with the agrarian question and does not speak of Russia," it is objected. "He would have said so had he spoken of our country,"

> reply your somewhat over-rash disciples. You will therefore understand, Citizen, the extent to which your opinion on this question interests us and what a great service you would be doing us by expounding your ideas on the possible fate of our rural commune and on the theory of the historical necessity of every country of the world passing through all the phases of capitalist production.

It is instructive to note that Marx thought over his response to this letter for several months during which he wrote four different drafts before settling on the final version (see Note 10). In response to Zasulich's question about the prospects for building socialism on the basis of the mir, the rural commune in Russia, Marx replies:

"In analysing the genesis of capitalist production, I said":

> At the heart of the capitalist system is a complete separation of ... the producer from the means of production ... *the expropriation of the agricultural producer* is the basis of the whole process. Only in England has it been accomplished in a radical manner. ... *But all the other countries of Western Europe* are following the same course.
>
> The 'historical inevitability' of this course is therefore *expressly* restricted to *the countries of Western Europe*. The reason for this restriction is indicated in Chapter XXXII:
>
> > '*Private property*, founded upon personal labour ... is supplanted by *capitalist private property*, which rests on exploitation of the labour of others, on wage-labour.'
>
> In the Western case, then, *one form of private property is transformed into another form of private property*. In the case of the Russian peasants, however, *their communal property* would have to be transformed into private property.
>
> The analysis in *Capital* therefore provides no reasons either for or against the vitality of the Russian commune. But the special study I have made of it, including a search for original source-material, has convinced me that the commune is the fulcrum for social regeneration in Russia. But in order that it might function as such, the harmful influences assailing it on all sides must first be eliminated, and it must then be assured the normal conditions for spontaneous development.

Akram-Lodhi and Kay (2010a, p. 184) note:

> This letter is more than a historical footnote. It shows that multiple

resolutions of the agrarian question facing small-scale petty commodity producing peasants located and operating within a dominant world capitalist economy were both possible and consistent with Marx's underlying logic.

PART TWO: INDIA

It should be noted at the outset that it is probably incorrect to speak about *one* agrarian question for all of India. Immense regional variation in ecological as well as economic factors ensures very different dynamics in different parts of the country. That said, we will discuss three big themes in the Indian agrarian question which apply to a greater or lesser degree to the whole economy, viz. the mode of production debate, the New Farmers Movements of the 1980s, and lack of structural change or whether the agrarian question has been bypassed in the neoliberal period.

Mode of Production Debate

The Indian 'mode of production debate' brought together some of the most prominent Marxist social scientists in the country to characterize the agrarian structure in India. Was it capitalist or was it semi-feudal? What were the main classes in rural society? How should India's relationship with imperialism be factored into the characterization of Indian society? What kind of revolutionary political strategy followed from the political economic analysis? These were some of the main questions around which the debate was organized. Occurring in the context of the eruption of the Naxalite movement in the late 1960s and its brutal suppression by the Indian state, this debate was from the start, academic as well as political. Today, the numerous peoples' movements, ranging from struggles against displacement and dispossession, to movements for rights over common property resources, to the Maoist movement, are political expressions of enormous rural churning. This provides a backdrop which is very similar to that provided by the late 1960s in India and makes the original debate worth appreciating and understanding.

It will not be possible to give a full account of this debate here. Interested readers are referred to Alice Thorner's (1982) comprehensive three-part survey. For our purposes, it is worth noting that the central issue at stake in the debate was the extent and nature of the development of capitalism in Indian agriculture. This makes the debate directly continuous with earlier writings in the Marxian tradition on the agrarian question, for e.g. Kautsky, Lenin's *Development of Capitalism on Russia* as also Dobb's *Studies in the Development of Capitalism*. But the Indian context also threw up new considerations. What if the economy under consideration was in the periphery of the world capitalist system and was industrializing under neo-colonial conditions? Would its laws of development be the same as for the early industrializers?

The political question was, what is the stage of the Indian revolution? If capitalism had already developed in Indian agriculture, then socialism would be on the agenda. But if pre-capitalist, 'feudal' relations dominated, then a bourgeois revolution was in order first, before socialism could arrive. Readers will recognize the stagism of historical materialism here.

The basic question on what is the prevailing mode of production in Indian agriculture gave rise to a host of theoretical and empirical concerns. For example, the disagreement between Ashok Rudra and Utsa Patnaik over the definition of capitalism, wherein Rudra attempts a statistically derived definition based on landholding patterns while Patnaik insists on a more theoretical definition which she bases not only on production relations (presence or absence of wage-labour) but the manner in which surplus is utilized. Only if surplus is reinvested in expanded production (and technical improvements) does it count as capitalism in Patnaik's view. For this she was criticized by other participants of the debate including Andre Gunder-Frank.

Amit Bhaduri, taking a different and highly influential position, characterized Indian Agriculture as semi-feudal by listing the following features which make it more like 'classic feudalism' than 'industrial capitalism': share-cropping, perpetual indebtedness of the small tenants, and concentration of two modes of exploitation viz. usury and land ownership in the hands of the same economic class; and lack of accessibility to the market for small tenants.

Bhaduri went on to argue that these relations of production create incentives for keeping productivity stagnant. For example, usurious landlords refusing to undertake technical improvements that will raise incomes for their tenants (and for themselves) because higher incomes would lead to lower indebtedness and thereby reduce interest incomes for landlords. These are the 'built-in depresors' of Daniel Thorner and can also be seen as an example of the relations of production acting as 'fetters' on the forces of production. As Byres has noted, the concern with presence of semi-feudal or feudal relations of production is that of, "obstacles to an unleashing of accumulation in both the countryside itself and more generally —in particular, the accumulation associated with capitalist industrialization." (Byres in Akram-Lodhi and Kay 2010a, pp. 179-80)

Revisiting this debate and commenting on the state of production relations in India at the aggregate level, Basole and Basu (2011) note:

> Over the past few decades, the relations of production in the Indian agrarian economy have become increasingly "capitalist"; this conclusion emerges from the fact that the predominant mode of surplus extraction seems to be working through the institution of wage-labour, *the* defining feature of capitalism. Articulated to the global capitalist- imperialist system, the development of capitalism in the periphery has of course not led to the growth of income and living standards of the vast majority of the population. On the contrary, the agrarian economy has continued to stagnate and the majority of the rural population has been consigned to a life of poverty and misery.
>
> Aggregate level data suggests that the two main forms through which the surplus product of direct producers is extracted are (a) surplus value through the institution of wage-labour (which rests on equal exchange), and (b) surplus value through unequal exchange (which mainly affects petty producers) where input prices are inflated and output prices deflated for the direct producers due to the presence of monopoly, monopsony and interlinking of markets. Semi-feudal forms of surplus product

extraction, through the institution of tenant cultivation and sharecropping, have declined over time. Merchant and usurious capital continues to maintain a substantial presence in the life of the rural populace, both of which manage to appropriate a part of the surplus value created through wage-labour, apart from directly extracting surplus value from petty producers through unequal exchange.

From a class perspective, a salient feature of not just Indian agriculture but of the entire economy is the incomplete nature of class differentiation and the presence of 'classes of labour' (Bernstein, 2004) rather than a clear bourgeoisie and working class. There is a continuum in which the producer retains or loses control over the means of production and the labour process as well as product to varying degrees. In the agrarian sector this can be seen through the mix of sources through which marginal and small peasants earn their incomes. Casual wage labour, own cultivation, and non-farm businesses all contribute to the family's livelihood.

The persistence of small capital in agriculture and elsewhere has been debated in both the Marxian and the mainstream development literature as the question of the informal sector and of delayed structural change in the Indian economy. An important question that this throws up is what shape anti-capitalist politics will take in the country in the presence of 'classes of labour'. What solidarities are present in the working classes which are divided not only by caste, gender, and ethnicity, but also by degrees of possession of the means of production.

The 'New Farmers Movements' in India

The 1970s and 80s saw large numbers of the peasantry in India mobilized against the Indian State. These peasants' or farmers' movements arose in many different states and at their height brought hundreds of thousands of peasants into mass rallies, demonstrations courted arrests and road and railway blockages (*rasta roko* and *rail roko*). Some principal organizations in the movement were Shetkari Sanghatana in Maharashtra led by Sharad Joshi, the Bharatiya Kisan Union (BKU) in Punjab,

Harayana and Uttar Pradesh (BKU-UP led by Chaudhary Mahendra Singh Tikait), and the Karnataka Rajya Raytha Sangh (KRRS) in Karnataka led by Nanjundaswamy (Sahasrabudhey 1986).

These 'new farmers' movements' (NFMs) challenged the classical agrarian question or transition narrative on several counts. First, they articulated a rural vision for India's future, second, they asserted the rights of the peasantry to its own surplus or in other words challenged the terms of trade between agriculture and industry, and third, the peasants were their own leaders and identified the principal locus of exploitation outside the village. They did not fight a class war with the landlords, but rather a 'terms-of-trade war' with the state.

Though the movements were a mixed success and eventually fizzled out in the 1990s, they raised some important questions regarding contradictions in Indian society, the type of industrialization needed in India, the relationship between large and small capital, and the place of peasants and artisans in the national economy.

The reluctance of the peasantry to be a 'handmaiden' to industrial interests and its identification of the principal contradiction as one between town and country rather than between classes both ran counter to the classical historical materialist narrative. The principal demands were for higher output and lower input prices. In contrast to traditional 'land to the tiller' peasant movements which identified local landlords as the class enemy, in the new 'remunerative prices' movements, the focus of attack was the Central Government in New Delhi (the Indian State) which was seen as the key actor is setting the terms of trade between agriculture and industry. As evidenced by the nature of the demands, the farmers who participated in these movements practised commercialized agriculture. They purchased many inputs from the market (seeds, pesticides, fertilizers, electricity, and water) and sold output to the market. Thus they were 'peasants' not in the sense that they practised subsistence agriculture and handicraft, but in the sense that they owned the means of production, employed family labour and a few (in some cases no) wage-workers (see Omvedt, 1993 for one overview of the movement).

From the beginning, these movements were controversial. They were seen as movements of 'kulaks' (Russian for 'rich peasant') explicitly drawing a parallel between the Preobrazhensky-Bukharin debate and the problem facing Soviet Union in the 1920s before Stalin's campaign against the rich farmers. The movement's spokespersons identified the principal contradiction plaguing the rural countryside as not class exploitation of the agricultural wage-workers but instead a conflict between 'town and country'. They argued that surpluses produced in the rural areas (i.e. largely in agriculture) should not be siphoned away via state policy to the urban areas to finance industry, but rather should be retained in the rural areas where they could finance development and industry. Polemically this was expressed as, 'We don't want your schools and hospitals, just give us our due and we will build our own.'

The movements were organized around the principle of non-violent mass action unlike the other peasant movement of the period, the Maoist Naxalite movement based on the strategy of armed struggle. In the movement's heyday in the mid-1980s mass rallies saw hundreds of thousands of peasants marching to Delhi and enacting various actions such as *rail roko, rasta roko, gherao* and *jail bharo* (stop trains, block roads, encircling officials, and courting arrest). Villages were closed to government officials, stocks of produce were held from the market leading to a steep rise in prices, and in some instances peasants refused to pay electricity bills and interest on loans from banks and credit cooperatives. Sahasrabudhey (1991) notes that these methods are distinct from strike methods in that they disrupt the market and do not disrupt production, "as if symbolically point out that it is not relations of production but relations of exchange that are the root evil." (p. 146).

Thus the terms of trade (real or perceived) between agriculture and industry played a very important role in these movements. One leader noted:

> ...our struggle is not for issues like electricity tariff or land legislation. We have a wider vision. The whole of the rural economy should be changed. It should not be a field of exploitation

> as it has been since British rule, a generating centre for the national economy. The surplus should remain in the villages, and from this the appropriate growth of village-based industries and development should be made rather than exploiting the villages to create a surplus for urban-based industries which only create unemployment and poverty. (Bipin Desai, a Gujarati peasant leader quoted in Lindberg, 1994, pp. 96-97)

Gail Omvedt, a participant of the mode of production debate and a prominent supporter of the NFMs argued that "The anti-state and decentralist thrust of the movement, the aim of retaining the accumulated surplus and its reinvestment in the village have challenged the traditional Marixst notion of industrialization, large-scale, urban-based 'collective' production as being progressive." (Omvedt 1994, p. 13)

The theoretical disagreements over the character of the movement of 'independent agricultural producers' (Rudolph and Rudolph, 1987) manifested themselves even over the issue of what to call it. Omvedt (1993) notes that left commentators have been reluctant to call it a peasant movement. Here is now she describes the movements:

> These were not sharecroppers or poor peasants fighting landlords; they were 'independent commodity producers,' peasants caught up in the throes of market production, dependent on the state and capital for their inputs of fertilizer, pesticide, seeds, electricity, and water and for the purchase of their products. So different was the situation from the traditional understanding of the peasantry that most scholars and left commentators have refused to call it a 'peasant' movement at all, but instead have described it as a 'farmers" movement, though there is no terminology for the distinction (presumable that between subsistence peasants and commercially oriented farmers) in any Indian language. (p. 101)

Rudolph and Rudolph (1987) in their extensive study of the political economy of post-independence India, posited the category of 'bullock capitalist' to describe farmers with landholdings from 2.5-15 acres, i.e. holdings too large to make them landless or marginal and too small to make them landlords or capitalist farmers. Thus they say:

> Bullock capitalists are not kulaks...Our definition of bullock

> capitalists as an agrarian class distinguishes them from kulak-like Indian farmers (large landowners) on the one hand and marginal farmers or landless agricultural workers on the other. Because they are neither capitalists nor workers, neither exploiters nor exploited, they pose a conceptual problem for liberals as well as Marxists concerned to identify suitable interests or classes with which to conflict or ally.

The view of the movement's ideologues was that remunerative prices would benefit all peasants who sold to the market, which was a vast majority of peasants. Better prices would lead to a chain reaction of higher wages for labourers, rural industrialization and employment generation. Thus the *peasantry as a whole* would benefit. This 'trickle down' theory was attacked by left intellectuals (see Banaji 1994 for one strong attack). First, the suggestion that higher prices would lead to higher wages was questioned since this ignored the class conflict inherent in the wage-setting equation. Second, the point was raised that small peasants may be net buyers of food-grains and thus might as likely be hurt by higher food prices as they might benefit.

The controversy over class differentiation within the peasantry versus the contradiction between town and country was encapsulated in Sharad Joshi's slogan 'Bharat versus India'. Most Marxist commentators interpreted the Bharat-India divide as a country-town divide. Bharat was the exploited countryside (the agricultural sector) and India constituted the cities and towns, the industrial sector. The state, by setting the terms of trade between the two was seen to be favouring India over Bharat. This 'populist' ideology was interpreted thus:

> There are no 'exploiters' in the villages; that all the villagers have essentially the same interest which assumed an economic form in the demand for remunerative prices for marketed produce; and that the Bharat/India divide is absolute, a situation whereby village and town do not share any common interests. (Dhanagare, p. 87)

Omvedt and Galla (1987), defending the movement pointed out that Sharad Joshi himself, at one of the Shetkari Sanghatana meetings had said: "I have never said that the Bharat-India divide was a village-city one." Omvedt and Galla discovered that all the movement's literature defined 'Bharat' as including 'refugees from the villages in the cities', while the elite-rulers of the villages were classed as part of 'India'. Thus they accused left commentators of reducing a more complex contradiction to a simple 'town versus country' issue. The authors go on to argue that the contradiction being highlighted by the farmers' movements was something akin to a 'formal-informal' divide. And further that the movement did not necessarily deny the existence of class, rather it identified another contradiction as being more important. This was a tough pill to swallow. As Omvedt (1993) notes:

> The fact is that while a traditional Marxist framework could to some extent handle the other movements by using concepts of 'nationality' or even 'caste' and 'gender' alongside of or supplementary to a 'class analysis,' the peasant movement directly challenged the class framework itself. It based itself on and theorized the exploitation of the 'peasantry' as a whole, but a 'Marxist' framework that took 'private property' in the means of production as the only factor for getting to the heart of exploitation and contradiction was simply incapable of seeing the 'peasantry as a whole.' (p. 104)

There is much to learn from the New Farmers Movements and related literature for those who want to understand the nature of the agrarian question in India. There are no easy answers here because what is at stake is nothing less than how to creatively apply Marxian theory in analyzing non-European societies. This question is still up for debate.

Neoliberal India: Agrarian Question Bypassed?

The debates we have looked at in the foregoing pages start from nineteenth century Europe and continue till India of the 1980s. What of the current neoliberal period? Is the agrarian question still relevant? During the hey-day of the NFMs agriculture still contributed over 30 per cent to GDP and accounted for over two-thirds of the labour force. Now the contribution to GDP is down to 15 per cent and falling. It is true that just under half of the labour-force still reports agriculture as the source of primary employment, but less and less do agrarian questions seem to occupy centre-stage in politics and policymaking except as rear-guard narratives of preventing forcible land acquisition and farm suicides.

Thus, Lerche (2013, p. 393) notes that:

> The overall role of the agricultural sector in India is changing, slowly but steadily. In the early 1980s, more than two-thirds of the working population were in agriculture and in 2009–10 this had fallen to close to the 50 per cent mark. However, this change does not seem to form part of a classical agrarian transition leading to dynamic industrial development. In fact – as in many other developing countries today – the shift in employment has been to the service sector and to construction, not to manufacturing.

The land question and primitive accumulation are still important (see chapters by Rajesh Bhattacharya and Pranab Kanti Basu), but the classical agrarian transition narrative seems less and less relevant. Many observers have noted that the transition (with which we started) has failed to occur in India. Unlike East Asian countries such as Japan, Korea, Taiwan, China and to some extent Vietnam, India did not witness a thoroughgoing land reform, nor a rapid development of the formal industrial and service economy, resulting in a bloated informal sector.

The contemporary Indian economy can be characterized by four well-known, stylized facts, related to structural change, employment patterns relating to the distribution between the formal and informal jobs, structure of landholding and resistance to land acquisition.

First, the sectoral employment shares have been changing far more slowly than output shares, resulting in a large proportion of the labour-force being trapped in low productivity agricultural work. Between 1987-88 and 2009-10, share of value added coming from the primary sector (composed of agriculture and allied activities) halved from 31.72 percent to 15.23 percent. Over the same period, the share of employment in the primary sector merely declined from 64.87 percent to 51.3 percent.

Second, over the past two decades there has been virtually no growth of formal sector employment, while the informal sector has grown in absolute and relative terms. Between 1991 and 2011, the total labour force in India increased from 338.67 million to 476.66 million (World Development Indicators Online Database). Over the same period, total (i.e., private and public) employment in the organized sector increased from 26.73 million to 28.99 million. Thus, over this two-decade period of rapid economic growth, more than 98 percent of the *increase* in the labour force was absorbed in unorganized sector employment.

Third, the average agricultural land holding is small and has been decreasing in size over time, and agricultural output and incomes in per capita terms are largely stagnant (or even falling). When we look at the structure of landholding we see that between 1961 and 2003, average area of ownership holding declined from 2.01 to 0.81 hectares. Over the same period, the proportion of households owning less than 1 hectare of land increased from 75.22 percent to 90.4 percent; the proportion of total area owned by such households increased, over this four-decade period, from 20 percent to 43 percent

Fourth, there is resistance by farmers to giving up land despite low incomes in agriculture. Whether for construction of Special Economic Zones (SEZs) or for industrial projects or for infrastructural development, recent years have seen dogged resistance by farmers to giving up their agricultural land. Struggles against land acquisition have flared up in different parts of the country.

But importantly as Lerche notes,

> Today, agriculture does not appear to significantly support growth in Indian non-agricultural sectors, neither through capital transfers nor through the creation of a major rural market for industrial produce. (ibid, p. 400)

Seeing the divergence between the growth rates of agriculture and the rest of the economy Lerche (2013, p. 391) observes:

> On the basis of this evidence, the non-agrarian Indian bourgeoisie does not seem to need to press for a solution to the agrarian question in the classical sense; its functionality has been taken over by non-agrarian, mainly foreign, finance and non-agrarian

markets. This, in Bernstein's schema, means that the agrarian question of capital has been bypassed.

Under these circumstances what is the future of the agrarian sector in India? The lowest point in recent history, the period between 1991 and 2004 that saw a vast increase in farm suicides and agricultural growth rates below 1 per cent may have been crossed (agricultural growth was back to nearly 3 per cent in the period 2004-2012 (Lerche, 2013). But new contradictions between the peasantry on the one hand and the global corporate food regime on the other, highlighted by organizations such as Via Campesina have arisen, which we have not had the time to discuss here but may become more important in the years to come.

I close with some questions. At the national policy level, why is there a complete lack of vision with respect to the sector that still employs nearly half the Indian workforce? Can India develop a path on her own that has a legitimate place for the vast majority of its workforce who are self-employed in agriculture or other petty production? And finally, returning to Vera Zasulich's query: what would new politics for building socialism look like if it did not follow the stagism of orthodox historical materialism but thought creatively about different possible futures?

Questions for Further Discussion

Note: These questions can either be used as prompts to start a general discussion or as debating issues between groups of students.

1. What do you see as the future of the peasantry in India? What about other small property holders who work in the informal sector?
2. Can peasants, artisans, and other small-property owners play a constructive role in the struggle against capitalism? What do we need from a theory of history so that such possibilities open up?
3. How can we theorize the class contradiction between small capital owners and their workers in the backdrop

of the larger structure of corporate capitalism and imperialism?

4. One of the main theses of the NFMs was that the principal locus of exploitation of the peasantry lay outside the village, not inside it. What is meant by this proposition? Contrast this with a Marxian understanding of rural society.
5. Do you agree that the agrarian question has been bypassed in India today? If yes, why? If not, why not?
6. Mitra (1977) notes that Preobrazhensky, 'turned Rosa Luxemburg on her head'. What is meant by this? If we take Rosa Luxemburg's assertion of the necessity of an 'outside' for capital seriously, how does it change our perception of rural struggles in general and the NFM in particular?

REFERENCES

Akram-Lodhi, A.H. and Kay, C. (2010a). Surveying the Agrarian Question (Part 1): Unearthing Foundations, Exploring Diversity. *The Journal of Peasant Studies*, *37*(1), 177-202.

—— (2010b). Surveying the Agrarian Question (Part 2): Current Debates and Beyond. *The Journal of Peasant Studies*, *37*(2), 255-284.

Banaji, J. (1994). The Farmers' Movements: A Critique of Conservative Rural Coalitions. In Tom Brass ed. New Farmers' Movements in India. *The Journal of Peasant Studies*, Special Issue 21: 3/4.

Basole, A. and Basu, D. (2011). Relations of Production and Modes of Surplus Extraction in India: Part I–Agriculture. *Economic and Political Weekly*, 46(14), 41-58.

Bentall, J. and Corbridge, S. (1996). Urban-Rural Relations, Demand Politics and the "New Agrarianism" in Northwest India: The Bharatiya Kisan Union. *Transactions of the Institute of British Geographers*, 21:1, 27-48.

Bernstein, H. (2004). 'Changing Before Our Very Eyes': Agrarian Questions and the Politics of Land in Capitalism Today. *Journal of Agrarian Change*, 4 (12), 190-225.

Bernstein, H. (2009). VI Lenin and AV Chayanov: Looking Back, Looking Forward. *The Journal of Peasant Studies*, *36*(1), 55-81.

Bhattacharya, R. and Basole, A. (2009). The Phantom of Liberty: Mo(der)nism and Postcolonial Imaginations in India. In Rajani

Kanth ed. The Challenge of Eurocentrism: Global Perspectives, Policy and Prospects. Palgrave: New York.

Brass T. (2000). Peasants, Populism and Postmodernism: The Return of the Agrarian Myth. Frank Cass: London.

Byres, T.J. (1995). 'Political Economy, the Agrarian Question and the Comparative Method'. *Economic and Political Weekly*, Vol. 30, No. 10, pp. 507-513.

Githinji, M. and Cullenberg, S.E. (2003). 'Deconstructing the Peasantry: Class and Development in Rural Kenya', *Critical Sociology*, 29:1, 67-88.

Griffin, K., Khan, A.R., and Ickowitz, A. (2002). 'Poverty and the Distribution of Land'. *Journal of Agrarian Change*, 2(3), 279-330.

Kanth, R.K. (1986). *Political Economy and Laissez-faire: Economics and Ideology in the Ricardian Era*. Rowman & Littlefield.

Kautsky, K. (1988). The Agrarian Question, 2 Vols., translated by Pete Burgess. Zwan Publications: London.

Lenneberg, C. (1988). 'Sharad Joshi and the Farmers: The Middle Peasant Lives!' *Pacific Affairs*, 61:3, 446-464.

Lerche, J. (2013). The Agrarian Question in Neoliberal India: Agrarian Transition Bypassed?. *Journal of Agrarian Change*, 13(3), 382-404.

Lindberg, S. (1994). 'New Farmers' Movements in India as Structural Response and Collective Identity Formation: The Cases of the Shetkari Sanghatana and the BKU' in Tom Brass ed. *New Farmers' Movements in India. The Journal of Peasant Studies*, Special Issue 21: 3/4.

Marx, K. (1987). Peasantry as a Class. Selections from the 18th Brumaire and Class Struggle in France, in Teodor Shanin ed. Peasants and Peasant Societies: Selected Readings. New York: Basil Blackwell

Mitra, A. (1977). *Terms of Trade and Class Relations: An Essay in Political Economy*. Frank Cass: London.

Omvedt, G. (1993). Reinventing Revolution: New Social Movements and the Socialist Tradition in India. ME Sharpe: London.

Omvedt, G and Galla, C. (1987). Ideology for Provincial Propertied Class? *Economic and Political Weekly*, 22:45, 1925-1926.

Patnaik, U. (2007). *Marx and his successors on the Agrarian Question*. LeftWord: New Delhi.

Preobrazhensky, E. (1926). *The New Economics*, translated by Brian Pearce with an Introduction by Alec Nove.

Rudolph, L.I and Rudolph, S.H. (1987). In *Pursuit of Lakshmi: The Political Ecoonmy of the Indian State*. The University of Chicago Press: Chicago.

Sahasrabudhey, S. (1986). *The Peasant Movement Today,* Ashish Publishing House: New Delhi.

Sahasrabudhey, S. (1991). *Science and Politics: Essays in Gandhian Perspective.* Ashish Publishing House: New Delhi.

Shanin, T. (1984). *Late Marx and the Russian Road: Marx and 'The Peripheries of Capitalism',* Monthly Review Press: New York.

Thorner, A. (1982). Semi-feudalism or capitalism? Contemporary debate on classes and modes of production in India. *Economic and Political Weekly,* 1961-1968.

NOTES

1. Note however the 'peasant' is a historically contingent category and lack of clarity on what is meant by this term can cause theoretical problems. Kautsky (1988) discusses the transformation of the largely self-sufficient peasant-artisan into a peasant (i.e. a farmer who owns small property, how small is small?) who is much more dependent on the market for a living. This is the distinction between independent producers and independent commodity producers. The word 'peasant' in the Chayanovian (after Russian economist A V Chayanov) sense describes self-sufficient producers who do not engage with the market is any significant degree. However as used in Kautsky 'peasant' is taken to mean a petty-proprietor who owns means of production in whole or in part, who engages in self-exploitation and exploitation of unpaid family labor, sells produce in the market, but does not hire wage-workers. In more recent literature terms such as 'middle peasant' or 'rich peasant' are used to describe classes that may hire in labour while working the field themselves.
2. This refers to the empirically observed relationship that as farm size decreases output per acre increases. In other words land productivity is inversely related to farm size. This has spawned a huge literature. See Griffin, Khan and Ickowitz (2002).
3. Marx, *Capital,* Vol. 1, Ch. 30: http://www.marxists.org/archive/marx/works/1867-c1/ch30.htm
4. P Patnaik, Socialism and the Peasantry at http://www.monthlyreview.org/mrzine/patnaik110209.html
5. 'Terms of trade' are basically relative prices, in this case, between agricultural products and industrial products.
6. It should also be noted that a few years later Stalin implemented Preobrazhensly's program with far more ruthlessness than

envisaged by the latter.

7. The question of small property has a deeply ambivalent position in bourgeois society. On the one hand capitalism is (falsely) equated with petty production ('self-employment') in popular discourse. On the other hand the majority of the working class owns no property other than a house.
8. Marx and Engels, Manifesto of the Communist Party http://www.marxists.org/archive/marx/works/1848/communist-manifesto/index.htm
9. V I Lenin, Economics and Politics in the Era of the Dictatorship of the Proletariat http://www.marxists.org/archive/lenin/works/1919/oct/30.htm
10. See Shanin ([1983] 2009) for various drafts of Marx's response to Zasulich, a Russian communist. Also available online at: https://www.marxists.org/archive/marx/works/1881/zasulich/

12

Development of Capitalism in India

Rajesh Bhattacharya

This chapter is partly based on 'Capitalism in Post-Colonial India: Primitive Accumulation Under Dirigiste and Laissez Faire Regimes' by Bhattacharya (2010) Unpublished PhD dissertation, University of Massachusetts, Amherst.

Introduction

Indian capitalism is often viewed through the Western lens. Ever since the two World Wars and the Great Depression rocked the Western economies in the first half of the last century, there has been an intense debate on the best way to manage capitalism—i.e. whether to have minimal or substantial government involvement in the economy. Thus, two distinct ideas of the state vied for supremacy in the West—the liberal state and the welfare state. The liberal state is premised on the idea that class contradictions in capitalism are automatically ameliorated through economic growth and economic growth is maximized in a free-market economy that encourages competition and innovation. The liberal view envisages a minimal role of the state committed only to protection of property rights, enforcement of contracts and minimal social safety net for the poor. The welfare state is premised on the idea that class-contradictions in capitalism need to be stabilized by the state through some sort of capital-labour accord. The state would ensure productivity growth and competitiveness as well as redistribution to the working class of resulting economic gains, thus facilitating rising profits for capitalists and rising well-being of workers.

The success of East Asian capitalisms has given birth to a new idea of the state—the 'developmental' state. The 'developmental' state is different from the liberal state in that economic growth is actively engineered by the state through purposive, selective and clinical interventions in specific markets coupled with a harsh reward-punish system for domestic capitalists to facilitate rapid capital accumulation and innovation. The 'developmental' state is different from the welfare state in that it is authoritarian; it represses democracy, and working class mobilization, in particular, and insulates the state from popular demands. The 'developmental' state is based on a state-capital accord unlike the welfare state which is based on a capital-labour accord. The idea of the 'developmental' state is firmly anchored in the traditional discourse on the relative merits of state and market in enabling capitalism. It exemplifies the opportunities for late industrializing countries in using state power to manipulate market forces to engineer rapid industrialization.

The Indian situation is arguably far more complex. Unlike the Western liberal and welfare states, democracy had taken root and consolidated itself in India at very low levels of per capita. This has resulted in unprecedented popular demands on the state and the state remains central to the life of the overwhelming majority of the Indian population. Unlike the East Asian developmental states, it was not feasible for the Indian state to subordinate politics to the problem of capital accumulation. The brief Emergency period of 1975-77 amply illustrated the impossibility of the triumph of bureaucratic governance over political democracy. But, even before that, clinical interventions in the economy by the Indian State through Five Year Plans to facilitate industrialization through rapid capital accumulation had to be abandoned by mid-1960s in response to emergencies, both external and internal. The political consensus that supported the Planning exercise had started to fray as early as mid-1960s. By early 1970s, the Indian State had decisively taken the so-called 'populist' turn, as much in response to rising poverty that accompanied early industrialization drives (Dandekar and Rath (1971)) as to the political crisis of the 1960s. Techno-bureaucratic planning turned out to be incompatible with democracy. Planning in the sense we have come to understand it died with Nehru.

While pro-business and pro-market reforms since mid-1980s have transformed Indian capitalism, the resulting social contradictions of free-market capitalism have once again brought the state back with vengeance through a series of public policies of unprecedented scale and significance—e.g. the NREGA, the Food Security Bill, the new Land Acquisition Bill and the Forest Rights Act etc, each of which can potentially be a game-changer not only for poverty-alleviation programmes, but development of capitalism in general. Just as the economic and political crises engendered by the early Five Year Plans (when the Indian business groups had a comfortable and trusting relationship with the Nehru-led government) precipitated the remarkable acts of state intervention by the Indian state (nationalization of bank, insurance and coal sectors, MRTP and FERA Acts, and reservation for small-scale sector etc.) in the late 1960s and early 1970s, the crisis of post-reforms Indian capitalism have precipitated the recent spate of policies. Every time the Indian state had moved close to the capitalist class, it had to suffer the political crisis of legitimacy.

The main contradiction in India is the contradiction inherent in the *co-evolution* of capitalism and democracy. Both capitalism and democracy are processes in a society, with their relative autonomy and mutually constitutive effects on each other such that they support and undermine each other at the same time. None can be reduced to the other in a causal framework. The Indian experience is an exemplar of this *co-evolution* of capitalism and democracy and defies characterization in terms of categories drawn from histories of Western and Eastern capitalisms.

For England, substantial re-organization of property had taken place before the advent of democracy. The development of capitalism in USA was as much dependent on explicit negation of democracy (annihilation of indigenous population and slavery) or indirect violation of it (restricting access of the

African-American population to voting rights). Where political culture was strong, say France, there was slow emergence of capitalism. In fact, France—the cradle of modernity and democracy—experienced the slowest transition to capitalism. Predominance of artisanal and peasant modes of production continued till Second World. Moreover, throughout the nineteenth century, France, vacillated between republican, Bonapartist and monarchical forms. Most late-industrializing countries had unstable relations with democracy – e.g. Germany, Italy, Spain in the twentieth century. In all or most countries of Europe, dispossessed, excluded and redundant/surplus labour force emigrated to new continents—settler-colonies of Europe across the world, where primitive accumulation was literally exported and targeted at indigenous populations. In short, these European countries could shield capital from democracy by exporting undemocracy abroad. In addition, most of these countries had access to non-democratic spaces outside their societies but within their sphere of control of national capital in the form of colonies.

The majority of twentieth century cases of successful industrialization or capitalism came at the cost of democracy—starting from Soviet Russia, Japan and East Asian countries and now China. In Latin America, parts of Africa and South-East Asia, the unstable relation between capitalism and democracy is well known. In certain cases where inequality has been extremely high, politics has been a spectacle itself—radical popular movements to civil wars to extreme authoritarianism. In short, we do not have a model of co-evolution of capitalism and (bourgeois) democracy that we see in India.

It is this history that sets the Indian state apart from the ones we refer to as liberal, welfare or developmental states. First, the institutionalization of democracy in early stages of industrialization in India effectively ruled out the emergence of the 'developmental' state which is based on a state-capital accord through suppression of democratic politics. Second, and this goes without saying, the low level of industrialization and consequently, the low level of capitalist surplus in the economy, ruled out the emergence of any welfare state based on a capital-labour accord supported by the state through tax-transfer policies. In Western liberal states, democracy had consolidated around capital which then brought into existence the liberal state to advance the interests of the capitalist class. The subsequent oscillations between the liberal and the welfare-state reflect the changing requirements of the conditions of existence of capital in the face of class-contradictions within capitalist economy. At the time of independence, the Indian capitalist class either lacked the political legitimacy or economic strength to embark on the path of rapid capital accumulation by itself and thus actively sought or otherwise necessitated the commanding presence of the Indian state in the economy to jump-start industrialization. On the other hand, legitimation of the new sovereign Indian state in a society scarred by a colonial past required the state to establish connections with the people through a series of welfare/development policies.

India: The Social Context at the Time of Independence

The historical experience of the colonial rule and the nationalist movement shaped the views of the new sovereign Indian state in matters of economic policy. The idea behind economic planning was to reverse the effects of the colonial rule—namely, to industrialize the Indian economy and reverse the long process of deindustrialization under the colonial rule, to develop an indigenous capital goods industry and thus reduce dependence on Western countries for technology and capital goods and to break out of the colonial pattern of trade. Jawaharlal Nehru, the first Prime Minister of India, and a Fabian socialist, was greatly influenced by the experience of Soviet industrialization. While choosing not to take sides with either the Soviet or the Western camp during the Cold War, he nevertheless adopted Soviet economic planning as the vehicle of economic development in independent India. The role of the state would be to directly undertake capitalist industrialization to achieve social objectives like eradication of poverty and generation of employment opportunities. In fact, the state could and did replace, restrain, regulate and circumscribe private capitalists in order to achieve its goal.

It must be remembered that it was Gandhi rather than Nehru who was the iconic leader of the struggle for independence; Gandhi mobilized the passion and energy of the Indian masses against British rule by privileging tradition over modernity and by explicitly rejecting the modern Western industrial future for India. Gandhi's economic views were the exact opposite of Nehru's; Gandhi was an anti-modernist, liked Ruskin, Thoreau and Tolstoy, shunned modern capitalist industries and labour-displacing technology, favored decentralized economically self-sufficient village republics and was a quasi-anarchist in his opposition to the strong state. Planning was initiated against these divergent and opposed views of economic development, which threatened to undermine the possibilities of any consensus on economic development.

Certain effects of the colonial rule shaped Gandhi's views and in turn helped him harness popular energy in the struggle for independence. First, the colonial rule severely dislocated the traditional economy of India consisting of stable, self-sufficient village economies, with its population ordered by the caste system and a village-level division of labour, largely dominated by non-market production and allocation of goods and services and a unity of agriculture and industry that had previously shielded them from the corrosive impact of trade. Second, the introduction of private property rights in land by the British led to erosion of many of the customary rights enjoyed by the peasants as well as the traditional social security systems that alleviated the misery of the peasants in times of crises in the pre-colonial social formation of the Indian sub-continent. On the other hand, the nationalization of forests in the name of scientific forestry and declaration of 'wastes' and 'commons' as state property for raising state revenues unleashed processes of primitive accumulation that undermined many traditional economic activities. Third, the very processes that led to the emergence of capitalist industries in Britain also led to destruction of Indian industries—for example, protective tariffs in Britain enabled capitalist industries to develop there while free imports of British manufactured goods undermined traditional non-capitalist and capitalist products of India. India was gradually inserted into the colonial pattern of trade—a supplier of raw materials and an importer of manufactured goods. This phenomenon is most starkly illustrated in the case of textile industries in the two countries. This colonial pattern of trade was further strengthened by the development of the railways. Fourth, with the fall of the pre-colonial surplus appropriators and subsumed classes, urban Indian industries patronized by them also declined. Luxury consumption by the Mughal imperial court and the maintenance of the army supported a large urban craft industry. With decline in the royal power, such demand for the whole range of urban manufactures declined leading to urban unemployment. Palace-factories (*karkhanas*) which were established to cater to the demand for the royal court and the urban nobility were closed down. The new Indian elite during the colonial period—including the new agrarian feudal class emerging after the Mutiny of 1857 and the end of the Company rule in 1858—tried to emulate the British lifestyle and consumed imported British goods. On the other hand, the new middle class, a product of English education, developed a taste for British goods.

Share in national income: Sivasubramanian, S. (1997)

	1900-01	*1910-11*	*1920-21*	*1930-31*	*1940-41*	*1940-47*
Primary	68.4	66.4	61.2	58	54.7	54.6
Secondary	10.8	12.1	10.5	14.2	13.4	14.9
Tertiary	22.3	23	29.3	29.4	33.2	30.5
			Share in work force			
Primary	75	75.6	76.8	76	73.9	76.2
Secondary	10.7	10.3	9.4	9	10.2	9.8
Tertiary	14.3	14.1	13.8	15	15.9	14

The colonial period had left a large population dependent on agriculture and an extremely low land-man ratio that hampered productivity of agricultural labour. By the last quarter of the nineteenth century, deindustrialization of India under colonial rule was complete. Modern capitalist industries were set up by both Indians and British starting from the second half of the nineteenth century. However, if we look at the occupational structure of India over the period 1900 to 1947, we find that while modern industries expanded, the sectoral location of labour hardly changed.

The pressure of labour force on agriculture lead to a steady decline in land-labour ratio and agriculture became the reservoir of surplus population as poor peasants desperately held on to rapidly fragmenting land as their only means of production in conditions of surplus population. At the time of independence, therefore, "there was much scope for further primitive accumulation".

Indian Business and Planning

Three years before independence, in 1944, seven leading Indian capitalists, aided by an economist, prepared 'A Brief Memorandum Outlining a Plan of Economic Development for India'—a document that came to be known as the Bombay Plan. The Bombay Plan unequivocally called upon the sovereign Indian state (foreseeable in the very near future) to intervene in the economy in promoting industrialization. Though wary of state ownership and management of business, big business nevertheless asked the state to have rigorous and extensive control over the economy. India was probably the first country outside the Soviet Bloc to experiment with comprehensive and extensive economic planning and it is interesting to note that economic planning—usually associated with socialist economies— was actually asked for by business houses in India (Sen, 1982, p. 92)[1].

There were several economic and political reasons for that. At the end of the British rule, particularly during and after the Second World War, private businesses did not enjoy a favourable public opinion in India because of the famine and falling real wages while business profits soared both due to wartime excess demand as also from black marketing. Private business also thought that Quit India Movement of 1942 might go out of control of Congress and turn against Indian private business as well. Even if that did not happen, independent India's government might be confronted with strong and violent demands for income redistribution, and therefore forced into adopting 'populist' policies not suited to the country's long run interest. At the same time, the experience of the two World Wars had impressed upon private businesses the reality that they were completely dependent on imports for capital goods and the war-time build-up of 'sterling reserves' and 'dollar pool' provided a unique opportunity to use the foreign exchange reserves to build up a domestic capital goods industry. They could not wait for the private sector to come forth with the necessary investment. The state was therefore called forth to seize the opportunity.

The idea of Planning had been around since 1930s in the ideas of Indian economists, business leaders and even colonial administrators. The National Planning Committee was created by Congress in 1938. Its idea of planning was essentially concerned with the question of industrializing the economy. Subhas Bose nominated the following among the members of the NPC—Jawaharlal Nehru, Sir M. Visvesvaraya, Sir Purushottamdas Thakurdas, Dr. Meghnad Saha, A.D, Shroff, K.T. Shah, A.K. Saha, Dr Nazir Ahmed, Dr V.S, Dubey, Ambalal Sarabhai and Dr. J.C. Ghosh. In 1939, NPC formed 27 sub-committees to look at different aspects of planning. Members of the sub-committees included leading industrialists like Lala Shri Ram, J.R.D. Tata, B.N. Mukherji, Kasturbhai Labhai, S.L. Kirloskar, Padamphat Singhania, D.P. Khaitan. NPC however became defunct by 1943 as the Congress leaders were in jail because of Quit India movement.

In 1941 a Post-War Reconstruction Committee was set up to 'prepare developmental plans for India', replaced by Reconstruction Committee of the [Viceroy's] Council in 1943. While the Congress leaders were in jail. Industrialists like Birla, Thakurdas etc. joined the committee. The Department of Planning and Development' was set up with Ardeshir Dalal (a director of Tatas as its head). Interestingly, socialism-leaning K.T. Shah and Meghnad Saha were excluded from it and 'socialist' Nehru was in jail. All the people who authored the 'Bombay Plan' were in the Policy Committees of the Government—JRD Tata, GD Birla, P. Thakurdas, AD Shroff, Lala Shri Ram, Ardeshir Dalal, Kasturbhai Lalbhai and John Mathai.

Before we come to a comparison of Bombay Plan and India's first three Five Year Plans, it is to be noted that the Industrial Policy of the Government of India, 1945 clearly acknowledged the influence of the Bombay Plan. The 1945 policy recommended central control over twenty categories of basic industries, (Iron and Steel, Machines, Plants and Tools, Electricals, Chemicals, Transport, Cement etc. and some consumer goods industries like Textiles, Sugar, Automobiles, etc) and nationalization of other 'basic industries of national importance' in which adequate private capital was not forthcoming (aircraft, automobiles and tractors, chemical machinery, machine tools etc.). In some industries (shipbuilding, locomotives and boilers etc.) both government and private industries would exist. Overall industrial development would be controlled, through industrial licensing. To allow freedom to small industrial enterprises, any new industry beyond a certain capital value would require licence from the Government to operate. This, the Government observed, would enable them to distribute industries all over the country and check over-concentration in certain places.

Amal Sanyal (2011) argues that the similarities between the Bombay Plan and India's first three Five Year Plans are striking. Both assumed a central role of the government. The Bombay Plan admitted that, "[i]n order to prevent the inequitable distribution of the burden between different classes which this method of financing will involve, practically every aspect of economic life will have to be so rigorously controlled by government that individual liberty and freedom of enterprise will suffer a temporary eclipse.". Both plans emphasised rapid development of the basic and core industries as part of overall strategy. Both denied any role to foreign direct investment. Both wanted to increase agricultural output by managing technology and inputs, through irrigation, modern inputs and bringing more land into cultivation. Land reform was not considered as part of the plans. Even sectoral outlays and time-sequencing of investments were similar.

Table: Actual Outlays in FIve-Year Plans, 1951-1965 and Proposed Outlays in the Bombay Plan. Source: Sanyal, 2011

	First Plan	*Second Plan*	*Third Plan*	*Bombay Plan*
Agriculture and CommunityDevelopment	15.1	11.0	14.0	8.3
Irrigation, and MultipurposeIrrigation and Power	28.0	19.0	22.0	45
Industry, including Small Industries	7.6	24.0	24.0	
Transport and Communication	23.6	28.0	20.0	9.0
Social Services	22.6	18.0	17.0	27.6
Miscellaneous	3.0	—	3.0	10.0

The similarities arise from the fact that the i) outlays on industry and irrigation and ii) agriculture and community development (the latter is included in miscellaneous items in Bombay Plan) are roughly similar. The dissimilarities, interestingly consist of i) a larger share to social services and ii) a smaller share to transport and communication in the Bombay Plan compared to Five-year Plans.

Even the time sequence of investment outlays was similar. In the Bombay Plan, the fifteen year period was broken into three five year terms. The first five year period was to give significant emphasis on agriculture and consumption goods, the second five year term to increase the allocation for heavy and core industries and the third to step up expenditure on transport and social services. The Indian government's first three Five Year Plans chalked out an identical intertemporal path. They stressed agriculture and consumption goods in the first plan, and then heavily invested in basic industry and transport from the second plan onwards.

The Nature of the Indian State

It would be a mistake to reduce the history of Planning in India to the bourgeois script. At the time of independence, there were two alternative plans of national development, drafted by the Gandhians and the Communists. The nature of economic development to be pursued in independent India was a politically contested question.

> [T]he very institution of a process of planning became a means for the determination of priorities on behalf of the "nation". The debate on the need for industrialization, it might be said, was politically resolved by successfully constituting planning as a domain outside "squabbles and conflicts of politics. (Chatterjee, 1995, p. 202).

Below, I list some views on the nature of the Indian state.

(a) Some authors (Ray (1982), Marathe (1986)) argued that Indian capitalists themselves upheld and encouraged planning. There was no contradiction between the aspirations of the Indian capitalists and the developmental and regulatory state. These authors argue that the Nehruvian Five Year Plans were a direct extension of the Bombay Plan of 1944 put forward by the leading capitalists of the time.

(b) Chibber (2003) contests the claims in a) by suggesting that Indian capitalists were opposed to any form of socialist planning and attempted and subverted the developmental goals of the state. Therefore, unlike in Korea, the Indian developmental state failed to win the support of the capitalists in its project of economic development.

(c) In an interesting book, Sen (1982) claims that the Indian state was independent of bourgeois control since the Indian capitalist class was too weak either to promote capitalist development by themselves or to subvert government policies by withdrawing support.

(d) A very powerful Marxist tradition in India (Patnaik 1979, Desai 1975) sees the role of the Indian state as facilitating private capitalist development, *even through large-scale social ownership of productive resources*, precisely because the Indian capitalist sector was economically too weak to embark on the kind of accelerated industrialization India needed or to eliminate the kind of structural bottlenecks that plagued the Indian economy.

(e) Certain authors (K.N. Raj 1973) have used the notion of 'intermediate regime' first developed in Kalecki (1972) in his class-analysis of states in developing countries. The 'intermediate regime' is theoretically counter-posed to the classical Marxian notion of transition where power is transferred from the ruling feudal classes to the capitalist class, often aided by the state. In the intermediate regime, the state represents the interest of two classes—the urban lower middle class and the rich peasantry—whose class interests lie in between the proletariat and the bourgeois (Byres, 1993, p. 33).

(f) Similarly, others have characterized the Indian state as mixed in class-character, but in terms of more conventional class categories. One such formulation, influenced by Maoist ideas, was the semi-feudal or semi-capitalist characterization of the Indian state where significant feudal class structures in Indian agriculture and the rising industrial capitalist class processes each contributed to the dominant political bloc in India and influenced Indian industrialization in contradictory directions (Bhaduri, 1973a and 1973b), Bagchi (1985), Prasad (1973, 1974)

(g) A different idea of the Indian state emerged, especially in and around the Subaltern Studies school of historiography, with the application of the Gramscian concepts of 'hegemony' and 'passive revolution'. For a full review and critique of this approach, see Chakravarty and Cullenberg (2003). The notion of Passive Revolution captures the nature of class – transformation in transitional societies where the Classic Revolution has failed to materialize. Instead of historical change by which the capitalist class takes over power and establishes its hegemonic rule and order, passive revolution refers to the case, where capitalist class manipulates the transformation in its favor through 'molecular' or incremental change. In the process, the capitalist class has to incorporate many non-capitalist elements in its social order. The hegemonic ideology is not the ideology of the bourgeois extended over the civil society, but rather the construction of a new ideology that represents the social order as standing for the entire society or nation. The socialist rhetoric or economic planning in India is seen as an exercise in passive revolution by the Indian bourgeois where interests of different groups in the Indian society were sought to be balanced in order to secure the conditions of slow yet advancing capital accumulation.

(h) In recent times, the developmental role of the Indian state has been analyzed in terms of the Foucauldian notion of 'governmentality' (Sanyal 2007, Chatterjee 2004). Sanyal argues that the *governmentalized state* does not function through repression or coercion as in the case of the *sovereign state*, but rather takes up the function of management of the 'population' in a welfare-enhancing capacity. The Indian state *manages* the economy by addressing the negative social consequences of capitalist development, and primitive accumulation in particular, by focusing the development efforts on the victims of capitalist development. Through welfare-activities, the Indian state secures the political and cultural conditions for the continuation of capitalist development. Instead of the coercive state in the context of primitive accumulation in England, we have the governmentalized state in India that navigates the society through primitive accumulation, while all the time shielding it from powerful currents that might destabilize the social order.

The Two Regimes of Capitalist Development in Postcolonial India

A useful way to construct a history of postcolonial India is to distinguish between two different 'regimes' with markedly different economic, political and cultural conditions—in effect, two different social contexts within which capitalist development proceeded in India. Economists agree that the New Economic Policy, announced by the central government in 1991, is a watershed in India's economic history.

At the political level, significant changes distinguish the period since the 1980s from the earlier period. The most important of these changes was the erosion of the hegemonic one-party rule of the Indian National Congress (hereafter, simply Congress) and the birth of an era of coalition politics—with shifting and unstable alliances between many smaller regional and major national political parties. For the first twenty five years after independence, a relatively patient electorate remained politically loyal to the Congress whose political morality and legitimacy, derived from its role in India's independence movement, went largely unchallenged. Congress represented a 'rainbow political philosophy'—i.e. a political philosophy that accommodated political views on the right, left and centre under a single umbrella, displaying all the colors of the political spectrum (with the notable exception of the Communist Parties of India). Congress's rainbow politics was an effective barrier to political crystallization around issues like caste, religion, ethnicity, autonomy etc. The heady days of Nehruvian planning coincided with the overarching ideological stance of the Congress founded on socialism, modernization, secularism and development.

In the late 1960s and the 1970s, the regime of economic planning and the political hegemony of Congress faced a series of crises. After two decades of impressive growth, the Five Year planning strategy ran out of steam in mid-sixties with resulting industrial deceleration, food crisis and soaring unemployment. Politically, the Congress hegemony faced parliamentary as well as extra-parliamentary challenges in several states[2]. The Congress Prime Minister Indira Gandhi responded by launching a nation-wide poverty eradication programme in 1971. In 1975, she declared national emergency—for the first and the only time—in India and tried to crush opposition. During the emergency, in 1976, the constitution of India was amended and the words 'socialist' and 'secular' were added to the Preamble. None of these could save the Congress. In the elections of 1977, after Emergency was lifted, Congress was routed in the national elections and the first non-Congress coalition government was formed in India.

Though Congress and Indira Gandhi returned to power in 1980, the small interregnum of coalition rule changed Indian politics forever. The breakaway fractions from that coalition developed into many of the smaller regional and national parties of India that secured political importance over succeeding decades. Early 1980s saw the first attempts at deregulation of the Indian economy leading to an economic environment for private capitalists to become economically powerful vis-à-vis state capitalist enterprises. Furthermore, growth rate of the economy picked up after a decade of slowdown.

Since 1991, neoliberal policy has actually helped the fracturing of politics. The fact that the central government no longer allocates capital investment between states or control private capitalist investment through licensing and other regulations as before means that states have to compete with each other to attract domestic and foreign investment. As a result, regional aspirations often provide the material motives to formation of regional parties. Moreover, the weak economic role of the centre means a single hegemonic party is not an essential political condition of local development. More important is the strategic alliance with one of the major parties to form a coalition government at the centre in order to secure for the region a larger share of Central funds. The shifting allegiance of smaller parties, often viewed as 'opportunism' and portrayed as a decline of ideology and morality in Indian politics is in fact partly explained by two phenomena—the neoliberal policy and the fractured political space.

Two significant political and cultural developments in the 1980s changed the Indian society in radical ways—the rise of lower castes as a particular political force and the rise of Hindu nationalist Right. One of the most significant events under the coalition government of 1977-1980 was the setting up of the Mandal Commission in 1979 with the mandate to 'identify the socially or educationally backward'. The Commission's report, submitted in 1980, recommended 'a positive discrimination' in favour of lower castes with a certain percentage of government jobs and educational seats reserved for them. This immediately led to a controversy as upper caste people protested against reservations which took away some of their social and economic privileges. Over the next decade, the lower caste people mobilized around new political parties who focused on the caste issue. The implementation of Mandal Commission's recommendations in 1990 was a watershed event that brought caste into the centre of Indian politics and it has remained central after that.

The rise of Hindu Right in the 1980s and the communal tension that it created through its aggressive assertion of Hindu nationalist identity and its attacks on the Muslim minority provides another traumatic experience in India. The Hindu right combined aggressive military posturing with laissez faire economic policies favouring private capitalists and at the same time promoted a conservative culture that asserted Hindu identity in an increasingly Westernized middle class. Even as they asserted the Indian identity at the cultural level, their economic policies undermined the same through rapid spread of global consumerist culture across Indian middle classes which undermined many of the traditional Indian cultural norms.

In the words of Yogendra Yadav (1999), the period since the 1990s has been dominated by three Ms—Mandal (caste), Mandir (temple, in English, i.e. religion) and Market (globalization). At the same time, class-based politics have weakened in India over the last two decades. However, movements against loss of livelihoods, dispossession through markets and displacement of traditional communities by state and private capitalist industrial projects have increasingly come into prominence over the same period.

If one has to demarcate the regimes—always at the risk of oversimplification—one can highlight the following differences. The period from 1947 to 1991 was a regime that combined centralized economic planning with one-party hegemonic rule of the Congress and social cohesion based on relatively controlled inequality of income and an inclusive culture of accommodation and appeasement of religious, ethnic, caste and class contradictions. The period since 1991 is a regime of free-market private capitalism with a fractured, uncertain and contested political space, cultural ambivalence due partly to the clash of global consumerism with an assertive Hindu chauvinism and a society in general torn apart by rising inequality, jobless economic growth and clashes around caste, religion, ethnicity and autonomy[3].

The period since 1991 is also unique in the sense that the contradictions of capitalist development are brought into sharp relief since an economically powerful, paternalistic and populist state is replaced by a state subjected to all the contradictory pulls and pushes of capitalist and non-capitalist class structures as well as other non-class processes, even as it increasingly loses its economic power to intervene in the society to maintain social cohesion. One particular manifestation of this contradictory development of the society is what is often referred to as a 'radical disjuncture' between economics and politics in India today, pulling the population in opposite directions. In the sphere of economic life, more and more people are excluded from the benefits of economic growth under the neoliberal regime—with jobless growth, increasing inequality and widespread dispossession brought about by accelerated capitalist accumulation—yet the same marginalized groups are included in the political processes of electoral democracy. "The rich dominate the economy now more than earlier, but the poor have a strong voice in the polity more than earlier. And there is a mismatch." (Suri, 2004, p. 5405).

More and more people have been voting and participating in the broader electoral processes in India in the recent times. Interestingly, oppressed and marginalized groups are voting in increasing numbers[4]. Despite state-level differences, at the national level, participation of women, dalits (lower castes), and adivasis (tribals) has increased. As Palshikar and Kumar (2004) observe, "in spite of all the limitations of the electoral process, people have succeeded in instituting their own democratic meaning in this process." (Palshikar and Kumar, 2004, p. 5417).

Persistent Dualism in the Indian economy

Planning in India proceeded on two fronts—one targeted at rapidly developing the basis of a capitalist industrial economy and the other targeted at preserving the non-capitalist economy (which harboured the huge surplus labour force of the country) from oligopolistic business houses for eventual transformation of the former into a decentralized, competitive capitalist economy. This economic objective required the planners to both facilitate capitalism in one sector and resist capitalism in another sector. Thus, for management of poverty, planning had to be both for and against capital.

Planning was not simply an instrument for economic development; more importantly, it was an instrument for nation-building. The path to nation-building—namely, industrialization— was given by the history of richer Western nation-states; Planning was to be the main instrument for avoiding the 'unnecessary rigors of industrialization'. This required balancing short term versus longer term objectives—e.g. balancing modern against traditional modes of production, investment against consumption, growth versus employment etc. In short, planning was an exercise in economic management that went far beyond the drive towards industrialization. The frequent reference to the 'socialistic' character of planning has more to do with the requirements of immensely complicated acts of balancing different objectives than with the substantive content of socialist transformation of the society itself.

> Planning essentially consists in balancing: the balancing between industry and agriculture, the balancing between heavy industry and light industry, the balancing between cottage industry and other industry. If one of them goes wrong then the whole economy is upset. (Nehru's speech to all-India Congress Committee, Indore, 4 January, 1957 quoted in Chatterjee, 1986/1999, p. 159).

This act of balancing—economic management of the highest order—was all the more difficult for the following reasons:

1) India had been a victim of 'primitive accumulation' (i.e. dislocatory effects on the traditional economy) that supported industrialization in Britain and led to *de-industrialization* in India. Therefore, industrialization had to be politically legitimized.
2) The adoption of universal adult suffrage at the time of independence meant that this legitimacy had to be

politically renewed on a continuous basis.

3) The political strategy of class-compromise—the foundation of Congress's nation-building process—ruled out major redistribution of productive assets and transformation of power-structures. The Congress Party had to deal with the opposition of big landlords as well as big industrial and merchant capitalist groups to any policy that threatened their freedom of business. Therefore, existing economic structures as well as continuous political resistance made the act of economic management all the more difficult.

For Nehru, socialism meant nothing more than 'equality' and equality meant equal opportunities—the foundation of bourgeois equality. This equality is to be achieved at the level of production, since "[s]cientific planning enables us to increase our production, and socialism comes in when we plan to distribute production evenly" (Nehru 1962): speech at a public meeting, Bangalore, February 6, 1962 quoted in Chatterjee (1986/1999, p. 159). Even though large-scale redistribution of property was found politically infeasible, planning could be used to provide avenues for the large mass of small commodity producers to prosper, accumulate and differentiate into competitive capitalists. Instead of taking on large monopolistic business interests directly, the planners turned to the non-capitalist segment, the small commodity producers and micro-entrepreneurs to establish the basis of economic democracy. However, such a political objective required a sophisticated temporal management of poverty.

The two-sector Mahalanobis model was a simple framework for allocation of investment—the policy variables being the proportion of planned investment going into capital-goods and consumption-goods sector. Mahalanobis initially formulated a one-sector model in 1951 and 1952, which was almost similar to the Harrod-Domar model in its minimalist formulation in terms of the incremental capital-output ratio and the investment ratio. In the two-sector elabouration, Mahalanobis decomposed total investment into sectoral shares of capital-goods and consumption-goods industries. Such an exercise yielded two benefits—a) the illustration of the possibility of maximizing growth rate of output for a given level of investment by careful allocation among two-sectors and b) illustrating the choice between alternative time-paths of consumption and hence the importance of the time-horizon of planning. Thus, the choice was clear—if the standard of living of the majority of the people was to be immediately increased, investment allocation in favor of growth would have to be compromised to a certain extent.

However, the four-sector model seemed to have been motivated by an entirely different concern. Reading the draft plan frame of the Second Five Year Plan, it would appear the problem had radically shifted to the problem of employment, clearly reflecting the objectives set forth by the government, which in Mahalanobis's words, was that of "(a) increasing employment and (b) attaining a satisfactory rate of increase of income which have been adopted in the Plan-frame" (Mahalanobis, 1955, p. 17). In fact Mahalanobis goes further in mentioning that "the objective of the Second Five Year Plan was to maximize employment rather than rate of growth."

It is this idea which motivated the four-sector model of Mahalanobis. If the two-sector model illustrated the possibility of maximizing growth with a given level of investment by allocating resources to the capital goods sector, the four-sector model illustrated the possibility for maximizing employment by allocating investment in the consumer good industries among a) factory production b) small and household industries (including agricultural products) and c) services (health and education). The four-sector model provided the planners with an intellectual apparatus to make allocation decisions regarding employment and income targets.

The striking feature of both the draft plan-frame and the final Second Five Year Plan was the space dedicated to small scale, household or 'hand' industries as compared to heavy industries, which was the major priority sector in the second five-year plan. In fact, more space is devoted to small and village industries in the draft Plan-frame compared to heavy industries which was the priority of the Second Five Year Plan. The small-scale industries would expand by supplying the increased demand for consumer goods generated by the investment in the capital goods industries. In this scheme of affairs, large private enterprises in the consumer goods industries were to be heavily regulated. Explicit recommendations included a) not undertaking any fresh investment to expand factories which compete with small and household units of production, b) temporary ban on further expansion of factory production which is competitive with small-scale or hand production (even if it results in idle capacity) and c) to impose excise duties on factory-made goods to protect the small-scale industries from cheaper factory products. Just as protective trade policies were used to develop indigenous industries, internal pricing policies were used to protect and develop small-scale against larger factory units.

Mahalanobis's views are not entirely clear on the exact temporal dimension of the strategy, even though its importance is heavily underlined. It would appear that in the short-run, small and household industries would expand, probably on the basis of unchanged technological basis, creating more jobs and higher incomes. Most of the additional employment generated was assumed to be self-employment rather than wage-employment.

> The tentative Plan-frame visualizes that about 10 to 12 million people would find employment during the Plan period, the investment pattern being specially designed to make this possible. It must be pointed out that the figure mentioned above does not refer to jobs as such in the sense of work on wages or salaries; a part will undoubtedly be jobs of this type; but a part will be in the form of employment opportunities that will enable so many more self-employing workers to obtain their livelihood. Even as it is, the number of self-employing workers is much larger than that of hired workers; and the position is not likely to undergo a material change during the Second Plan period. (Memorandum prepared by a Panel of Economists 1955) in Mahalanobis (1955), p. 121.

The problem of disguised unemployment was treated as a problem of inadequate social demand for the products of the small and household industries. Only when the workforce is relatively gainfully employed— through expansion of demand

–can one talk about modernization of production in small scale industries. At that point, it is assumed that a differentiation within the small industries sector as well as competition from the factory sector would be socially manageable. Interestingly, in his review of Gunnar Myrdal's *Asian Drama*, Mahalanobis talked about industrialization of agriculture as a process that would take forty to fifty years to complete. Therefore, the pacing of change, intimately tied to the management of poverty, was the central concern behind the Second Plan. Partha Chatterjee had noted the parallel with the French history of industrialization.

> It is curious that in the one country of Europe where a 'bouregois' political revolution was carried out under the slogan of liberty, equality and fraternity, the protection of small-peasant property after the Revolution meant the virtual postponement of industrialization by some five or six decades. Chatterjee (1995/ 1999, p. 209)

Agriculture had also to act as a 'sink' of surplus labour power. Therefore, processes of dispossession or differentiation cannot be allowed to destroy the 'sink'. These led to same contradictory policy interventions in agriculture as in industry. The following rather long quote admirably captures the contradictions and the compulsions that drive state intervention in agriculture.

> Indeed the problem of India's agriculture lies outside agriculture, namely that the other sectors did not grow fast enough to withdraw sufficient population out of agriculture. ....The non-agricultural sector is in part an 'organized' sector and entry into that sector is highly restricted. That sector does not take in any more people than it can remunerate at the relatively high level. All the rest must stay behind in agriculture and share whatever may grow there. *Agriculture is a parking lot for the poor*.
>
> Underlying this fact is the agrarian reform and policy pursued in the last four decades. It failed to make a distinction between abolition of feudal elements and elimination of enterprises. For instance, not only were intermediaries abolished but lease and sale market in land also abolished. Ceiling limits on landholdings were imposed with the ostensible purpose to distribute the surplus land to the landless. Whatever the success of these measures, they tended to freeze the situation in agriculture and inhibit movement

> in and out of agriculture. Special agencies were created called Small Farmer Development Agency (SFDA) and Marginal Farmer and Agricultural Labourer (MFAL) development agency to administer programmes initiated to make essentially non-viable small and marginal farmers and agricultural labourers viable by providing them with credit. Subsequently, these were supplemented by the Integrated Rural Development Programme (IRDP) to provide them with additional self-employment. There were also programmes providing additional wage employment, such as the Cash Scheme for Rural Employment (CSRE), Pilot Intensive Rural Employment Programme (PIREP) and the Food for Work programme. *The intention had been to give to the surplus population, which agriculture could not support, some succour, without withdrawing it from agriculture* (Dandekar, 1992, pp. 54-55, Italics mine).

The ceiling laws, by restricting concentration of landholdings, had killed the land market. The law prevented "the possible dispossession of numerous small and marginal holders which would probably have occurred through a competitive process in the land market in the absence of a ceiling on landholdings" (C.H. Hanumantha Rao quoted in Chandra, Mukherjee and Mukherjee, 2000, p. 391). Thus, while conditions for development of capitalist production in certain branches of production were being created, the management of surplus population required that the same conditions be prevented from emerging in other areas of production. We have already seen how reservation of commodities for traditional non-capitalist industries prevented private and state capital to make inroads into the production of those commodities. In the same way, land reforms policies led to a 'freezing' of agriculture as a sector dominated by small peasant farms.

Despite these efforts, productivity of agriculture remains very low in India even in comparison with other developing countries and Indian agriculture is still dominated by peasant farms. It is fair to say that by the end of the Planning regime, agriculture was exhausted as a 'sink' of surplus labour power. There was no more land to distribute to the landless and industrial growth was unable to absorb the landless rural labour force. The only viable option was to distribute homestead land, encourage animal husbandry that required minimal land and ancient production of non-agricultural wage goods[5].

Outside agriculture, the huge and expanding informal sector consists of small family 'businesses'; the majority of them are petty production units without hired labourers and hence belong to the non-capitalist sector of the economy. Since the publication of NCEUS report in 2007, the share of informal sector in total employment (more than 90%) has become a salient point in public debates on the Indian economy. Recently, in their book, *Poor Economics*, Abhijit Banerjee and Esther Duflo, have questioned the idea that the poor informal entrepreneurs act like 'entrepreneurs' in the conventional sense. After reviewing the evidence on microfinance-led development projects, they conclude that:

> Microcredit and other ways to help tiny businesses still have an important role to play in the lives of the poor, because these tiny businesses will remain, perhaps for the foreseeable future, the only way many of the poor can manage to survive. But we are kidding ourselves if we think that they can pave the way for an exit from poverty. (Banerjee and Duflo, 2011, p. 234)

According to the NSSO survey on unorganized manufacturing enterprises in 2005-2006, almost 87% of the enterprises are Own Account Manufacturing Enterprises (OAMEs), i.e. enterprises without any hired workers. These are run by owner-workers using family labour, where possible. A few quick facts regarding these OAMEs:

a) Less than a third of them have any sub-contracting linkages with the formal sector and this is surely an upper limit.
b) Their median total assets is Rs 11610.
c) Their median annual household income per participating worker is Rs 6520 for sub-contracted OAMEs and Rs 9024 for non-subcontracted OAMEs, i.e. Rs 543 and Rs. 752 per month.
d) Almost 80% of the OAMEs reported their enterprises as stagnant or contracting over the last three years.

It is clear that we are not only looking at poor people, but also looking at a vast non-capitalist segment of the economy. At the time of planning, it was noted that 58% of the labour force was self-employed. The picture has hardly changed. In terms of the structure of the Indian economy, we must therefore think of two sectors—a capitalist economy dominant in terms of surplus, accumulation and growth and a petty producers' economy dominant in terms of employment and subsistence. Almost twenty-five years after the 1991 reforms, this structure of the Indian economy has stayed remarkably resilient. Just as the Farm Management Surveys in 1950s brought to light the large-scale existence of peasant farms with negative economic profits, similarly the successive rounds of NSSO surveys on the unorganized manufacturing sector show preponderance of enterprises with negative profits once minimum wages are imputed to family labour.

Conclusion: Capitalism and Democracy

Protection of petty commodity /small capitalist production was integral to the economic model of growth adopted during Planning. Planning, therefore, had to be for capital and against capital at the same time. This vision enshrined in the Mahalanobis four-sector model was never implemented by Nehru. The conditions for capitalism and democracy grew, but antagonistically and outside the plan, leading to the abandonment of planning and emergence of the quintessential feature of Indian politics— so-called 'populism'.

Ironically, it was in the radical days of Indira Gandhi that many of the original components of the Second Plan were implemented, but outside the Plan frame. It was around this time that attacks against the interventionist state by business groups intensified, but they failed to dislodge the state from its prominent position in Indian society, because by then, democracy had consolidated itself around the state, rather than capital. The continued 'enchantment' with the Indian state (Kaviraj (2005)) ruled out the emergence of a standoffish liberal state. Any discussion of postcolonial capitalism in India requires a fundamental rethinking of the theory of state.

REFERENCES

Bagchi, A. (1985). *Of Semi-feudal Democracy and Military-Bureaucratic Authoritarianism* in (ed.) Mitra, A., *The Truth Unites: Essays in Tribute to Samar Sen*, Subarnarekha: Calcutta.

Banerjee, A. and Esther Duflo (2011). *Poor economics: A radical rethinking of the way to fight global poverty*. Public Affairs.

Bardhan, P. (2008). 'Democracy and Distributive Politics in India.' In I. Shapiro, P.A. Swenson, and D. Donno (eds.), *Divide and Deal: The Politics of Distribution in Democracies*. New York University Press: New York and London.

Bhaduri, A. (1973a). A Study of Agricultural Backwardness under Semi-feudalism, *Economic Journal*, 329, 83, pp. 120-137.

Bhaduri, A. (1973b). An Analysis of of Semi-feudalism in East Indian Agriculture, *Frontier*, 6, 25-7, (29 September).

Chandra, Bipan, Aditya Mukherjee and Mridula Mukherjee (2000). *India After Independence*. Penguin Books: New Delhi.

Chatterjee, Partha (1986). *Nationalist thought and the colonial world: A derivative discourse*. Zed Books: London.

Chatterjee, Partha (1995). *Nation and its Fragments*. Oxford University Press: Delhi.

Chatterjee, P. (2004). *The Politics of the Governed: Reflections on popular politics in most of the world*, Columbia University Press: New York.

Chibber, V. (2003). *Locked in Place: State-Building and Late Industrialization in India*, Princeton University Press: Princeton.

Dandekar, V.M., and N. Rath (1971). *Poverty in India*. Indian School of Political Economy: Pune.

Dandekar, V.M. (1992). 'Forty years after Independence'. In *The Indian Economy: Problems and Prospects*, ed. Bimal Jalan. India, 33-84. Penguin Books: New Delhi.

Desai, A.R. (1975). *State and Society in India.: Essays in Dissent*, Bombay.

Jenkins, Rob. (1999). *Democratic Politics and Economic Reform in India*. Vol. 5. Cambridge University Press: Cambridge.

Kalecki, M. (1972). *Selected Essays on the Economic Growth of the Socialist and the Mixed Economy*, Cambridge University Press: Cambridge.

Kaviraj, S. (2005). 'On the enchantment of the state: Indian thought on the role of the state in the narrative of modernity.' *European Journal of Sociology* 46.02: 263-296.

Mahalanobis, P.C. (1955). 'The approach of operational research to planning in India.' *Sankhyâ: The Indian Journal of Statistics*: 3-130.

Marathe, S. (1986). *Regulation and Development: India's Policy Experience with Controls over Industry*, Sage: Delhi.

Palshikar, Suhas and Sanjay Kumar (2004). 'Participatory Norm: How Broad-Based Is It?' *Economic and Political Weekly*, 39(51): 5412-5417.

Patnaik, P. (1979). Industrial Development in India since Independence, Social Scientist, Vol. 7 No. 11, June 1979, pp. 3-19.

Prasad, P.H. (1973). Production Relations: Achills Heel of Indian Planning, *Economic and Political Weekly*, VIII, 19, (12 May), pp. 869-72).

Prasad, P.H. (1974). Reactionary Role of Usurer's Capital in Rural India, *Economic and Political Weekly*, Special Number IX, 32-33-34 (August), pp. 1305-1308.

Raj, K.N. (1973). The Politics and Economics of Intermediate Regimes, *Economic and Political Weekly*, VIII, 27 (7 july), pp. 1591-5.

Ray, R. (1982). *Industrialization in India: Growth and Conflict in the Private Corporate Sector, 1900-1947*, Oxford University Press: Delhi.

Sanyal, Amal. "The Curious Case of the Bombay Plan." *Contemporary Issues and Ideas in Social Sciences* 6.1 (2011).

Sanyal, Kalyan K. (2007). *Rethinking Capitalist Development: Primitive Accumulation, Governmentality and The Post-colonial Capitalism.* Routledge: New Delhi and UK.

Sanyal, K., and R. Bhattacharyya (2009). 'Beyond the factory: globalisation, informalisation of production and the new locations of labour.' *Economic & Political Weekly*: 35-44.

Sen, A. (1982). *The State, industrialization and class formations in India*, Routledge and Kegan Paul: London.

Sundaram, T.R. (1961). 'Utilization of Idle Manpower in India's Economic Development'. *Pacific Affairs*, 34(2): 131-140.

Suri, K.C. (2004). 'Democracy, Economic Reforms and Election Results in India'. *Economic & Political Weekly*, 39(51): 5404-11.

NOTES

1. In a recent book, Vivek Chibber comments that, "Virtually all commentators also agree that there is a direct line of continuity from the Bombay plan of 1944-45 to the First Five-Year Plan in 1950" (Chibber, 2003: 88).
2. The Maoist leftist movements in West Bengal, Bihar and Andhra Pradesh and the social justice movements in Tamil Nadu shook the Congress in late 1960s. Further, there was an internal split of the Congress into Right Congress and Left Congress in 1967. By 1974, there was nationwide mobilization, led by one of the most

respected political leaders, Jayaprakash Narayan against the Congress Prime Minister Indira Gandhi.

3. These changes were gradual, rather than discontinuous and hence the choice of the year 1991 as the point of discontinuity is purely arbitrary—being significant only to the extent that the formal change of policy regime was a 'statement' of how things were to move in the coming decades, an official acknowledgement of a new vision of capitalist development.
4. Rural participation exceeds urban, and hence poorer sections of Indian society are voting in greater numbers than the richer. In the 1991 national elections, 61% of the rural and semi-urban electorate voted as against 53% of the urban electorate. In 2004 national elections, 60% of *dalits* (lower castes) voted as compared to 56% of upper-caste voters. (Palshikar and Kumar, 2004)
5. "Perhaps the only viable programme left for the landless was the one which has been to some extent taken up in recent years, of distributing homestead lands or even just home sites, ensuring the payment of minimum wages, as well as providing security of tenure and fair rents to sharecroppers and tenants. Other answers are to be found in increasing off-farm employment in rural areas, in increasing animal husbandry and other activities associated with cultivation but not requiring land." (Chandra, Mukherjee and Mukherjee, 2000, pp. 391-392).

13

Concept of Caste and Practices of *Jati*: Exploring Roots of Incomparability

Padmanabh Samarendra

Caste is widely regarded as a social reality of India. In academic literature produced over the last hundred years and more, it is often recognized as the institution that separates society in India from that of the other countries.* It is said, and one does not require to cite the authors of this opinion given its universal acceptance, that society in India is divided into hundreds of castes. The Kammas, Nadars, Namboodiris, Okkaligas, Pulayas, etc. in southern states; Chitpavans, Kunbis, Mahars, Mangs, etc. from western region; Banias, Jats, Telis, Thakurs from northern provinces; and Dosadhs, Barujiwis, Kayasthas, Khandait, Kurmis, etc., in eastern part of the country represent some of those castes. The scholars trace the existence of caste from almost the very beginning of India's known history; referring to early Sanskrit texts they have written about the presence from the Vedic period onwards of Brahman, Kshatriya, Vaishya and Shudra castes as parts of the *varna* order. But, what is caste? What are its characteristic markers? How do we know that Kammas, Kunbis, Jats and Kurmis are caste groups? Given the certitude of knowledge on the theme, backed by extensive fieldwork and voluminous reports, one would expect that these questions must be long settled in academic writings. Surprisingly, as I explain below, that is not the case.

I. Practices of Caste: In Texts and in Fields

Various scholars have tried to define caste over the last hundred years. In 1901, the then Census Commissioner of India, Herbert Hope Risley wrote that caste was 'a collection of families' that claimed 'common descent' and was 'associated with a specific occupation'. Most importantly, however, caste was 'invariably endogamous' (Risley 1903, p. 517). Three decades later, in 1932, G.S. Ghurye observed that despite 'all the labours' of the scholars, 'we do not possess any real general definition of caste'. He added that 'any attempt at definition is bound to fail because of the complexity of the phenomenon' (Ghurye 1932, p. 1). Hence, instead of formulating a definition, he listed the following six 'features' that characterized caste: 1. Segmental division of society 2. Hierarchy 3. Restrictions on feeding and social intercourse 4. Civil and religious disabilities and privileges of the different sections 5. Lack of choice of occupation 6. Restrictions on marriage (Ghurye 1932, pp. 2-18). Drawing upon the experience of his fieldwork, Andre Beteille, in 1965, wrote: 'To begin with, caste may be defined as a small and named group of persons characterised by endogamy, hereditary membership, and a specific style of life which sometimes includes the pursuit by tradition of a particular occupation and is usually associated with a more or less distinct ritual status in a hierarchical system' (Beteille 1971, p. 46). Similarly, in 1974, McKim Marriott and Ronald B. Inden stated, 'Caste systems resemble the much more widespread systems of social and economic classes in containing ranks that tend to be culturally marked, occupationally linked, hereditary, and endogamous' (Marriott and Inden 1982, p. 982).

Underlining the commonalities in these explanations, M.N. Srinivas wrote, 'A sociologist would define caste as a hereditary, endogamous, usually localized group, having a traditional association with an occupation and a particular position in the hierarchy of castes. Relations between castes are governed, among other things, by the concepts of pollution and purity and generally, maximum commensality occurs within the caste' (Srinivas 1962, p. 3). Birth, occupational specialization, a clear hierarchy and endogamy are thus some of the features that have been associated with an academic conception of caste. But how far these features associated with the concept actually match with the beliefs, customs and practices of communities in society? Do these help us in identifying a caste? Can, for instance, the Kammas, Kunbis, Jats and Kurmis, be identified as castes on the basis of these features? Let us examine the situation by trying to locate these features in the lives of the communities we call caste.

Birth

Caste, it is often said, is decided by birth; by birth one is a Kamma, Kunbi, Jat or Kurmi. Implied here is the argument that it is the operation of the principle of birth that separates castes from other communities. However, birth is not specific to caste. For instance, one could also be an Oraon or a Lepcha or a Hindu or Muslim by birth. These are regarded as tribal and religious communities. Even national identities: Indian, American, etc., pass on to the next generation through birth. Hence, the criterion of birth cannot demarcate caste. Further, the type of any community is identified from the way it functions in society; when seen as a biological act, birth does not tell us about the social function of a community.

Occupation

Many scholars argue that caste division was initially based on the principle of occupational specialization. The *varna* order, in their opinion, represented this principle: Brahmans were ritual officers, Kshatriyas controlled the political domain, Vaishyas produced economic wealth, while Shudras served the other three. The presence in the society today of caste groups, such as, potters, goldsmiths, ironsmiths, oil-pressers, etc. is further taken to confirm the hypothesis that occupation decides the identity of a caste. However, the assumption that every caste is associated with a traditional occupation where the latter provides the basis for the existence of the former finds little support in society. Thus Diane Mines writes that "There is no way that most castes in India can be or could ever have been matched with occupations. There are thousands of *jatis* in India.

In comparison, standard list of occupational service castes are small" (Mines 2009, p. 14). There are two further inconsistencies that beset the equation of occupation and caste. First, as Quigley writes, 'it is never the case that *all* members of a given caste perform a particular occupation (Quigley 2002, p. 147; emph. orig.). For instance, the communities called by a single caste name Bania are actually engaged in different occupations. The reverse of this situation, as Quigley once again points out, is equally true: "Many people who perform the same occupation belong to quite distinct castes" (Quigley 2002, p. 148).[1] Thus, the Kammas, Jats and Kurmis share a common occupation: agriculture; yet, they denote three different communities. Evidently, the principle of one occupation/one caste never operated in the Indian society. In fact, if occupation were the basis of caste, then, a majority of Indians should be belonging to a single caste of agriculturists.

Hierarchy

Hierarchy, many scholars believe, constitutes the structure of the caste system. Every caste, they argue, occupies a definite position on the caste ladder; the top position on this ladder is occupied by Brahmans, while the so-called untouchables are relegated to the lowest rung. The structure of hierarchy has been interpreted to be based on the principle of purity and impurity: Brahmans embody the former and the so-called untouchables the latter. The presence of a Brahman-untouchable bound uniform hierarchy is taken to be the defining feature of the institution of caste.

The acceptance of a uniform hierarchy as a marker of caste, however, is misleading because of several reasons. The academic assumption that every caste carries a definite and fixed rank is not supported by evidence. Thus, it is not correct to say that Brahmans are uniformly regarded as most pure. Within Brahmans exist numerous communities all of whom do not share a uniform status. In fact, as Quigley wrote, many of these "continually dispute each others' status" (Quigley 2002, p. 143). Further, many Brahman communities, for instance, those who help in the performance of the last rites for the dead and who are found generally on cremation grounds, are regarded even by non-Brahmans to be very impure. Secondly, rank of a caste in society is subject to constant contestation, negotiation and change. The castes that are placed lower on the ladder rarely concede their own inferiority and often challenge other's superiority. Dipankar Gupta thus writes that none of the so-called 'low caste' or 'middle caste', actually 'see themselves as inferior in any essential sense' (Gupta 2004, p. ix). The notion of a uniform hierarchy, he continues, "stands bereft of empirical support from practically every quarter of Hindu India. As assertive caste identities articulate alternative hierarchies, there is hardly any unanimity on ranking between *jatis*" (Gupta 2004, p. vi). Finally, the evidence collected by Srinivas in the context of Okkaligas or Dipankar Gupta in the context of Jats shows that the landowning dominant castes do not accept the superiority of Brahmans. In fact, sociologists generally agree that caste hierarchy is shaped by local factors and therefore cannot be uniform in structure.

Endogamy

Endogamy or marrying within is considered as one of the most distinctive features of caste. Members of a caste, it is widely acknowledged, choose spouses from within their community and not outside. For instance, a person belonging to the Bhumihar caste in Bihar or Vaidya in Bengal would generally marry another Bhumihar or Vaidya and not a Rajput or a Kayastha. In the present times, when any link that might have existed between occupation and caste is barely adhered to and any sanction representing caste hierarchy is hardly observed, the matrimonial columns in the newspapers specifying the community identity of the prospective bride or groom appear to be the most visible sign of the existence of caste. However, can we say that communities called caste are necessarily endogamous? Let us examine the evidences.

First, Lepchas and Mundas, Hindus and Muslims, and Parsis regarded respectively as tribal, religious and ethnic groups also tend to marry within. Endogamy thus is not specific to caste. Secondly, and more importantly, large numbers of communities coming from all parts of India which are recognized as castes do not appear to be endogamous. For instance, according to the Census Report of 1891 cited by Edgar Thurston, in Madras Presidency, 'Gampa, Illuvellani, Godajati, Kavali, Vaduga, Pedda, and Bangaru' communities claimed to be a part of the Kamma caste (Thurston 1909, 96). However, despite claiming to be a part of the same Kamma caste, these groups observe restrictions on intermarriage. A Gampa or an Illuvellani thus marries only another Gampa or Illuvellani. The situation leads us to ask which is the real caste—Illuvellani or Kamma? The first is the actual endogamous group, but it is the second that is acknowledged by others in society as a caste.[2]

The academic notion of caste, the above discussion illustrates, does not seem to match with the social situation. Not one of the markers of caste uniformly correspond to the beliefs, customs and practices of communities living in India. And, yet, in academic writings and beyond, these communities are called caste.To recapitulate, let us consider the situation of Kammas, Kunbis, Jats and Kurmis whose names have been recurring above.Though recognized as castes, these communities do not engage in any specific occupation, rather, agriculture is their common vocation; these do not recognize any uniform hierarchy with Brahmans at the top; and these are not strictly endogamous groups.

Why is there a mismatch between the academic understanding of caste and the social situation? Why when we have shelves full of books that tell us that caste exists in India, that it is the steel frame of the Hindu community, and that it has been in existence for centuries, we fail to accomplish the most elementary task of identifying a caste? I propose the following hypothesis to explain the riddle. I believe that caste as conceived in contemporary academic writings is a new *idea*. It emerged towards the end of the nineteenth century in the course of and because of the census operations. By implication, then, I submit that the social form that is imagined through the term caste had never previously existed in the Indian society. Hence, the concept of caste fails to correspond to social realities. I elaborate the hypothesis below.

II. Caste, *Varna* and *Jati*

Caste is a foreign word; derived perhaps from the Portuguese 'casta', this word could not have been in circulation for more than past three to four centuries. The would-be critics of this article might respond by stating that even if the word is new, its connotation is not so. What does caste connote? The scholars, in general, have interpreted caste as an equivalent of *varna* or/ and *jati*. Both *varna* and *jati* have indeed been parts of indigenous traditions. If it can be demonstrated that the attributes of caste match with that of either *varna* or *jati* then the hypothesis that I propose would certainly stand rejected.

In order to illustrate the distinction between caste vis-à-vis *varna* and *jati*, I briefly look into their meanings. Caste has been variously defined as an endogamous, ethnic, occupational, ritualistic or racial division. Underlying all these definitions are present the following two assumptions: that caste actually exists and can be observed in society, and that it has a fixed and uniform boundary implying that communities called castes across India have something in common. The *varna* order, when compared, seems to share the definitiveness of caste: as mentioned in the Sanskrit texts there are four groups within this order the attributes of which are more or less consistent. Yet, unlike caste, the scholars point out, the *varna* system is text-based and does not exist on the social plane in the same form. No society across the Indian subcontinent is actually divided into merely four groups of Brahman, Kshatriya, Vaishya and Shudra. The presence of the *jatis*, on the other hand, can be observed in society. It is possible to empirically verify the presence of *jatis*, such as, Bania, Barujiwi, Chitpavan, Dosadh, Jat, Kamma, Kayastha, Khandait, Kunbi, Kurmi, Mahar, Mang, Nadar, Nambooderi, Okkaliga, Pulaya, Teli, Thakur.The similarity with caste however ends here. The connotation of *jati*, in contrast to caste, is far from uniform. For example, in vernacular literature, we come across the Lohar and the Sonar *jati* (professional communities), the Maratha and the Bangla *jati* (linguistic or cultural communities), the Hindu and the Mussalman *jati* (putatively, religious communities), the Munda and the Oraon *jati* (communities presently registered in the government documents as tribes), the Vaidya and the Bhumihar *jati* (communities which are endogamous), *mardon ki jat* and *aurat jat* (community of men and community of women), *manav jati* (community of humans), etc. *Jati* thus denotes professional, regional, linguistic, religious, only locally recognizable and even gendered communities. Evidently dissimilar, these communities are not necessarily endogamous either. If *jati* is to be equated with caste, as many contemporary scholars believe, then we might ask which of the above-mentioned *jatis* could be treated as castes? And what would be the criteria of selection? So, what is caste – *varna* or *jati*? Further, when the scholars write about the pan-Indian caste system what are they referring to – a system of *varna* or that of the *jatis*? In this article I argue that caste is neither *varna* nor *jati* though it masquerades as one or the other or both at the same time. And since caste is not the same as the other two, it must be a new category deployed for imagining the Indian society.

The genesis of the concept of caste is directly linked with the census operations in colonial India. Beginning around the middle of the nineteenth century, the census because of its methodology and agenda was a unique project. It was a direct survey of population; instead of surmising or using textual references, the enumerators went to the people with a questionnaire to know about their number and attributes. This meant, for instance, that the acceptance of the *varna* order in the census would depend not on the textual citations that could be mustered in its support but on its observed presence in society. The purpose of the census was to count the population and classify it under different heads—age, sex, religion, caste, occupation, etc. The conduct of these two interrelated processes depended on the fulfilment of certain preconditions. First, an entity to be counted had to be definite and discrete with no overlapping boundaries. For example, people that were to be enumerated as Hindus must first be defined as such and separated, say, from the Sikhs, Buddhists or animists. Classification, on the other hand, referred to the practice of sorting and arranging the data in different columns and rows to be presented in a tabular form. The first step relevant in this regard was to formulate the classificatory principle/s. The principle/s would be derived from the defining attribute/s of the entity to be classified. For example, if caste was recognized as an occupational division then different types of occupation would be used to name the columns or rows in a table within which the numerous castes enlisted during a survey would be placed. An accurate classificatory table demanded that the name describing a column or a row should match with the nature of data pigeonholed therein. The census was a serialized pan-Indian project. The data that was collected was put to comparison across the provinces as well the various editions of the census operations. The fulfilment of this very basic exercise hinged on consistency in the use of the classificatory models. Uniformity in the criteria of identification and classification of communities thus was essential for a proper conduct of enumeration. And once again, keeping in view the empirical nature of the project, these criteria had to be drawn not from texts but from the lived social experience. These features of the census, I argue, were instrumental in producing the idea of an empirical and uniform caste.

III. Beginning of Census and Problems in Enumeration

The assessment of population in colonial India had started from the early years of the nineteenth century (Cohn 1990, pp. 233-36). These however were indirect appraisals with no uniformity in the method followed. The first census based on a direct survey of population took place on January 1, 1853, in the North Western Provinces (called the NWP hereafter, the province covered parts of the present day UP). In the following decade census was also held in several other provinces including Oudh and Punjab, though as yet it was neither a regular nor a pan-Indian affair. The enumeration of caste started from the census of the NWP in 1865; it continued to be a prominent part of the colonial census till 1931.

The introduction of caste in census was accompanied with serious problems of identification and classification. The enumerators discovered during the surveys that society was not patterned according to the four-fold *varna* division comprising Brahman, Kshatriya, Vaishya and Shudra. Instead in their localities they encountered *jatis* – communities with unfamiliar names, uneven status and unalike characteristics. For example, the report on the census of the NWP in 1865 showed the Sikh, Jain, Goshain, Jogee, Sunni, etc. to be sharing the same space in the caste table along with the Brahman, Kshatriya, Vaishya and Shudra (Plowden 1867, pp. 80-81). The caste table in the report on the census of Oudh in 1869 presented a similar picture. The group of 'higher caste of Hindu' included 'the following thirteen castes': Brahman, Bengali, Jat, Jain, Kshatriya, Kayasth, Khatri, Kashmiri, Marwari, Punjabi, Sikh, Sarawaks, Vaishya (William 1869, p. 86).The *jatis*, these examples indicate, have never been homogenous though our *caste-conditioned* minds have failed to appreciate the significance of the situation or even take this into account in the first place. Nonetheless, the census officials were now faced with a serious challenge: which of those diverse *jatis* enlisted in the census schedules were castes, and how were these to be classified in view of the fact that the *varna* framework was not considered relevant anymore? The problem was to assume acute proportions with the inauguration of the pan-Indian decennial census series and the manifold rise in the collection of data.

The pan-Indian decennial census series, which commenced from 1871-72, suffered from several defects. It was not conducted all over the country on the same day, nor did it cover all the regions of British India. However, its most crucial shortcoming, as evident from the columns used in the reports on different provinces was the want of consistency in the classification of castes. I cite below the arrangement of castes as followed in the NWP (Plowden 1873, p. lxxxviii), Central Province (Neill 1873, p. 33), Bengal (Waterfield 1875, p. 21) and Madras Presidencies (Waterfield 1875, p. 21):

Classification of Castes During the Census of 1871-72

North Western Provinces	*Central Province*	*Bengal*	*Madras*
1. Brahmans	1. Brahman	1. Superior Castes	1. Priests
2. Rajpoots	2. Agriculturists	2. Intermediate	2. Warriors
3. Buniyas	3. Pastoral Castes	3. Trading	3. Traders
4. Other Castes of Hindoos	4. Artisans	4. Pastoral	4. Agricul-turists
	5. Merchants	5. Engaged in Preparing Cooked Food	5. Shepherds and Pastoral Castes
	6. Scribes	6. Agricultural	6. Artisans
	7. Small Traders	7. Engaged in Personal Service	7. Writers and Accounṭant Castes
	8. Servants and Labourers	8. Artisan	8. Weavers
	9. Manufacturing Castes	9. Weaver	9. Labourers
	10. Mendicants and Devotees	10. Labouring	10. Potmakers
	11. Dancers, etc.	11. Occupied in Selling Fish and Vegetables	11. Mixed Castes
		12. Boating and Fishing	12. Fishermen
		13. Dancer, Musician, Beggar and Vagabond	13. Palm Cultivators
			14. Barbers
			15. Washermen
			16. Others
			17. Outcastes

The outcome of the process of classifying castes, it was admitted in a memorandum on the conduct of the first decennial census in India that was presented before the British Parliament, was 'not satisfactory, owing partly to the intrinsic difficulties of the subject, and partly to the absence of a uniform plan of classification, each writer adopting that which seemed to him best suited for the purpose' (Waterfield 1875, p. 20). Such a lack of consistency in the classificatory columns, the author of the memorandum regretted, permitted only 'a few particulars' (Waterfield 1875, p. 20) to be aggregated. The very purpose of the census operations was in jeopardy as questions arose about the feasibility of deducing all-India figures from the provincial reports on the issue of caste.

Before moving on to the census of India in 1881, I briefly underline those procedures of enumeration that played a critical role in constituting a new idea of caste. The understanding of caste in colonial literature in the early decades of the nineteenth century was primarily text-based. The colonial officials like William Jones and Henry Colebrook, writing from towards the close of the eighteenth century, considered Sanskrit texts as the authentic sources of knowledge about the Hindus. Hence these officials, also called the Sanskritists, despite being aware of the presence of the *jatis* treated the text-derived *varna* order to be representing the original and the authentic caste system. The empirical approach of the census led to a fundamental change in the outlook: the focus shifted from text to people. The social space was marked as the habitat of the real; the verification of truth came not from the pages of the Sanskrit tomes but the experience of the lived lives of men and women. As per the new norms the *varna* model was put through the empirical test, and rejected. The society was populated not only with the Brahmans, Kshatriyas, Vaishyas and Shudras. Simultaneously started the questioning of the credibility of the propagator of this model: Manu. Let me cite in this regard some of the officers associated with the census of different provinces in 1872. Referring to the 'Code of Manu and some of the Puranas [that] profess to give an account of the institution of castes' (Cornish 1874, p. 121), Cornish who supervised operations in the Madras Presidency commented: "It is plain that in a critical inquiry regarding the origin of caste we can place no reliance upon the statements made in the Hindu sacred writings. Whether there was ever a period in which the Hindus were composed of four classes is exceedingly doubtful" (Cornish 1874, p. 122). Similarly C.F. Magrath, the officer entrusted with the compilation of castes from Bihar, stated, "It was necessary, if the classification was to be of any use, that the now meaningless division into the four castes alleged to have been made by Manu should be put aside" (cited in, Beverley 1872, p. 155).

The critique of Manu, in a broader sense, was addressed to the text-based exposition of the Indian society as presented by the Sanskritists. Yet, as Trautmann points out, the legacy of William Jones, Henry Colebrook and later Max Muller and John Muir continued to figure in and configure the terms of investigation at a time when anthropological interpretations had begun to displace the text-based versions of caste (Trautmann 1997, pp. 26, 191-206). Furthermore, in the face of the presence of the divergent *jatis* during the surveys, the anthropological theories found corroboration of the idea of caste as a single entity in concepts drawn from Sanskrit texts. Hence, the allusion to the ideas of *varna samkara* (narrowly interpreted as miscegenation) or the separate functions of Brahman, Kshatriya, Vaishya and Shudra when caste was interpreted respectively as an endogamous or occupational division. Thus the textual categories, though disputed, could not be discarded during the empirical shift in the understanding of caste. At the same time the bases and the connotations of these categories were radically altered. For example, while the *varna model* was refuted, some of its components could still find a place in the census reports. The Brahmans and the Rajputs were indeed included in the classificatory table of the NWP in 1872. However, the inclusion took place not before the physical presence of these communities could be verified. Thus F.S. Growse who had helped Plowden in preparing the caste table of the NWP, wrote that in the province the Brahmans numbering around 3,234,342 were 'still a living entity' and the Kshatriyas were 'adequately represented in modern speech by the word Thakur, or Rajput' though the Vaishyas and the Shudras had 'completely disappeared' (cited in, Plowden 1873, p. lxxix). The integrity of the *varna* order was broken; hollowed out of the earlier connotations, the constituting groups when individually appropriated were suffused with new meanings. The census, I believe, was accompanied with a process of *empiricalization* of textual traditions. In the course of enumeration, the components of the *varna* order, *i.e.*, Brahman,

Kshatriya, etc., were *empiricalized*: attributed a visible and verifiable body. Caste, henceforth, was recognized necessarily as an empirical category. It is in the context of empirical inquiry, I should also add, that the academic tradition of counterpoising *varna* and *jati* in terms of textual vs. real (or for that matter, ideal vs. actual, original vs. contemporary) started. The tradition continues in the writings on caste even today.

Let us return to the census of India in 1881, which also happened to be the first synchronous survey of population to be conducted in the country. The question that had assumed seminal significance for the project was that of maintaining uniformity in the classification of castes. However, despite all efforts to ensure statistical consistency on the various issues connected with the enumeration of caste, discrepancies persisted in the census. The conflicts in numbers cast a shadow of doubt on the very authenticity of the project of census. It was increasingly being acknowledged that to count it was first necessary to know what caste was. In 1882, W.C. Plowden, the outgoing Census Commissioner, recommended that in every province 'some officer who has a taste for, and a knowledge of, archaeological research' should be deputed to compile information about caste. The 'advantage of having such information at hand at the next census', he concluded, needed 'no comment'.[3] Responding to the recommendation, the Government of Bengal appointed H.H. Risley, in 1885, to conduct a survey of castes and occupations of the people of the province.[4] Subsequently, Risley was appointed as the Census Commissioner to supervise the 1901 edition of the census operations in the country.

I briefly digress here to ask why the empirical surveys which underlined the divergence of *jatis* and exposed the mismatch between the social situation and textual representation of society leading to a questioning of the relevance of the *varna* model failed to dislodge the belief of the colonial officials in the existence of a pan-Indian caste structure? Several reasons can be cited here. The first relates to the burden of history. In the body of knowledge about the Indian society that the census officials had inherited from the Sanskritists, the existence of caste had already been recorded. Further, the Sanskritists used to address both *varna* and *jati* as caste; so, even when the continuance of the *varna* order was doubted the *jatis* remained present to be counted as castes. The second reason is linked to the functioning of the state. The census operations launched by the colonial state produced a social map of the country reconstituting pan-Indian identities of caste, tribe, Hindu, etc., within its very format. The design of these operations replicated the model of the administrative edifice of India: the district census reports were compiled to produce a provincial report; the provincial reports together, in turn, generated the general report on the census of India. Implicit in the format was the assumption about the universality of caste; that castes from different parts of the country could be added up and presented in a master table. The obligation on the census officials was to uncover the essence of caste, to abstract those defining features on the basis of which castes across the regions could be identified, counted, compared and classified. Thus in the wake of the questioning of the text-based *varna* model, attempts were made in the course of the successive census operations to sift and identify castes from amidst the multifarious *jatis* and construct for these an alternative pan-Indian classificatory grid.

The conclusion of the census of 1881 marked a watershed in the history of the project in India. Till now the collection and compilation of data were understood to constitute the field of enquiry of census. However, the persistent problems in statistical computations had rendered the continuation of this project with its older focus untenable; the colonial state under the circumstances was *compelled* to make an ethnographic move. The results of the survey of Bengal undertaken by Risley were published in 1891 in four volumes entitled the *Tribes and Castes of Bengal*; subsequently, under the generic title of *Tribes and Castes* glossaries of communities were compiled and published for the North-Western Provinces and Oudh (1896), Southern India (1909), Punjab and North-Western Provinces (1911) and the Central Provinces (1916). Generally, the glossaries came prefaced with a long essay where the respective authors attempted to explicate caste: its origin, history, salient characteristics, etc. These essays aimed to investigate and discover the defining feature/s on the basis of which castes could be identified and separated from amongst the diverse *jatis* living in society. Three brief qualifications need to be added here. First, when formulating their respective anthropological explanations of caste, the colonial scholars did not and could not exclude the concepts found in the Sanskrit texts. Secondly, prior to the beginning of the ethnographic surveys sponsored by the provincial governments, some census officials like James Bourdillon and Denzil Ibbetson did try to investigate caste. However, such attempts were borne out of personal curiosity and were not parts of the colonial state's initiative. Finally, despite consenting to conduct a survey of tribes and castes in certain provinces, classification remained the primary concern of the colonial state. Accordingly, the state tried to limit the investment, both material and academic, in anthropological researches and keep it germane to the specific problem. In short, while the moves made by the state in the post 1881 phase were ethnographic, the same cannot be said about its nature. Nonetheless, change had come to mark the project of census; unlike their predecessors, the Census Commissioners in the following decades, before embarking on the exercise of classification, engaged in clarifying what caste was.

IV. Need of a Definition

The census of India in 1901 witnessed the most comprehensive attempt made by any Census Commissioner yet to understand caste. Using anthropological concepts and the data relating to physical features of local population collected during the survey of Bengal and later from a few other provinces, Risley forged his racial theory of caste. He presented the initial version of this theory, in 1891, in an essay entitled 'Caste in relation to marriage', included in the first volume of his ethnographic glossary of Bengal (Risley, 1891). However, it should be mentioned here that he was not the first scholar to discuss the idea of race in the Indian context. The genesis of caste, according to this explanation, lay in the 'fact' (Risley 1903, p. 555) of racial difference. Briefly, when the tall, fair and sharp-nosed Aryans entered India from the north, they encountered the short, dark and stub-nosed Dravidians. In order to prevent intermixture of blood and loss of purity of their race, the Aryans instituted restrictions on marriage with the local race. From such restrictions evolved the structure that we know as caste (Risely 1903, p. 555).

The responsibility of the Census Commissioner, however, was not to provide an academic explanation about the origin of caste in the remote past. The onus rather was to specify the criteria that could be used to identify and classify castes in the present. Once again Risley was confronted with the same question that had tormented his predecessors. What was caste? And once again Risley was presented with the same answer: the *jatis* on the ground were far from homogenous. Let us hear the Census Commissioner himself dwelling upon the dilemma: "In a country where the accident of birth determines irrevocably the whole course of a man's social and domestic relations... one thing that he may be expected to know with certainty, and to disclose without much reluctance, is the name of the caste... to which he belongs." Yet when asked about his caste, wrote a dismayed Census Commissioner, a respondent might actually give the name of "an obscure caste... a sect... a sub-caste... an exogamous sect... a hypergamous group... may describe himself by... occupation or... the province or tract of country from which he comes" (Risley 1903, p. 537). So, which name from among these was that of caste? Circumstances demanded clarity on the issue; to count and collate, it was necessary to fix the identifying marker. Hence, in the census report of 1901, appeared a 'definition' (Risley 1903, p. 517) of caste. Caste had several characteristics, Risley wrote; it "may be defined as a collection of families... associated with a specific occupation; claiming common descent". But more than anything else, caste was 'almost invariably endogamous' (Risley 1903, p. 517). Alongside Risley also declared that castes should be classified according to the 'principle' of 'social precedence' (Risley 1903, p. 538).

Neither the criterion of identifying castes nor that of classifying these could deliver the desired results. Endogamy could not be the defining marker of caste; as we know a large number of *jatis*, perhaps a majority of these, are actually not endogamous.In the beginning of this article, I have explained that Kamma, Kunbi and Kurmi are not endogamous groups, though these are indeed recognized as castes. I have also mentioned there that within these exist smaller communities which are the actual endogamous groups. Hence, Risley's definition of caste remained inapplicable. Risley also failed in his attempt to classify castes on a pan-Indian scale according to the principle of 'social precedence'. The divergence in the nature of *jatis* naturally implied the absence of a singular scale to measure status or construct hierarchy. The Census Commissioner himself later observed: "Castes can only be classified on the basis of social precedence. No scheme of classification can be framed for the whole of India" (Risley 1903, p. 557). No pan-Indian classificatory table was presented in the report on the Census of 1901.

Risley had criticized the classificatory tables in the preceding censuses for being inconsistent; yet even a small sample from the census report prepared under his guidance reveals a similar situation. Thus some of the names included in the caste table of the report on the census of Bengal in 1901 were the following: Chamar, Halwai, Baniya, Madrasi, Marwari, Manipuri, Burmese, Chinese, Japanese, Bengali, Maratha, Sikh, Baishnab (Bairagi), Buddhist, Munda, Santal, Oraon, Ahir, Kurmi, Barnasankar, etc. (Gait 1902, pp. 192-266). Tentatively these communities can be described as professional, regional (both from within and outside the country), linguistic, religious/ sectarian, tribal (according to the records of the state), and only locally known groups. Risley indeed was able to compile a list of castes made up of the heterogeneous *jatis* as his predecessors and successors had done. In fact, in a similar manner the state as well as the academicians in contemporary India also has been producing caste lists. However the question that must be asked is the following: what is it that is common between, say, Chamar, Marwari, Munda and Kurmi that qualify these to be parts of a list of castes? How can we decide whether Baniya is a caste or not? The only factor that seems to be uniting the names that form the list of castes cited above is that these are seen to belong to different communities. *Jati*, in the first place, then, signifies a community. Caste on the other hand is also imagined as a community but a community of a *particular* type. The particularity of caste is inscribed in the features attributed to it: a definite and singular hierarchy with perhaps the Brahman at the top and the untouchables at the bottom, a specific set of practices relating to endogamy or commensality, etc. These particularities do not uniformly apply to the *jatis* and this is why *jati* as understood in indigenous traditions and society is not the same as caste.

In the midst of lengthy academic expositions and scores of classificatory tables, caste had a troubled presence in the pages of the census reports. No exhaustive list of castes could ever be prepared for any province, let alone for the country as a whole; every such list was completed only by adding columns named as 'other castes', 'castes not specified/not known', etc.; no list was ever submitted without questions being asked whether those enlisted were really castes; no two reports on the census of India ever matched in the way these classified castes were identified; no inventory of caste was ever compiled without the presiding Census Commissioner expressing misgivings about the whole project. The enumeration of caste continued given its deemed administrative relevance; however, no sooner had the pan-Indian census started that the state was compelled to try and trim down its engagement with the subject. During the census of 1881 it was decided that only those castes having a numerical strength of minimum 100000 would be classified; after 1901, following the failure of Risley to construct a pan-Indian classificatory table, the practice of classifying castes in census itself was given up, castes from now onwards were enlisted alphabetically; in 1931, the last general counting of castes took place. Thus, after more than six decades of enumeration, the census authorities failed to provide the criteria to identify caste and classify these groups. Yet, the very structure of census first generated and then sustained the belief that caste was a uniformly definable and empirically verifiable entity. These two premises continue to configure the varying interpretations of caste today.

Conclusion

The *idea* of caste, as conceived in contemporary academic writings and within the policies of the state, was produced in the course of the census operations in colonial India. In the text-based explanations offered by the Sanskritists in the early decades of the nineteenth century, the Brahman, Kshatriya, Vaishya and Shudra were treated as authentic castes; *jatis* enjoyed no distinct conceptual status, the assumption being that these could be subsumed, at least theoretically, within the *varna* order. The onset of the census operations from the middle of the nineteenth century signalled fundamental changes. Empirical surveys showed the *varna* division to be non-existent; the focus now shifted onto the numerous *jatis* populating the social space. The project entailed that the diverse *jatis* be first counted, and then classified within a new pan-Indian template. The obligation was novel and unparalleled. The *jatis*, along with their assumed numerical strength, had been listed earlier too; however these communities stood in such lists as discrete units. The summing up of number in the census, on the other hand, was possible only if the entities counted were made comparable. The compulsion, under the circumstances, was to find the feature/s common to the otherwise divergent *jatis*, so that these could be defined and demarcated uniformly. In search of the defining features, the state started investing in ethnographic surveys and was gradually drawn into a nexus, which was not always complementary, with the western academic complex. Consensus eluded (and still eludes) any definition of caste; nevertheless, the ethnological investigations in the context of statistical requirements eventually produced the dogma—the dogma of caste being an empirically verifiable entity with a uniform and fixed boundary across the country. Once delimited, caste was endowed with a singular history of origin (racial, occupational, etc.), a set of common practices, and a structure. Its pan-Indian architecture included the *varna* names; though much doubted on empirical grounds, these categories, because of being known beyond a locality, could still serve the state's agenda of classifying the *jatis*. However, in the course of their selective appropriation, Brahman, Kshatriya, Vaishya and

Shudra were first *empiricalized* and then interpreted to be merely denoting ranks. Boundary and hierarchy thus became the two dimensions characterizing the new caste system conceived in the context of counting and classification.

The image of caste moved from the pages of the census reports into the domain of the state and the wider academia. The census was an official project and its impact on the state policies was only understandable. Further, the census remains till date the only non-sample based pan-India survey. Hence, it constituted the ground from which it became possible to talk of an empirical and uniform pan-Indian caste. It is not a mere coincidence, as Cohn has pointed out, that most of 'the basic treatises on the Indian caste system written during the period 1880 to 1950' (Cohn 1990, pp. 241-242) were by men entrusted with the supervision of the census operations either at the provincial or all-India levels. Denzil Ibbetson, J.A. Baines, H.H. Risley, E. Thurston, E.A. Gait, J.H. Hutton are a few of those names that can be cited in this regard.

Caste, I believe, cannot be equated either with *varna* or *jati*. The components of the *varna* order are not indeterminate; yet, these are not empirically verifiable. The presence of *jatis*, on the other hand, can be observed; however, these never had a singular and uniform identity in the Indian society. Caste thus is fundamentally different from both *varna* and *jati*; yet, because of its associations with both *varna*-names and *jati*-practices struck in the course of the census operations, it has been misconceived as a component of indigenous society. To illustrate this, let us explore what the expression 'Brahman caste', so commonly used in both academic and everyday parlance, could mean. Translated textually, 'Brahman *varna*' cannot denote a group of people physically existing, though, that is the idea the word caste labours to convey. Its empirical rendering as 'Brahman *jati*', on the other hand, would be fallacious; there has never been nor could there ever be a *jati* in the Indian society called Brahman. Kanyakubja Brahman, Maithil Brahman, Namboodiri Brahman, Chitpavan Brahman, etc., are some of the groups regarded in the census reports as Brahman castes. Significantly, in all these names, the word Brahman neither comes alone, nor as a prefix; conjoined as a suffix, it actually appears as part of the identity of the diverse *jatis*. In a similar fashion, the question 'what is caste?' routinely asked in classrooms and beyond generates an ambiguous sense. Is the question about *varna* or is it about *jati*? These two, I have repeatedly emphasized, are not identical questions and therefore anticipate different answers. Caste, hence, is an idea of recent origin that emerged by displacing the text-based *varna* order on the one hand and suppressing the multifariousness of the *jatis* on the other. Though there was no prior design shaping its production, a pan-Indian caste system in its empirical avatar appeared initially towards the close of the nineteenth century in the documents of the state. Hence, the use of the category of caste in place of *varna* and *jati* in historical explanations of the Indian society or the framing of policies by the state in contemporary times can only be misleading. I should perhaps add before I conclude that I am not trying to suggest that there was no hierarchy or discrimination in society before the birth of caste. Both *varna* and *jati*, which have been different and yet interacting parts of indigenous traditions since ancient times, carry their respective notions of hierarchy. In fact, I believe that by avoiding the generalized structure of hierarchy as presented within the caste system, we could understand better the specific constituents of authority that have been operating in the Indian society.

REFERENCES

Beteille, Andre, 1971 (1965). *Caste, Class and Power: Changing Patterns of Stratification in a Tanjore Village*, University of California Press: Berkeley and Los Angeles, California.

Beverley, H. (1872). *Report of the Census of Bengal*, Bengal Secretariat Press: Calcutta.

Cohn, Bernard S., 1990 (1987). 'The census, social structure and objectification in South Asia', in his,*An Anthropologist among the Historians and Other Essays*, Oxford University Press: Delhi, pp. 224-254.

Cornish, W.R. (1874). *Report on the Census of the Madras Presidency, 1871, with Appendix*, The Government Gazette Press: Madras.

Enthoven, R.E. (1922). *The Tribes and Castes of Bombay, Vol. II*, The

Government Central Press: Bombay.

Gait, Edward A. (1902). *Census of India, 1901: The Lower Provinces of Bengal and their Feudatories, Vol. VI A, Part II: The Imperial Tables*, Bengal Secretariat Press: Calcutta.

Ghurye, G.S. (1932). *Caste and Race in India*, Kegan Paul, Trench, Trubner & Co. Ltd.: London.

Gupta, Dipankar (2004). 'The certitudes of caste: When identity trumps hierarchy', *Contributions to Indian Sociology*, N.S., Vol. 38, No. V, pp. v-xv.

Klass, Morton, 1993 (1980). *Caste: The Emergence of the South Asian Social System*, Manohar: New Delhi.

Marriott, McKim and Ronald B. Inden (1982). 'Caste Systems', in *The New Encyclopaedia Britannica: Macropaedia, Volume 3*, Chicago: Encyclopaedia Britannica, pp. 982-991.

Mines, Diane P. (2009). *Caste in India*, Ann Arbor, Michigan: Association for Asian Studies Inc.

Neill, J.W. (1873). *Report on the census of Central Province*, Bengal Secretariat Press: Calcutta.

Plowden, W.C. (1867). *Census of the North Western Provinces, 1865, Vol. I: General Report and Appendices, A, B, C, and D*, North Western Provinces' Government Press: Allahabad.

——, (1873). *Census of the North Western Provinces, 1872, Vol. I: General Report and Statements and Tables*, North Western Provinces' Government Press: Allahabad.

Quigley, D. (2002). 'Is a theory of caste still possible?', *Social Evolution and History*, 1:1, pp. 140-170.

Risley, H.H. (1891) *The Tribes and Castes of Bengal: Ethnographic Glossary, Vol. I*, Bengal Secretariat Press: Calcutta.

——, (1903). *Census of India, 1901, Vol. I: India, Part I: The Report*, Bengal Secretariat Press: Calcutta.

Samarendra, Padmanabh (2011). 'Census in colonial India and the birth of caste', *Economic and Political Weekly*, XLVI:33, 51-58.

Srinivas, M.N. (1962). 'Introduction', in his,*Caste in Modern India*. Asia Publishing House: Bombay.

Thurston, Edgar (1909). *Castes and Tribes of Southern India, Vol. III*, Government Press: Madras.

Trautmann, Thomas R (1997): *Aryans and British India*, Vistar: New Delhi.

Waterfield, Henry (1875), *Memorandum on the Census of British India of 1871-72, presented to both Houses of Parliament by Command of Her Majesty*, George Edward Eyre and William Spottiswoode: London.

Williams, J.C. (1869), *The Report on the Census of the Oudh, Vol. I: Report*, Oudh Government Press: Lucknow.

NOTES

* The essay draws on Samarendra (2011) published in the *Economic and Political Weekly*. A modified version of the paper was presented, in July 2015, at the 'Summer School on Marxism', organised by the Department of Sociology, South Asian University, New Delhi, in collaboration with Rosa Luxemburg Stiftung, Germany. When writing the initial and the present versions of the paper, I have received comments and support from Amit Basole, Atul Chandra, Gautam Bhadra, Neeladri Bhattacharya, late M.S.S. Pandian, Paresh Chandra, Pranab Kanti Basu, Rajesh Bhattacharya, Ravi Kumar, Rohan D'Souza, Sangeeta Dasgupta and Tanika Sarkar. I am thankful to all of them. I also thank the ICSSR, New Delhi, for the award of the postdoctoral fellowship which gave me the time to work on this article.

1. Morton Klass had raised the same objection earlier. He wrote: "In all parts of India today, and clearly in the past as well, we find instances of two or more endogamous groups engaged in the same occupation living side by side, without any indication whatever of a propensity toward amalgamation because of their common occupation" (Klass 1993, p. 78).
2. Similarly, in Maharashtra, R.E. Enthoven wrote, Maratha Kunbis, Konkani Kunbis, Khanndeshi kunbis, Talheri Kunbis and Kane Kunbis, all of them claimed to be Kunbis; yet, instead of intermarrying these married within their own group (Enthoven 1922, p. 285). In Bihar, Risley informed that Awadhiya, Chanaur, Ghamela, Jaiswar, Kachaisa, Ramaiya and Sanswar claimed to be Kurmis; yet, each of these groups married within and not outside (Risley 1891, p. 530).
3. Asia, Pacific and Africa Collection, British Library, London (hereafter, APAC), Statistics and Commerce Department (hereafter, SCD), L/E/7/73, Register 521, No. 1840, August 1882.
4. APAC, SCD, L/E/7/73, Register 521, No. 91½, January 1884.

14

Understanding Caste

Anand Teltumbde

Many theories of origin of caste are in vogue. None however enjoys concurrence among scholars. Most explain or describe caste but none is oriented to tell us how to annihilate this monster. To me it is a waste of effort to pontificate over the origin of caste not because of the infeasibility of the task but because an erroneous assumption seems to inform it, which is that castes are static and hence if one knew its roots, it would be possible to strike at them to annihilate them. As I would argue, the caste have been changing all through their history and hence if one is concerned with their annihilation, one needs to focus on their contemporary manifestations and not their historical forms. From the Marxist perspective, we may not need a precise theory but an approximate but plausible explanation of its materialist basis so that we may be able to articulate strategies for its annihilation.

The source of the caste code is contained in the amorphous ideology of Brahmanism and is typically traced to the *Purusha Sukta* of the *Rig Veda*, regarded as the earliest Hindu text. All the Vedas are supposed to have been brought in by Aryans, the people who came from outside, and who conquered the native people of the subcontinent and imposed their own hierarchical system on them. While it is entirely plausible, what the Purusha Sukta speaks about is the hierarchy of four *varnas* and not of the numerous castes. Moreover, such imposition may not last unless it is sustained by the material basis. According to me, attributing castes to *Purusha Sukta* is confusing castes with *varnas*. While *varna* is a system of social stratification that is found approximately in all ancient societies, castes are unique to the Indian subcontinent. It therefore implies that if one wants to understand castes, one has to look at the distinguishing material characteristics of this subcontinent.

The distinguishing material characteristics of this subcontinent can be seen in terms of its unique natural endowments, such as the vast fertile and flat tracts of land, and plenty of sunshine, water, and congenial climate. When the nomadic tribes began settling for agriculture, they had to undergo changes in their social formation everywhere. As for instance, a narrow window of congenial climate in Europe necessitated huge intensity of labour over equally huge tracts of land, giving rise to a system of lords and serfs to carry out the cultivation. However, the tribes in the Indian subcontinent did not have to undergo any change while settling for agriculture as they could easily get a piece of land for the sustenance of their own family. Castes were these tribal identities, which continued from pre-agriculture phase. There might not have been any hierarchical sense in these identities. The Aryan system actually superimposed their *varna* system over these then existing castes, effectively instituting the sense of hierarchy.

Agricultural societies needed magic and rituals, which brought importance to the priestly class. The Brahmans, India's priestly class, took advantage of this fact and consolidated their supremacist position by creating an elaborate body of scriptures, in course, making the caste system as the lifeworld of people. It was legitimated with the doctrine of *Karma* and *Dharma*. That one was born in a particular caste was due to one's *Karma* in previous birth and if one wanted next birth in a better caste, one should observe one's caste *Dharma* in the present birth. While this ideology held sway over the minds of people, the dynamics of the system also lent the system longevity. While castes within each *varna* internalized their respective hierarchical position they contended within their *varna* for superiority. As such, while the castes busied fighting within their vicinity, they never challenged the macrostructure of *varna*.

Caste as the lifeworld of people remained intact even during the heydays of Buddhism. Buddhism and Jainism belonged to Shraman stream, which was opposed to Brahmanism. Both gained royal (state) support, got institutionalized as religions and remained the dominant ideologies of the subcontinent for almost a millennium, but they, contrary to the commonplace notion, did nothing to root out the poison of caste from the society. Its remained content with creating a no-caste island of Jainism had adopted Brahmanic system of varna (and also castes) right from the biginning and only Buddhism maintained its ideological anti-caste stand. However, it monastic order. Its anti-casteism remained a passive ideology and did not have much impact on society.

Castes were disturbed only during the alien rule starting from the mediaeval times, firstly under the Islamic rule and thereafter the colonial rule. During the Islamic rule in the subcontinent, the lower castes were first time exposed to an alternate religious system that did not have castes. The Sufis, Islam's mystics, with their liberal spirituality and their preference for the company of the poor, attracted a multitude of *shudras* and *avarnas* to Islam. Apart from religio-cultural appeal of Islam to the lower castes, the Muslim rule brought in an advanced feudal system that systematized land revenue administration, promoted manufacturing guilds and established cities, which provided further avenues to the lower castes to escape the bondage of the village caste system. A virtual exodus to Islam resulted with Hinduism losing almost a fifth of its followers.

During the same period, one more wave of anti-caste movement emerged in the form of *Bhakti* movement, which originated in South between the sixth and tenth centuries. *Bhakti* movement was not a unified movement but in relation to caste, it reflected, at least in some of its radical strands like *Kabirpanth*, an individualistic and anti-corporatist rebellion against caste. It raised many low caste individuals like Ravidas and Chokhamela to the stature of sainthood and did not distinguish people by caste. Though these individuals broke caste restrictions imposed upon the Dalit communities to become *Bhaktas*, they could only preach human equality and criticize caste practices. Their influence on the society was limited only to spiritualism and prescribed *moksha* as the salvation.

Later, in the fifteenth century, when Sikhism, assimilating the lofty ideals of the *Bhakti* movement and Islam, was born—directly promising the banishment of caste distinctions—Dalits in the Punjab region rushed in to embrace it. However, other than being bestowed with such new appellations as Mazhabi Sikhs and Ravidasias, Sikhism made no substantive difference to their lives. It proved that the ideology or religious tenets were incapable of arresting the material interests of people.

The very advent of the colonialists provided many employment opportunities to Dalits in the army, the colonial establishments, and their households to escape their caste bondage. Dalits in many parts of the country entered the British Army and came to realize their own military prowess, when they won series of battles for the British. The army and other employments certainly lifted Dalits economically. But the big difference came in through education they received in military schools; it opened up new horizons giving them a glimmer of hope for emancipation from their oppressive existence. Many early anti-caste reformers were shaped by the missionary education. Mahatma Jotirao Phule, who pioneered these anti-caste revolts himself was a product of missionary education. The access to education during the colonial period has been the revolutionary development in the history of Dalits. Education opened up the world to them; it made them understand their status vis-à-vis others; it also helped develop the consciousness of being wronged and lent them psychological strength to resist it. This is the precise process one finds in various agitations articulated by Dalits before Ambedkar.

Besides, the colonial rulers tried to directly tinker with the caste system with their own colonial logic. The 1857 sepoy drove the British to consciously strategise for controlling the native population. They followed the basic dictum in control theory: you cannot control what you cannot measure. They brought in a battery of anthropologists and sociologists to launch measurements and thereafter instituted caste-wise census. It resulted in three things: one, it created pan-Indian caste identities, which were further facilitated by efficient modes of transport, two, it solidified hierarchies, and three, it transformed caste, hitherto a socio-cultural category, into an administrative and political category.

These developments brought in many unintended benefits to the lower castes, which resulted in their incipient movements. They were further helped by the colonial strategies of 'divide and rule'.

Post-1947, the ruling classes have been more manipulative in exacerbating the caste question than ever before, paradoxically in the name of eradicating it and establishing an egalitarian society. They outlawed untouchability but cunningly legitimized castes in the Constitution with an alibi of doing social justice to traditionally 'backward' castes. They intrigued by using policy making to systematically further the interests of the incipient bourgeoisie. They clandestinely adopted their Bombay Plan in the first three Five Year Plans. They implemented the convoluted land reforms legislation in a calibrated manner to create a congenial class of rich farmers in rural India to make a bourgeois-landlord state. In caste terms, these moves led to transferring the baton of Brahmanism to the most populous *Shudra* castes. They brought in the capitalist strategy of Green Revolution that enriched this class and spread capitalist relations in vast structure of the countryside. In caste terms, it transformed the villages with interdependent ethos into virtually warring groups; the populous *Shudra* group led by the rich farmers who consolidated their base using their caste ties and Dalits, fragmented into sub-castes as the rural proletariats. It gave rise to a new genre of caste atrocities starting from Kilvenmani in 1968.

The adoption of the first-past-the-post type of election system for the parliamentary democracy also was not an innocent act although it appears to have been adopted by all the erstwhile British colonies. It was a deliberate choice to ensure the continuance of the rule of the ruling classes.

By 1970, the class of rich farmers, hugely enriched by the

government policies, developed their political ambitions leading to the emergence of regional parties that made electoral politics increasingly competitive. It further aggravated the caste question because the ruling classes intensified their intrigues to strengthen caste identities among people so as to lure them as caste blocks. The Mandal phenomenon, that opened up the can of caste worms was just part of the process.

The above run-up should bring us to a certain understanding about caste. Foremost, caste is basically a hierarchy-seeking category, that splits like amoeba and hence it cannot be the basis for articulating any radical struggle. Caste is not based on any religio-ideological dictum but has a material basis which came to be reinforced by the ideology. Hence, the viable anti-caste struggle ought to be aimed at eradicating the material basis of castes. Castes have been changing all through history and are still changing. The changes have been majorly brought about by the forces of political economy and not by any ideological matters. Capitalism, in fact, brought in changes in castes, in terms of eliminating ritual differences among castes that came under its influence. The resultant change is seen in terms of contemporary castes having been essentially reduced to a class like division—Dalits versus non-Dalits, their hardest manifestation being the caste-atrocities. Caste identities are promoted by the ruling classes and have acted as an intoxicant for the masses. The annihilation of caste would be possible only through the class unity of people. In other words, the anti-caste struggle has to be integrated with the class struggle and as a corollary, made a part of the revolutionary project.

List of Contributors

Amit Basole is Assistant Professor of Economics at the University of Massachusetts, Boston where he teaches Development Economics and Political Economy. Amit holds a PhD in Economics from the University of Massachusetts, Amherst. His research addresses poverty and inequality, political economy of structural chance and the informal sector, and the economics of informal knowledge. His work has been published in several edited volumes and in journals such as *Economic and Political Weekly*, *World Development*, *Development and Change*, *Rethinking Marxism*, and *International Review of Applied Economics*. Amit also writes for general audiences at ideasforindia.in, sanhati.org, and other online fora, and has recently edited a book titled *Lokavidya Perspectives: A Philosophy of Political Imagination for the Knowledge Age* published by Aakar Books, New Delhi. Prior to switching to Economics, Amit completed a PhD in Neuroscience from Duke University where his research on the neurophysiology of the mammalian visual system was published in journals such as *Nature* and *Progress in Brain Research*.

Anand Teltumbde is a writer, political analyst and civil rights activist with the Committee for Protection of Democratic Rights (CPDR), Mumbai. He has been associated with various people's struggles right from his student days and reflecting on them from a theoretical perspective through his writings. An author of over 20 books he writes a column Margin Speak in *Economic and Political Weekly*. Currently he teaches Business Management at IIT, Kharagpur.

Anjan Chakrabarti is Professor of Economics, University of Calcutta. He has authored and edited six books and has to his credit over fifty academic articles in journals and edited books.

Among his major books are *Transition and Development in India* (with Stephen Cullenberg) from Routledge and *The Indian Economy in Transition: Globalization, Capitalism and Development* from Cambridge University Press (with Anup Dhar and Byasdeb Dasgupta). He has been awarded the VKRV Rao Prize in Economics in 2008.

Anne-Kathrin Krug is a lawyer in Berlin (Germany). She organizes reading groups for Karl Marx's *Capital* in the Rosa Luxemburg Foundation and works on Marxist theory of law.

Anup Dhar is Associate Professor at the School of Human Studies, Ambedkar University, Delhi. He is also director of the Centre for Development Practice in the same university and currently a member of the editorial board of the Annual Review of Critical Psychology. Among his major books are *Dislocation and Resettlement in Development: From Third World to World of the Third* (with Anjan Chakrabarti) from Routledge and *World of the Third and Global Capitalism* (with Anjan Chakrabarti and Stephen Cullenberg) from Worldview Press.

Jakob Graf is studying social sciences in Jena (Germany). He is a member of the editorial board of *Prokla*, a journal for critical social science, and of the German left party Die Linke. In 2014 he stayed in India for five months, doing an internship at Rosa Luxemburg Foundation in Delhi. He works on the topics of Latin America's left, informal sector in India and global political economy and Marx's critique of political economy in general.

Padmanabh Samrendra is Associate Professor at the Dr. K.R. Narayanan Centre for Dalit and Minorities Studies, Jamia Millia Islamia, New Delhi. He has been working for the past several years on themes, such as, the concept of caste, caste movements and processes of knowledge formation in colonial India. He has contributed articles on these themes in journals and edited volumes.

Paresh Chandra teaches at the Department of English, Hindu College, Delhi. His research areas are English and French modernism, literary history, critical theory, and continental philosophy. For the past many years he has been part of the Radical Notes collective, and over the last two also of "The University Worker".

Pranab Kanti Basu has taught at Asutosh College, Kolkata. He is presently Professor, Department of Economics and Politics,

Visva-Bharati where he teaches teaches *International Economics and Marxian Political Economy* among other courses. His latest works include *Globalisation: An Anti-Text* (Aakar Books, Delhi, 2008), 'World of the Third, (*EPW*, 2015), 'Inclusive Growth: A Lacanian View' (forthcoming, *Rethinking Marxism* 28(2)),'From Hegemony to Governmentality' (*International Critical Thought*, Academy of Marxism, Chinese Academy of Social Sciences, Beijing). His areas of interest include Marxism, community and critical thought.

Rajesh Bhattacharya is Assistant Professor in the Public Policy and Management Group at the Indian Institute of Management Calcutta where he teaches Indian economic and political history, Indian political economy and public policy. He has also taught development economics, political economy and history of economic thought at South Asian University, University of Calcutta and Presidency University. He obtained his PhD in Economics from the University of Massachusetts, Amherst. His research areas include urban political economy, capitalism and dispossession, tribal rights, educational policies and reforms in India, informal economy and financialization.

Ravi Kumar teaches at the Department of Sociology, South Asian University. His works include *Neoliberalism, Critical Pedagogy and Education* (2016, Routledge: London); *Education, State and Market: Anatomy of Neoliberal Impact* (2014, Aakar Books: Delhi); *Social Movements: Transformative Shifts and Turning Points* (2014, Routledge: Delhi); *Education and the Reproduction of Capital: Neoliberal Knowledge and Counterstrategies* (2012, Palgrave Macmillan: New York); *Global Neoliberalism and Education and its Consequences* (2009, Routledge: New York & London); He is co-editor of a book series on *Social Movements, Dissent and Transformative Action* (Routledge: Delhi). His area of research includes Political Economy of Identity Politics, Social Movements, neoliberal impact on education and processes of knowledge production. He is Associate Editor of *Society and Culture in South Asia* (published by Sage).

Rohit teaches Economics at the Centre for Economic Studies and Planning, Jawaharlal Nehru University. His research interests include political economy of growth, heterodox macro-economics, monetary theory. His book titled *It's Not Over: Structural Drivers of the Global Economic Crisis* has recently been published by Oxford University Press.

Surajit Mazumdar is currently at the Centre for Economic Studies and Planning (CESP), Jawaharlal Nehru University. Prior to this he has served on the faculties of Ambedkar University Delhi (AUD), Hindu College, University of Delhi and the Institute for Studies in Industrial Development (ISID), New Delhi. Surajit studied at the University of Delhi and then at Jawaharlal Nehru University, Delhi. His research focuses on studying the corporate sector and the political economy of Indian industrialization, patterns of growth and structural change in India, and the impact of globalization on India's economy.